THE ANTINOMIAN CONTROVERSY, 1636–1638

The Antinomian Controversy, 1636-1638

A DOCUMENTARY HISTORY

Second Edition

Edited, with Introduction and Notes, by

David D. Hall

Duke University Press

Durham and London

1990

F
67
. H92
A58
1990

Library of Congress Cataloging-in-Publication Data
appear on the last printed page of this book.

For Edmund S. Morgan

Contents

Preface to the Second Edition

THE Antinomian controversy has come into its own. Three hundred and fifty years after the magistrates and ministers in early Massachusetts crushed a movement of protest, the events of 1636 to 1638 are regarded as crucial to an understanding of religion, society, and gender in early American history. The dispersal of the "Antinomians" and the reassertion of "orthodoxy" fixed the path that religion and society would follow for the next century, if not longer. And the harsh reaction to Anne Hutchinson, a lay religious leader who challenged the authority of the ministers, exposed the subordination of women in this culture—a subordination some, like Mrs. Hutchinson, tried to challenge.

We know more about the main actors in the controversy—Anne Hutchinson, her chief clerical supporter John Cotton, and the other ministers who confronted both of them—than we knew when this collection of documents was published in 1968. The progress of scholarship is amply evident in the bibliography of recent work appended to this preface. But let me comment briefly on a few crucial matters of interpretation.

Anne Hutchinson, her husband William, and their children arrived in Boston in 1634. The little that we know about her spiritual life before she emigrated to America is embedded in the report of her "examination" by the magistrates and ministers in 1637. During that examination Mrs. Hutchinson broke into the mode of spiritual autobiography, telling how, back in England, she had come to question the truthfulness of godly ministers in the Church of England who never seemed to act according to their principles. Separating from the established

ix

church and ministry, Mrs. Hutchinson fell into an "Atheisme" that ended when she heard the voice of God: "at last he let me see how I did oppose Jesus Christ ... and how I did turne in upon a Covenant of works ... ; from which time the Lord did discover to me all sorts of Ministers, and how they taught, and to know what voyce I heard. . . ."[1] Thereafter, she depended on this clarifying voice for guidance.

Anne Hutchinson came to trust one minister, John Cotton. Before he left England for New England in 1633, Cotton preached in Boston (Lincolnshire) not far from the town of Alford where the Hutchinsons lived. It may have been from Cotton that Mrs. Hutchinson learned to question the significance of the "law" and the "covenant of works." He may also have encouraged her to conceive of the Holy Spirit as "indwelling" in the elect saint. Once they reached New England she and Cotton shared the same dissatisfaction with the spirituality of the colonists. Many of these people seemed to think that "affliction of Spirit" and "restraining from all known evil" were the signs of "saving Union, or Communion" with Christ. Together, the minister and the lay woman challenged this reasoning, reminding those who used it that the performance of moral duties was unrelated to divine mercy. To think otherwise, the two warned, was to proceed in the way of "works" and not of "free grace." Looking back on the moment when he and Mrs. Hutchinson were collaborators, Cotton remembered the good consequences of this message: "And many whose spirituall estates were not so safely layed, yet were hereby helped and awakened to discover their sandy foundations, and to seek for better establishment in Christ. . . ."[2]

Anne Hutchinson was representative of Puritan spirituality in placing so much "emphasis on the need for an inner experience of God's regenerating grace as a mark of election."[3] But

---

1. See below, pp. 271–73.
2. Ibid., p. 412.
3. Sydney Ahlstrom, *Theology in America* (New York, 1967), p. 27, quoted in Endy, *William Penn and Early Quakerism,* p. 16. Note: full bibliographical information for this and all subsequent references is provided in the bibliography.

she was also a "radical" critic of that movement, and her fuller message was similar to the apocalyptic spiritism of the left wing of the Protestant Reformation. No historian has connected her directly to sixteenth-century radicals or to the "familists" who existed on the margins of English society.[4] But like these radicals Anne Hutchinson devalued the outward material world and exalted the submersion of the self in the Holy Spirit. Like many of them, moreover, she espoused the doctrine of mortalism: when the body dies the soul dies also. James F. Maclear, the historian who has done the most to explicate her mortalism, is surely right to argue that "Anne forged a connecting link between the 'radical reformation' of the sixteenth century and the 'realized eschatology' of the Quakers" in the mid-seventeenth century.[5]

Anne Hutchinson was also radical in being a prophetess. If the testimony of her enemies may be trusted, she had prophesied in England—warning, just before she left, that God intended to destroy that country—and prophesied anew while crossing the Atlantic. At the climactic movement of the 1637 "examination" she likened herself to Daniel in the lion's den and foresaw her own deliverance.[6] As recent work has demonstrated, the popular religious culture of Elizabethan England sanctioned certain kinds of prophesying.[7] But the practice always made the authorities uneasy. It did so again in New England, for the woman who prophesied was openly defying the hierarchical authority that men derived from their gender, and from gender-restricted learning. (No women received the same level of academic training as the ministers.) We may therefore place Anne Hutchinson

4. At her church trial there was testimony that Anne Hutchinson admired the "Woman of Elis," a person of whom, unfortunately, almost nothing is known (see below, p. 380). Mrs. Hutchinson's allusion to separatist Puritans in her spiritual autobiography suggests, however, an awareness of the crosscurrents (some of them incipiently "radical") that pervaded English Puritanism in the 1620s and 1630s.
5. Maclear, "Anne Hutchinson and the Mortalist Heresy."
6. See below, pp. 273, 338, 339, and Hall, *Worlds of Wonder*, pp. 95–97.
7. Thomas, *Religion and the Decline of Magic*, ch. 5; Hall, *Worlds of Wonder*, ch. 2.

in the company of other saintly women who, throughout the history of the Christian church, have claimed the "authority of inspiration" as the one alternative left open to them. Anne Hutchinson proved able to match verse for verse when her interrogators accused her of defying Scripture. But in the end she rested her empowerment as teacher and prophet on the direct witness of the Holy Spirit.[8]

The magistrates and ministers rejected the authority of such inspiration. They feared its consequences for their own authority; in some congregations in New England, lay men and women were casting aside their customary deference and challenging the ministers on issues of faith and doctrine. Time and again in the "examination" of Anne Hutchinson, and throughout the introduction and conclusion that Thomas Weld added to the first edition of *A Short Story of the Rise, Reigne, and Ruine of the Antinomians,* the magistrates and ministers accused Anne Hutchinson and her followers of recklessly endangering civil and religious order. Accordingly, her enemies insinuated that she was an agent of the Devil,[9] and they compared "Antinomianism" to other discredited movements—the Familists, and the sixteenth-century Anabaptists who seized control of Münster, Germany—all of which were seen as turning "all things upside down among us."[10]

Three hundred and fifty years later, we discern in *A Short Story* a rhetoric of "heresy" that rested on assumptions about gender, learnedness, and order. This rhetoric entailed a sharply dualistic understanding of the good and the bad: orthodoxy and heresy, the forces of God on the one side, the forces of Satan on the other. Once this rhetoric was unleashed, the flow of abuse was almost unstoppable. As Stephen Foster has cogently argued, we must not confuse the hysteria about heresy with what "really" happened; the heresy hunters always painted with a broad brush and were quick to accuse their enemies of holding

---

8. Huber, *Women and the Authority of Inspiration.*

9. The magistrates associated Mrs. Hutchinson and one of her followers, Jane Hawkins, a healer, with witchcraft, a crime that was closely linked with gender. See Karlsen, *Devil in the Shape of a Woman.*

10. See below, p. 253.

every kind of bad idea. When we peel away the excess, it is clear that Mrs. Hutchinson was not a "libertine" who advocated sexual license.[11] Yet in another sense the rhetoric of the controversy *is* the reality, for it explains why the magistrates and ministers retaliated so vigorously against the "Antinomians." Moreover, Anne Hutchinson and her other clerical ally, John Wheelwright, relied on the same rhetorical pattern: in his fast-day sermon of January 1637, Wheelwright invoked the image of a holy war between the true followers of Christ and their enemies who taught a covenant of works.

John Cotton ran afoul of his fellow ministers for different reasons. Not until the "Elders Reply" and Cotton's "Rejoynder" were published for the first time in this documentary collection was it possible for historians to understand the quarrel between the most prominent minister in New England and most of his colleagues.[12] As several historians have established, this quarrel had to do with the order of salvation, or the ways in which God accomplished the "work of grace." All of the ministers agreed that this work of grace was the doing of God. Christ's death on the cross had satisfied God's justice, and the risen Christ proclaimed the gospel. Even so, these ministers reasoned (in keeping with Christian tradition) that there must be repentance on man's part. Redemption involved the willing, active self and the struggle to achieve repentance. Repeatedly in their sermons the Puritan ministers in England and New England urged people to "reach out for the promises," "close with Christ," perform certain duties. To give force to these commands, the clergy cited such verses as 2 Peter 1:10: "Wherefore the rather, brethren, give diligence to make your calling and election sure: for if ye do these things, ye shall never fall"—a verse they would cite again in debating John Cotton.[13]

---

11. Foster, "New England and the Challenge of Heresy."

12. One scholar, misled by my naming of the documents, has said that I omitted to include Cotton's "Revisall," the final text in the manuscript at the Massachusetts Historical Society. This document appeared in print in 1646 as *A Conference Mr. John Cotton Held at Boston,* and I reprinted it (corrected against the manuscript text) under that title.

13. See p. 72; and for John Cotton's own interpretation, see pp. 93, 124–25, 406.

But where did this activity fit within the sequence of "justification" and "sanctification"? The first of these terms refers to the imputation of Christ's righteousness to the sinner; without this righteousness there is no way of escaping condemnation. The second of these terms refers to the godliness that elect saints manifest after being justified. In the debates that took place in 1636 and 1637, most of the ministers in New England argued that justification was consequent upon "faith." They defined faith, accordingly, as an "active instrument." In making faith "active," and in placing it before justification, they relied on distinctions in logic among several kinds of causes (formal, efficient, material, final), and on a concept of divinely instituted "order." William Stoever has shown that, from their point of view, God worked through an "ordained" sequence and a "means of grace" (the church and ministry) he himself had constituted and controlled.[14] The ministers' answer to Error 43 ("The Spirit acts most in the Saints, when they indevour least") contains their thinking about means and order:

> Reserving the special seasons of God's preventing grace to his own pleasure, In the *ordinary constant course of his dispensation,* the more we indevour, the more assistance and help we find from him . . . by indevour be meant the *use of lawfull meanes and ordinances commanded by God, to seeke and find him in.* . . .[15]

The Aristotelian language in the "Elders Reply" was an additional way of explaining how the sovereignty of God encompassed and made room for man's activity in the process of salvation.

This language may seem abstract to us. But not to these ministers, who in their everyday experience as pastors had to advise people on assurance of salvation. I argued in 1968, and would argue again, that assurance of salvation was the central issue in the controversy. It is important to recognize that most of the ministers regarded assurance as something that did not arrive all at once, but piecemeal, over time. This was a conclu-

---

14. Stoever, *"Faire and Easie Way."*
15. See below, p. 231; emphasis added.

sion they reached after long experience with the vicissitudes—the ups and downs—of the spiritual life. Assurance seemed to wax and wane. When uncertainty prevailed, the ministers counseled the remedy of "practical reasoning," or in theological language, the "practical syllogism": "he that repenteth and believeth the Gospel shall be saved/But I repent and believe the Gospel/ Therefore I shall be saved."[16]

The great historian of Puritanism, Perry Miller, interpreted the issue in the controversy otherwise: it was "preparation for salvation" that the ministers were insisting on. Miller regarded "preparation" as making inroads on the Calvinist doctrines of free grace and unconditional election. But in point of fact there was almost nothing said about preparation in the controversy. More recently, a number of historians have insisted that the ministers never proposed that actions taken prior to justification were "meritorious" in regard to grace. Others disagree, and interpret Thomas Shepard, Thomas Hooker, and Peter Bulkeley as tending toward a "works righteousness."[17]

The task of understanding John Cotton seems more daunting—and to yield a greater variety of interpretations—than the task of interpreting his fellow clergy.[18] We can safely say that Cotton never passed over into "radical" religion. He accepted the performance of "prayer and other holy duties, whereby we may after come to the sight of our Sanctification," and, in contrast to Anne Hutchinson, he regarded the Bible as the sole basis of truth, though he emphasized the priority of "Spirit" over

---

16. See below, pp. 75, 148.

17. See the citations in Hall, "On Common Ground," pp. 207–8. These differences of opinion have much to do with different understandings of the meaning and significance of "preparation." Stoever has carefully distinguished four meanings of the term: "Appendix: Preparation for Salvation," 'Faire and Easie Way,' pp. 192–99. It may help to note that the ministers, in debating Cotton, argued the priority of grace: "For it is grace that works the Condition, it is grace that reveals the condition, it is grace that makes the promise . . . and what danger is there hereby, to a well instructed Christian of derogating from free grace?" (see below, p. 67).

18. See Hall, "On Common Ground," p. 212. Literary historians have essayed to contrast Cotton's understanding of language and the sermon with the practice of his colleagues. See the work by Delamotte, Habegger, Knight, and Toulouse listed in the bibliography.

form. He had his own perspective on the "sad doubts of their own estates" that perplexed so many of the colonists. Assurance of salvation could and should arrive with "fullness," he argued, and not bit by bit.[19] Disagreeing with his fellow ministers on the nature of "sanctification," he regarded it as "the fruit of the Spirit of Christ dwelling in true Believers," and accordingly minimized the significance of "duties." When he wondered aloud whether lay people and the ministers were falling into a "covenant of works," he was warning about a possible *tendency:* should people reason that "first Assurance" stems from moral behavior, "it will unavoidably follow that our works are the grounds and causes of our first Assurance," a conclusion which would violate "Protestant doctrine."[20]

Reading through these documents anew, I am struck by the rhetorical quality of the charge that so-and-so was preaching a "covenant of works." Like its twin, the charge of "familism" and "antinomianism," it conveyed a broad uneasiness that we cannot always translate into issues of doctrine. The elasticity of the phrase enabled lay men and women to use it against clergy they distrusted, though we know from other evidence that these clergy were orthodox on the relationship between works and grace.

Throughout these documents we must beware of rhetorical excess—and perhaps of distortion. Stephen Foster has argued that the eighty-two errors pulled together by the synod of 1637 are a classic example of excess; he interprets them as deriving more from the tradition of heresy-hunting than from real-life "Antinomians" in New England.[21] (Indeed, the members of the Boston Church complained of being credited with opinions that they did not hold.) At her church trial Anne Hutchinson was initially charged with sixteen mistakes in theology, a number Thomas Weld inflated to twenty-nine in his preface to *A Short Story.* Every reader should compare two of the documents in

---

19. See below, pp. 121, 129.

20. See below, pp. 56, 133; John Cotton, *A Treatise of the Covenant of Grace* (London, 1671), pp. 177–79.

21. Foster, "New England and the Challenge of Heresy," pp. 647–50.

this collection, the unedited transcript of Mrs. Hutchinson's "Examination" and the highly edited version published in *A Short Story*. But the most intriguing text is one that is not included here, John Winthrop's journal history of New England. Partisan of one side in the controversy, Winthrop may have shaped his narrative accordingly.[22]

The war of words lasted well beyond the formal ending of the Antinomian controversy in 1638. Philip Gura has reminded us that "radical" Puritans of several kinds moved in and out of New England throughout the early decades.[23] John Cotton and certain other ministers may have continued to emphasize "free grace." A year after the controversy had ended, Thomas Shepard wrote in his "autobiography" that

> Mr. Cotton repents not, but is hid only. (1) When Mistress Hutchinson was convented he commended her for all that she did before her confinement and so gave her a light to escape through the crowd with honor. (2) Being asked whether all revelations were lost because all revelations were either to complete Scripture or for the infancy of the weak church, he answered that they were all ceased about particular events, unless to weak Christians, and seemed to confirm it now; whereas in the sermon it was to the weak church under the old testament, he did extend it to weak Christians also under the new. (3) He doth stiffly hold the revelation of our good estate still, without any sight of word or work.[24]

In Rhode Island Anne Hutchinson remained intransigent. And in the colony she had left, other women continued to defy the rules about gender, and to suffer for their independence.[25]

How far in American history may we trace the echoes of the Antinomian controversy? As the seventeenth century came to an end, a nonconformist (Puritan) minister in England, disputing

22. Lewis, "Sweet Sacrifice."
23. Gura, *Glimpse of Sions Glory*, ch. 9.
24. *God's Plot: The Paradoxes of Puritan Piety Being the Autobiography & Journall of Thomas Shepard*, ed. Michael McGiffert, p. 74.
25. Koehler, *Search for Power*; Karlsen, *Devil in the Shape of a Woman*.

"free grace" with another writer, quoted the synod of 1637 against his opponent.[26] When the Great Awakening broke out in New England in the 1740s, a minister who viewed the revival as a manifestation of "enthusiasm" and not as a work of grace, cited in his favor the findings of the synod.[27] Nathaniel Hawthorne was more sympathetic; in *The Scarlet Letter* (1850), he likened Hester Prynne, a rebel for the sake of "heart," to Anne Hutchinson.[28] And in our day Anne Hutchinson has become emblematic of the possibilities—long thwarted, though never wholly suppressed—for women to assert spiritual leadership.[29]

Preparing these texts for publication many years ago, I had the skillful assistance of Avi Soifer. This time around, I want to thank Michael McGiffert for aid of many kinds over the years, and in particular for reviewing this new preface. I am grateful to Janice Knight for other comments, and to Stanley Fish and Jane Tompkins for recommending a new edition of this book. A few errors crept into the first edition, and these have been corrected. I have provided some additional commentary in the form of new footnotes. These notes, introduced into this edition of *The Antinomian Controversy*, appear on the pages listed below. Each note is indicated by an asterisk at the bottom of its respective page.

Notes to the Second Edition

P. 51: The theological and philosophical language in Question IX is explicated in two useful articles: "habit" in Norman Fiering, "Benjamin Franklin and the Way to Virtue" and "The Image of God in Adam" in Jesper Rosenmeier, "New England's Perfection."

---

26. Daniel Williams, *Gospel-truth Stated and Defended* (London, 1692).

27. Charles Chauncy, *Seasonable Thoughts on the State of Religion* (Boston, 1743).

28. Colacurcio, "Footsteps of Anne Hutchinson."

29. Two words of caution are in order. Anne Hutchinson was probably not a practicing midwife, since that name is never used in connection with her in the records. And while she opposed the authority of the ministers, she may not have been an egalitarian. Her theology seems to involve the distinction between the few gathered saints, and the hypocritical worldly.

"Habit" or "habitual grace" signifies the infused virtues and gifts of the Holy Spirit and is an aspect of sanctification. See pp. 40, 45, 103, 143, 195–96, 401, 411.

P. 58: The Latin phrase *proxima potentia* was translated by John Cotton as "nearest power" (see p. 158).

P. 58: Question XV has to do with the validity of the "practical syllogism," for which see also pp. 76, 182, 237. From Calvin onward, the Reformed (Calvinist) tradition debated the proper uses of the "practical syllogism." See Hall, "Understanding the Puritans," p. 345 n. 17; Stoever, *'Faire and Easie Way,'* pp. 126–29.

P. 63: See pp. 74 and 107 for other references to 1 John 5.

P. 65: Compare John Cotton's rearrangement of the sequence "word, work, and object" to (p. 86) "object (ground, or justification), word, work."

P. 117 n. 17: John Cotton translated the Latin (p. 183) as "a latter, or secondary proof."

P. 142: When John Cotton wrote that "I have the gift of faith . . . in order of nature before I be justified," he was using a Scholastic term that Stoever explicates in *'Faire and Easie Way,'* p. 125. The term is used elsewhere in these documents. See also pp. 194, 401.

P. 165: The Puritans (like most other Christians in this period) reckoned that the conversion of Jews to Christianity was foretold in the Book of Revelation and would occur shortly before the Second Coming. See also pp. 155, 308, 380.

P. 174: Francis Cornwell was "a Kentish vicar who became a leader among the Baptists and a considerable author," as Geoffrey Nuttall pointed out in his review of the first edition. *Journal of Ecclesiastical History* 20 (1969), p. 358.

P. 197 n. 44: John Cotton translated this same passage from Chamier (see below, p. 410) as "Chamier . . . denyeth Faith to bee a cause of Justification; 'For if it were (saith hee) Justification should not be of Grace, but of us.' "

P. 200: The 1692 reprinting of *A Short Story* was occasioned by a theological controversy, the so-called "Crispian" or "Neonomian" dispute, that broke out within English nonconformity in that year. The various polemical contributions to this debate by Daniel Williams, Isaac Chauncy (a Harvard College graduate), and others throw an interesting and largely unexplored light on the debates of the 1630s.

P. 214: Anne Hutchinson was either pregnant (as contemporaries assumed) or suffering from a hydatidiform mole, as modern medical opinion holds. Her physical weakness during the church trial (see p. 351) arose from this condition.

P. 219: An independent manuscript copy of the Synod of 1637's deliberations was consulted by Charles Chauncy as he prepared *Seasonable Thoughts on the State of Religion in New-England* (Boston, 1743), his onslaught against the Great Awakening. He quoted a passage (p. vi) on "the Reasons given for the meeting of the Synod" that was not carried over into *A Short Story:* "the Opinionists pretended such a New Light as condemned all the Churches, as in a Way of Damnation; and the Difference to be in Fundamental Points, even as wide as between Heaven and Hell: And hence it was conceived, that all the Churches should consider of this Matter, that if it were a Truth, it should be universally embraced; but if it were an Error of Heresy it might be universally suppressed, so far as such a Meeting could reach.' "

P. 226: Error 24 can be connected to the accusation against Mrs. Hutchinson (p. 308) that she boasted of being able to know "infallibly . . . the election of others." Wheelwright's fast-day sermon, John Cotton's *Sermon Preached at . . . Salem,* and Error 22 (restricting the scope of the minister's sermons to the elect) are relevant to an understanding of the ecclesiastical implications of spiritism.

P. 247: "All the Churches unanimously consented to the Condemnation of them [these errors], except diverse of Boston, one or two at Charlestown, one at Salem, one at Plymouth, one at Duxbury, two at Watertown: And although Mr. Cotton set not down his Hand as the rest of the Elders did; yet he thus expressed himself, in Disrelish of them, *that some were blasphemous and heretical, many erroneous, and all incongruous."* Chauncy, *Seasonable Thoughts,* p. vii.

P. 255: According to Samuel Groom, John Cotton protested that "Brother Wheelwright's Doctrine was according to God, in the Points Controverted, and wholly, and altogether; and nothing did I hear alleged against the Doctrine proved by the Word of God." *A Glass for the People of New England,* repr. in *The Magazine of History* 37 (1929), pp. 10–11.

P. 268: Mrs. Hutchinson was quoting Joel 2:28: "I will pour out my Spirit. . . ."

P. 280: The publicizing of Mrs. Dyer's "monster birth" is described in Hall, *Worlds of Wonder,* pp. 100–102. See also Anne Schutte, " 'Such Monstrous Births': A Neglected Aspect of the Antinomian Controversy," *Renaissance Quarterly* 38 (1985): 85–106.

P. 350: I would eliminate all of the italicization in the transcript of the church trial; I now think that the apparent underlinings in the manuscript were not meant to be transcribed as italics.

P. 378: Geoffrey Nuttall has suggested that the reference is to the English "free grace" Puritan Joshua Sprigges; but Stephen Foster has pointed out that Sprigges matriculated at Oxford in 1634, which makes him too young. Nuttall, review of this book, *Journal of Ecclesiastical History* 20 (1969): 358; Foster, "New England and the Challenge of Heresy," p. 646 n. 47.

P. 398: Robert Baillie renewed the charge of "Montanism" in *The Dissuasive from the Errors of the Time, Vindicated from the Exceptions of Mr. Cotton and Mr. Tombes* (London, 1655), alleging (pp. 22–24) that Cotton was known to have expressed "Montanist" ideas at Cambridge, specifically the indwelling of the Holy Spirit.

P. 398 note 3: Samuel Gorton's theology is described in Gura, *Glimpse of Sions Glory,* ch. 10.

P. 410: Baillie, who believed that it is "one of the grosse errors" that "the union of Christ with the soul is compleat before and without all acts of faith," questioned Cotton's interpretation of Chamier and Pemble (*Dissuasive ... Vindicated,* pp. 26, 29).

P. 413: "My information was that Mrs. Hutcheson [*sic*] did visite M. Cotton in his house much oftner then by any other of his whole flock was wont to be done...." Baillie, *Dissuasive ... Vindicated,* p. 29.

THE ANTINOMIAN CONTROVERSY, 1636–1638

Introduction

THE purpose of this volume is to bring together the essential documents of the Antinomian Controversy that took place in Massachusetts between 1636 and 1638. Antinomianism in its root sense means "against or opposed to the law." In theology it is the opinion that "the moral law is not binding upon Christians, who are under the law of grace." In New England it denoted the opposition between man's obedience to the law, or his works, and the saving grace communicated by the Holy Spirit. But the colonists in Massachusetts who stood for "free grace" against the "legall" preachers did not call themselves Antinomians since to them, as to most seventeenth-century Protestants, the term implied licentious behavior and religious heterodoxy. Together with those other common terms of abuse, "Anabaptist" and "Familist," it was used, rather, by the opponents of the "Antinomians" to discredit them. *A Short Story of the Rise, reign, and ruine of the Antinomians, Familists & Libertines, that infected the Churches of New-England* was John Winthrop's way of linking the proponents of "free grace" in Massachusetts with these disreputable movements. Such language suggests how deeply the interests and feelings of the colonists were engaged in the Controversy. To them its significance was plain. It was a struggle for control of Massachusetts, and when control was assured the victors showed little mercy to the vanquished. In truth, the Antinomian Controversy is one of those events historians speak of as crises or turning points. Coming at a time when the new society was still taking shape, it had a decisive effect upon the future of New England.

Most of the documents of the Controversy were brought together in a single volume by the New England historian Charles

Francis Adams in 1894.[1] Others have remained uncollected, and a few are published here for the first time. This volume contains all of the documents in Adams's collection as well as most of the remaining published materials. Those reprinted here, but not in Adams, include the *Sixteene Questions of Serious and Necessary Consequence,* John Cotton's *A Conference . . . at Boston,* and John Wheelwright's fast-day sermon. Five other documents are drawn from unpublished manuscripts: the letters between Thomas Shepard, John Cotton, and Peter Bulkeley, the ministers' "Reply," and a major statement by Cotton of his theology, here entitled his "Rejoynder." The sum total of new material nearly equals the size of Adams's original collection. The significance of these new materials, though less easy to measure, seems just as great. In the traditional view of the Antinomian Controversy, Anne Hutchinson assumes the leading role as the chief antagonist of the orthodox party. But in the new documents, the major figure is John Cotton. Strictly speaking, he was not an Antinomian, yet the evidence gathered here clearly indicates that his differences of opinion with the other ministers in Massachusetts were at the heart of the Controversy.

The remainder of this introduction falls into three sections. The first contains a brief history of the Antinomian Controversy. The second pursues a few of the theological issues involved, and the last summarizes the principles followed in the editing of the documents.

I

THOUGH the documents cover a period of nearly three years, the Antinomian Controversy took place essentially in the seventeen months between October, 1636, and March, 1638.[2] The story of

---

1. *Antinomianism in the Colony of Massachusetts Bay, 1636–1638* (Boston, The Prince Society, 1894).

2. The dates in the introduction and headnotes are Old Style, following the Puritans' calendar, with the exception that the beginning of the new year has been changed to January 1. This narrative of the Controversy is based on the account of John Winthrop, whose *History of New England* is the essential source of information about what happened, and when. The edition prepared by James Savage (Boston, 1853) has been followed. The *Records of the Colony of Massachusetts-Bay,* ed. N. B. Shurtleff, *1* (Boston, 1853), is the source of other details.

what occurred during those months must begin with a woman, Anne Hutchinson. She was a Puritan, like most of the other emigrants to Massachusetts, but because her Puritanism took a different turn she was eventually banished from the colony as a heretic. For her, as for the founders of New England, Puritanism meant an insistence upon an evangelical ministry preaching the Word of God. Anne's father, Francis Marbury, was such a minister in the Church of England. When she was born in 1591 he was preaching in the town of Alford, Lincolnshire. Later the Marburys moved to London, but in 1612 Anne returned to Alford as the wife of a local merchant, William Hutchinson. That same year the Reverend John Cotton left Emmanuel College, Cambridge, where he had been a tutor, to become the minister of Boston, Lincolnshire, a town some twenty miles from Alford. Cotton was just twenty-seven years old, but his vigorous and incessant preaching soon established him as one of the leading Puritans in England. Among his admirers was Mrs. Hutchinson. When Cotton, to avoid imprisonment for his nonconformity, fled to New England in 1633, "it was a great trouble unto" her. Like hundreds of other English Puritans in the same predicament, she felt she "could not be at rest" until she followed her beloved minister across the sea. For this reason the Hutchinson family sailed from England in May, 1634.

In the two years between their arrival and the outbreak of the Antinomian Controversy, the Hutchinsons established themselves as leaders in the new Boston where Cotton was now preaching. In November, 1634, William Hutchinson was elected a deputy from Boston to the Massachusetts General Court, the highest political authority in the colony. Anne took on the role of spiritual adviser to others of her sex. At first she visited around, usually to women in childbirth. Then, at some unknown date, she began to hold meetings in her home for the purpose of repeating and discussing the previous week's sermons. These meetings became so popular that she had to organize another series for men. In all, some sixty or more persons crowded into the Hutchinson home each week to hear Anne comment on the sermons not only of Cotton, but also of the other ministers who were preaching in nearby towns.

Much of what Mrs. Hutchinson heard from those other min-

isters was not to her liking, and she said so to the people gathered
in her house. She complained that, with the exception of Cotton,
the ministers were "legalists" who argued for some necessary connection between man's own works and his redemption by Christ.
They took the outward evidence of "sanctification" — leading a
righteous life — to mean that Christ had redeemed, or justified, a
person's soul. Needless to say, the ministers did not agree with
Anne's interpretation of their preaching. Nor did they like the
other ideas she was spreading among her listeners. As early as September, 1634, the Reverend Zechariah Symmes, who came to New
England with the Hutchinsons, had questioned her orthodoxy;
but it was not until the spring of 1636 that the other ministers in
the colony warned Cotton of the strange opinions circulating
among his parishioners. At the same time Cotton's colleagues
were having doubts about his preaching. Was he the source of
Mrs. Hutchinson's ideas?

In October, 1636, the ministers confronted this question directly. That month they gathered in Boston for a "conference in
private" with Cotton, Mrs. Hutchinson, and her brother-in-law,
the Reverend John Wheelwright, who had just arrived in the colony. The results of the conference were encouraging, for Cotton
"gave satisfaction to them, so as he agreed with them all in the
point of sanctification, and so did Mr. Wheelwright; so as they all
did hold, that sanctification did help to evidence justification."
But in the Boston Church differences of opinion were still unre-
solved, and when a majority of the members, "being of the opinion of Mrs. Hutchinson," proposed that Wheelwright join the
Church's ministry, these differences erupted into a public quarrel.
Boston already had a second minister, the Reverend John Wilson,
who was unsympathetic to Anne Hutchinson. By nominating
Wheelwright, her supporters clearly meant to insult — and replace — Wilson. This was too much for John Winthrop, the leading layman in the church and a friend of Wilson. Taking advantage of a rule requiring unanimity in a church vote, he was able to
thwart Wheelwright's election, though he did so at the price of increasing the bitterness in the church.

Two months later the ministers again met in Boston with Cotton and Mrs. Hutchinson. This time their conference failed to

produce agreement. Answering a question about sanctification, Cotton warned that if taken wrongly as evidence of justification it amounted to a "Covenant of Works." Mrs. Hutchinson was more blunt; she told the ministers directly that many of them were preaching "works," not "grace." In the meantime the Controversy had entered the General Court. On December 7 the governor of Massachusetts, Henry Vane, announced his resignation to a special session of the deputies. Vane was an admirer of Mrs. Hutchinson, and the reason he gave for wanting to leave the colony — his fear that "God's judgments" would "come upon us for these differences and dissensions" — contained the implication that her indictment of the ministers was correct. After Vane withdrew his resignation at the request of the Boston Church (the members knew the value of a friend in power), the Court began debating who was to blame for the colony's troubles. Vane pointed to the ministers, but they, in turn, accused him of provoking the Controversy. In a "very sad speech of the condition of our churches," John Wilson spoke for his colleagues in laying "the blame upon these new opinions risen up amongst us, which all the magistrates, except the governour and two others, did confirm, and all the ministers but two." Finding itself divided like the colony, the Court concluded its session with a call for a general fast on January 19. There was still the hope that repentance would restore peace.

But the fast-day served only to deepen the lines of division. That it failed to bring peace was largely the doing of John Wheelwright. Attending services at the Boston Church, he was called up out of the congregation by Cotton and invited to preach. Wheelwright responded with a sermon in which (to quote Winthrop's summary) he "inveighed against all that walked in a covenant of works, as he described it to be, viz., such as maintain sanctification as an evidence of justification etc. and called them antichrists, and stirred up the people against them with much bitterness and vehemency." Encouraged in this fashion, the Antinomians intensified their crusade against the "legalists" among the clergy. During lectures and church services, they asked "public questions" of ministers who preached "doctrines, which did any way disagree from their opinions; and it began to be as common here to distinguish between men, by being under a covenant of grace or a covenant of works, as in other countries between Protestants and Papists."

This was the situation when the General Court met again on March 9. To his great relief, Winthrop could report that "the greater number far [of the deputies and magistrates] were sound," and the actions of the Court bear him out. One of the Antinomians, a man named Steven Greensmyth, was fined £40 and ordered to "acknowledge his fault in every church" for saying that "all the ministers (except Mr. Cotton, Mr. Wheelwright, and hee thought Mr. Hooker) did teach a covenant of works." After voting its approval of the speech John Wilson had made in December, the Court called upon Wheelwright to answer for his sermon. When he "justified it, and confessed he did mean all that walk in such a way," the Court asked the other ministers what this meant, and learned that "such a way" referred to the message they were preaching. Wheelwright was promptly judged guilty of "contempt & sedition" for having "purposely set himself to kindle and increase" bitterness in the colony. Wheelwright's friends did not let this vote pass without a fight: "much heat of contention . . . between the opposite parties," was Winthrop's laconic reference to the ensuing struggle. The minority within the Court protested formally, and the Boston Church, which had petitioned for procedural changes favorable to Wheelwright at the beginning of the session, now "tendered a petition in his behalf, justifying Mr. Wheelwright's sermon." None of these protests was accepted, nor was Henry Vane able to prevent the Court from deciding it would hold its next session in Newtown (Cambridge). That session would be a "general court of elections," and the orthodox party knew it stood a better chance of winning if the elections for governor and magistrates were held in a town other than Boston.

The excitement of election day, May 17, still lives in Winthrop's narrative. No sooner had the session begun than a clash occurred over a petition presented in defense of Wheelwright.

> The governour [Henry Vane] would have read it, but the deputy [John Winthrop] said it was out of order; it was a court for elections, and those must first be despatched, and then their petitions should be heard . . . but yet the governour and those of that party would not proceed to election, except the petition was read. Much

time was already spent about this debate, and the people crying out for election, it was moved by the deputy, that the people should divide themselves, and the greater number must carry it. And so it was done, and the greater number by many were for election. But the governour and that side kept their place still, and would not proceed.

A majority of the freemen then went with Winthrop to one side of the Newtown common and elected him governor in place of Vane.

Other measures against the Antinomians followed. In the election of magistrates, the two incumbents who had supported Wheelwright were left out, and when one of them, together with Henry Vane, reappeared in the Court as one of two deputies from Boston, the majority "found a means to send them home again." On a second try the two gained admission, but their presence failed to deter the Court from ordering that no "strangers" could be received in the colony for longer than three weeks without the permission of the Court. This law was necessary, Winthrop declared, in order to prevent the Antinomians from adding new immigrants to their number.

Meanwhile the ministers were trying to settle the theological aspects of the Controversy. About the time of the election, they emerged from a new round of conferences bearing an agreement with Cotton on the issue of sanctification. But the list of other doctrines in dispute was now so long that they decided to hold a special "synod." Meeting at Cambridge on August 30, the synod took up the business of identifying and refuting some ninety "errours" of the Antinomians. Another of its tasks was to deal with various problems of church order that the Controversy had exposed. Because the Antinomians had abused two of the privileges of church members, the liberty to question the minister and that to hold "private" meetings, the synod warned against their continuance. With tighter control of doctrines and church order assured, the ministers adjourned on September 22.

If the synod was a demonstration that the ministers had closed ranks, the colony as a whole still suffered from the aggressive challenges of the Antinomians. Many of their acts were petty. After Winthrop replaced Vane as governor, the honor guard that Boston provided the office-holder refused to escort him. In July, Vane turned down an invitation from Winthrop to attend a state dinner on the grounds "that his conscience withheld him." More serious was the fact that "though Mr. Wheelwright and those of his party had been clearly confuted and confounded" by the synod, "they persisted in their opinions, and were as busy in nourishing contentions . . . as before." Realizing, finally, that "two so opposite parties could not contain in the same body, without apparent hazard of ruin to the whole," Winthrop and a majority of the colonists determined to adopt a sterner policy. At the next General Court session, which began on November 2, the leaders of the Antinomian party were disfranchised and banished from the colony. A variety of lesser penalties was imposed upon the other signers of the petition presented to the Court in March, and the Court concluded by ordering that all "guns, pistols, swords, powder, shot, and match" be collected from Mrs. Hutchinson's sympathizers.

Then it was Anne Hutchinson's turn. Since she had not engaged in any of the political protests, the Court had to find some other basis on which to punish her. Her trial by the Court was nearly a disaster, for Mrs. Hutchinson made the various charges brought against her seem ridiculous. Not until she spoke of receiving revelations from God did the Court find an issue on which she could be banished from the colony. With her proscription, the Controversy drew to its close. In the winter months, the churches were busy disciplining members who had taken part in the affair. Thus the last chapter of Mrs. Hutchinson's life in Massachusetts was her "trial" before the Boston Church, from which she was excommunicated on March 22, 1638. Six days later she left the colony. Like many of the other exiles, the Hutchinsons went to Rhode Island. A few years later, they moved near present-day Rye, New York, where in August, 1643, Anne Hutchinson and a dozen members of her family were killed in an Indian raid.

II

In the opinion of Charles Francis Adams, the Antinomian Controversy could not be properly appreciated if it were approached from a theological point of view. "As a rule," suggested Adams, "theological controversies are . . . among the most barren of the many barren fields of historical research; and the literature of which they were so fruitful may, so far as the reader of to-day is concerned, best be described by the single word impossible." Such a statement may reflect Adams's urbane scepticism more than a realistic understanding of history, yet Adams found confirmation for his rule in the Antinomian Controversy. To him the theological language employed by the ministers was "a jargon which has become unintelligible." The "mis-called" controversy was, in any case, not about matters of doctrine but about power and freedom of conscience. Anne Hutchinson and John Wheelwright, declared Adams, were rebels against the dogmatic tyranny of the ministers. Their revolt was the first step toward the "emancipation" of Massachusetts from the heavy burden of Puritanism.[3]

Crude though it was, Adams's interpretation is partly borne out by some more recent investigations.[4] Leaving aside the social and political dimensions of the Controversy which are explored by these investigations, the following discussion addresses itself to the theological issues that Adams dismissed as "jargon." What were these issues? The most complete guide to them is the catalogue of "erroneous opinions" compiled at the synod of 1637. But this list is repetitious and indiscriminate; it also lumps together the opinions that emerged later on in the Controversy with those that circulated from the start. In searching for the root issues, this chronological distinction must be kept in mind, as well as the difference between the issues debated by the ministers and those injected into the Controversy by the more radical members of the Boston Church. In the beginning there were only two issues involved, according to Winthrop's reckoning: "1. That the person of the Holy Ghost dwells in a justified person. 2. That no sanctification can help to evidence to us our justification."[5] The second of these statements figured as the major issue in the debate between John Cotton and his fellow ministers. Replying to the sixteen questions, Cotton answered "more largely and distinctly" to

3. C. F. Adams, *Three Episodes of Massachusetts History* (Boston, 1892), 366–367; Brooks Adams, *The Emancipation of Massachusetts* (Boston, 1887).
4. The Bibliographical Note following the documents refers to these studies.
5. Winthrop, *History, 1*, 239.

question thirteen, "Whether evidencing Justification by Sanctification, be a building my Justification on my Sanctification," it being, as he said, "exposed to greatest Agitation and Exception."[6]
According to Thomas Shepard, the "principall opinion & seed" of
all the "monstrous opinions" condemned by the synod of 1637 was

> that a Christian should not take any euidence of gods speciall grace
> & loue toward him by the sight of any graces or conditionall euan-
> gelicall promises to fayth or sanctification; in way of ratiocination;
> (for this was euidence & so a way of woorkes,) but it must be with-
> out the sight of any grace fayth holines or speciall change in him-
> selfe. by immediat reuelation in an absolute promise. & because
> that the whole scriptures do giue such cleare plaine & notable eui-
> dences of favour to persons called & sanctifyed; hence they sayd
> that a second euidence might be taken from hence but no first
> euidence.[7]

To this same issue, finally, Winthrop referred most often in his
running account of the Controversy.

If we accept this testimony, the problem is then to understand
why the relationship between justification and sanctification became so debatable in the 1630s. Part of the explanation lies in the
background of the colonists. Like other English Puritans, they assumed that everyone could know whether or not he was saved, or
of the elect. The blunt question of the revivalist — "Brother, are
you saved?" — had its analogue in the evangelical preaching of the
spiritual brotherhood, the fraternity of Puritan preachers in England. To help their listeners answer that question, the preachers
wrote scores of books describing the process of conversion in
which the elect came to know "experimentally" of their salvation.
But no one who listened to the "painfull" sermons of the ministers could take his salvation for granted. The conversion experience was too variable, the "heart" of the sinner too shifting, for
assurance to be complete. The result of the ministers' preaching
was thus to arouse an acute anxiety in many of those who lacked

---

6. *Sixteene Questions of Serious and Necessary Consequence* (London,
1644), 14.
7. "The Autobiography of Thomas Shepard," *Publications of the Colonial Society of Massachusetts, 27,* 385.

assurance. The preachers could not resolve the problem by declaring that anxiety was inevitable. They had to provide some objective measure of grace, some outward sign of inner holiness. One such sign was sanctification, the daily course of living a godly life. Though the Puritans recognized that a hypocrite could simulate the life of righteousness, they reasoned that only the person whose heart had been transformed could sustain his obedience to the will of God. Outward behavior could therefore be taken as a sign — albeit a confusing one — of justification.

The colonists brought the problem of achieving assurance with them to New England, and in the new world a special set of circumstances made it more intense. One of these circumstances was the religious excitement that prevailed in Massachusetts during the early 1630s. While the colonists remained in England, they lived in the fear that the government would deprive them of their spiritual "food," the preaching of the spiritual brotherhood. When Archbishop Laud made that fear a reality by driving the Puritan preachers out of the Church, Puritan laymen risked their lives to found a new society in which evangelical preaching would be unrestrained. For the first time in their lives, these Puritans could indulge themselves in sermons, and there is ample evidence to suggest that they did so.[8] It was not only a feeling of release that inspired indulgence of this kind; the colonists also turned to their ministers for comfort to make up for that denied them by the bleak New England wilderness. If the shock of their encounter with that landscape drove some colonists back to England, others responded by seeking consolation from the Holy Spirit.

Out of this heightened longing for grace came a revival, a period of exaggerated piety. According to Roger Clap, who placed the beginning of this revival in 1633, it served as a means of relieving the anguish of dislocation:

> God's holy spirit in those days was pleased to accompany the word with such efficacy upon the hearts of many, that our hearts were taken off from old England and set upon heaven. The discourse not only of the aged, but of the youth also, was not, "How shall we

---

8. Winthrop, *History*, *1*, 390; 4 *Collections of the Massachusetts Historical Society*, *1*, 211.

go to England?" . . . but "How shall we go to heaven? Have I true grace wrought in my heart? Have I Christ or no?" O how did men and women, young and old, pray for grace, beg for Christ in those days. And it was not in vain. Many were converted, and others established in believing.

The Boston Church Records bear Clap out on the number of conversions. In the six months following John Cotton's admission to membership in September, 1633, sixty-three persons — or nearly half the number of members acquired during the previous three years — joined the church.[9]

An increase in church membership was not the only consequence of the revival. At the time it occurred, the colonists were debating what standards of church membership they should adopt. The revival was to shape that debate in a crucial direction. The colonists wished to restrict the church to the godly, but they were not sure what terms to demand of prospective church members. By 1633, they had set up two requirements, soundness in doctrine and evidence of good behavior. Some of the ministers, among them John Cotton, wanted to go further by requiring candidates to testify before the church about their experience of conversion. Since the revival seemed to guarantee an abundance of conversions, the other ministers agreed, and in February, 1636, when Thomas Shepard formed a new church in Cambridge, the advice of the ministers present was "that such as were to join should make confession of their faith, and declare what work of grace the Lord had wrought in them; which accordingly they did."[10]

But by 1636 the revival itself was over. For the first time in America, the ministers learned the lesson that the tide of grace soon ebbs. The reasons seemed clear. As the hardships of life in the new world diminished, the colonists were turning to other interests. Piety declined as the lure of prosperity grew stronger. As early as 1635 the new mood had disheartened John Pratt of Water-

9. Alexander Young, *Chronicles of the First Planters of the Colony of Massachusetts Bay* (Boston, 1846), 354–355; Boston Church Records, *Collections of the Colonial Society of Massachusetts, 39*, 12–18.

10. Edmund S. Morgan, *Visible Saints* (New York, 1963), Ch. 3; Winthrop, *History, 1*, 215.

town. Haled before a court for complaining about the spiritual depression, Pratt explained that the "many folde occasions & businesses, which here att first wee meete withall" prevented the colonists from keeping their "hearts in that holy frame which some tymes they were in, where wee hadd lesse to doe in outward things."[11] Similarly the ministers were discovering that the feeling of release had a disappointing consequence. "Does not plenty of means make thy soul slight means?" Shepard asked his Cambridge congregation. "When you went many miles to hear, and had scarce bread at home, O, you thought, if once you had such liberties; but when they are made yours, now what fruit?"[12]

The collapse of the revival engendered a mood of acute religious anxiety. As Clap's account indicates, the revival and the new requirement for church membership were forcing everyone in the colony to ask himself, am I saved? In the aftermath of the revival many were not sure of the answer. How could they tell if they were saved or not? What evidence could they rely upon? How could they gain assurance of salvation and escape from anxiety about their spiritual estates? For one member of the Boston Church the answer to these questions was a desperate one. "A woman of Boston congregation, having been in much trouble of mind about her spiritual estate, at length grew into utter desperation, and could not endure to hear of any comfort, etc., so as one day she took her little infant and threw it into a well, and then came into the house and said, now she was sure she should be damned, for she had drowned her child."[13] Others, less desperate, found relief in cursing the ministers. Nowhere else in the world, remarked Shepard, had there been "such expectation to find the Lord," and for those who found Him not, the reaction against the ministers was intense: "They give in and therefore care not for . . . that food which they find nourisheth them not."[14]

Thus the spiritual depression of 1635–1636 gave rise to an an-

11. *Records of the Court of Assistants of the Colony of the Massachusetts Bay, 1630–1692* (Boston, 1904), 2, 111.

12. Thomas Shepard, *The Parable of the Ten Virgins Opened & Applied,* in *The Works of Thomas Shepard,* ed. J. A. Albro (Boston, 1853), 2, 92.

13. Winthrop, *History, 1,* 281–282.

14. Shepard, *Works, 2,* 170–171.

tiministerial attitude and an anxiety about the knowledge of God. All that was needed to turn these two ingredients into Antinomianism was the preaching of John Cotton. Cotton's sermons in Boston had touched off the revival of 1633, and in those he preached during the summer of 1636 he tried to get it going again. Piety had declined, declared Cotton, because the colonists had become too proud of New England's "Reformation" in manners. He reminded them that good behavior itself, or "walking in the wayes of God," as the various church covenants expressed it, was a "work" that any hypocrite could perform. Such "sanctification" could amount to no more than a "righteousness of ones own." In short, "Reformation is no assurance that God hath made an everlasting Covenant with us."

Against pride in "works" Cotton set the true measure of the saint. He was "Meek in Spirit & Merciful, and Mourning for Sin." He was overcome with a sense of his helplessness.

> Now then, doth the Lord draw you to Christ, when you are broken in the sense of your own Sins, and of your own Righteousness? When you look at duties you are not able to do them, not able to hear or pray aright.

Rather than counting upon "duties" for assurance, the sinner must look to God.

> If the Lord do thus draw you by his Everlasting Arm, He will put a Spirit into you, that will cause you to wait for Christ, and to wait for Him until He doth shew Mercy upon you.

The person who waited for Christ, whose heart was "emptied of every thing besides," could be judged one of the elect, and hence be eligible for church membership: "You may safely receive him into your Church fellowship."[15]

These themes reappeared in the conversation of Anne Hutchinson. Before the Controversy broke out, she had won Cotton's "loving and dear respect" for her efforts to overcome the spirit-

---

15. John Cotton, *A Sermon Preached...At Salem* (Boston, 1713), 30–33; John Cotton, *A Conference Mr. John Cotton Held at Boston with The Elders of New England* (London, 1646), 7.

ual deadness that he was also attacking. In her efforts to arouse the colonists "to seek for better establishment in Christ," Mrs. Hutchinson insisted that those who turned for comfort to the performance of "duties" were resting their assurance on "sandy foundations."[16] To this extent her message was useful and legitimate. Even John Winthrop admitted that "the Doctrine of free justification lately taught here took me in as drowsy a condition, as I had been in (to my remembrance) these twenty yeares."[17] But Anne Hutchinson did more than revive the colonists from their "drowsy" state. Taking up Cotton's warning against confidence in "works," she turned his denunciations of moralism into the specific charge that the other ministers in the colony were preaching a "Covenant of Works." By this term she meant that the ministers were letting people "thinke [themselves] to be saved, because they see some worke of Sanctification in them."[18] More broadly, the term she used referred to the covenant God had made with Adam. As a man without sin, Adam could ensure his salvation by fulfilling the condition of perfect obedience, but after the Fall man's "works" no longer earned him any merit with God. In the new "covenant of grace" that God established with Abraham, the sole reasons for salvation were the Gospel of Christ and the free gift of grace.

Mrs. Hutchinson based her attack upon the "legall" preachers on the difference between these covenants. Between free grace and man's own righteousness she saw no connection, and therefore insisted on treating sanctification as a "work." From the radical disjunction between grace and "duties" flowed the rhetoric of the Antinomians:

> Here is a great stirre about graces and looking to hearts, but give mee Christ, I seeke not for graces, but for Christ, I seeke not for promises, but for Christ, I seeke not for sanctification, but for

---

16. John Cotton, *The Way of Congregational Churches Cleared* (London, 1648), Pt. 1, 51–52.

17. *Winthrop Papers* (Boston, 1943), *3*, 344; [John Winthrop], *A Short Story of the Rise, reign, and ruine of the Antinomians, Familists & Libertines* (London, 1644), 31.

18. *John Wheelwright*, ed. Charles Bell (Boston, 1876), 164.

Christ, tell not mee of meditation and duties, but tell mee of Christ.[19]

On it was also based Anne Hutchinson's personal sense of communion with the Holy Spirit. Since her own piety rested upon an immediate awareness of the Spirit, she could deny that the ministry was needed as an intervening "means of grace" between God and man. And she could solve the problem of assurance by declaring that those who received the Spirit never had to doubt their estate again. In her system, any striving after "signs" of grace was a sure sign that grace had not been granted.[20]

Anne Hutchinson brought most of these beliefs with her to New England, but they owed their currency in the colony to the spiritual depression of 1635–1636. The "Antinomians" in Massachusetts were primarily those who sought relief from their religious anxiety and support for their anger at the ministers. Antinomianism provided them with both. Yet there was an alternative route to assurance and one that, in the end, the majority of the colonists chose to follow. As described by Thomas Shepard in a series of sermons he began to preach in the summer of 1636, this route involved a ceaseless striving after grace by the saints and the unregenerate alike. In Shepard's view, the spiritual journey of the saint on earth became a constant growth in grace as he struggled to fulfill the commands of God. Given this ceaseless struggle, the reason for the spiritual depression and the rise of Antinomianism was obvious. Antinomianism was simply a way for the "slothful" sinner to escape the demands of the law. Shepard had no patience with the argument that man was helpless; to the cry of the Antinomians, "We can do nothing, and why are we pressed to it?," he replied that God made room for man's own striving within the larger framework of the divine initiative. God and man worked together in the process of salvation: "Whereunto I also labor, striving according to his working, which worketh in me mightily" (Colossians 1.29). Since the grace of God made possible the efforts of the saint, Shepard argued that sanctification could be used as a valid sign of justification, or election. The same reasoning led

---

19. Winthrop, *Short Story*, 19.
20. Cotton, *The Way . . . Cleared*, Pt. 1, 52; [Winthrop], *Short Story*, 6, 8.

him to his doctrine of assurance. Though anxiety was part of the "trial" of life in this world, the saint, said Shepard, could gain assurance from his own striving after righteousness. The answer to anxiety lay in constant activity.[21]

The Controversy touched on other issues besides the relationship between justification and sanctification. One was the significance of "preparation" as a stage in the process of conversion. Did God demand that man prepare himself to receive grace? Did man's response to the "Law" have any saving efficacy? Cotton did not think so, but most of the ministers were "preparationists" to one degree or another.[22] Another problem was determining the relationship between faith and grace. Like all Protestants, the colonists believed that salvation was the gift of a merciful God who only asked of man that he have faith. Could faith be considered the "condition" of the covenant of grace, the response man must make to the offer of the Gospel before God would grant him grace? Or was faith an aftereffect, a consequence of justification? Cotton held to the latter opinion, but his opponents believed that faith was the "active" instrument for receiving grace.[23] Other issues besides these were involved in the ministers' debate, but all of them came around eventually to the original question: How is the saint to know he is saved? The rhetoric and theology of the Antinomian Controversy were never far away from the immediate problem of providing assurance for the troubled souls of the colonists.[24]

The differences of opinion between the ministers were a serious threat to the unity of Massachusetts so long as Cotton stuck to his position. But at the synod of 1637 he agreed to recognize the

---

21. Shepard, *Works, 2,* 250–251.

22. Cf. Perry Miller, " 'Preparation for Salvation' in Seventeenth-Century New England," *Nature's Nation* (Cambridge, 1967); Norman Pettit, *The Heart Prepared* (New Haven, 1966).

23. Cf. the exchange of views between John Cotton and Peter Bulkeley, below, and [Winthrop], *Short Story,* 6.

24. The Scriptural texts that figure most often in the Controversy were those dealing with the "witness" of man's salvation (1 John 5.10), with man's striving (2 Peter 1.9–10; Ephesians 1.13–14), with the opposition of grace and the law (Romans 8.14–16), and with the relationship between works and grace (Matthew 7.17; Romans 4.4–5).

validity of the other side; "The Spirit," he now affirmed, "doth Evidence our Justification in both wayes, sometime in an absolute Promise, sometime in a conditionall."[25] This was really a concession, not a compromise. Though his opponents may have agreed to tolerate Cotton's theology, it was their own synthesis of moralism, activism, and voluntaryism that came to prevail in New England.

In this sense the Antinomian Controversy was a turning point in the religious ideas of the colonists. But the Controversy was not the point at which New England left the mainstream of the Reformed tradition. The Antinomianism of Anne Hutchinson was the real departure, for it prefigured the radical stance of the Quakers. The New England ministers, on the other hand, remained officially faithful to the Westminster Confession for a hundred years. When the liberal movements of the eighteenth century reached New England, they had to do battle with Jonathan Edwards, the greatest champion orthodoxy was to have; and in his *Treatise Concerning Religious Affections,* Edwards quoted more from Thomas Shepard than from any other writer.

The effects of the Antinomian Controversy were rather upon the elusive "temper" of the New England Puritans and the region's church history. In the aftermath of the Controversy, the standards of church membership seemed to need revision, and by the 1640s the ministers were easing the requirement that candidates testify about their conversion experiences. Equally important was the shift in the ministers' thinking about the nature of their authority. The Congregationalism of the thirties was radically experimental in the way it allowed the minister and church members to share authority. But the shock of the Controversy recalled the ministers to a more traditional assertion of their prerogatives. Thus the Congregationalism of the Cambridge Platform (1648) reflected the temper of the forties, just as the Antinomian Controversy had reflected the temper of the thirties. Gone was the spiritual enthusiasm that had prompted the revival and the experiments in church order. In its place was a formalism that the ministers in New England would lament for another century.

---

25. Cotton, *The Way . . . Cleared,* Pt. 1, 45.

III

THE editorial principles followed in this volume depart from Charles Francis Adams's practice in several respects. Within the limits of nineteenth-century typesetting, Adams tried to achieve a literal reproduction of the texts. This meant that he repeated obvious printers' errors and employed the long s, in addition to leaving contractions and abbreviations as they appeared in the manuscripts. Scholarship no longer rests upon such antiquarian exactness. In the texts based on printed copies, errors have been silently corrected and the long s has been changed to the modern form. All contractions, abbreviations, and ampersands in manuscripts have been written out. Superior letters have been brought down to the line of text. Spelling has been regularized for the interchangeable letters u, v, w, i, and j. Biblical citations all follow the same form, while book titles and Latin phrases have been italicized. In the manuscript of John Wheelwright's fast-day sermon, would, should, and could were spelled without the u; here the missing letter has been restored. The first words of sentences have been capitalized. When material is quoted in the documents, the form of quotation has been changed to conform to modern usage. One text, the report of Mrs. Hutchinson's church trial, required extensive editing of punctuation. Otherwise the spelling, punctuation, and capitalization of the originals, whether printed texts or manuscripts, have been followed exactly.

These documents pose the problem of what is an "original" text in the first place. For several of the texts we depend upon a book written by a colonist but printed in England without his supervision, perhaps even without his consent. In December, 1637, John Cotton wrote to an English minister complaining of an unauthorized printing:

> One thing, let me intreate further of you. I heare there is a written Booke goeth up and downe in England under my Name, as my Catechisme. I did indeede goe over the Principles of Religion in way of Catechisme here. . . . But what Notes [have] bene taken of it from my mouth, I know not: Sure I am I never perused any Copy to be sent for England. And therefore if you heare of such a writing, I pray you, doe me this Christian favor, to beare witnesse from

me, I doe not owne it, as having never seene it: although [it] may
be; sundry things in it, were delivered by me, which I doe Acknowledge.[26]

In the 1640s, Thomas Shepard disowned the first edition of *The
Sincere Convert* on the grounds that "it was a collection of such
notes in a dark town in England, which one procuring of me, published them without my will or my privity. I scarce know what it
contains, nor do I like to see it, considering . . . the confession of
him that published it, that it comes out much altered from what
was first written."[27] Even the absence of such complaints does not
mean that a given text is accurate. In the case of the Antinomian
documents we should rather expect the opposite for the reason
that their seventeenth-century printings were based on one of the
many *copies* in circulation, not on the *originals*. Thanks to the
existence of independent copies of two of the following documents, the problem of establishing the original text has been
partly overcome. Besides the London printing of *A Conference
. . . Held at Boston,* there exist two contemporary manuscript versions. And there are handwritten emendations, drawn from the
"original MSS," in a printed copy of *Severall Questions of Serious
and necessary Consequence.* Only with the first of these did colla-
tion of the different copies turn up much material missing from
the printed version, but in both there are many changes that make
opaque paragraphs and sentences intelligible once again.

The editorial annotation in this volume also varies from
Adams's practice. He consistently commented upon the family
backgrounds of the persons involved in the Controversy and upon
what might be called its historical geography, the setting in terms
of nineteenth-century Boston. His notes on both of these subjects
are still worth consulting, since the information in them has not
been carried over into these pages. The biographical sketches included in the notes to this volume may be located in the index.

Adams assumed, and no doubt correctly, that his antiquarian audience cared not a whit for theology, and that it could read

---

26. John Cotton to John Dod, December (1637?), Cotton Papers, Prince
Collection, Boston Public Library.

27. Cotton Mather, *Magnalia Christi Americana* (Hartford, 1855), *1,* 389.

Latin. For modern readers these conditions exist in reverse. In the texts below, Latin passages have been translated unless a translation follows in the document itself or the phrase is a familiar one. I have identified as many as possible of the authors and books that were cited in the debates, using the editions available in the Yale University Library. The annotation of the theological "jargon" is selective. The principal aim has been to alert the reader to certain important terms, to interrelationships between the documents, to key passages of Scripture, and finally, to the vast literature of Puritanism that surrounds the Controversy.[28] Since the references to Scripture run into the hundreds, I have assumed that the serious student will often turn to a concordance and a King James Bible.

In the present volume, the pagination of seventeenth-century printings has been indicated, using numbers in brackets. The limited cross-referencing in the notes is supplemented by the index, which includes a number of theological categories.

The task of preparing these documents has been greatly eased by the assistance I have received from Mark Thomson, Gay Little, David Richards, and, most especially, my wife. I am grateful to Leo Curran for help in translating the Latin, and to Miss Marjorie G. Wynne for facilitating my use of the Stiles Papers, Yale University Library. The Massachusetts Historical Society has kindly granted permission to reproduce the documents in its possession.

---

28. The Bibliographical Note at the end of this volume refers to this literature.

CHAPTER I

Letters between Thomas Shepard
and John Cotton

THE letters that Thomas Shepard[1] and John Cotton[2] exchanged sometime before June, 1636, are perhaps the earliest documents of the Antinomian Controversy. In the first of these letters, Shepard expressed his dismay at the themes of Cotton's sermons and asked him to explain his views more fully. Over the next several months Cotton's opponents were to learn that pinning him down was not an easy business. Shepard may have learned this lesson already, for he requested that Cotton "give us satisfaction by way of wrighting rather then speech." Though both men were confident that the differences between them could be resolved, the exchange served only to clarify their disagreement on three points: the relationship between the Word and the Spirit; the activity of a sinner before he received the Holy Spirit; and finally, the life of righteousness as evidence of redemption. All three became major issues in the Controversy.

The letters bear no dates, but the time of the exchange may be fixed approximately from other information. Shepard arrived in Massachusetts in October, 1635. Thomas Hooker,[3] to whom Cot-

---

1. Thomas Shepard (1605–1649) emigrated to New England in 1635 and spent the rest of his life as pastor of the church in Cambridge.

2. John Cotton (1584–1652) was vicar of St. Botolph's, Boston, Lincolnshire before coming to New England in 1633. He was the outstanding minister among the founding generation.

3. Thomas Hooker (1586–1647), minister at Newtown and subsequently at Hartford, Connecticut, was a distinguished preacher in England before emigrating to Massachusetts in 1633. His daughter Joanna married Thomas Shepard in 1637.

ton refers as if he were living with Shepard, left Newtown (Cambridge) at the beginning of June, 1636. These two dates would seem to fix the period within which the letters were written. Shepard would not have been prepared to comment on Cotton's preaching immediately after arriving from England; thus 1636 seems more likely than 1635. And the reference he makes to "our church" may place the exchange after February 1, when he and a group of friends formed themselves into a church in Newtown.[4]

The manuscripts of the two letters are in the Cotton Papers, Prince Collection, Boston Public Library. Their condition is such that a full text cannot be established. Words in brackets represent readings warranted by fragments of letters or by the sense.

Thomas Shepard to John Cotton

Dear Sir

It is the earnest desire not only of my selfe, but of diverse of our members, whose harts are much endeared to you, that for the farther clearing up of the truth, you would be pleased to give us satisfaction by way of wrighting rather then speech for this on time to these particulars

1: Whether the man Christ Jesus in suffring the death of the soule, did not only loose the life of Joy; but also (to his own feeling) the life of righteousnes, or of the first Adam, and so lived by faith in the Duity; and hence [he puts] out the life of legall righteousnes and extinguisheth Adams righteousnes in all his members, and causeth him to live by that faith of the son of god.

2: Whether A Christian finding a qualification of a promise saving [wrought] in him; can, or should lay hold or close with the Lord Jesus according to that promise; but rather to stay for a more full, and clearer Revelation of the spirit: for if he is thus to set that promise by, and so to wait for the spirit; [then] doth he not refuse to give present honour to gods truth and love revealed in the promise; and on the other side; if he is to stay and rest his soule upon the promise before the spirit comes, doth he not then build on somewhat in him selfe, and receives the promise before god

---

4. Winthrop, *History, 1,* 202–203, 214–215, 223.

gives it to him? I doe gladly consent [to] that which you delivered last Thursday,[5] that he that stayes his soule upon the promise is bound to wait for a farther revelation or declaration of gods mind to him by the spirit in the ordinances and in the promise; and I thinke there is little love in that woman to her absent husband, that is quieted with his letters of his purpose to returne; and [longs?] not the more from the receiving of them, to see and enjoy himselfe; but my question if you observd it, is different from this;/

3: Whether this revelation of the spirit, is a thing beyond and above the woord; and whether tis safe so to say; because the spirit is not seperated from the woord but in it and is ever according to it:/

4: Whether a man can Truly lay hold on any promise, but that either he must be *de facto* in Christ, or *in fieri*,[6] immediatly and nextly preparing for Christ: for if he truly lay hold on a promise and never meet with Christ, then I would gladly know, [how] you can free the Lord and his [promise] from Falshood; for the promise speakes plainly that Christ is come to seeke and save the lost;[7] now if he that is truly lost beleeves this promise, and yet Christ never come to save him, then where is the truth of the promise? and on the other side: if he cannot truly lay hold on it, then I doe humbly desire you, to cleare your owne speeches this last Thursday; for you sayd (if I mistook not) a man might be truly lost (mentioning the promise first) and yet Christ never seeke nor save him, for then you sayd all the woorld which is lost, should be saved; and then Judas who not only was lost but felt himselfe also lost, is saved: to which I conceived I had no call publikely to reply; that Judas was not lost neither felt [himself] lost, in the sence and meaning of the promise; for lost men are [willing and] glad to follow there guide; which he was not; therefore is it not safer to say that a man may misapply the promise, and so thinke he doth truly close with Christ and the promise, rather then to say plainly

5. Every other Thursday was lecture day in Boston.
6. In the process of.
7. Luke 19.10: For the Son of man is come to seek and to save that which was lost.

that a man may truly lay hold on a promise, and yet misse of Jesus Christ? for under correction I doe perceive that the inferences made upon such speeches, will be very dangerous: not that I goe about to instruct you, whom god hath so greatly enriched what you should speake; for the Lord knowes I account it one of the greatest New England mercies that the providence of the Lord hath placed me so neare unto you; to be taught and to learne of you, but this that I speake tis from that due respect I beare to your selfe, and love and tendernes to your precious ministry, that it may suffer no blur; and also to cut off all seeming differences and jarrs: I make no question, with you, but a man may not only lay hold upon a promise, [but] also upon Christ himselfe, yet loose and misse of Jesus Christ; yet the truth is cleare to me that whosoever Truly layes hold of or closeth with a promise; but that either he hath Christ, or shall have Christ and the promise:/

5: Whether a Christian having once his sonship sealed to him by the spirit ever doubts agayne of Gods love to him as a son, though he fall into diverse grosse and scandalous sins:

6: Whether a Christian may be so far clensed by the blood of Christ, that although he comes not to the perfection of Adams righteousnes, yet he may come to attayne the same essence and truth of righteousnes that Adam had, and yet fall away: for I doe willingly consent thus far with you,

1: That by Christs blood a man may be sanctified, and set apart from prophane and common use, to speciall use in the church, in the judgement of which he may be truly sanctified, as all the churches Paul writ to were Saints and sanctified: yet many reall hypocrites among them that were visible Saints.

2: [That] a man may not only outwardly [and] in the judgement of the church be sanctified, but the man in his own feeling and in the sight of god himselfe be inwardly sanctified, or made [legally] righteous; but yet Inward legall righteousnes seemes to me to be far different, in Essence from Adams righteousnes: Aehues inward seale was far different from Adams seale; tis true Adams righteousnes was not immortall seed, but the same true holiness and righteousnes, those that are in Christ are only renewed unto, and being sown agayne in their harts by Christ it is so far cherished by Christ that its made now immortall seede; of which true holines and righteousnes I know no grounds as yet to thinke that any unregenerate man is renewed unto.

3: [I doe?] also grant that many professors do cozen themselves with inward legall righteousnes, either wrought in them by vertue of the spirit of bondage or fetcht from Christ himselfe, and take legall acts and dispositions as sure signes and markes of being in Christ; but yet still I desire to know of you whether this is the same righteousnes that Adam had for essence, differing from it only in degree; and whether tis the same holines and righteousnes that true beleevers have differing on from another only in the efficient, faith woorking the one, the law and the spirit of bondage woorking the other: I beseech you for speedy satisfaction send a speedy answer to these; for we shall not be able to stir out this weeke many sad imployments being now upon our church; on thing more I doe with submission desire you not to [be] mistaken in; as if that the Familists doe not care for woord or ordinances but only the spirits motion; for I have bin with many of them and hence have met with many of there bookes; and I doe know thus much of them, that scarce any people honour woord and ordinances more, for they will professe that there they meet with the Spirit and there superlative raptures; H.N:[8] the author of them cites scripture abundantly, and Jesabell Revelation 2: who hath her depthes, calls her selfe a prophetesse, tis her glory to interpret scripture; and but that I should hold you too long I could send you diverse of there *Theses de Sacra Scriptera,* by which you might soone see what honour they put upon the woord; and if your servant, after his mariage would not heare you, because the spirit moved him not; it was not its likely out of any contempt to the woord, but Because he might happily account your selfe a legall preacher; so (as they tearme them) to heare whom the spirit never mooves them; or if he did not thus judge of you, he had not fully learned his lesson; and he may well stand for an exception agaynst a generall rule; this I speake from the enforcement of my conscience, least under this colour of advancing woord together

---

8. Hendrik Nicholas or Niclaes (fl. 1502–1580), founder of the religious community known as Familists. Niclas, a mystic, claimed that he received revelations from God.

with the spirit, you may meet in time with some such members (though I know none nor judge any) as may doe your people and ministry hurt, before you know it; and thus I have plainly writ my hart unto you, being persuaded that in the spirit of meeknes, you will not thinke I have thus writ to begin or breed a quarrell; but to still and quiet those which are secretly begun and I feare will flame out unles they be quenched in time; I desire therefore that you would answer me in wrighting as soone as ever you can; and I do beleeve we shall not differ when things are hereby ripened for we are desirous and glad to learne; thus beseeching the god of all grace and peace to fill blesse and prosper you; with remembrance of my respect to that precious gentleman with you,[9] and to your wife I rest. Yours in the Lord Jesus

Tho. Shepard:

From New town:/

Addressed: To the reverend his deare friend Mr Cotton teacher at Boston be these ld

John Cotton to Thomas Shepard

Deare brother,

I thanke you unfeignedly for this labor of your love, to acquainte me with such passages in my ministery, as through eyther misexpression on my Part, or misconstruction, or misreport of others, might hinder the worke of christ amongst us. The particulars you enquire of are many, and the Returne of your Messenger is short, and therefore I shall (god Helping) returne you (as I may) short, and plaine Answers there unto.

1. Your 1. Quaere concerneth me not, nor any Doctrine or opinion of mine. I have some times heard it, and pleaded against it, as not safe if it should be receyved; But I know noe man that holdeth it, or even mentioned it, but by way of Inquiry, and Disputation.

2. To your 2d. I looke at all Promises as given us by the covenant

---

9. Sir Henry Vane (1613–1662) came to Boston in October, 1635. He was living with Cotton at the time Shepard wrote his letter. Elected governor of Massachusetts in May, 1636, Vane was defeated in his bid for re-election a year later and returned to England in August, 1637.

of grace, and the covenant of grace as given us by christ. So that
I doe not satisfy my selfe in closeing with a Promise, or with
the covenant of grace but as I first close with christ, in whom
the covenant, and the Promise is made, and confirmed, Isaiah
42.6: Galatians 3.16: 2 Corinthians 2.20:

And I conceyve the soule closeth with christ, by feeling himself
[a] poor desolate soule, lost for want of christ, sensible of his
owne Insufficiency to reach him, and unworthy also to receyve
him, yet seeking, and [1 word mutilated] for him in every ordi-
naunce, and spirituall Deuty, though finding it selfe unable to
beginne, or continue seeking or waiting, farther then christ
shall helpe, and worke with him.

Thus closeing with christ wee safely close with every Promise
so farre as the Lord revealeth it, and applyeth it to us: which
also stayeth the soule though not from searching farther after
christ, and the seale of his spirit, yet from sinkeing. [I suppose]
David closed with the Promise applyed to him by Nathan 2.
Samuel 12.13. and so gave honor to the trueth, and love of god
revealed in the promise, yet rested not so, but searched after
farther sense of the sprinkeling of the blood of christ, and comfort of the spirit Psalms 51.7.8.

3. The word, and Revelation of the spirit, I suppose doe as much
differ, as letter, and spirit. And therefore though I consent to
you, that the spirit is not separated from the word, but in it,
and ever according to it: yet above, and beyond the letter of the
word it reacheth forth comfort, and Power to the soule, though
not above the sence, and Intendment of the Word.

4. I doe not conceyve, that any man can truely lay hold of a [sav-
ing] Promise, till he lay hold of christ, and so the promise never
fayleth him, nor his takeing hold of it.

As for that Promise, that christ came to seeke, and to save that
which is lost, if he that is truely lost, doe truely beleive this
Promise, I doubt not, christ certainly came to save him; the
promise to such is a word of trueth.

Nor doeth this crosse (to my Remembrance) any speach delivered by me the last lecture. For though I saide, A man might
be truely lost (as I saide, all men were by the fall) yea and feele
him selfe to be lost (as I saide, Judas did, and others doe, by a

spirit of bondage, or Despayre) yet I spake not of men truely
lost according to the full meaning of the promise, but according to the common apprehension of it, when sundry seeing
their lost estate by a spirit of bondage, hearing that word doe
fo[rth] with beleive it belongeth to them. As for that sence
which you give of truely lost, I refuse it not: though I conceyve
the promise may reach lower then to such. For what if the soule
can not finde it selfe glad to follow his guide but feeleth it selfe
lost for want of a guide, and of grace to follow him: is it in such
an estate, as Christ [will] seeke and save if it feele it selfe lost
[for want of Christ? I doe not remember nor doe I beleive that
. . . hath saide . . . may truely lay hold on a Promise and yet
misse of Christ . . .]¹⁰
against mine owne judgment who doe not see how a man can
truely lay hold of any promise before he have layde hold of
christ. I blesse the Lord for your love to me, and tender respect
to my unworthy labors: and I truely returne you this office of
thankfullnesse, your person and worke findeth a large roome in
my heart, though my heart it selfe be straite, and narrow. As for
differences, and jarres, it is my unfeigned desire to avoide them
with all men especially with Brethren: but I doe not know, I
assure you, any difference, much lesse jarres, betweene me, and
any of my Brethren, in our Publique ministery, or other wise,
to any offence.

5. Your 5th Quaere I more affirmed, but doe conceyve that a
   childe of god sealed by the spirit falling into divers grosse, and
   scandalous sinnes may doubt againe of gods love; onely this I
   would say, that the sonnes of god so sealed doe more rarely fall
   into such sinnes (for it is some what contrary to their sealing)
   (which stampeth a character of christs Nature upon them:) yet
   sometimes such as doe so fall may yet reteyne or doubtlesse
   clayme unto gods fatherly love, as Isaiah 63.16.17. Neverthelesse I have found by some experience (more wayes then one)
   that god doeth leave his sealed children some times to such re-

---

10. The manuscript is mutilated at this point; the material in brackets is
supplied by a nineteenth-century transcript at the Massachusetts Historical
Society.

newed doubtings, the better to rayse up their hearts rather to
lay up all our joy in christ, then in our owne songs in the Night.
6. In your 6th Quaere you grant in your 3 propositions as much
(in a manner) as I desire to hold forth, for it is the desire of my
heart by the grace of christ [to provoke?] christians (in this
Countrey of universall Profession) not to rest in any such
. changes or graces, or Deutyes or ordinances (as church-fellow-
ship etc.) as may leave them short of saveing fellow-ship with
Jesus christ. But whether the common graces, and gifts of tem-
porary beleivers differ onely in degree, and in the efficient, I
am not for the present able to determine. All that I have saide
about it, is this, that I would not wish christians to build the
signes of theire Adoption upon [any] sanctification, But such as
floweth from faith in christ jesus; for all other holynesse, and
righteousnes, though it were as true as that of Adams in Innocency may be as his was a mortall seede, and fall short of perse-
verance: whereas the least seede of fayth, and of that holynes
which floweth from it abideth for ever.

As for the Familists, I onely expressed what I have found, not
onely from my man, but from a Ring Leader of that sect, Mr.
Townes of Notingham-shire[11] who is wont to say, he knowes
how farre our scripture learning can leade us, as haveing him
selfe found a more perfect way; also in the confession of fayth
published with the Life and Death of Mr John Smyth[12] I finde
they abuse that Place in 2 Peter 1.19: to say, that christians doe
well to hearken to the word as to a Light shining in a Darke
Place, till the Day Starre arise in theire hearts: but then they
are free from the word and sacraments etc: save onely for offence sake. If they please them selves in their Revelatyons, and
Raptures comming upon them in the word but not from the
word, their delusion is manyfest, but [good] Brother, doe not

---

11. Probably Robert Towne, author of *The Assertion of Grace* (London,
1644/45).

12. Thomas Piggott, *The Life and Death of John Smith* and *Propositions
and Conclusions . . . containing A Confession of Faith* (1613?), reprinted in
Robert Barclay, *The Inner Life of the Religious Societies of the Common-
wealth* (London, 1877), following p. 117. John Smith (d. 1612) was a separatist
Puritan who became a Baptist shortly before his death.

Resemble such a delusion to the faithfull Practise of such christians [why by?] feeling [their] neede of christ, and finding a
[Promise applyed to them by his word though they close there
with . . .][13]
give god the glory of his trueth, and love, yet doe not rest
therein till they have gott this Promise sealed unto them by the
further Annoyntment of the spirit. I persuade my soule with
out doubting, it is farre from your intention so to doe, though
your expressions seeme to feare some such danger in this manner of holding out of christ, which I have applyed my ministery
unto these many yeares both in old Boston, and in New; where
in if any error be discovered to me, God forbid I should shutt
mine eyes against it, but I suppose wee differ not here in, nor
any of my Brethren if wee understand one another. Nor doe I
discerne (though after diligent search) that any of our members, (brethren or sisters) doe hold forth christ in any other
way, so that if my ministery be hurt by this kinde of Declaration of the way of christ, or if any quarrells or stirrs be breed
there by, I hope even this also will tend to the farther service of
christ in the issue.
Meane while I hartily thanke you for this pretious fruite of
your unfeigned brotherly love, desireing you to helpe me further, with any such advertisements as may prevent any hin-
drance of the worke of christ in my hand, and may advance his
kingdome who is god over all blessed for ever.
Your salutations to Mr Vane I will god willing present to him
anon, who hath bene a broade all this Day.
Remember my Deare affection to your selfe, Brother Hooker
and others with you whom I deepely honor in the Lord; the
Lord Jesus fill us with him selfe, and leade us in his owne way
to his heavenly kingdome. In him I rest,

Your affectionate though weake
Brother

J C

---

13. Material in brackets comes from the Massachusetts Historical Society
transcript.

CHAPTER 2

Peter Bulkeley and John Cotton: On Union
with Christ

THE document below represents another stage of the dia-
logue between Cotton and his fellow ministers, in this case
with Peter Bulkeley.[1] Undated, it probably was written in mid-
1636 when the ministers were sounding Cotton out on his theological views. The form of the document is somewhat confusing.
In the first part (prior to "My Answer") conflicting arguments are
mingled, while Cotton's "Answer" embodies objections to his
point of view. This arrangement probably means that the document is a composite summary of earlier exchanges.

The issue between Bulkeley and Cotton is whether faith on
man's part is in any way antecedent to or a cause of "union" with
Christ. Behind the theological and scholastic terminology lies the
deeper question of man's role in the process of salvation. Bulkeley
believed that a person seeking Christ must make an active response to the divine initiative, and he argued that this active response, or faith, bore a causal relationship to salvation. In *The
Gospel-Covenant*, a treatise Bulkeley wrote in answer to the Antinomians, he explained the relationship in this way:

> But here a further question is made by some, what manner of con-
> dition faith is; It's granted (will some say) that faith is a condition,
> but it is a condition only consequent to our Iustification, and so to
> our being in Covenant with God; but its no antecedent condition;

---

1. Peter Bulkeley (1583–1659) emigrated to New England in 1635 and
was one of the founders of Concord, where he remained as minister until his
death. Together with Thomas Hooker, he presided over the synod of 1637.

ON UNION WITH CHRIST 35

wee are (as they conceive) in a state of Grace and salvation before
faith, and then faith comes and believes that Iustification and salvation which was before given . . . In opposition whereunto, I lay
down this conclusion . . . That we are not actually justified, nor in
a state of grace and salvation, before faith . . . . Its not a condition
only consequent, but antecedent to our actuall justification, and
being in state of grace before God.

In *The Gospel-Covenant* and in his exchange with Cotton, Bulkeley based his argument that faith was a "Cause" of justification
upon a distinction between justification as "purposed and determined in the minde and will of God," and justification as made
"actuall" in the life of the saint.[2] He and the other ministers
would also rely on Aristotle's four classes of causes — the formal
cause, or that into which something is changed; the efficient cause,
or that by which a change is wrought; the material cause, or that
in which a change is wrought; and the final cause, the end or purpose for which a change is made — in order to explain the "active"
role of faith. But from Cotton's point of view all of these distinctions simply meant that the ministers were introducing "works"
as a condition of grace. In his answer to Bulkeley he invoked the
four classes of causes himself, but only to prove that faith, if somehow involved in union with Christ, was a consequence of grace.

The manuscript of the text is in the Cotton Papers, Prince
Collection, Boston Public Library.

Received from Mr B.

THE spirit of God sent in to the soule worketh fayth.——that is
the union. If (sent) there must be a (Recevinge) Else a notionall
consideration of one Relative without the other. But in this union
our soule [neither] receives nor comprehends christ by Faith.

For by this declaration of the union, the spirit of God gives a
being to Fayth only, but noe power to actuall receivinge for that
comes after as a fruite of this union.

---

2. *The Gospel-Covenant; or The Covenant of Grace Opened* (London,
1646), 321–322.

If Fayth be wrought in the Soule then it must be effectuall Faith to make the bond of this union on our part: Else it is an Empty faith, without the power of it.

But this faith hath noe Efficacie of worke in this union.

For this union is made before Faith worketh, and the worke of this Fayth is but an effect of the union, and not any Cause of it.

It is not the Formall Cause of this union: for *forma esse, Animal rationale*[3] gives the beinge to a man. Nor is it Passive only

But this faith doth not give the forme to this union for it doth nothinge till the union be made, which yet can never be true union without the true Causes

Such a faith as this (as it hath Relation to this union) is not a livinge faith because it doth not his office, but leaves the soule mainly defective in point of our union for want of a concurrent act to helpe the soule to close with christ which makes up the true union on our parte, which Fayth the spirit of God gives and alsoe acts effectually, for that end in the Soules of his people.

If it be (the union) betweene Christ and the soule then there
must be a mutuall
{ giving
  and   each other: but in this union there is
  taking }
a mere taking on Gods part, noe givinge: because here the fayth hath not power to receive; But on mans part neither receiving of Christ, nor giving back himself to christ again, for fayth doth nothing till the union be compleated, and soe a consideration of one to be active in this union without the other   Soe that by the same reason that the spirit of God may unite it selfe to the soule before faith doth any thing in the union, By the same reason may the spirit of God unite it selfe to the soule without such a faith, and soe be united to an unbeleever, and soe to a Reprobate etc.

The working of faith by the Holy Ghost
This is the Union

---

3. Form gives being; the rational soul (gives being to a man).

The worke of faith in us to apprehende
This the fruit of the union

My Answer./
The Spirit of God sent into the Soule worketh Faith,
That is the Union.

Ob. "If sent, there must be a Receyving, Else a Notionall Consideration of one Relative without the other."

Ans. There is a Receyving, to wit, a Passive Reception (as Dr Ames calleth it in his *Medulla cap. de vocatione num* 20, 21:)[4] in that wee are Receyved as Paul saith, I am apprehended (that is, taken hold of, and receyved) by christ Jesus, Philippians 3.12.

"But in this union the soule neither Receyveth nor Comprehendeth christ Jesus."

Ans. In this union the soule Receyveth Christ, as an empty vessell receyveth oyle: but this receyving is not active, but passive.

"By this declaration of the union the spirit giveth onely a being to Faith: but noe power to actuall Receyving: for that cometh after, as a fruit of the union."

Ans. 1. The Spirit giveth a Power to actuall Receyving, that is, it giveth such a being to Faith, whereby it hath Power, (or is able) actually to beleive, and so actively to receyve Christ, as it did receyve him passively, it being created in the soule.

Ans. 2. There is [this] Difference betweene Actuall Receyving and active Receyving: A soule may actually receyve Grace as it doeth in receyving all the Gifts of Grace wrought in it in his first Conversion, wherein nevertheless the soule is merely passive. But it doeth actively receyve Grace, when it acteth upon Christ and stryveth by it self to receyve Christ for any helpe unto further measure of Grace. The first of these is in union, the latter is a fruite of union. An empty vessell actually receyveth oyle poured

---

4. William Ames (1576–1633), a Puritan theologian. Cotton cites his *Medulla Theologica* (Amsterdam, 1634), Bk. 1, 84–93. Though Cotton here attributes the distinction between passive and active faith to Ames, he would later declare that the term passive faith was "rarely hard of out of my mouth"; see p. 195. Ultimately the term derives from Aristotle's ten categories. Calvin speaks of believers acting "passively" in the *Institutes of the Christian Religion,* trans. F. L. Battles (Philadelphia, 1960), II.v.11.

into it, when it self is passive: but a child actively receyveth milke out of his mothers brests when by sucking it, it is active.

Ob. "If Faith be wrought in the soule, it must be Effectuall Faith, to make the bonds of the union on our parts, or else it is an Empty Faith, without the Power of it. But this Faith hath noe Efficacy in this Union."

Ans. 1. Effectuall the Faith is, though not to make the union, yet to Take, or Accept the union, and to bring forth the fruits of it.

2. Faith in union is also Effectuall, though not as an Efficient Cause to Effect the union, yet as a Formall cause to constitute the union: which it doth not by Acting upon christ unto union, but by acting upon the Matter, as a consentany Argument, consenting to dwell in the humbled soule where it is, as a forme in the *Formatum,* so making the soule alive in christ: 2. as a Consentany Argument unto Christ, as consenting to union with christ, as an Empty vessell is a consentany Argument to Receyve Oyle poured into it.

Ob. "This Faith is not the formall Cause of this union. For *forma dat esse. Anima rationalis* giveth the being to the man, nor is it passive onely.

"But this Faith doeth not give the Forme to this union. For it doeth nothing till the union be made: which yet can never be true union without the true Causes."

Ans. As *Forma dat Esse formato,* So doeth Faith to a true Faithfull christian making him alive in Christ, and so a member of him. As *Anima rationalis* giveth being to a man and so union with the first Adam: so doeth Faith give Being to a christian and so union with Christ. Nor is it Passive in that sence, nor did I ever say it was: I said indeede that it was not Active to Beleive upon Christ [unto] union, but Passively receyved him: but active upon man, as a consentany Argument dwelling in him, and so of a naturall man constituting him a christian, and so consenting formally to the Receyving of Christ. It is true, Faith doeth not give the forme to this union: for it self is the forme. But when you say, Faith doeth nothing till the union be made: be pleased to understand it doeth not Beleive upon Christ, till the union be made: but Acteth upon the Supposition, to wit, upon the man in whom it is, By making and constituting him of a carnall man, a spirituall and Faithfull man, a true christian, and so a member of christ. So that thus the union consisteth of all the 4 Causes completely.

The spirit of God is the principall and next Efficient cause, the word[5] of Grace the Instrumentall Cause:

The humbled Sinner, the materiall Cause:

The Grace (or Habit) of Faith the Formall Cause.

The Glory of Grace, and the Salvation of the Sinner, the finall Cause.[6]

The Habit of Philosophy maketh a man a Philosopher, though he never yet kept a Philosophy Act.

Anima rationalis makes a man to be what he is, a man, and so united to Adam, as a member and Hayre of his, though he have not yet putt forth any Rationall act upon Adam, but upon it owne Body, consenting to dwell in it, and so making it a man. So Faith maketh a christian man that which he is, a true christian and so united to christ as a member and Hayre of his, [though] he have not yett putt forth an Act of Beleiving upon christ, but the Act of a Consentany Argument upon the person in whom it is and consenteth to be, and so an Act of a Consentany Argument to christ, to wit an Actuall [Fitnesse] to Receyve him, and to close with him.

Ob. "Such a Faith as this (as it hath Relation to this union) is not a living Faith, because it doth not his office, but leaveth the soule mainly defective in point of true union, for want of a concurrent Act to helpe the soule to close with christ, which maketh up the true union on our part: which Faith the spirit of God giveth, and also Acts Effectually to that End in the soules of his People."

Ans. It is a living Faith, or else it could not so Act upon the soule in which it is, as to make it a true living faithfull soule. Nor doeth it leave the soule mainely defective in point of true union, for want of a concurrent Act to helpe the soule to close with Christ to the making up of true union on our parts. For though God hath ordeyned Faith to helpe the soule to close with christ, yet not to

5. The term may be worke; the original wording has been written over in another hand.

6. Calvin cites these same four causes in discussing the relationship between grace and works, *Institutes,* III.xiv.17.

make up our union with christ by Actuall Beleiving on Him, but
on our parts to say Amen to what God hath done, and to receyve
what God hath given and wrought in us. These Scriptures seeme
to me as Thunderbolts to cast downe all contrary Imaginations.
Wee must be abiding in Christ, or else without him (to wit, without his abiding in us) wee can doe nothing, John 15.5. And wee
must be good Trees before we can bringe forth good fruit, Matthew 7.18. If then closing with christ be a good fruit, wee must be
good Trees before wee can bring it forth. And how wee can be
good Trees, before wee be Engrafted into Christ, wee must looke
for it in Aristotles [1 word unintel.]: for it is not Revealed in the
Gospell of Christ.

Ob. "If it be the union betweene christ and the soule then
there must be a mutual $\frac{\text{Giving}}{\text{Taking}}$ each other. But in this union,
here is a meere Taking on Gods part, noe Giving or Act on mans
part, neither Receyving nor giving etc."

Ans. Here is not onely a meere taking on Gods part, but a giving also. For God giveth us his Sonne and his spirit in a Promise of
Grace, when he giveth Faith to the soule. And the Faith receyved
hath power to Receyve christ, the Habit of Faith habitually, the
Act of Faith actively. For the very Habit and gift of Faith is of an
Emptying Nature, emptying the soule of all confidence in it self
and in the Creature, and so leaving and constituting the soule as
an empty vessell, empty of it owne worth, and goodnesse, but full
of Christ.

On mans part therefore, It cannot be said that there is noe receyving: for there is an Habituall Receyving of christ, by the
Habit of Faith. But for the soule to give it selfe back againe to
christ, before it be united unto christ, It is so spirituall and gratious a worke, that if the soule can doe that before union, I know
noe greater worke that it can doe after union. And so wee shall
bring in a Power of Faith to doe as great a worke before union, as
after union: yea and a greater worke too; by how much a greater
worke it is to gett life in christ when wee are dead, then to keepe
it, when wee are alive. I dare not acknowledge any *liberum Arbi-*
trius to close with christ, till *Arbitrius* be liberated. And *libera-*

tum Arbitrius[7] is not, but by christ and in christ, John 8.36. For out of christ we are servants [in] Sinne.

"But then say you, It will follow, that if the spirit of God may unite it selfe to the soule before Faith doeth any thing in the union, then by the same Reason it may unite it selfe to the soule, without such a Faith, and so may be united to an unbeleiver, to a Reprobate, etc."

Ans. Two things you [doe here mistake]:

1. Wee doe not say that the spirit unites it selfe to the soule at all, but that it uniteth the soule to christ.

2. Wee doe not say, That the spirit uniteth us to christ before Faith doeth any thing in the union. For Faith being in the soule giveth Being to a christian unto union with Christ: as *Anima rationalis* being in the Body, giveth being to the child unto union with Adam. Now noe Reprobate, no Unbeleiver hath such a Faith being, or constituting such a Being in him: and that preventeth the Consequence of your Argument.

To cleare this point a little more unto you   All union is of two (or more things) into *aliquod Tertium,* As the 3 Persons in Trinity are united into one Godhead: the humane and Divine Nature of Christ are united into one Person: two marryed Persons are united into one Flesh. Now what is the Third thing into which christ and the soule is united? Not into one divine Essence, or Essentiall Nature, for then we were noe lesse then Gods. Nor into one Person, for then wee were capable of Divine worship, as the Humane Nature of christ is: nor into one flesh, for so all wicked men are of the same humane flesh with christ, as well as the Faithfull. It remayneth then, that wee are united into one spirit, according to that in 1 Corinthians 6.17. He that is joyned to the Lord is one spirit. Now what is that spirit into which wee are Joyned, or united? not into the Holy Ghost. For by the Holy Ghost wee are united into one spirit, 1 Corinthians 12.13.   The spirit therefore into which christ and wee are united, is noe other but the Created spirit of Grace and Holynesse, or a Created spirit-

---

7. *Liberum Arbitriu(m):* free judgment; *liberatum Arbitriu(m):* (and) freed the judgment (is).

uall life of spirituall Gifts of Holynesse and Righteousnesse, which in our first Parents, as also in the Regenerate is called the Image of God. Not that the same spirituall Gifts of Grace, which dwell in the humane Nature of christ, are found the same *numero* in us, but the same in kinde, the same in Resemblance, and Proportion. Of his Fullnesse wee all Receyve Grace for Grace, John 1.16: the like Faith, Hope, Love, Zeale, meekenesse, Patience etc. being found in us in our measure, which are found in him above measure. Now then the Holy Ghost by the Gospell working and creating Faith, and with Faith all the like spirituall Gifts of Grace in us which are founde in christs humane Nature, wee are thereby formally united unto christ, that is, wee are made to be of one and the same spirituall and holy Nature and Disposition with the Lord Jesus, by the worke of the same Holy Ghost. In regard of both which wee are said to be made partakers of the same Divine Nature, to wit, both of the same Holy Ghost dwelling in us, and of the same spirituall Gifts of the Holy Ghost (for the kinde and nature of them) which are found in Christ. So that to constitute this union, there needeth not our Acting of those Graces upon Christ: but the Holy Ghosts working of these Graces in us, which make us fitt to Act upon Him.

CHAPTER 3

John Cotton, *Sixteene Questions of Serious and Necessary Consequence*

IN October, 1636, John Winthrop noted in his journal that Anne Hutchinson had become the cause of a debate over certain points of theology. After listing several "errors" Mrs. Hutchinson had expressed, Winthrop added that "there joined with her in these opinions a brother of hers, one Mr. Wheelwright, a silenced minister sometimes in England." To deal with these errors the "other ministers in the Bay" held a "conference" with Wheelwright and Mrs. Hutchinson at Boston in October. John Cotton also attended and "gave satisfaction to them [the ministers], so as he agreed with them all in the point of sanctification."[1]

This agreement proved illusory. Not only did the "point of sanctification" remain controversial, but Cotton also continued to preach sermons that disturbed his fellow ministers. Meeting again in December, they drew up a list of "points, wherein they suspected Mr. Cotton did differ from them, and . . . propounded them to him, and pressed him to a direct answer, affirmative or negative, to every one." Winthrop describes this December confrontation a second time in the *History:*

> About this time the rest of the ministers, taking offence at some doctrines delivered by Mr. Cotton, and especially at some opinions, which some of his church did broach, and for he seemed to have too good an opinion of, and too much familiarity with those persons, drew out sixteen points, and gave them to him, entreating him to deliver his judgment directly in them, which accordingly he did.

---

1. Winthrop, *History, 1,* 239–240.

43

"And," concludes Winthrop, "many copies thereof were dispersed about."[2]

One of these copies found its way to England, where it was published in 1644 as *Sixteene Questions of Serious and Necessary Consequence, Propounded unto Mr. John Cotton of Boston in New-England, Together with His Answers to each Question.* A second edition with a slightly altered title and text appeared in 1647.[3] A copy of this edition at the Massachusetts Historical Society contains emendations in a seventeenth-century hand, the source of which was an independent manuscript text. The person making the corrections thought this manuscript was the original; "The printed Part I corrected by the MSS. Original," he wrote on the inside of the title page. Whether the original or simply another of the "many copies" Winthrop mentions, his text supplied a number of valid corrections to the printed versions. As reprinted below, the *Sixteene Questions* follows the form of the first edition with material from the corrected copy added in brackets.

One of the minor documentary puzzles of the Antinomian Controversy is the status of a different list of sixteen questions (without answers). There are two manuscript versions of this list, one in the Belknap Papers, Massachusetts Historical Society, printed in the *Proceedings of the Massachusetts Historical Society, 46, 275–276,* the other in the Stiles Papers, Yale University Library, printed below for the first time. The two lists are identical save for punctuation and capitalization.

[FROM THE STILES PAPERS]
Questions of the Elders

"New England 1637   Questions agreed upon by all the Elders of the Bay to be conferred upon at a Meetinge

---

2. Ibid., 249–253. In *Saints and Sectaries* (Chapel Hill, 1962), 129–133, Emery Battis declares (on what authority it is not clear) that the ministers met with Cotton on December 12, and "that evening, or early the next day" drafted the list of sixteen questions.

3. *Severall Questions of Serious and necessary Consequence, Propounded by the Teaching Elders, Unto M. Iohn Cotton of Boston in New-England. With his respective Answer to each Question* (London, 1647). This edition

1 Whither Christ with all his Benefits be dispenced in a Covenant of Workes?

2 Whither all the promises bee made to Christ himselfe, and the conditions fulfilled in him personally?

3 Whither there be any conditionall promises, in the Covenant of Grace, or only absolute?

4 Whither all the Commandements in Scripture be legall, and none Evangelicall?

5 Whither there be Union betweene Christ and the soule before, and without Fayth?

6 Whither Fayth in Justification bee meerely passive?

7 Whither wee are justified before wee believe in Christ?

8 Whither Justification bee an Acquittinge of a sinner, or the Declaration to the soule that it is acquitted?

9 Whither Habits of Grace doe not differ a sainte from an Hypocrite?

10 Whither justifyinge Fayth, and sanctification, bee in Christ, as in the subject, and not in the soule?

11 Whither a Beleever ought to stirre up himselfe to act holilye, before hee feele the spirit of God to act him?

12 Whither Union with Christ, and Justification by him, must bee first fully seene, and assured to the soule, by the immediate Witnesse of the Spirit, before hee cann see the truth of his Fayth, or sanctification, soe as to evidence his Justification thereby?

13 Whither our first Assurance must bee from an absolute promise, not from a conditionall?

14 Whither a beleiver hath not right to a Blessinge by a conditionall promise of the Gospell: and may not pleade the same in a Covenant of Grace?

15 Whither hee that hath savinge Grace, may without sinn denye it?

16 Whither hee that hath received the Witnesse of the Spirit ought not to trye it by Witnesse from sanctification?"

---

omitted the opening paragraphs, "Deare and Reverend Sir," and "Reverend and beloved Brethren," as well as the preliminary list of questions. Otherwise the two editions are identical.

Sixteene Questions

Deare and Reverend Sir,

WEE doe humbly and earnestly desire a short and plaine Answer of those Questions under-written, and at the hand of you, those things we desire your speedy Answer unto: and though some of these wee know your judgement in, yet not for ourselves onely, but for others sakes we put them all in.

Reverend and beloved Brethren,

FOR an Answer unto your (Interrogatories, shall I call them?) or Questions. Though I might without Sinne referre you (as our Saviour did the *High-Priest* when his Doctrine was questioned) to what *I* have ever taught and spoken openly to the world, as having in secret said nothing else, *Iohn* 18.20.21. Yet   [2] because you are much more deare and precious to me, than the *High-Priest* was to him; and because *Love* thinkes no Evill, and *Truth* feareth not the *Light:* I have (by the helpe of Christ) sent you (according to your Desire) a plaine and short[4] Answer to each particular: wherein if I erre, let me see mine Error, and try if I shut mine Eyes against the Light. If in your judgement *I* hold forth the Truth, then beare witnesse with me to the Truth, for the Honour of the Name of Christ, and for the Peace and salvation of the Churches in our Lord Jesus, your Lord and ours.

CERTAIN QUESTIONS

Propounded by sundry of the teaching Elders in the Bay, to Mr. *Iohn Cotton* Teacher in the Church of   [3] *Boston.*

Quest. 1

WHAT the seale of the Spirit is?

2. Whether every Beleever be sealed with it?

3. What ground from the Word of that distinction, a Broad Seale, and the other seale; and the differences between them?

4. Whether a man may or ought to see any saving work of

---

4. Homely: ms.

Christ in himself, and take comfort from it, before he be sealed by the Spirit?

5. Whether the Testimony or Seale of the Spirit be so clear as witnesse immediately by it selfe, without respect of any Work of Christ in a man; or so constant, that it being once obtained, a man doth never after question his Estate?

6. Whether a Christian may maintain like constant comfort in his Soule, when he hath fallen into some grosse Sinne, or neglected some knowne Duty, as when he walked most closely with God?

7. Whether a weak Beleever may not warrantably apply some Promise to himself, as given him by God although he doth not yet discern his interest in it by the Broad Seale of the Spirit?

8. Whether a Christian must of Necessity have his first Assurance from an absolute and not from a Conditionall Promise?

9. What you mean by Christian Sanctification, whether immediate Acting of the Spirit, or infused Habits; if Habits infused; whether such as are contrary to corrupt Nature, and all vicious Habits: and if so, whether you must not mean   [4] the Image of God in *Adam* renewed in us, to be our Sanctification?

10. Whether this Sanctification being discerned by us, be not a true Evidence of Justification?

11. Whether this Sanctification being discerned may not be, and often is a Ground of Primitive Comfort, as it is an Evidence of our being in Christ?

12. Whether when my Justification lyeth prostrate, I may not prove my self in a state of Grace by my Sanctification?

13. Whether evidencing Justification by Sanctification be a building my Justification on my Sanctification: or a going on in a Covenant of Works?

14. Whether a Christian be not further active after Regeneration, then before; if there be a difference, wherein it lyeth.

15. Whether it be not a safe way to conclude my safe Estate by my Practicall Reasoning.

16. Whether a Christian may not presse the Lord for Spirituall Mercies, with Arguments drawn from the Graces of Christ himselfe.

NOW FOLLOW THE ANSWERS.

Quest. I.

WHAT *the Seale of the Spirit is?*

Answer.

The Seale of the Spirit is taken by some good Divines to be the Sanctification of the Spirit, as that which like a Seale:

$$\left\{\begin{array}{l} \textit{1. Distinguisheth,} \\ \textit{2. [Concealeth],}^5 \\ \textit{3. Confirmeth.} \end{array}\right\} \text{ the faithfull:}$$

Others take it for the Witnesse of the Spirit it selfe, as it is distinguished from our Spirit, *Rom.*8.16. In which sense it is commonly used by our Brethren in the Church: Though [5] I my selfe doe generally forbeare to call it by that Name [i.e. the seal], and doe⁶ usually call it, the *Witnesse of the Spirit,* least I might give offence to any, who may conceive the Seale of the Spirit to be more generall.

Quest. II.

Whether every Beleever be sealed with it?

Answer.

Every Beleever is not sealed with the Seale of the Spirit, if the Seale be taken for the Witnesse of the Spirit it selfe, but in the former sense, all Beleevers be sealed with it.

Quest. 3.

What Ground from the Word of that Distinction, a Broad Seale, and the other Seale, and the differences betweene them.

Answer.

I know no such Distinction betweene the Broad Seale and the other Seale: Nor was that Distinction propounded by any of our Members, but by one of your selves, who expressing his Conception in that Speech, one of our Members⁷ answered him according

---

5. Consenteth: printed text.

6. The printed texts read, "doe not usually call it," but the emendator has crossed out the not.

7. Concurrently with the meeting of the ministers, the members of the Boston Church were exchanging views with the members of other churches. A summary of their debate with the Cambridge Church is printed in the *Winthrop Papers* (Boston, 1943), *3,* 324–326.

to his meaning in his own word, if you call it so, saith he; Neverthelesse thus much may truely be said: There is a difference betweene the Witnesse of the Spirit, as it regenerateth and reneweth our Spirits; and the Witnesse of the Spirit [itself] as it comforteth us with evident Assurance of our *Adoption, Rom.* 8. 16.

Quest. IV.

Whether a man may or ought to see any saving Worke of Christ in himselfe, and take Comfort from it, before he be sealed by the Spirit?

Answer.

A true Beleever may and ought to see (if it be declared to him in the use of the means) any Worke of Christ in himselfe that accompanieth Salvation (as *Cornelius* did) before he be sealed with the Witnesse of the Spirit it selfe: yet full setled Comfort he cannot take, nor rest in, till it be witnessed unto him by the Spirit: for Comfort without the Word is false Comfort, [and the Word without the Spirit yieldeth but dark comfort] and neither Word nor Spirit, doe teach us to take any[8] Comfort so much from the Worke of Christ in us, as from the Object of it.

Quest. V.

Whether the testimony or Seal of the Spirit be so clear, as to witnesse immediately by it self, without respect of any work of Christ in a Man: or so constant, that it being [6] *once obtained, a man doth never after question his Estate?*

Answer.

The Testimony of the Spirit [it self] is so cleare, as that it may witnesse immediately, though not without some worke of Christ in a man, yet without respect unto [that][9] Worke: Neverthelesse it is not so constant or permanent (at least not in all Beleevers) but that a man after he hath received it, may come in time of Temptation [and desertion to] question his Estate, though not so frequently nor so desperately as before.[10]

---

8. Our: ms.

9. The: printed text.

10. "These last words not in the MSS.": ms. note concerning the phrase, "though . . . before."

Quest. VI.

Whether a Christian may maintaine like constant Comfort in his Soule, when he hath fallen into some grosse Sinne, or neglected some knowne Duty, as when he walked most closely with God.

Answer.

A Christian man cannot find like constant Comfort maintained to his Soule, [upon any gross][11] sin, whether of Commission or Omission, as when God keeps him in a close walking with him: For the Spirit of God in him being grieved (and grieved it is by any grosse sin especially) it will not speak wonted *Peace* and *Comfort* to him. If David fall into such grosse Sins, as *Adultery* and *Murder*, it cannot be, but the Bones of his Comfort will be broken, *Psal.* 51.8. Neverthelesse, the assurance of a [Christian] mans good Estate, may be maintained to him, when the frame of his Spirit [and Course][12] is growne much degenerate, *Isa.*63.16.

Quest. VII.

Whether a weake Beleever may not warrantably apply some Promise to himselfe as given by God, although he doth not yet discerne his Interest in it by the Broad Seale of the Spirit.

Answer.

A weake Beleever may warrantably apply some Promise to himselfe, and may have it also given him of God, even whilest he is yet waiting for it, before he can [yet] discerne his Interest in the Promise, by the Witnesse of the Spirit it selfe: For the Soule that waiteth for Christ, may come to see and know (by his renewed knowledge) that he doth waite; and may from thence conclude, that he on whom he waiteth, will not absent himselfe for ever.

Quest. VIII.

Whether a Christian must of necessity have his first   [7]
assurance from an absolute, and not from a Conditionall Promise?

Answer.

A Christian mans first assurance doth arise from the Spirit of

---

11. After he hath fallen into: printed text.
12. "And Course" comes after "frame": printed text.

God, applying Gods free grace in an absolute Promise. Or if in a Conditionall Promise, it is not to Workes, but to *Faith*, and to faith, not as it is a Worke, but as it [receiveth][13] the free grace of God offered, and applyed in Christ Jesus.

Quest. IX.

What you meane by Christian Sanctification, whether imme-diate acting of the Spirit, or infused Habits: *If habits infused, whether such as are contrary to corrupt* Nature, *and all vitious* Habits: *and if so, whether you must not meane the Image of God in* Adam *renewed in us, to be our Sanctification?*

Answer.

I meane by Christian Sanctification, the fruit of the Spirit of Christ dwelling in true Beleevers, working and acting in us, both infused *Habits* and actions of *Holinesse*, contrary to all vitious *Habits* and actions of corrupt *Nature*. And yet I doe not [there-fore] meane, that the Image of God in *Adam* renewed in us (and no more then so) is our Sanctification: our Sanctification in Christ hath in it this more; Faith in the Righteousnesse of Christ, and Repentance from dead Works, (and that which is the Root of [both])[14] the indwelling Power of the Spirit, to act and keep Holi-nesse in us all, which Adam wanted.

Quest. X.

Whether this Sanctification being discerned by us, be not a true Evidence of Justication?

Answer.

If this [true Christian] Sanctification be evidently discerned, it is a true evidence of Justification, *a Posteriori*; as Justification is likewise a true Evidence of Sanctification, *a Priori*.

Quest. XI.

Whether Sanctification being discerned, may not be, and often is a ground of Primitive Comfort, as it is an Evidence of our being in Christ?

---

13. Revealeth: printed text.
14. All: printed text.
* See new note p. xviii.

Answer.

I doe not beleeve that this Sanctification being discerned, is a
ground of Primitive Comfort, though when it is evidently discerned, it be an Evidence of our being in   [8]
Christ. I conceive our faith depending on Christ is as
soon discerned, and sooner then our Sanctification by Christ; and
yet, neither will discerning of it yeeld setled Comfort to the Soule,
till the Spirit of God doth witnesse from Christ, Gods thoughts of
Peace towards him.

Quest. XII.

Whether when my [Justification][15] *lyeth prostrate, I may not
prove my self in a state of* Grace *by my Sanctification?*
Answer.

If my Justification lyeth prostrate (that is, altogether dark and
hidden from me) I cannot prove my selfe in a state of Grace by my
Sanctification: For whilst I cannot beleeve that my Person is accepted in Justification, I cannot beleeve that my Works are accepted of God, as any true Sanctification.

Quest. XIII.

*Whether evidencing Iustification by Sanctification, be a
building my Iustification on my Sanctification: or a going on in a*
Covenant *of* Workes.
Answer.

To evidence my Justification by my Sanctification, though it
may seem at first blush a plain and [familiar][16] *Phrase*, yet it is indeed ambiguous, or at least obscure: Give me leave to cleare the
sense of it, and then give you mine answer. To evidence my Iustification by my Sanctification, is no more at first hand than to give
or hold forth my Sanctification for an evident Argument of my
Iustification: Thus farre the *Phrase* is plain. But now when I give
it for an evident Argument, I may give it either for an evident
cause or ground of my Iustification, or for an evident Sign or Effect of it. Again, when I give it for an evident sign of Iustification,
I may either give it [for an only][17] sign (having nothing else to

---

15. In the printed text the word is "sanctification," an obvious error.
16. Evident: printed text.
17. "Alone for an evident": printed text.

shew for my Iustification) or I may give it for a concurrent Sign, together with other Signs and Witnesses, which may make both my Iustification and my Sanctification evident and cleere to my selfe and others. Having thus cleered the ambiguity and obscurity of the *Phrase*, I give you mine Answer distinctly in these severall *Propositions*.

Proposition. I.

To give my Sanctification for an evident ground,   [9]
[and][18] cause, or matter of my Iustification, is to build
my Iustification upon my Sanctification, and to go on in a Covenant of Works. [This is the foundation of Popery, and will be the ruine and destruction of it.]

Propos. 2.

To give my Sanctification for an evident ground or cause of my Faith, whereby I am justified, as when I doe not, or[19] dare not depend upon Christ for my *Iustification*, till I evidently see my *Sanctification*, this is also to build my Iustification on my Sanctification, and to go on in a Covenant of works. For Sanctification (or which is all one) good works are not the Cause of justifying faith, but justifying faith the Cause of them.

Propos. 3.

To give my Sanctification for an evident cause and ground of my faith (not whereby I am justified, but) whereby I beleeve my selfe to be justified (which they call the *Faith of Assurance*) this may be a building my Iustification on my Sanctification, or a going on in a *Covenant of Works* two wayes:

1. If the Soul have no Evidence of his Dependance upon Christ for Righteousnesse, nor no Evidence of his Effectuall Calling unto Christ, and unto faith in Christ (by the Fathers drawing him to come to him) but onely he seeth an evident Change [wrought] in himselfe, from a prophane [or][20] civill course to a sanctified Conversation; [This is still a building of Justification upon Sanctification], or at least, upon that which is worse, to wit, upon that which seemeth true Christian Sanctification, which in-

---

18. Or: printed text.
19. Nor: printed text.
20. And: printed text.

deed is not, but [only] a legall Reformation. For when a man hath bin humbled under the Spirit of Bondage by the Terrors of the Law, [and] yet never came[21] to feel his need of Christ, nor his own insufficiencie or unworthinesse to receive him,

Though he may obtain

{

1. Restraining grace to keep him from known Sinnes.

2. Constraining (or exciting) Grace to provoke him to Duty (or else his Conscience sometimes terrified by the Law would flye in his face.

And though in this way he may find Comfort (as the Stony ground did, and Thorny Soyle much more) and so   [10] from this great Change he may build up to himselfe the faith or *Assurance* of his *Justification*,[22] yet in truth, in so doing he buildeth upon such a Sanctification which is indeed a sandy Foundation.

2. To give[23] *Sanctification* for an evident ground or Cause of faith, whereby a man beleeveth himselfe to be justified, may be a building of *Justification* upon *Sanctification* in another Case: to wit, when we shall give a man no other ground or Evidence of his *Justification*, but onely from the Evidence of his *Sanctification*: For the Publican did not (as the Pharisee thought himselfe did) see any evident fruits of his *Sanctification*, but was deeply affected with the sense of his Sinnes, so that he smote his Breast with the Anguish of sinne, and durst not lift up his eyes to Heaven through Confusion of face for Sinne, but only cryed out to God to be mercifull unto him in this sinfull estate: and yet by our Saviours own judgement this man went home justified rather then the other (*Luk.* 18.) though he saw no Evidence of his *Sanctification*, but rather Evidence of his sinfull Corruption. If any of our Brethren doubt hereof, I would pray them to call to mind what some of them that lived in *Essex* have heard our Brother *Hooker* and Mr. *Rogers*[24] also teach soundly, and [acutely][25] out of the Word; that

---

21. Yet he may never come: printed text.
22. The emendator seems to propose sanctification as an alternative.
23. Give my: printed text.
24. John Rogers (1572–1636) and Thomas Hooker made their reputations as preachers in Essex County, England.
25. Argue: printed text.

there be saving graces which are not sanctifying, but are wrought before *Sanctification*, which yet may beare Witnesse to a safe estate (and I may adde[,] to Fellowship with Christ, for there is no safety [at all] but in him) before the Soule can see any Evidence of his *Sanctification*.

Propos. 4.

A man may give his *Sanctification* for an evident ground or Cause of his faith whereby he is justified, and yet sometimes not build his *Iustification* upon his *Sanctification*, nor be under a *Covenant* of *Workes*, [but of Grace], but onely sometimes goe aside to a *Covenant* of *Workes*: As in Case, when a man is truely justified, and seeth it not, he doth then betake him to his Workes for the hastning of his *Assurance*. As *Abraham* when he had long waited for the promised Seed, [though][26] he was justified by beleeving the free Promise: yet, for the more speedy satisfying of his Faith and Hope, he turned aside to goe into *Hagar*, (who was a *Type* of the *Covenant* of *Workes*)[27] for the   [11] hastning of his sight and fruition of the promised Seed:
So there be sundry Children of *Abraham* (even of his elect Seed [by Her]) that having beene driven out of their Sins by a Spirit of Bondage, and finding a need of Christ, and their owne insufficiencie and unworthinesse to receive him: doe therefore seek and wait for him (by the mighty Power of God) in every Ordinance and Duty. Such men are already truely justified (though it may be as yet they doe not know so much) because this their seeking and waiting for Christ, in the Sense of their own Need & Emptines, and unworthinesse, is a true Act of a lively justifying faith. But now if such souls, because God may tarry long, before they can see and feele Christ given to them, shall therefore seeke Christ in

---

26. Thought: printed text.
27. Galatians 4: ms. In chapter 4 of the Epistle to the Galatians Paul interprets typologically the story of Abraham's sons by Hagar and Sarah. Hagar, a slave woman, was Abraham's concubine; she and her son Ismael represent life under the law, or covenant of works. Sarah, a free woman, was Abraham's wife. She and her son Isaac represent life under the promise, or the covenant of grace. Arguments involving Old Testament "types" were frequent in Puritan literature; cf. Sacvan Bercovitch, "Typology in Puritan New England: The Williams-Cotton Controversy Reassessed," *American Quarterly* 19 (1967), 166–191.

their owne Workes of *Sanctification,* and in the Promises and Blessing given to such Workes, [and finding such works find peace] and not finding such Workes, can finde no Peace nor *Assurance*: Such Soules, though they doe not build their *Justification* upon their *Sanctification,* (for indeede they were truely justified before, while they depend[ed] on Christ for Righteousnesse, according to the free Promise of Grace, and so are truely under a *Covenant* of Grace) yet they goe aside to a *Covenant* of *Workes* (as [it were,] unto *Hagar*) to bring forth to [them] the sight of Christ (the seed of [the] Promise) whom they so long waited for. The fayling of such Soules is this, that they having Christ layd in their Hearts, as the Foundation of their *Justification* (though they know not so much.) Upon this golden and precious Foundation, they build Hey and Stubble, in seeking, and setling, and grounding their faith of *Assurance* not upon Christ, nor upon the free Promise of Grace, nor upon the *Witnesse* of the Spirit it selfe applying the same, but upon the Holinesse of their owne Workes. In which Case, they are often put to many[28] sad Doubts [of their own Estates], ever and anon renewed upon them, till the faith and confidence, which they had built upon their owne Workes, be at length burnt up with the Fire of Temptation, and the clearer Daylight of Gods Word and Spirit. And then, though their owne Workes, and their owne[29] Building thereupon be burned, yet their Soules will be saved in the Day of the Lord Jesus.

Propos. 5.

The Soule that hath lyen under the Terrors of the Law, and commeth afterwards to see and feele his need of Christ, and his owne [want of] strength and worth to receive him, and doth depend upon Christ for *Righteousnesse* and   [12] *Mercy,* he may come in this Estate to see (by his[30] renewed Knowledge) his dependance on Christ, and withall some fruits of *Sanctification* that flow there-from, as Prayer (sometimes) with unutterable Sighes and Groanes, Brokennesse of Spirit, Mourning for sight of Christ, Longing desire after the sincere

---

28. Many and sad: printed text.
29. Owne is crossed out before Workes and Building: ms.
30. His is crossed out: ms.

Milk of the Word[,] love of the Ministery that wounded him, &c. And seeing God helping him here[in],[31] he may thereby gather, that he that hath begun to helpe him, will go on to helpe him still. But yet to give these for certaine Evidences of his *Justification*, the poore Soule dare not, though another Christian of better discerning, may justly so apply [them] to him as good Evidences of his justified estate. But neverthelesse he will still seeke and wait for further and clearer Fellowship with Christ, till the Spirit of God himselfe doe witnesse to him, the gracious thoughts of God towards him in a free Promise of Grace, before he can plead his owne good workes, (whether after [his] Conversion or before) for good Evidences of his *Justification*. For (as it hath beene observed by one of our godly learned Countrymen) the graces of Gods Spirit in our Soules, are like the Stars in the *Firmament,* which shine but with a borrowed Light from the *Sun*: If the *Sun* were hid from them, their Light would be obscure: so is the light of our graces, if the Spirit of God doe hide his light from us.

Propos. 6.

But now if the Spirit of God [himself] do shed[32] abroad his Light into such a Soule, and give him a cleare sight of his estate in a free Promise of grace in Christ; such a one evidently discerneth both his *Justification* and his *Sanctification*; and the one of them giving good Evidence to the other, the Blood to the Water, and the Water to the Blood, and the Spirit to both, 1 *John* 5. 6. 8. And thus in evidencing his *Justification* by his *Sanctification*, he doth not build his *Justification* upon his *Sanctification*, nor hereby goe on in a *Covenant* of workes, [no] nor goe aside to it.

Propos. 7.

But though the Soule may gather *Knowledge* of his estate, from such Evidences of *Sanctification*; yet if he shall therefore build his justifying Faith upon such evidences, he shall againe goe aside to a *Covenant* of Workes, though his Person may be under a *Covenant* of grace; For justifying Faith cannot safely build or rest upon any ground, save onely upon Christ and his *Righteousnesse*.[33]

---

31. A correction in the second edition, as was the preceding comma.
32. Shew, an obvious printer's error: printed text.
33. "This Prop. was not in the MSS.": ms. note.

Quest. XIV.

Whether a Christian be not further active after Re-   [13]
generation, then before; if there be a difference,
wherein it lyeth?

Answer.

A Christian is more active after *Regeneration* then before, before *Regeneration* we are not active at all in any spirituall Chris-
tion [work],[34] no nor in *Proxima Potentia*, Passive to receive helpe
from God to doe it, but after *Regeneration, Acti Agimus*.[35] If we
act and goe forth in the strength of our own spirituall *Giftes*, without looking up to Christ, we fall as *Peter* did, *Matth.* 26.33. 39.
etc.[36]

Quest. XV.

Whether it be not a safe way to conclude my safe estate by my
practicall Reasoning?

Answer.

It is not an unsafe, but a lawfull way to conclude a mans safe
Estate by way of Practicall Reasoning, so [be it][37] the Reason be
not carnall but spirituall. One proposition being expressed in the
Word, or safely deducted thence; the other being the experimen-
tall observation of a good Conscience, enlightened by the Spirit of
God, and looking up to Christ to cleare the Conclusion from both.
Neverthelesse a good Conscience will not satisfie [it][38] selfe in this
way, till it be established by the *Witnesse* of the Spirit [it self]; or
if it should so satisfie and rest it selfe for a Season, God will [in
time][39] awaken it, to a Sense [of his] further need of Christ.

Quest. XVI.

Whether a Christian may not presse the Lord for spirituall
Mercies, with Arguments drawne from the Graces of Christ in
himselfe?

---

34. Action: printed text.
35. *Proxima potentia* (corrected in ms. from *proximam potentiam*): immediate power; *acti agimus:* acted upon, we act. See note 26, p. 143.
36. The Scriptural reference is corrected from Matthew 26.23: printed
text.
37. So it be: printed text.
38. Himself: printed text.
39. In time follows awaken it: printed text.
   * See new note p. xix.

Answer.

A Christian Soule is more usually wont to presse the Lord for spirituall Mercies, by Arguments drawne from his owne spirituall Miseries and Infirmities, then from the Graces of Christ in himselfe. Neverthelesse, the Saints doe also make use of Arguments drawne from the Graces of Christ, when they do discerne the same in themselves, but they are usually such Graces whereby they goe out of themselves, and their owne *Strength* and *Worth*, (as Faith, Hope, Desire, Seeking, Waiting, &c.) or such as doe expresse their spirituall Bent and Inclination, or Affection, which they desire might be quickned and satisfied with their spir-   [14] ituall proper *Object* or *End*, but the force of their Arguments from those Graces, is fetched, not from the Force, or Fulnesse, or Power of them, but [rather] from the Weaknesse and Emptinesse of them.

Thus have you (according to your Desire) a plain and short Answer to all your Demands, except the thirteenth; which being exposed to greatest Agitation and Exception, I have spoken the more largely and distinctly to it; that so, I might avoid carefully (as I see it needfull) all Suspition of Ambiguity and Obscurity.

Now the *God of Truth and Peace* lead us by his *Spirit of Truth* into all *Truth*, through *Him*, who is made unto us of *God* the *Way*, the *Truth* and the *Life*.   AMEN.

FINIS

CHAPTER 4

The Elders Reply

AFTER Winthrop had mentioned the list of sixteen questions he went on to remark of Cotton's answers, "Some doubts he well cleared, but in some things he gave not satisfaction. The rest of the ministers replied to these answers, and at large showed their dissent, and the grounds thereof."[1] The "Elders Reply" to Cotton's answers is published below for the first time. The text comes from a manuscript at the Massachusetts Historical Society, the same manuscript that contains the emendated edition of *Severall Questions of Serious and necessary Consequence,* Cotton's "Rejoynder," and a copy of *A Conference,* the last two of which follow in this collection. A reference to "this Winter season" that had complicated the elders' "meeting and staying together" would suggest that the "Reply" was written soon after Cotton handed in his answers, probably in January. The brackets in the text appear in the manuscript.

Winthrop's description of the "Reply" fits it perfectly: on some points the ministers agreed with Cotton, on others they spelled out their differences. The main point of their arguments is to defend the use of sanctification as an evidence of justification. They accused Cotton of arbitrarily "straitning the freeness of Gods spirit," and protested the reductionism of the Antinomians' position: if the "great disputes of late" had initially been premised on the assumption that there was, indeed, some connection between faith, justification, and sanctification, now "all are taken up in this one conclusion, That we can see neither Sanctification

---
1. Winthrop, *History, 1,* 253.

nor faith no nor Justification, before the witness of the Spirit; but all at once by it." To this sharp dichotomy between the Spirit and man's activity, the ministers opposed distinctions of their own between two forms of "works," "Evangelical, Saving works" and legal works, and two forms of sanctification, "false" and "true." In general their strategy was not to overwhelm Cotton with theological arguments, but to alert him to the dangerous conclusions others were drawing from his position. Besides defending sanctification as evidence of salvation, their other concern was to vindicate their reputations as orthodox Protestants who believed in "free grace."[2]

The Elders Reply.

Reverend and Beloved in the God of Love!

These few things that we have replyed to your Answer we entreat you to accept of, as fruits of our love to your self, and of our desires of the establishing of Truth and peace in the Churches of Christ. We have the rather embarked ourselves in a busines of this nature because of your own desire, and of the offense of diverse who have made account that our silence all this while, hath spoken our consent to all you said. The truth is, we have been tender of your honour, and have made conscience of dissenting in the least from you, wherein Truth might not be wounded: And for this, we appeal to the Searcher of all hearts. You cannot be ignorant which way the stream of most Divines, both of our own Country and others runs. From whose steps if any turn aside, they had need bring sound proof from the Scripture, or else fear they tread awry in so doing. Now Dear Sir, we leave these things with you, hoping that the Lord will honour you, with making you a happy Instrument of calming these storms and cooling these hot contentions and paroxysmes that have begun to swell and burn in these poor Churches. We had written sooner, but that we were delayed partly by the expectation of your grounds, and partly by the difficulty of our meeting and staying together this Winter season,

---

2. Cf. ibid., 254–255.

to advise of what we should do herein. The God of Peace create peace for us, and help us to love his Truth together in Christ Jesus our Prince of Peace, Even so Amen.

To your Preface

Which we desire to take in the best part, though we see no ground why you should conceive we gave you the Questions as so many High-priest-like Interrogatories, contrary to our free ingenuous profession made in private to you. viz. That sundry opinions (intimated in those Questions) going up and down as yours in the repute of some, we might have from your own hand what you hold, whereby to stop their mouths that raise up any slander of you, or prejudice against the Truth. And this the Lord knows was the true intent of our Hearts. Nor see wee, why you should conceive it needless to answer sith you say nothing privately, which you have not publickly preached, as neither Christ had. For though you speak nothing, yet others might publicly conceive you to be of this or that Opinion, which they father on you. And sundry things which you have publickly uttered, were darkly and doubtfully delivered; whereof as we have privately besought you to consider, so we desire to see them interpreted: Nor know we why you should so express yourself, as to profess us dearer to you, than was the High Priest to Christ. Should we so have mentioned our affection to your self, it would have come very short of that which we find in our hearts. But to conclude, as you desire us to bear witness to what we shall apprehend you hold forth as true, which we have done and are resolved in the Lord for ever to do; so we beseech you to bear witness with us against those Opinions which shall appear to be false, and the defenders thereof: for we need, not only your Consent with us in the truth, but your seasonable reproof of those that dissent.

To your Answer to the First Question.

In propounding that Question (that there might be no strife about words) our desire was to know of you, What the seal of the Spirit is? Which if you had clearly explained it would have been very acceptable and usefull, many other things depending thereon. Your Answer consists of 3 things. (1.) You tell us, what other Divines diversly think it to be. (2.) In what sense it is commonly used by your Brethren. viz. for the witness of the Spirit itself. (3.) That yourself do not call this Witness of the Spirit, the Seal of the Spirit. But usually the witness of the spirit itself; lest you should offend those that conceive the Seal of the Spirit to be more general. So that you do not plainly set down what your self apprehend it to be. Whether therefore you conceive Sanctification to be any part of the Seal; Or whether you conceive the Witness of the Spirit to be the Seal; Or whether you conceive the Seal of the Spirit to bee somewhat else, which some (as we have heard) do, is doubtful unto us.

To your Answer to the Second Question.

Herein you grant that every Believer is sealed, if sealing be taken for Sanctification. And therein we consent with you. But 2ly That every Believer is not sealed, if it be taken for the witness of the Spirit itself. Which We grant thus far, viz. that every believer doth not sensibly hear the Witness or take notice of it, no more than the Israelites listned to Moses testimony of their Redemption from Egypt when they felt their anguish and hard bondage, Exodus 6.9. Yet every believer being a Son John 1.12. he hath the Spirit of a Son, Galatians 4.6. and therfore he calls God Father; and this he could not do unless he had this witness in some measure, according to the dispute of the Apostle Romans 8.14.15.16. And if this be thus We see no reason why some Christians are said by diverse to be sealed, and some not, when as all have the impression of Sanctification, all have the witness in themselves 1 John 5.10. But some are made to be under the work of the Father, some under the work of the Son, and others under the work of the Holy Ghost, and these only sealed, and yet the first and 2d sort confessed to be believers.

To your Answer to the Third Question.

The broad seal of the Spirit was not first mentioned by any of us, but by our Brother Wheelwright. For our Brother Shepard almost in the begining of the discourse that day,[3] desired of him an

---

3. The reference is probably to the conferences held in December.
* See new note p. xix.

Answer to this Question, Whether the seal of the Spirit was common to all believers, or special to some. He answered, not common
but Special. Thereupon it was replied, If the Earnest of the Spirit
be common, then the Seal is common; for the Apostle interprets
the Seal of the Spirit to be the Earnest of the Spirit Ephesians
1.13.14. But the Earnest of the Spirit is common to all believers;
Ergo etc. To which he answered, after some hesitation thus,
Though every Christian believer hath this kind of Seal, yet he has
not the broad seal of the Spirit; and being pressed to prove such
a difference of the Seal, he said That though the Seal mentioned
in this place might be common, yet the 17th verse sheweth us the
broad seal of the Spirit.   Now it may be, some one of the Elders
might speak that word over again, having taken it first from Mr.
Wheelwright, and your self might hear it first spoken then, and so
mistake.   As for the latter clause of your Answer, We agree with
you, That the Consolation of the Spirit is a further degree of witness than Regeneration is of itself alone.

To your Answer to the 4th Question.

Herein (first) you grant a true believer may and ought to see, if
the Lord manifest it, (and we take it you mean that he sometimes
doth) any work of Christ in himself which accompanies Salvation;
as Cornelius did, before he be sealed with the Witness of the Spirit
itself. If so, We then desire, That they may be reproved who say a
man must see nothing in himself until sealed with the Spirit, and
censure those Christians as under a Covenant of Works that
gather any evidence of their safe Estate from any work of Christ,
before the conceived seal comes; who should rather be encouraged
and meekly instructed to look for more of Gods Spirit, not taking
up their rest in what they have. (2.) You say, Full and setled comfort he cannot take nor rest in, untill it be witnessed to him by the
Spirit. Which we grant to be true, if you mean most full comfort;
for every believer hath need of all the 3 witnesses, Spirit, Water,
blood, 1 John 5.8. to give him most full comfort.   But that which
you add is doubtfull; viz. That neither Word nor Spirit do teach
us to take our Comfort so much from the work of Christ in us, as
from the Object of it. To which we answer, Work, Word and Ob-

ject, which God hath joyned together to comfort, We dare not separate; for let a man look upon his Work of Grace, and comfort
himself in having the same, and not look to a Word, it will be but
confused comfort: Let a man look to a word of promise, made to
one that hath such a work in him; and not look upon the promise
as it is in Jesus, it will yield but little solid comfort. If a man receive comfort from beholding the Object the Lord Jesus himself,
and hereupon is fully persuaded, and looks not to the Word and
Work of Jesus; this will yield him little more than deluding comfort. Therfore all these are put together John 14.21. He that hath
my comandments and keepeth them loveth me (here is the work)
He shall be loved of my Father, (here is the word of promise) I
will manifest my self unto him (There is the object.)

To your Answer to the Fifth Question.

Herein you say, That the Spirit may witness imediately; not
without a work, but without respect to a Work in us. Now, in saying it, you do not affirm that it alwaies is or must be so, but only
that it may. But if your judgment be further, viz. That the testimony of the Spirit is or must be only or usually immediate without respect to a work, that is, without the sight of any work discovered by the Spirit (for we hope, none do conceive us, by respect
to a work, to have meant worth or merit of a work which we de-
test.) then we humbly entreat to see your grounds for it. For we
fear such an opinion may be a seed of much hypocrisie and delusion in the Churches, and that it may train up people to a plain
forsaking of the Scriptures indeed, while they cleave to them in
shew.

To your Answer to the Sixth Question.

Whereas in the latter clause hereof you said, A Christian may
have Assurance of his good Estate, maintained to him, when the
frame of his Spirit and course is grown much degenerate: We
much want satisfaction. For though we dare not easily in this or
other cases peremptorily determine that God may not, or doth
not this or thus, but leave an unlimited liberty to the Spirit of
God, yet on the other side it leaves us in the dark to say only, it

---

* See new note p. xix.

may be; which usually implyeth a possibility out of ordinary way. Because some may take it for the common wonted dispensation of God to Christians, we must needs reply thus much, That as we conceive it not to be his usual course with his people, to maintaine their Assurance in such a frame, the Lord carrying on all parts of his work both of Faith and holiness in some nearer Symmetry and proportion: So that position doth seem to open a wide door of temptation, as into Sin with less fear, so into a bold continuance and slight healing of sin, and breaches thereby. Neither doth the Lord use to maintain Assurance of peace to men, whilest they neglect to walk in the way of peace before him, Psalms 85.6.7.8 Galatians 6.16. which way those degenerate ones you mention Isaiah 63.16.17, were now returned into; who when they called God Father were then deeply affected with their degenerated frame and course. Neither did the Lord by Nathan testifie pardon to David till he had humbly confessed his sins, 2 Samuel 12.13.

To your Answer to the Seventh Question.

Herein you grant, (1.) That a man may see a work of waiting (2) A promise of peace to him in that condition. (3) That by renewed knowledg he may come to conclude peace provided for him: And all this before the Spirit witnesseth his interest in the Promise. To all which we consent, (taking the witness of the Spirit here for most full Assurance, which we conceive you do.) but many people deny; and therefore we desire they may be informed herein.

To your Answer to the 8th Question.

We grant (1) That the Lord by absolute promises (as they are called) may and doth oftentimes work faith of dependence or adherence. (2) That after a man is in Christ by faith, God may work by them faith of Assurance, if withall he clear up unto him his faith, or some other saving grace, to which these promises do belong: Or at least if such a grace be presupposed by the Soule though for the present not minded. But to take our first Assurance to arise from the Spirit in an absolute promise only, is not only difficult to us to believe (and therefore desire your grounds) but seems dangerous to maintain, as straitning the freeness of Gods Spirit in working and destroying the comfort of many, whom Christ himself doth speak comfort unto, Matthew 5.3. etc. Only this we add, That Gods free grace may be reveiled and received as freely in a conditional (where the Condition is first wrought by Gods free grace and not trusted to, as we desire ever to be understood when we mention conditional promises) as in an absolute promise, Romans 4.10.16. Revelation 22.17. Isaiah 55.1. For it is grace that works the Condition, it is Grace that reveals the Condition, it is grace that makes the promise, it is grace that sets on the promise; and what danger is there hereby, to a well instructed Christian of derogating from free grace?

To your Answer to the 9th Question.

To the last part hereof, wherein you add other things besides the Image of God in Adam concurring to the making up of Christian sanctification, we cannot assent; because we conceive that faith is the medium whereby we are sanctified Acts 15.9. and 26.18. and the indwelling power of the Holy Ghost the procreant and conservant Cause[4] 1 Peter 1.5. and therefore no material of our Sanctification. And as for Repentance, it seems rather to be the act or exercise of Sanctification, than any particular habit or part thereof, and is as large, in the Subject, the whole man, and object, good and Evil, as Sanctification itself.

To your Answer to the 10th Question.

We here desire you to interpret these words [evidently discerned] for if you mean Sanctification cannot be evident unless a man see his Justification first, (as once you publickly exprest your self) then your words bear this sense, if this true Sanctification be evidently discerned by seeing our Justification first, then it is a true evidence of justification; and so a man shall evidence by sanctification only that which was evident before; and thus upon point its no more an evidence than a Candle to the Sun. And if so, we see not, of what use those many passages, in the Epistle of John,

---

4. For the significance of these terms see note 11, p. 103.

and many other Scriptures that hold forth evidence of Sanctification can be, unto babes in Christ and such as believe and know
not that they do believe; nor can we think the signs delivered by
the Holy Ghost in Scripture, should be of use only to them that
are assured already, and so have least need, and of no use to them
that want assurance and so have most need of them. And thus
Sanctification will become of little or no account in point of Evidencing (which the Scripture layes so much weight upon) seeing
the strong have little or no need of it, if the weak who much need
it, can have no use at all. But if you mean that Sanctification may
be discerned by such other essential properties which are in its
own nature, and so be a true evidence of Justification *a posteriori;*
then we consent with you.

To your Answer to the 11th Question.

Here are diverse things doubtful to us. First, That though
Sanctification discerned in us may be an Evidence of being in
Christ, yet it is no ground of primitive Comfort. To which we answer, that these 3 things seem clear to us, (1) That there be many
Everlasting promises made to Sanctification in the Scripture 1
Timothy 4.8. (2) That one main end of these promises is strong
consolation Hebrews 6.17.18. (3) That the Lord is free to breathe
consolation in what promise he pleaseth, John 3.8. Hence a mans
primitive consolation may arise from his Sanctification, supposing
it to be such as accompanieth Salvation.

The 2d thing we doubt of is, That Faith in Christ is sooner
discerned than Sanctification by Christ. We grant that sometimes
it is so, not alwaies. And yet where faith is discerned it will give
little evidence in sad houres, for it will be suspected to be but a
dead faith, unless the presence of Sanctification be seen with it;
and then it may give stronger evidence.

The 3d thing doubtful is, That the sight of faith will give no
setled Comfort till the Spirit witnesseth Gods thoughts of peace.
Answer; If the Lord give a setled constant sight of a lively faith,
which every one ought to seek to maintain, together with a setled
sight of the promise made to Faith, the Lord Jesus Christ (if he
pleaseth) may give as setled comfort to that soul, by speaking and

breathing those words of peace as well as by witnessing imediately thoughts of peace. Unless he thinks and meanes not as he speaks; which be far from us to imagine.

We pray you also to consider, (1.) How this will stand with that in answer to the ninth Question, where faith is put into Sanctification: and here they are made contra-distinct. (2) Whether it be *ad idem,* to argue from primitive comfort to setled comfort, as here you do. (3) If it be a prejudice to free Grace to receive primitive comfort from the witness of the Spirit to or by a work; why not the like in after comfort, which must be still as much from free Grace as the first.

To your Answer to the 12th Question.

Herein you affirm, First. That a man cannot prove himself in a state of Grace by his Sanctification when his Justification is altogether dark and hidden from him.   Answer. We confess it is difficult to a man, to prove his Sanctification good that cannot prove how he came to his justification by Vocation;[5] but suppose a man savingly sanctified, we thus conceive, (1) That when Justification is hid from the eye, Sanctification and faith are there in the heart and oftimes effectually working. For a sincere heart doth not alwaies forsake the Lord, when the Lord seems to forsake him, Isaiah 50.10. Jonah 2.4. Jonah said he was cast out of Gods sight as not accepted, yet he did look unto the Temple, which argued faith, holy desire and unfaigned love. (2.) That when Sanctification is working it may be seen; because others may see, as your self grant; and the Lord may so bless their speech, that the party trying cannot but acknowledg Gods work and from thence may behold the Lords love. (3.) That when God hides his face most, there is oft in a justified soul, very deep and unfeigned sorrow, very lively faith of dependence on the Lord, and oftimes very close and humble walking before the Lord. Therefore grace being now in a special manner operative, if search be made, it may be through Gods help plainly discerned, James 2.22.

---

5. Vocation (Ephesians 4.1) means God's effectual call to man to respond by faith to the Gospel. The ministers assumed that this call and man's response were stages of salvation that preceded justification.

2. You herein affirm, That while a believer cannot see his person accepted he cannot see his work accepted. And this is made the reason of the former.   Answer. (1.) Though it be true, that my person is accepted before my work, yet it is not necessary, that what first is, should be first seen. Which seems otherwise 2 Peter 1.5, to 10. 1 Thessalonians 1.4.5. (2.) I may know my work to be accepted by knowing it is sound, Isaiah 56.6.7. Except any will say that the difference between a sound work and an unsound lyeth not in the being of the work, but in the acceptation of it; which is erroneous. (3) And lastly, We see not how this Answer will stand with your Answer to the 7th Question viz. That a weak beleever that hath not the witness of the Spirit may see his work of waiting for the Lord, and the promise made thereto, and conclude from thence his safe Estate; and therefore we inferr, that he must see this his waiting to be a work accepted. But here you say, A man can see no work accepted till he see his person accepted. Which we conceive, you hold to be, by the imediate witness of the Spirit itself, without respect to a work, in your Answer to the 5th Question.

To your Answer to the 13th Question

Herein after some distinctions you have thought it fit to express yourself in sundry propositions.

First Proposition we wholly consent with you in.

Second Prop. We grant here, That it is a great folly and sin against the Covenant of Grace, for a man not to come to, and depend upon Christ for Justification untill he evidently see his Sanctification: For this is, as if a sick man should refuse to go to the Physician untill he be well. And so we go fully out with you in such a kind of building.

Third Prop. The summe of it is this. (1) To evidence our Justification by a counterfeit Sanctification or Legal Reformation is to build on a Covenant of Works. Which we likewise affirm, or rather call it a self delusion: and such an ones error is in his false building rather than in his ground as thus; He that is truly sanctified is Justified; But I am so; Ergo. His proposition here is a good bottom; but his Assumption is faulty, by a false judgment of Himself. So that his Error is not in making Sanctification alone a ground of his Assurance but in taking a false Sanctification for a true. (2) That when we shall give no other evidence of Justification but sanctification etc. To which We cannot consent. For, To give no other Evidence of my Justification but Sanctification, at the most, is but to build the Assurance of my Justification on my Sanctification. And the being of Justification is much different from the seeing of it. Arguments from the Consequents (as Effects and Adjuncts etc.) may ground my knowledg of a thing; whereas only Causes, which are precedent, do make up the being of it. As for your Argument from the publican, We cannot reach whereto it tendeth. For, the Scripture saith not, [1.] That the Publican saw himself justified at all. Nor [2] That our Saviour gave him rather the sight of his sinful corruption than of his Sanctification for an Evidence of his Justification. Nor [3] Can any more be concluded thence in our apprehensions, but this, viz. That a man without sight of his Sanctification may be justified. And that such an one is more likely to us to be justified by God, that sees his wretchedness and confesseth it, than he that boasteth of a righteousness that he hath not. [4.] We know not how this instance can prove, That he that gives a man no other ground to evidence his Justification but from the evidence of his Sanctification; buildeth his justification upon his Sanctification, and goeth on in a Covenant of Works. [Lastly] Supposing he saw himself justified while he saw no Sanctification but only sinful corruption; Surely he might have been much more assured if he had seen his Sanctification. Neither do we see how your two Arguments from Mr. Hookers and Mr. Rogers testimony doth confirme your Proposition: For though they taught that there were saving graces which were not sanctifying; yet that Doctrin doth not bear witness, That to give no evidence of his justification but from his Sanctification, is, to build his justification upon his Sanctification. If indeed the Question had been, Whether he that makes Sanctification the sole evidence of a safe Estate doth judge truly? Then this Testimony would have evinced the Negative. But we cannot make these two equivalent; For, building justification upon Sanctification is a far more dangerous matter, than, to make fewer evidences of our justification than the truth affords. We therefore doe (1.) acknowledg with you That they have taught soundly and acutely out of the Word,

That there be saving graces which are not sanctifying, but are wrought before Sanctification, which yet may bear witness to a safe estate. (2) We acknowledg, That they who deny all evidences of Justification besides Sanctification, do err, in not acknowledging all the evidences of Free grace given by God: But we see no reason to say That such therefore do go on in a Covenant of Works, though they take their evidence from one of the witnesses of the Covenant of Grace.

Fourth Prop. The summe of it is this. That for a justified Soul to seek Consolation or Assurance of the Lords love, and of his Justification, by seeking to clear up his Sanctification and promise made unto it; is a going aside to (though not a building upon) a Covenant of Works, like Abraham to Hagar, a sinful hastning to see the promised seed, the Lord Jesus, and a building hay and stubble on that golden foundation; and a way wherein they are oft put into sad doubts.

First Answer. If by betaking himself to works you understand, to Works as a way whereby he may after attain unto the sight of his Justification; And that this is a going aside to a Covenant of Works; Then these five things seem to follow.

1. That David did ill to confesse his sin and to be humbled for it, when it hid the Lords face and favour from him; that so he might again see Gods face and favour in his Justification. Psalms 32.1.2.3.4.5.6. for he sought Consolation and peace in the way of Repentance.

2. That then the Lord hath done ill to command his people to humble themselves and pray and seek his face and turn from their evil waies that so he might forgive their sinns 2 Chronicles 7.14. 1 John 1.9.

3. That the Apostle Peter hath sent us aside unto a Covenant of Works in exhorting us to use all diligence, adding one grace to another thereby to make our calling and Election sure. 2 Peter 1.5 to 11.

4. That Christ hath done ill to command us to pray for the Spirit (prayer being an act of Sanctification wherein so many graces are acted) and to believe the promise of receiving it when we have so done.

5. To seek assurance from a divine witness (which the water

of Sanctification is made to be 1 John 5.8.) is a going aside to Hagar.

Secondly. But if by betaking himself to Works you understand Evangelical Saving Works, wherein together with the promise and Spirit of Grace I behold the Lords love as in a glass: yet still we conceive it no going aside to Hagar. For, To settle our Assurance on Christ or his faithfulness, and so to see the promised seed in a free promise revealed by the Spirit unto us that have such a work; is no going aside to Hagar, but rather a resting on Christ. We confess indeed, a justified Soul in this estate when he feels the Lord Jesus sanctifying his heart, he finds peace; and so he ought to do, as being a sensible expression of the Lords great love in removing sin so great an evil by the Spirit of his son; and we confesse that some Christians when they feel it not, do fall to doubting; which We say is their ignorance weakness and sin, being an act of unbelief and therefore are to be better instructed in the Covenant of Gods free Grace, not to be condemned as going aside to a Covenant of Works. And whereas you say such Christians ground not their faith of Assurance on Christ, nor on the free promise of Gods grace, nor on the witness of the Spirit. We answer, (1) That by clearing up their Sanctification, as the means and way, they come to see the face of Christ, as the End and bottom on whom their Peace is setled and grounded. (2) Although Christ is to be the chief matter of our Consolation yet a Christian ought to seek to see his interest in Christ, not only in beholding the face and hearing the voice, but also in feeling the gracious work of Christ 1 John 2.3. and 3.14.19. And therefore thus to do is no more building hay and stubble on a golden foundation, than to seek to see and be assured of our interest in Him in an absolute promise or in beholding his face. And if Christians in this case are often put to sad doubts of their own Estate, It is not because they sought to see Christ in clearing up their Sanctification; but because they are not abundantly exercised in that way 2 Peter 1.9.10. Or if they are, and yet have been continually doubtful, we conceive it hath been their ignorance and weakness so to be; and mans sin ought not to make us the more negligent in seeking to behold Christ in this glass and so to find him in his own way. As for the Alegory of Abraham and Hagar, it will not prove what is here said, but thus much only, That for any man to go aside to a Covenant of Works whereof you make Hagar to be a Type to seek to see the promised seed there, is to go aside to a Covenant of Works: But to seek to see the Lords face by seeking to feel the Lords own Work in us, is not going aside to Hagar. All doing or use-making of Works implyes not straightway a Covenant of Works. And we cannot but disrelish in these points of Evidencing Justification by Sanctification the frequent urging the term of Works, and our own Works. Which though there may be a fair construction of, yet to some it may seem to savour more strongly of Popish leaven than Protestant Doctrine doth imply.

Fifth Prop. The summe of it is this, 1. That a justified Soul seeing and beholding by renewed knowledg certain Evidences of Justification as prayer and brokenness of Heart etc. dare not, nay cannot, take them as certain Evidences of his Justification.

Answer. (1.) If he dare not take these as Evidences of the Lords love according to his promise of Love, then tis his sin and unbelief, for which he deserves to be rebuked, as making God a lyar. 1 John 5.11.12. (2) A poor believing Soul sometimes dare say that which the word saith: But the word saith that the poor hungry etc. are blessed: Ergo. (3) If he cannot take these as Evidences he is to lament his unbelief, and to seek to the Lord to persuade his heart as the man in the Gospel did, Mark 9.24.   Again, The Lord never makes promises whereby to comfort a man in a poor drooping condition, but they can and shall sometimes comfort him in that condition; Otherwise the Lord shall provide means for an end out of infinite love and pitie to his people, and yet they shall never attain that end.

2ly. The second part of the Proposition is summarily this. That such a soul will seek and wait for further and clearer fellowship with Christ till the Spirit of God doth reveal Gods thoughts of love in a free promise of Grace.

Answer. We say the same, if by a free promise you understand as well a conditional as an absolute promise. Which kind of promises if they be not free they should abolish rather than make parts of the Covenant of Grace. Yea, He ought to seek for evidence of the Lords love, not only till he hath once received the witness of the Spirit; but for clearer and clearer manifestations, untill he see

Gods face in Heaven. As touching the similitude of starrs shining only with a borrowed light from the sun. We answer you in the words of the same learned Countryman[6] of whom you speak. When the Sun is set the Star light appeareth, yet though the imediate presence and evidence of his favour shines not on the Soul, yet his graces therein appear as tokens of that his Love, So as the Soul knows there is a Sun still that gives light to those stars though it sees it not, as in the night we know that there is a Sun in another Horizon, because the Stars we see that have their light from it, and we are sure it will arise again.

Sixth Prop. You seem to hold forth (1) That Sanctification can not be seen. (2) That Justification cannot be seen without going upon, or aside unto a Covenant of Works, unless the Spirit of God itself do shed abroad his light into the soul, to give him a clear sight of his Estate in a free promise of Grace in Christ. And the conclusion of all these Propositions appears to be this, viz. That no man goes straight in a Covenant of Grace, but he that either sees nothing to evidence his good estate, or that sees what he doth see by the immediate witness of the Spirit itself.

Here also it farther appears. That whereas the great disputes of late have been, Whether Sanctification may be discerned by any properties in itself. Whether Justification may be seen in the evidence of faith. And whether Sanctification may be seen before Justification. All these have been in vain; and all are taken up in this one conclusion, That we can see neither Sanctification nor faith no nor Justification, before the witness of the Spirit; but all at once by it. And whereas it hath been wont to be argued thus, He that believeth shall be saved, He that is justified shall be saved, He that is sanctified shall be saved. Now it is thus, He that shall be saved is justified is sanctified hath faith. viz. He first seeth his good Estate in Gods thoughts of peace, (or in Election) testified to him, and therein reads himself a believer, justified, sanctified; and this is the only way, all others going on in or aside to a Covenant of Works. Which if they be the truths of God we would gladly be convinced thereof by sound proof.

---

6. In the *Sixteene Questions* the reference is to "some . . . of our . . . Countrymen"; the "some" is probably a printer's error.

To your Answer to the 14th Question

We believe the best man without Christ can do nothing and through Christ can do all things Philippians 4.13. John 15.5. and therefore after Conversion *acti agimus;* yet so as that Christ hath given to his people more than *proximam potentiam* to receive help from him; for the graces of Christ in his members are in part like Christs, John 1.16, spiritual and heavenly, and Ergo active in their proper nature, sometimes more, sometimes less. Yet because sin in us is too strong, grace in us (nakedly considered in itself) and the feebleness of Grace received, is such, that it is subject to many alterations and changes. And the dispensation of God now having appointed us a life of faith, which stands in receiving new supplies by piece meal, and not in being possessed of the whole portion at once, we therefore need a dayly assistance of the Spirit to help, and of faith to go out to Christ for dayly power and life.

To your Answer to the 15th Question

We do also conceive it sinfull to rest satisfied in the witness of our own Spirit, untill the Spirit it self bears witness with it, That we are sonns. But we have heard of some that think it an unsafe way to conclude a mans safe Estate by way of practical Syllogism and so quench Gods Spirit in themselves, by seeking a Spirit without any work of the Spirit in themselves, imagining the Lords spirit should bear witness without not with their Spirits, which we take to be contrary to Romans 8.16.

To your Answer to the 16th Question.

The Saints do use arguments both from their own Spiritual miseries and infirmities, and from the graces of Christ in them. And both these may well stand together in the same prayer: And they make use of these not rarely but frequently, and of these not some sorts only, but all sorts, and that ordinarily. Which is easie to shew by induction of many places of Scripture.

Thus Dear Sir, We have according to our light received, briefly plainly and uprightly, as in the sight of God laid down what we conceive concerning your Answers to all these points in

Question, Wherein we do in some things consent with you, and that we do most really and freely: In other things we are forced to dissent; and that we do unwillingly and sadly. Now We bow our knees to the Father of Lights, to clear up all our judgments in one truth, that we may all think and speak and preach the very same thing, which will advance the glory of his blessed truth, and the comfort of many a Soul who else will not be a little disheartned and unsetled in their holy course and frame by any apparent difference that may be between us.

CHAPTER 5

Mr. Cottons Rejoynder

THE third document in the Massachusetts Historical Society manuscript is John Cotton's "Rejoynder" to the "Elders Reply." Because of its length the "Rejoynder" must be considered the most important exposition of Cotton's theology at the time of the Controversy. Throughout the document, as in those that preceded it, the argument over the relationship between faith and grace turned on the nature and kinds of causality. The differences of opinion between the ministers and Cotton were partly a matter of Scriptural interpretation, as, for example, of Ephesians 1.13: ". . . in whom also, after that ye believed, ye were sealed with that Holy Spirit of Promise." In their commentary on the third question, the ministers cited this verse to support their contention that faith was somehow prior to, and a condition of, receiving the Holy Spirit. In the "Rejoynder" Cotton drew on Calvin and Piscator to argue that the English translation was misleading, and that "in order of causes" the Spirit came first. But Cotton's major concern was to rebut the logical distinctions that the ministers were employing to explain the role of faith. To him the scholastic arguments of the ministers led inevitably to the conclusion that "our works are the grounds and causes of our first Assurance," a conclusion "disallowed by the chief Protestant writers."

The "Rejoynder" here appears in print for the first time. Brackets in the text are in the original. The seventeenth-century form of setting off quoted material has been changed to conform with modern practice. Periods have been added to sentences ending in abbreviations.

Mr. Cottons Rejoynder.

To my Reverend and dearly Beloved Brethren the Elders of the Churches in the Bay:

Reverend and Beloved

To the First.   Because you say it would be very acceptable to you and useful, if I would clearly explain what I conceive the Seal of the Spirit to be, Thus take it in a word. I conceive the Seal of the Spirit is the Spirit himself, even as the name of Christ is often put in Scripture for Christ himself.

For, The Scripture to my remembrance doth never speak of the Seale of the Spirit as of a distinct thing from the Spirit: neither is this phrase The Seal of the Spirit a Scripture speech; but we are said to be sealed by the Spirit (to wit as any writing is sealed by a Seal) Ephesians 1.13. and 4.30. And when God is said to have sealed us, How did he that, but by giving the earnest of his Spirit in our hearts, 2 Corinthians 1.22? The Spirit is as fitly called a Seal as it is called the earnest, or the unction, Ephesians 1.13.14. 2 Corinthians 1.21.22. 1 John 2.20.27.

And because you conceive that the clearing of this point may conduce to the clearing of many others (many others as you say rightly depending thereupon) therefore I shall willingly tell you how and in what respect I take the Spirit to be the Seal.

First. As confirming all the Promises of Grace and the whole Word of God unto us; it being an authentical witness of the divine truth and power thereof unto our hearts, and thereby begetting and confirming faith in us. For though the Translators so turn the Apostles words (Ephesians 1.13) as if believing went before, and sealing by the Spirit followed after faith; yet if you consult with Calvin and Piscator on the place,[1] they will tell you that in time faith and the sealing of the Spirit go together, and in order of causes the sealing of the Spirit goes before faith, as being the Efficient cause of it. And so indeed may the word be better translated (as Piscator would have it) when you believed, or, in believ-

---

1. John Calvin, *Commentarius in Epistolam Pauli Ad Ephesios,* in *Opera Quae Supersunt Omnia* (Brunswick, 1895), *51,* cols. 152–153; Johannes Piscator, *Analysis Logica Sex Epistolarum Pauli* (Herborn, 1593), 99.

ing you were sealed, or, having beleeved you have been sealed
with the Holy Spirit of promise.   I consent with them, and do
take the Spirit himself to be ever *proxima efficieus causa fidei,*
both *procreans* and *conservans,*[2] The principal proper and effectual cause of faith. Whence the Spirit is called the Spirit of faith
2 Corinthians 4.13. The word and promise of God though mighty
through the Spirit yet without it is but a dead letter; and all the
six witnesses (of which the Apostle John speaketh) three in
Heaven and three in Earth which are brought to beget and confirm faith in Christ, do all of them bear witness nextly and imediately only by the testimony and efficacy of the Spirit who though
he hath a peculiar and distinct witness of his own, in which regard
he is made one of the six witnesses, yea two in a several consideration, yet he himself applyeth and conveyeth the testimony of all
the rest imediately to the Soul. Imediately I say though not without the word of God nor without (sometimes in some cases) the
work of God, yet with his own imediate power above the power
which either the word hath of it self, or the work of any creature.
Thus the Father when he draweth the Soul to Christ, teacheth and
learneth the soul to know Christ and to believe on him John
6.44.45. Galatians 3.15.16. but it is by the Spirit applying this
work of the Father, as he doth all the good things of God to us,
1 Corinthians 2.10.11.12. Thus also the Son revealeth the Father
to the Soul (Matthew 11.27.) and thereby giveth us ease and refreshing and liberty (Matthew 11.28.29. John 8.36) but it is by the
work of the Spirit applying the work of the son in his name (2 Corinthians 3.17.) And the Spirit himself also beareth a peculiar and
distinct witness of his own revealing the grace of God in greater
peace and power: In greater peace, for it is he that sheddeth
abroad the love of God into our hearts Romans 5.5. and he speaketh peace to us Psalms 85.8. even peace that passeth understanding Philippians 4.7. from whence springeth the joy unspeakable
and glorious, which is therefore called the joy of the Holy Ghost
because it floweth immediately from him and his testimony Romans 14.17. Whence also it is that he is often called the Comforter

---

2. Literally, "the proximate and efficient cause of faith, both creating and
preserving"; but in Cotton's paraphrase, "the principal proper and effectual
cause of faith."

John 14.16.26. and 15.26. and 16.7. Again, He revealeth the grace of God in greater power to us in Christ, Acts 1.8. to wit, above the power they had received whilst Christ was conversant with them upon the Earth.

As for the Water and the blood (the witnesses on Earth) they cannot confirm and ratifie their own testimonys, nor make them authentical to faith, unless the Spirit bear witness in them also: and therefore when they are named (as waies in which Christ cometh into the Soul) yet the Efficacy of their witness is attributed to the Spirit 1 John 5.6. And thus by ratifying and confirming all the witnesses of Christ and of our life in him, and by making them authentical unto our Souls, so as to beget or confirm faith by them, the Spirit of God is therefore called a Seale.

2. Again 2ly. The Spirit of God is called a Seal as engraving and writing the image of Christ in us (unto which the Father hath predestinated us to be conformed Romans 8.29.) Jeremiah 31.33.34. with 2 Corinthians 3.3. Ezekiel 36.26.27. Which image consisteth in our likeness to him in his death and resurrection Philippians 3.10. In perfecting whereof the Spirit useth not only the word and other Ordinances but also the two seals of the Covenant of Grace, baptism and the Lords Supper Romans 6.4.5. Our likeness to Christ in his death and resurrection consisteth in the mortifying of Sin, and in living unto righteousnes, whereof we shall have occasion to confer further in answer to your 9th Question.

3. I need not adde that the Spirit is also called a seal as distinguishing us from the World Revelation 7.2.3. and yet withall concealing us from it, 1 John 3.1. Which together with the former do make up all the offices of a Seal and demonstrate the Spirit himself to be the Seale.

To 2d.

Whether every believer be sealed with it? I answered Every believer is not sealed with it, if the seal be taken for the witness of the Spirit itself: But I pray you take my meaning aright, to wit, that every believer is not sealed with the Spirit Expressing his own proper and peculiar witness and work, distinct from the witness and work of the Father and of the Son. For every believer hath not received the fulness of joy of the Holy Ghost, and that power of the Spirit from on high which is the witness of the Holy Ghost himself, distinct from the witness of the Father and of the Son. But if the witness be taken for the Spirits manifestation and impression of the work of the father and of the son upon the Soul, so every beleever is sealed by the Spirit himself: For (as I have said) though the father reveal Christ in us, and draw us to him, yet it is by the Spirit applying the Fathers work to us; and though Christ reveal the father to us, and bring us to some ease and refreshing and son-like liberty (as hath been shewed) yet it is by the Spirit stamping and engraving a son-like disposition and Spirit in us. In this point I suppose there will be no difference, unless it be in what sort of promises the Spirit doth witness the work of the father or of the Son unto us.

But say you, "if it be so, we see no reason why some Christians are said by diverse to be sealed, and some not, (when as all have the impression of Sanctification and all have the witness of the Spirit in themselves, 1 John 5.10.) but some are said to be under the fathers work, some under the work of the Son, and others under the work of the Holy Ghost, and these last only sealed, and yet the first and 2d sort confessed to be beleevers."

Answer. They that say, these last sort only are sealed, I have conference with some of them, and find this to be their meaning, that these last only are sealed with the Spirit sealing his own proper and peculiar witness unto them, otherwise, they do confess both the former sorts have received the Spirit himself, who is the seal of the living God, revealing and confirming the work both of the father and of the Son in them before his own. Neither need it offend any Christian ears to speak of a distinct work of the father and of the Son, and of the Holy Ghost. For though all the persons in the Trinity do concur in all their works *ad extra*[3] (in their works upon the creature) yet every person hath his distinct manner of operation in every work upon the creature. And some works are more properly and eminently attributed to one of the persons rather than to another. They are made 3 distinct witnesses 1 John 5.7. which necessarily implieth a distinct manifestation of the life

---

3. On the outside.

of Christ to the Soul, in their several operations. In every comon Catechism, when the Question is made, What hath God the father done for you? Children are taught to answer, He hath created me; which if it be extended to our new creation also, it is but according to Scripture phrase, which maketh it God the fathers work to draw us to Christ. John 6.44. and to beget us that we should be the first fruits of his creatures, James 1.18. And when a 2d Question is asked, What hath God the Son done for you? They are taught to answer, He hath redeemed me: And what is Redemption but restoring to liberty? And if it be said, these to be the Sons work to give ease and refreshing and son-like libertie unto the Soul; it is but according to Scripture phrase, John 8.36. And when a 3d question is asked; What hath the Holy Ghost done for you? They are taught to answer, He sanctifieth and comforteth me. Which if it be in eminent manner ascribed to the Holy Ghost as sanctifying and comforting us in greater power and fulness, it is but according to Scripture phrase, John 14.16. and 16.22. and Acts 1.8.

To 3d.

Our brother Wheelwright professeth, He remembreth no such speech of his: The matter of distinction in some sense he doth own: the expression (though he should have used it) he disclaimeth. The words following in your Reply (that though the seal mentioned Ephesians 1.13.14. might be common, yet the 17 verse sheweth the broad seal) He utterly denyeth, professing he never had such a conceit in his heart, as being a gloss contrary to his own judgment.

To 4th.

When I said, A beleever may and ought to see (if it be declared unto him) any work of Christ that accompanieth salvation (as Cornelius did) before he be sealed with the seal of the Spirit itself. You must ever understand me as I have already spoken, before he be sealed with the Spirit expressing his own proper and peculiar work in the fullness of comfort and power: Otherwise no man can have, nor can truly by faith see any saving work of Christ in himself, till by the Seal of the Spirit itself it be engraven upon him, and witnessed unto him: for there is no work in us accompanying

Salvation, but it is a fruit of the Spirit and the things that are freely given unto us of God are revealed unto us by the Spirit 1 Corinthians 2.10.12.

But if it be so, say you, "then we desire that they may be reproved who say, a man must see nothing in himself, untill he be sealed by the Spirit and who censure those Christians as under a Covenant of works, that gather any evidence of their safe estate from any work of Christ in them, before the conceived Seal cometh; who should rather be encouraged and meekly instructed to look for more of Gods spirit not taking up their rest in what they have."

Answ. Reproof you know doth rather belong to the Pastors office:[4] The truth of the Doctrin, as I have here expressed it to you, our Church can bear me witness I have plainly taught it (according to my place) and have refuted the contrary. But as you express the contrary doctrin, which you would have me to reprove, I see no just matter of reproof in it. For I cannot see how a man can by faith see any thing in himself till it be instamped and ingraven and so sealed in him by the Spirit and also that it be witnessed (and so sealed) to him by the same Spirit himself. It is not any work from which we can gather any evidence to our faith of our safe estate by any light of our own Spirit and Conscience, unless the Spirit itself bear witness to that work in some word of grace. For as the Word without the Spirit cannot beget faith, so neither the work without the Spirit; unless we ascribe greater efficacy to a work created in us, than to the Word; which we may not do: For faith rather cometh by the word heard Romans 10.17. than by the work seen: yea neither word nor work (being both of them creatures) are able to beget or confirm faith, unless the Spirit himself (which is the Spirit of faith and life) breathe in both his own witness with them.

And this let me add, Though the Spirit may (and doth often)

---

4. Puritans distinguished between the offices of pastor and teacher in the ministry of a particular church. "The Pastors special work is, to attend to exhortation: . . . the Teacher is to attend to Doctrine." Williston Walker, *The Creeds and Platforms of Congregationalism* (New York, 1893), 211. Since Cotton was teacher of the Boston Church, he did not have to reprove unruly members.

bear witness to a word and a work in the evidencing of Sanctification, yet in the evidencing of Justification he beareth witness in
the word of free grace only without works, as I hope we shall see
hereafter.   Meanwhile, When you would have me and our other
brethren to encourage those Christians who gather the evidence
of their safe estate from the work of Christ in them, before any
former evidence of their justification by the seal of the Spirit I
must profess, though a child might lead me (and much more the
least of you) according to God; yet herein I dare not hearken to
you my self, nor persuade our brethren thereunto: For I know not
how to excuse it from going in a way of the Covenant of Works,
first to see a work before the seal and witness of the Spirit (and so
he must needs see it only by enlightned Conscience) and then to
see a promise made to that work; and then from both to gather a
faith of my justified estate: Such a faith is not a work of Gods almighty power begotten by the divine testimony and operation of
the Spirit of God, (for it is before it) but hammered it is and en-
gendred out of the concurse of three creatures, 1st. from the work
or fruit of our own Spirit then from the letter of the word (which
without the power of the Spirit of God is not able to beget faith)
and then from the help of an enlightned Conscience reasoning
and concluding from both. The danger whereof is evident, and
will also by Gods help further appear in the sequele.   Meanwhile, the best encouragement I can give to such christians is, not
to bless themselves in such an estate, or in such a faith of it, but
timely to understand that in kindling such sparks of comfort from
our selves, and walking in the light thereof this they shall find at
Gods hand, they shall lye down in sorrow, Isaiah 50.11.

When I said, that neither word nor Spirit do teach us to take
comfort so much from the work of Christ in us, as from the object
of it. This you say is doubtful to you: But wherefore should you
doubt? Doth any good Christian take as much comfort from his
faith, or from his hope, or from his love, or from his hungering
and thirsting after Christ, as he doth from (the object of all these)
Christ him self? Can any man take as much comfort in thirsting
after the water of life, as in drinking of it?

But say you, "The work and word and object which God hath
joyned together to comfort, you dare not separate."

Answ. 1. Be it so, yet when they are all joyned together, dare you then take as much comfort in the work as in the object of it? Did Abraham rejoyce as much in the work of his faith, whereby he saw Christs day, and in his seeing of that work, as he did in the blessed seed seen by him? Let the blessed seed himself speak and put it out of question, your father Abraham rejoyced to see my day, he saw it, and was glad, John 8.56. He rejoyced therfore not so much in the sight of his sight of Christs day, as in the day of Christ which he saw.

2. That work and word and object should not be separate, but all go together to comfort, I like it well; but only desire that every one of them may take his own place in his own order. In the comfort of Justification, let the object (or ground) of our comfort go before, and it revealed and given in a free promise of grace, then let faith receive it, and see it and rejoyce in it. In the Comfort of Sanctification, let the object or ground of our comfort go before, to wit our union with Christ, and it revealed to faith, and received before, then let the works of Sanctification follow according to the comandment of the word; and then settle not your comfort on the works, but expect your comfort in the object again to be revealed; who being revealed will acknowledg his acceptance both of you and your works: and such comfort will be sound and durable. An Example of the former you have in Abraham: The object or ground of his comfort, the blessed seed was revealed to him in a free promise of grace without works: This Abraham received and saw by faith, seeing and beleeving on this seed and the promise of it he rejoyced with joy unspeakable and glorious. An Example of the latter, the place you quote will yield us John 14.21. No man can keep the comandments of Christ but he that first loves him; and so much the words of the text imply, He that keepeth my commandments saith Christ is he that loveth me. Now no man can love Christ except he first beleeve in Christ, and by believing be united to him, and know the love that Christ hath towards him, 1 John 4.16.19. Here is then the ground of our comfort, first laid in our union with Christ, and in our knowledg of his love towards us: thence follows our love of him, and this fruit of our love we keep his commandments. And then though a word of comfort followeth, yet the comfort is neither laid up in the work, nor in the

word, but in the object promised again to be revealed, who when
he cometh according to his word will manifest himself and his renewed love to us. There is no fear of delusions in such comforts,
where works are made neither ground of our comfort first nor last,
and yet are not wanting in their place, that as it is written, He that
rejoyceth let him rejoyce in the Lord.

To 5th.

To the fifth. When I said, The Spirit it self may witness,
though not without a work, yet without respect to a work; I do
mean that it doth witness not only without respect to the merit
or worth of a work (as you explain it) but also without our sight of
any work of ours in some case; and yet in some other case it may
(and doth often) witness upon the sight of some work, of which
God by his Spirit doth witness and seal his gracious acceptance,
and of the person that wrought it.   My plain meaning is; In case
of Justification when the Spirit doth witness, and apply and seal
that unto the Soul, it witnesseth without sight of any work of ours
foregoing as any way preparing us thereunto: yea the witness
thereof upon the only sight of Christs righteousnes imputed to us
(not upon sight or work of any righteousnes of ours) is the cause
of our faith, and the good works that follow it, not they of it.
When Peter preached that through the name of Christ whosoever
beleeved on him should have remission of sins, it did not presuppose faith in all them that heard the word; but in holding forth
that promise the Holy Ghost went along with it, and fell upon
them all, and so begat faith in them and the fruits of it, Acts
10.43.44.

But in case of Sanctification, the Lord himself doth often witness (and so his Spirit) to a person formerly justified and assured
of his justified Estate, his acceptance both of the holiness of his
person and of his work, upon sight of his work. As it was granted
to Abraham, So the like I doubt not is granted to his faithful seed
also. To wit, when he was justified before (Genesis 15.6) and assured of it with full rejoycing (Genesis 17.17. compared with John
8.56.) afterward upon the offering of his son at Gods command,
the Lord testified his acceptance of his fear of God upon the sight
of that work Genesis 22.12.18.

But in the point of our free justification you need not fear that the gracious witnessing thereof unto our Souls by the Spirit of God breathing in a free promise without sight of any work, will breed any hypocrisie or delusion in the Churches, unless that such a witness were held forth as left the Soul as barren of good works after it, as it looketh at none (in the point of justification) before.

To 6.

In answer to your 6th Question. I said, Though a Christians comfort and sense of it will be darkned and shaken by falling into any gross sin; yet the assurance of his justification may be still maintained to him, even when the frame of his Spirit and course is grown much degenerate Isaiah 63.16.17.

"This speech you conceive (in summe) to be dark and dangerous. Dark, because [may be] doth usually imply a possibility out of ordinary way"; But (with your leave) modall propositions expressing possibility are opposed only to necessity of being so, and imply a possibility of being otherwise, whether it be in an ordinary way or an extraordinary. No rule in Logick or reason implyeth [may be] to express usually a possibility out of ordinary way, unless other circumstances of the Speech enforce it. But to clear this darkness (if any darkness be in it) my meaning is, that howsoever a Christian man fully assured of Gods favour formerly upon sure grounds may afterwards fall into some gross sin, and thereby through temptation and desertion and ignorance may come to doubt of his Justification, yet if he know the riches of Gods grace in Christ, he ordinarily both may, and (by ordinary rule) ought to beleeve that his justified estate doth still remain unshaken, notwithstanding his grievous sin. For as Justification and the faith of it doth not stand upon his good works, so neither doth it fall or fail upon his evil works.

I deny not (if it be taken with a grain of salt) that the Lord carrieth on all his works both of faith and holiness in some near Symmetrie and proportion; so that the stronger faith cleaving more stedfastly unto Christ, bringeth forth the purer holiness, the weaker faith the less purity of holiness; whence it is that Christians of strong faith living by their faith in Christ do seldom fall under such strong corruptions as weaker Christians do. But because men of great measure of holiness be apt to live besides their faith, in the strength of their gifts and not in the strength of

Christ, it pleaseth the Lord sometimes to leave them to greater falls, then other weaker Christians, who being of weaker gifts do find more need to live by faith in Christ than upon the strength of their gifts.   But this I conceive, though a Christian assured of his good estate in Christ upon safe grounds, should fall into gross sin, yet his sin is no just ground why he should weaken the assurance of his justified estate. Is there any text in Scripture that calls a true Christian to strengthen or weaken the assurance of his justified estate according to the strength or weakness of the holiness of his life? Neither will this open (as you fear) a wide door to fall into sin with less fear, or lye under it with slighter healing: nay rather it is the riches of this grace that breedeth this holy ingenuity in every child of grace, that where grace doth more abound, sin should abound the less. How should I commit (saith the Soul) this great wickedness and sin against the father of mercies, the God of all grace? And in case he be prevented by temptation and fall into sin, it is that which soonest and deeplyest woundeth his heart, and bringeth him home with the soundest and livelyest Evangelical Repentance, that he hath abused so rich grace unto wantonness, and hath loved him so little, who hath so much, and so freely, and so unchangably loved him.

When you say, "The Lord doth not use to maintain Assurance of peace, while men neglect to walk in the way of peace before him, Psalms 85.6.7.8. Galatians 6.16."

It is true, if you speak of that peace and tranquillity of soul which the consolations of God are wont to speak to a faithfull and holy life. But there is a peace of Justification by faith Romans 5.1. which may and ought to remain inviolate when the soul neither seeth nor feeleth his wonted consolations: for we live by faith not by sight (2 Corinthians 5.7.) and Davids challenge is no less safe than confident (Psalms 49.5) wherefore should I fear in the day of evil when the iniquity of my heels compasseth me about? The reason of which fearless confidence in the midst of his iniquity he giveth in v. 15. God will redeem my soul from the power of the grave, he shall receive me. It would exceedingly streighten the life of faith in Gods redeeming love if the assurance of faith might not stedfastly rest upon Christ, aswell to redeem him from gross sin and from an hard heart under it, as from outward calamities and ordinary iniquities, which may befall him in his close walking with God.

The place which I quoted out of Isaiah 63.16.17. doth still make good that for which I alleadged it. For though those degenerate ones were now in a way of returning unto God, when they complain of their degenerate estate, and of their estrangements from the waies of God, and of the hardness of their hearts under it; yet even still the frame of their Spirit and Conscience* [*q. num course]⁵ fell far short of that close walking with god, upon which you seem to make the Assurance of a Christian mans good estate to depend. That the Lord did not by Nathan testifie pardon to David, till he had humbly confessed his sin 2 Samuel 12.13. it will not therefore follow that David ought not before that to have beleeved it. If a Brother offend me I am not bound to testifie I do forgive him, before he testifie it doth repent him: and yet I am bound to forgive him (if I look to be forgiven at Gods hand) though I do not testifie it: So I doubt not, God had forgiven Davids sin, and David had ground to beleeve it before Nathan came to him. For Justification is *Perennis actus,* a perpetual act of God never interrupted: and therefore the Assurance of it ought not to be interrupted in our faith, unless faith may be allowed to beleeve a falshood. It is one thing for God to be at peace, another thing to speak and declare peace. It is one thing to declare a present act, The Lord doth put away thy sin, as if a while ago he had not done it another thing to publish an act past still continued, The Lord hath put away thy sin. It is one thing to speak of an act in itself, The Lord hath put away thy sin; another thing to speak of the effect of it, in regard of the exempting David from the punishment of Death, which else he might justly have feared by the Law (Leviticus 20.10.)

To 7th.

In my answer to your seventh Question I desire you plainly to conceive me as I plainly speak. First I say, A man that waiteth upon Christ may come to see and discern the Lord helpeth him to waite. 2ly He may see a promise of peace laid up in Christ for such

---

5. As in the manuscript. Here, and again further on, the copyist suggests another reading of the word.

as wait for Christ, and for peace in him. 3ly He may come to conclude that peace is provided and laid up for him in Christ on
whom he waiteth, and will still wait till he hath found him more
fully, and peace in him.   All these are plainly to be gathered out
of Psalms 130. 5. to 8. But still here are two things to be attended;
1st. That such a soul hath first seen Christ and mercy and pardon
laid up in him, v. 4. and this he hath seen by the Spirit of God
witnessing the same unto him, whence that waiting frame cometh
to be sealed and stamped upon him. 2ly In the midst of his waiting, his faith on Christ is not built on his own waiting but on
Christ, in whom he hath seen mercy and peace laid up for him;
and who having helped him to wait, will help him still to wait,
and will at length more fully give and reveal him self to him. The
author and object of his waiting is the ground both of his faith,
and his waiting, which is the act of his faith. It is not his act of
waiting that is the ground either of his faith in Christ, or of the
accomplishment of the promise to his waiting estate. Furthermore, when you take it from me, that the soul may see all this before the Spirit witnesseth his interest in the promise; conceive me
aright (as I think you do) before the Spirit itself in his own proper
work doth witness this interest in full Assurance with comfort and
power.

To 8.

You grant first "That God by absolute promises may and doth
oftentimes work faith of dependance or adherence; 2ly That after
a man is in Christ by faith God may work by them faith of Assurance, if with all he clear up unto him his faith or some other saving
grace to which these promises belong; or at least if such a grace be
presupposed by him, though for the present not minded. But to
take our first Assurance to arise from an absolute promise only, is
not only difficult to beleeve but dangerous to maintaine."

To your first grant I answer, If you mean by faith of Adherence, that faith whereby we receive Christ and our first union with
him, I do conceive that God not only may and doth often, but
even alwaies work that faith by his Spirit coming and breathing in
absolute promises; or if in conditional, it is alwaies without respect to any such condition as pre existent in the soul, though by
the promise the condition will be wrought in us. For I demand,

upon what condition can that promise be made upon which our faith is grounded to receive union with Christ? Is the Condition found in the Soul before union with Christ or after? All conditions before union with Christ are corrupt and unsavoury, as the corrupt fruits of a corrupt tree; and to such no promises are made at all. And all conditions after union with Christ are effects and fruits of that union, and of that faith which floweth from that union, and therfore faith was before them, and before the promises made to them. Yea faith itself and our adherence to Christ by it, is a fruit of that union; or else we might be beleevers, i.e. good trees, and bring forth good fruit before union with Christ which the Gospel accounteth impossible.

To your 2d grant I answer, If our first Assurance may be wrought by a conditional promise, I demand again, whether we be assured of that Condition before we be assured of our union with Christ or after? If after then our first Assurance was before it. If before, I demand How the Soul can be assured that such a condition is any saving grace peculiar to Gods elect, before he be assured both himself to be in Christ, and his grace to spring from union with Christ? If it be said that any saving grace may be discerned to be peculiar to Gods Elect by some peculiar characters whereby it is discerned from the common graces of the forwardest hypocrites; I answer, True, such peculiar characters there be, whereof this is alwaies one, without discerning whereof the rest can never be discerned, that, such graces spring from a lively faith, and do work from faith in Christ without which it is impossible to please God; And then we see our Justifying faith before we see our Sanctification pleasing to God.

Again, If all the promises whether absolute or conditional be first made and fulfilled in Christ, so that we have no right unto them by right of any condition or qualification or work in ourselves, but only by right of union with Christ; then we must first assuredly discern our union with Christ before we can assuredly discern, that the right of such a conditional promise belongeth unto us. Now I take it for granted on all hands, that all the promises are first made and fulfilled in Christ, and that we have no right unto any of them by right of any condition or qualification or work in ourselves; but only by right of our union with Christ, for in him are all the promises yea and amen, 2 Corinthians 1.20. Galatians 3.16. A wife hath right to her husbands goods not by her chastity or helpfulness to him or observance of him, but by her marriage union with him: So neither have we any right to the blessings of the grace of Christ laid up in any promises, nor can we challenge any assurance thereof, till we can first hold forth and plead our assured union with himself. Hence it is, that when Catharinus (a learned Papist)[6] went about to prove that a beleever in Christ might be assured of his Salvation by his good works, out of 2 Peter 1.5. to 10. Bellarmine answers him, This testimony will not help the Lutherans, because (saith he) *Ipsi certitudinem suam priorem operibus esse volunt non posteriorem. (de Justif.* l.3. c. 9) i.e. The Lutherans will have their assurance to be before works of Grace, not after. Whereto Pareus replyeth, We (saith he) acknowledge our former Assurance to be before works, from the testimony of the Spirit bearing witness to our Spirits that we are sound. Our latter Assurance to be of Works as of the signs and effects thereof.[7]

To which I might add the testimony of Calvin in his *Institutions* l.3. c.2. § 29. where he maketh the free promise the foundation of faith or assurance, because (as he there saith) a conditional promise whereby we are sent to Works, doth not promise life but as we see the condition found in ourselves. And therefore (saith he) unless we will have our faith to be trembling and shaking it behooveth us to support it with such a promise of Salvation which is offered freely and liberally of the Lord, and hath rather respect to our misery than worth. What kind of free promise he meaneth, he plainly expresseth in the words following, by instancing in that 2 Corinthians 5. 18. There is nothing (saith he) that can establish or assure faith but the liberal Embassaye whereby God in Christ reconcileth the world unto himself, which promise neither requireth faith nor works to go before it, though it doth require and will produce both to follow it.

A clear instance of this Faith of Assurance wrought by the

---

6. Ambrose Catharinus (1487–1553), a Catholic theologian and author of *Apologia Pro Veritate Catholicae ac Apostolicae Fide* (1520), an attack upon Luther.

7. David Pareus (1548–1622), *Roberti Bellarmini . . . De justificatione . . . Explicati et Castigati studio* (Heidelberg, 1615). Pareus was a Reformed theologian, Robert Bellarmine (1542–1621) a Catholic theologian.

Spirit of God in an absolute or free promise of Grace, the Book of Martyrs recordeth in Thomas Bilney, who in his Epistle to Cuthbert Tonstall B. of London[8] witnesseth that the first peace and assurance he found was by the sweet comfort which the Holy Ghost shed abroad into his heart upon reading that precious promise (free from all conditions of works) 1 Timothy 1.15. This is a faithful saying and worthy all acceptance that Jesus Christ came into the World to save sinners of whome I am cheif. Let not therfore any man professing the fear of God, profess in solemn Assemblies that the gathering of our Evidence and first assurance of Justification from Sanctification or from the promises made thereto, is a doctrin sealed by the blood of Martyrs; since this blessed Martyr testifieth the contrary in his own experience, and none of all the other Martyrs (to my best remembrance) do dissent from him.

You object, "That to make our first Assurance to arise from the Spirit in an absolute promise only, seemeth dangerous to maintain, as straitning the freeness of Gods Spirit in working, and destroying the Comfort of many whom Christ himself speaketh comfort unto, Matthew 5.3.4."

Answ. 1. My words in my former answer do plainly express that I do not so limit the Spirit as alwaies to work assurance only in an absolute promise; For thus they run: A Christian mans first Assurance doth arise from the Spirit of God applying Gods free grace in an absolute promise; or if in a conditional (as they call it) it is not to Works but to Faith, and to faith not as it is a work but as it receiveth the free grace of God offered in Christ Jesus.

Yea and this let me add further, In a mans first conversion the conditional promise to faith is not to faith at all as extant and pre-existent in the Soul, but as to be wrought and to be begotten in us by the power of the Spirit who breatheth in the promise of Grace, and coming into us uniteth us to Christ, from whom both faith and every spiritual grace and blessing is derived to us. An instance hereof I gave above out of Acts 10.43.44. where Peter having

---

8. John Foxe, *The Acts and Monuments,* ed. George Townsend and S. R. Cattley (London, 1837), *4,* 635. Thomas Bilney (d. 1531) was a proto-Protestant martyr.

preached and promised remission of sins to every one that beleeveth in Christ, he did not presuppose faith in all his hearers that so they might apply Christ and remission of sins unto themselves: but the Holy Ghost going along with the word and coming down upon their hearts with it, did indeed beget faith in them and assurance thereof.   And for a man that is in Christ, as God did not presuppose his faith but wrought it in him when he gave him Christ in an absolute promise at his first Conversion, so God may as well build him up to more full assurance by giving him a fuller and greater measure of his Spirit in a like absolute promise. And therfore you seem to me to fall into that fault which you blame in me, that is, to "limit and straiten the freeness of Gods Spirit when after that a man is in Christ by faith you allow God that he may work by absolute promises faith of Assurance if withall he clear up unto him his faith or some other saving grace to which those promises belong, or at least if any such grace be presupposed by him, though for the present not minded."

Why? May not God by an absolute promise as well increase faith as beget it? Or is it not as free for the Spirit of Grace to build up faith unto full Assurance by revealing clearly the free love of God in a promise of free grace as by clearing faith or any other saving grace in the Soul? Must some grace in us be at least presupposed (though for the present not minded) and may it not as well be wrought by the Spirit together with full Assurance, or after it, as be presupposed before it?

But finally, I would say, it is no straitning to Gods Spirit to say He revealeth free grace freely; which he doth if he reveal it in an absolute promise: But if he reveal grace in a conditional promise, to wit, upon any condition presupposed in us, look how much the condition is stood upon before grace revealed, so much is grace vailed and obscured in the revelation of it.

Answ. 2. Neither will the Spirit giving us our first assurance in an absolute promise, destroy the comfort of any whom Christ speaketh comfort unto in Matthew 5.3.4. etc. For two things there be found in the estate of such as Christ there speaketh comfort unto, which preventeth the destroying of their comfort though their first Assurance be given in an absolute promise.

1. There is none of those poor, or mourning, or hungry, or

thirsty souls there spoken of, that were brought into such an estate but by a former Assurance that all riches and comfort of satisfying grace and mercy is wholly and absolutely laid up in Christ, which the Spirit coming into their hearts sealeth up unto them, and some secret possibility of their interest therein, whence they receiving Christ in truth (though not in sense) do feel themselves poor for want of fellowship with him, and so come to mourn after him and hunger and thirst for him. Men are not brought to mourn after Christ or for him, till after a gracious sight of him wrought by the Spirit of Grace, Zechariah 12.10.

2. There is none of these that shall find their first assurance of the riches of Christ, and of his favour and righteousnes bestowed upon them in their poverty: nor their first assurance of Comfort in their mourning for him: nor their first satisfaction or filling in their hungering or thirsting after him: for it would imply a contradiction to find riches in a mans poverty, comfort in mourning, filling in hunger. It would indeed make that which is indeed but the way to further fellowship with Christ to be the end of our journey; as if a suitor should satisfie his desire in conversing with the waiting maid, when he longeth for fellowship with her mistress: or as if a man should find his hunger and thirst satisfied, by hearing that hunger and thirst is a sign of a healthfull body. But our Saviour in such a case telleth us, how men in such a condition shall first come to enjoy the blessings promised, when he saith (John 7.37.38.39) If any man be athirst, let him come unto me and drink; he that beleeveth in me, out of his belly shall flow rivers of water of life; this he spake of the Spirit etc. He doth not send men that are thirsty, to consider of their thirst, what a gracious disposition it is, and to drink well of their thirsting till they be filled with it, and such satisfaction out of it: No, no, but let them come (saith he) to me, (even unto me) and drink; not drink their consolation out of their thirst, but out of Christ. And the same word that calleth them to Christ, giveth them in a renewed measure the Spirit of faith, by which they do come to Christ, and do drink to the satisfaction of their Souls in the full Assurance of his grace and righteousnes freely given to them of God. So that when men come to be first thus qualified (as poor and mourning and hungry) it is from the revelation of free grace in Christ, and when they come to

be first satisfied with Christ and with the assurance of his love, it is not from their good conditions or qualifications, but from the same free promise of Grace, bringing them again to come to Christ, and to drink again of him, and of his free grace more abundantly.

Obj. But say you, "Gods free grace may be revealed and received as freely in a conditional promise (where the condition is first wrought by Gods free grace and not trusted to) as in an absolute, John 4.10. Revelation 22.17. Romans 4.16. and Isaiah 55.1. for it is grace that worketh the condition, it is grace that revealeth the condition, it is grace that makes the promise, it is grace that sets on the promise; and what danger is thereby to a well instructed Christian of derogating from free grace."

Answ. I profess ingenuously in the simplicity of my heart, that to my understanding it implyeth a contradiction: To be first assured that Grace worketh the condition in me, and grace revealeth the condition in me, that grace maketh the promise to me, and revealeth and setteth on the promise to me, and yet not to trust to it. For here is a work and a word; a condition wrought and revealed, a promise made and revealed and set on; and what hindreth now but I may safely trust partly to this work (though not wholly) and partly to the promise made to it. And though I trust not at all to the worth of the work (as deserving any thing at Gods hand) yet I cannot but trust (at least in part) to the right of the work, and unto the promised blessings by reason of the promise made to it. Yea, so much do I trust to that work that if I see not that work in myself I dare not trust a promise nor the grace and blessing offered in the promise to belong to me; But if I take the promise to belong to that work (though given of grace) and find that work and feel it in me, then upon the sight of that work I may claim my right to the promise and to the comfort and blessing pronounced in it. Be not deceived (I beseech you) that because you profess to take all from grace, condition, promise, and the revealing of both, that therein* [*q. if not therefore] you do not derogate from grace. It was that which deceived Bellarmine to plead that Justification by works doth not derogate from Justification by Grace, "For the works themselves (saith he) are not works of nature but of Grace, and therfore though we be justified by them,

yet still we be justified by Grace, unless we make Grace to fight
against Grace." Bellarmine *de Justif.* l.1. c. 21. Whereto you know
our Divines are wont to answer, That Grace and Works, (not only
in the case of Justification but) in the whole course of our Salvation from Election to Glorification, are not subordinate one to another, but opposite: so that whatsoever is of Grace is not of Works,
and whatsoever is of Works is not of Grace, according to that divine maxim of the Apostle Romans 11.6. If it be of grace it is not
of works, otherwise Grace is no more grace: and if it be of Works
then it is not of grace, otherwise works is no more works.[9]

Think not to say, The Lord speaketh not simply of Works, but
of the merit of Works; for he speaketh of right by works aswell as
of the merit of works; for so Romans 4.4. he opposeth grace not
only to merit but to debt; To him that worketh the reward is not
reckoned of grace but of debt: and yet no true Christian but
knoweth that even to him that worketh, wages is not due of debt
but only in respect of the promise of God made to works in the
Covenant of Works: otherwise though we should work exactly the
whole will of God all our daies, we could challenge no reward of
debt from Gods hand: for all we are, or have, or can do, is of God
and not of our selves. If he that worketh claim any reward for his
work, it is out of promise made to the work, which before God and
man, of truth, is due debt: And therefore if we claim or gather our
first Assurance of blessing and comfort from any works of Sanctification, though we trust not to the merit of the work but to the
grace and faithfulness of the promises, yet if we claime, I say, and
gather blessings and comforts to ourselves from the promises
made to the good works wrought in us, and by us (though of
grace) before we see our union with Christ and right to all promises and comforts and blessings in him; we then do receive them
not of Grace but of debt; and that in very truth must needs derogate from free grace.

And this I take to be one main difference between the promises of the Law and the Gospel: In the Law, the promise is made
to the Condition or qualification of the creature, though given
him of God: so that, give me the condition and I claime my right

9. Pareus, *Roberti Bellarmini ... De justificatione,* 5, 326–329.

to the promise. In the Gospel the promise is made to Christ, so that, give me Christ and I claim my right to the promise and to all the comforts and blessings thereof: And therefore that which maketh the accomplishment of all the promises of the Gospel to be of grace, is not because we have the condition from God and the promises from God, and the revealing of both from God (for so it is in a Covenant of Works) but because all the promises are given to Christ, and all the conditions are fulfilled in Christ, and the revealing of both is by the revealing of Christ given of grace freely to the Soul. He is the door that must be first opened to me, and revealed to me, and entred in by me, before I can see any Assurance that the treasures of Gods House belong to me.

As for Conditional promises which you instance in, wherein you say, "Gods free grace may be revealed and received as freely as in those which are absolute (as John 4.10. Revelation 22.17. Romans 4.16. Isaiah 55.1.)."

I answer, Gods free Grace is not then received and revealed freely, when it is revealed and given to a condition of works first going before in the creature; but then, when grace being first freely given, and absolutely, without any condition, doth work such conditions in the creature: and yet not such conditions whereto promises of further comfort is due (for then our ensueing comforts were laid up in such conditions,) but such conditions doth grace freely work in us wherein our souls are carried to Christ in whom our last comforts as well as our first are laid up. For I do believe, as Christ is the first and last in other respects, so

in this that he is the first and last condition $\frac{of}{in}$ the promises. Christ

is the first condition, who being first given and united to us, giveth us our first right and inheritance of promises and blessings and conditions appertaining thereunto: and when we have received such conditions from him, then we look for further comfort, not in the revealing of such conditions, but in the further revealing of Christ freely.

To apply this to the conditional promises alledged by you; The conditions mentioned in them are faith in Christ, and thirst after him, and prayer for him. Now no man hath had these conditions given to him, or revealed in him, but he hath had Christ first

given and revealed to him freely who hath wrought these conditions in him. Now he having received these conditions, looketh
not for his further comforts in these conditions (no more than a
thirsty man looketh for his comfort in his thirst) but as he found
his first tast of comfort in Christ (who wrought in him this faith
and thirst and prayer for him) so hee beleeveth and prayeth and
thirsteth and findeth it more abundantly in him.

To 9th.

You cannot as you say assent to the last part of my Answer to
your ninth Demand. For whereas I said, That our Sanctification
in Christ hath in it this more than the Image of God in Adam,
Faith in Christ, Repentance from Dead works, and (that which is
the root of both) the indwelling power of Christ by the Spirit to
act and keep holiness in us (all which Adam wanted) You conceive
"Faith in Christ is the medium by which we are sanctified (Acts
15.9 and 26.18) the indwelling power of the Spirit is the procreant and conservant cause and therefore no material of our Sanctification. And as for Repentance, it seemeth rather to be the act or
exercise of sanctification, than any particular habit or act thereof,
and is as large in the Subject (the whole man) and in its object
(good and evil) as Sanctification itself."

Answ. Though Faith in relation to the object, to wit, as it receiveth Christ, belongs to Vocation, and so is a medium whereby
we are sanctified: yet as a quality setting us apart from all confidence in our selves and resigning us to Christ, it hath a place in
Sanctification. And so Dr Ames taketh it; who also speaking of
Repentance as it is a real change of the disposition of the Soul, so
saith he, *Resipiscentia idem sonat cum sanctificacone,* Repentance is the same with Sanctification, *Medul:* l. 1. c. 29 §. 8.[10]

If an unbelieving and impenitent heart (as such) be a common
and unclean heart, then a believing and repentant heart (as such)

---

10. Ames, *Medulla Theologica,* Bk. 1, 133. As translated in *The Marrow
of Sacred Divinity* (London, [1642]), the passage referred to reads: "But this
sanctification is distinguished, from that change of a man which is proper to
the calling of a man in Faith and repentance, In that that Faith there is not
considered properly as a quality, but in relation to Christ: neither is repentance there considered as a change of disposition; for so it is all one with sanctification: but as a change of the purpose and intent of the mind. But here a
reall change of qualities and dispositions is looked unto."

is holy and sanctified to the Lord. If the good fruits which John Baptist exhorteth his hearers to bring forth worthy of Repentance (Matthew 3.8) be fruits of sanctification then is there an habitual Repentance from whence such fruits spring, as well as an actual. To speak of Repentance as an act or exercise of Sanctification, and not an act or exercise of the gift or habit of Repentance putteth a strange and causeless difference between Repentance and all other spiritual gifts of grace abiding in us. For whereas all other spirituall gifts of grace abiding in us are distinct infused habits, which by the quickening power of Christ through faith do put forth their proper acts and exercises, only Repentance is made an act without an habit, or at least without any habit that is properly and peculiarly disposed to bring forth such acts.

But be it as you say, That Repentance is the act and exercise of sanctification, and so is as large as sanctification itself both in the subject and object, then it will follow that in all the acts of sanctification Repentance is acting and putting forth itself; which if it be so, therein will appear a manifest difference of our Sanctification from that of Adams, which was wholly exempt from all entercourse and exercise of Repentance. In the Sanctification of Adam there is no act or exercise of faith and Repentance. In all our Sanctification there is an act and exercise of faith and Repentance. Therfore our Sanctification is not the same with that of Adams.

Furthermore, To speak properly, I conceive that Sanctification is rather an act or exercise of Repentance than Repentance an act and exercise of Sanctification: For in every act of Sanctification we are but turning from sin and from our selves, and returning to the Lord. And that which setteth both Repentance and Sanctification on working is faith in Christ which deriveth renewed life and power, will and deed and all from Christ. So that faith doth not concur in duties of Sanctification as an external efficient but as a formal ingredient in every holy Christian duty; whence the just is said (aswell in his Sanctification as in his Justification) to live by his faith: and Paul saith, the life that he now liveth, he liveth by the faith of the son of God Galatians 2.20. Which holdeth forth to me a broad difference between our sanctification and that of Adams, in which he neither lived by faith

nor put forth any act of an heart repenting and turning to the
Lord.

As for the indwelling presence and power of Christ by his
Spirit, which is the root of our Sanctification, not so of Adams;
You answer, "It is the procreant and conservant cause, but no ma-
terial of our Sanctification."

If your meaning be (as your words will bear no other) That
the power of the Spirit is the procreant and conservant cause of
our Sanctification, by begetting and preserving the habits of Sanctification in us, but not in producing the acts of Sanctification, so
that we our selves produce the acts of Sanctification by vertue of
those habits received by us and preserved to us; you doe then indeed make our Sanctification the same with that of Adams; but
not the same with that of Pauls who bringeth in Christ not only
as a procreant and conservant cause of his spiritual life but as
joyntly concurring with him in every act of spiritual life as much
as himself, yea more; I live (saith he) yet not I but Christ liveth in
me Galatians 2.20. and again, to me (saith he) to live is Christ Philippians 1.21. Your judgment in this point jumpeth with Grevin-
chovino, *A dominio (inquit) peccati nos sanat spiritus sanctus non
ut causa formalis sed efficiens.* Whereto I joyn with Ames in returning you this Answer, *Immo omnis efficiens movens efficien-
ter, vim aliquam in eo genere motivam et quasi formam in re
motâ relinquit semper impressam. Hoc in projectione lapidis fieri
voluit subtilissimus Scaliger, Exercitatione 28. In actionibus autem illis quae ad alterationem et perfectionem objecti tendunt
apertius est quam ut negari possit. Formalis igitur sanandi vis in
anima imprimitur per vim hanc Spiritus extrinsecus efficientem.*
If then the indwelling power of the Spirit do imprint a formal
healing power upon the Soul, this power concurreth not only as
a procreant or conservant cause of our Sanctification, but as a formal ingredient in its healing of the Soul, which in Adams holiness
it did not.[11]

---

11. "The Holy Spirit heals us of the rule of sin, not as a formal cause but
as an efficient cause." Ames: "Indeed every efficient cause that moves effi-
ciently leaves, in that respect, a certain motive force and as it were a form impressed upon the object moved. This is what the most subtle Scaliger [Julius
Caesar Scaliger, a Catholic humanist] thought happened in the throwing of

You may not put me off with a distinction between material and formal: For when you make the indwelling power of the Spirit to be the procreant and conservant cause and not the material of our Sanctification, you do much more deny it to have any formal ingrediency or concourse in our Sanctification. But the truth is, the Holy Ghost doth not work in us gifts and habits of Sanctification to act and work by their own strength, nor doth he with them give faith in Christ to go forth of it self to him for renewed strength to set these habits awork. But he himself setteth faith awork and stirreth it up to look forth to Christ and to wait on him, who being waited on, quickeneth by his Spirit all our gifts in his name to bring forth fruits of righteousnes unto God. So that the Holy Ghost hath not only an external efficacy in begetting and preserving our Sanctification; but also an internal concourse and cooperation in the duties of Sanctification. Whence that which our Saviour saith of his Apostles is true concerning all his Disciples (though not in like measure) It is not you that speak (and consequently not you that think or do) but the Spirit of your Father that speaketh in you, Matthew 10.20. Which I suppose could not have been said of Adam in his holy duties which in the state of innocency he might have put forth. Besides Consider (I pray you) with me (because the point in hand is of great consequence)

---

a rock, Exercise 28. But in those actions that aim at the alteration and perfection of the object, it is too evident to be denied. Therefore the formal power of healing is impressed upon the soul by this force of the Spirit acting externally." William Ames, *Guil. Amesii ad Responsum Nic. Grevinchovii Rescriptio Contracta* (Leyden, 1617), 148–149. Nicolas Grevinchoven (d. 1632) was a Dutch Arminian.

In this and the succeeding paragraph Cotton again denied the validity of a logical distinction that might allow for man's activity prior to grace. The ministers were distinguishing between the Holy Spirit as the "procreant and conservant cause" and faith as the "material" cause of sanctification. In this context the material cause meant a power within a subject (man) to perform the work; it is an internal power, as opposed to an external, or "formal." Again Cotton jumped the distinction by attributing the entire work to the Spirit: "So that the Holy Ghost hath not only an external efficacy in begetting and preserving our Sanctification; but also an internal concourse and cooperation in the duties of Sanctification." In a paragraph in the *Institutes*, II.v.14 just above the one Cotton quoted at the end of the "Rejoynder," Calvin discusses the relationship between God's will and man's activity in terms of the throwing of a stone.

Is not our Sanctification the Image of God renewed in us? Is not this Image of God the new man opposite to the old corrupt through deceivable lusts? Is not this new man a tree of Righteousnes? Is not the root of this tree Christ dwelling and working in us by the power of his Spirit? And is the root no material of the Tree? no part of it, but only a procreant conservant cause of it?

Moreover, As our Sanctification is the new man created in us after the Image of God; So after the image of Christ especially, unto whose image as well in Sanctification as in affliction God hath predestinated us to be conformed Romans 8.29. Now, the image of Christ sealed and engraven upon us by the Spirit of Christ consisteth in our conformity and likeness to him in his death and resurrection, Philippians 3.10. And our likeness to him in his death and resurrection consisteth in our dying to sin and to this world and to the Law and to our selves, and in living unto Christ. Whence it is that Perkins [margin: Perkins *Gold.Chain.* ch.38[12] *Medul* l. 1 c.29] and Ames and others have given these two for the two parts of Sanctification; Mortification and Vivification. Now how the Sanctification of Adam could consist of such two parts as these I must confess it is past my capacity.

To 10.

I said, That true Christian Sanctification evidently discerned is an evidence of Justification *a posteriori,* as Justification is a true evidence of Sanctification *a priori.* You demand, "Whether I mean that Sanctification can be evident unless Justification be first Evident?"

Answ. I conceive not. For seeing all true Sanctification is wrought by Faith in Jesus Christ, even by that faith whereby we are justified and our persons accepted in Christ Jesus. And seeing the life of this faith is a necessary ingredient not only in every habit but in every act of Sanctification, it is not possible that our Sanctification or any duty of it should be evident to us to bee wrought in God unless it first evidently appear to be wrought in faith; and then our justification will of necessity be evident to us before our Sanctification can be truly evident.

---

12. William Perkins (1558–1602), a Puritan theologian; Cotton cites *A Golden Chaine, or The Description of Theologie* ([Cambridge], 1597).

You'l object; "Thus (upon the point) Sanctification is no more an Evidence then a Candle to the Sun."

Answ: You might have said than a Candle to a candle; for there is not so great difference between Sanctification and Faith, as betwixt a candle and the Sun, unless it be in regard of the Object of faith, Christ himself, and him revealed by the witness of the Spirit it self. And it is no dishonour to Sanctification to light his candle at Justifying Faith, which receiveth his light imediately from Him who is the light of the Word. But of this more hereafter.

Ob: But (say you) "If it be so, we see not of what use those many passages in the Epistle of John and other Scriptures that hold forth Evidence by Sanctification can be unto babes in Christ and such as beleeve and know not that they do beleeve."

Answ. I hope it will be no offence to you, no more than to myself, if we borrow light from Calvin to clear the meaning of the Holy Ghost in such passages of Johns Epistles from which your objection is taken. In 1 John 2.3. hereby (saith John) we know that we know him if we keep his comandments. Upon which place saith Calvin, "We must not hence gather that faith doth relye upon Works; for though every beleever have a witness of his faith from his works; yet it followeth not that it is founded there, seeing this as a latter proof cometh in over and above in steed of a signe. Therfore (saith he) the Assurance of faith doth only rest on the grace of Christ, but Godliness and holiness of life doth show a difference between true faith and feigned, and dead knowledge of God." Again, in 1 John 3.14. By this (saith John) we know that we are translated from death to life because we love the brethren. Upon this place (saith Calvin) "A man should praeposterously conclude, That Life may be acquired by love seeing love is latter in order. The Argument would have more colour to argue, If Love do certifie us of our Spirituall life, then the Assurance of faith may lean upon our works. But (saith he) the solution of this also is not difficult; For although faith be confirmed by all Spirituall gifts of grace as by some helps; yet it doth not cease to take for its foundation the only mercy of God in Christ. And a little after, After that faith be once founded on Christ other things may be added over and above which may help faith. Nevertheless in the mean while it resteth only on the grace of Christ." In 1 John 3.19. By this (saith John) i.e. by the love of our brethren in truth, we know that we are of the truth and shall before him persuade our hearts. Whereupon (saith Calvin) "But let us alwaies remember that this knowledg of our estates which the Apostle here speaketh of, we have it not from our love, as if from thence were to be fetched certainty of Salvation; For surely we do not know that we are the Sons of God by any other means than because he sealeth to our hearts by his Spirit our free Adoption out of his grace. And when the Apostle addeth, Hereby we shall persuade our hearts before him; He doth (saith he) advertise us that faith doth not consist without a good Conscience; not that from thence our persuasion springeth or dependeth thereupon: For it is alwaies meet, to weigh what the Apostle driveth at. Though a good conscience cannot be severed from faith yet no man can thence rightly collect that we must have respect to our works that our persuasion may be firm."[13]

It appears therfore evidently by the Judgment of Calvin, That these places which give signs of our good estate from Sanctification, were not given at all to such Christians as are doubtfull of their estates, from thence to gather the first Assurance of their good estates: but to such only as are formerly assured of their good estates by the seal of the Spirit and to them they are of notable use to declare to themselves and to all the world, by such holy fruits, that their faith is not feigned nor themselves hypocrites. And in that respect they are of special use even to weak Christians also (even to those whom you call babes in Christ) that whereas many teachers and professors do bear themselves forth as worthy Christians, they may know them to be counterfeit Christians no better than hypocrites, if they see them destitute of brotherly love, and devoid of conscionable care to keep Gods comandments.

The Lord Jesus who best knows with what milk to feed his babes, doth not send them to gather knowledg and assurance of their estates first from their Sanctification or good works, but first from the knowledg of himself and of God as their father; I write

---

13. John Calvin, *Commentarius in Iohannis Apostoli Epistolam*, in *Opera Quae Supersunt Omnia* (Brunswick, 1896), 55, cols. 310–311, 339–342.

unto you babes because yee have known the father 1 John 2.13. And he that knoweth God as a father knoweth his Adoption out of the free grace of God in Christ Jesus. If you ask by what means? John answereth by the unction which they have received by the holy one, whereby they know they were in Christ, and should abide in him, 1 John 2.20.27.

If any man object (as I hear some do) 1 John 5.13. That the scope of Johns Epistle is, that beleevers may know they have eternal life, and that they may beleeve on the name of the Son of God. I answer; It will not thence follow that beleevers do come on first to believe, or do first come on, to know that they do beleeve, by the witness of their works of Sanctification: But that coming to beleeve, and to know that they do beleeve by the unction of the Spirit revealed in the word of grace that abideth in them, they may be further confirmed in faith by the same Spirit and word, and may make the same known to themselves and their brethren, by their brotherly love and their faithfull keeping of Gods comandments.

To 11.

Whether true Sanctification discerned by us may not be (and often is) a ground of our primitive comfort etc. I answered, No; as conceiving our faith whereby we depend on Christ, to be as soon discerned (if not sooner) than our Sanctification; and yet neither faith nor Sanctification to yeild setled comfort to the Soul, till the Spirit of Christ doth witness to the Soul Gods thoughts of peace towards him.

You reply that diverse things are here doubtfull to you; as (1) That though Sanctification evidently discerned by us (as before) is an evidence of our being in Christ, yet it is no ground of our primitive comfort. (2) You doubt Whether faith in Christ be sooner discerned than Sanctification by Christ. (3) You doubt Whether it be true that the sight of faith will give no setled comfort till the Spirit witness Gods thoughts of peace.

For Answer, I do refer you to my former answer above, in clearing the 8th Question. For the same grounds upon which our first assurance is built, upon the same is our primitive comfort built; and the clearing of the one cleareth the other.

Yet something let me add soe far as you here insert any new

matter. I said, Though Sanctification evidently discerned be an evidence of our being in Christ, yet it is not a ground of our primitive comfort. My reason was because a man hath his primitive comfort from some former work of God before Sanctification, to wit, from Gods giving him Christ in his effectual calling, and the righteousnes of Christ in his justification; and both in a free promise of grace (Isaiah 43.22. to 25.) which we receiving by faith have peace with God, Romans 5.1. and this peace is our first comfort.

You reply. "That there are many everlasting promises in Scriptur made to Sanctification 1 Timothy 4.8. 2ly That one main end of these promises is to beget strong consolation Hebrews 6.17.18. 3ly That the Lord is free to breathe consolation by what promise he pleaseth, and therfore a mans primitive comfort may sometimes arise from his Sanctification."

Answ. To your first doubt I answer; Though Godliness (and so Sanctification) hath the promises of this life and that which is to come (as the Apostle saith in the place you quote) yet all the promises are not made to it; not the promise of union with Christ, not the promise of Regeneration, not the promise of Justification, not the promise of faith, whether of dependance or Assurance. And therefore if our primitive comfort spring (as it doth) from any of these blessings, we cannot seek for it in the promises made to Sanctification.

2ly. I have denied above, that in proper speech the promises of the Gospel are made imediately to our Sanctification, So as by right of our Sanctification to challenge any blessings promised to us. But indeed all the promises are made first and imediately to Christ, and by right of our union with him they come to be communicated to us in a way of faith and Sanctification: So that if any promises be made to us either to clear our Sanctification to us, or to comfort us in it, we must first see our selves united to Christ before we can see our comfortable right in the one or in the other.

3ly. Though it be true that you say, that one end of the promises is to convey strong consolation to us, according to Hebrews 6.17.18. Yet the consolation there spoken of is consolation to Sanctification not to Justification, whereof Abraham (who is there spoken of) was comfortably assured before. God promiseth and

sweareth strong consolation to Abraham upon his sanctified obedience in the oblation of his Son, Genesis 22.12.16.17.18. but he
beleeved in Christ before, Genesis 15.6. and rejoyced in beleeving, Genesis 17.17. compared with John 8.56.

4ly. Though it be true, The Spirit is free to breathe consolation in what promise he please, (John 3.8) yet it is not his pleasure
to breathe the comfort or Assurance of our Justification in works;
lest any flesh should rejoyce in itself, before it have learned to
fetch all his rejoycing and consolation from Christ, in whom we
must first find both our Justification and Sanctification laid up,
and from him set over unto us by God, that no flesh might glory
in his presence, and that he that glorieth might glory in the Lord
1 Corinthians 1.30.31.

To your 2d doubt (whether faith in Christ be sooner discerned
than Sanctification by Christ) You grant that sometimes it is so,
not alwaies. For when faith is discerned it will yield little comfort
in sad hours, yea it will be suspected to be but a dead faith unless
the presence of Sanctification be seen with it, etc.

Answ. In sad houres, if faith be suspected Sanctification will
be suspected much more. For seeing the Just liveth by his faith,
the life of faith putteth life into Sanctification: If faith seem dead
and suspected, Sanctification cannot appear lively and evident. In
this case the faithfull Soul doth not go about to revive his dead
faith by looking at the presence of his Sanctification, but by looking at Christ, and the free promise of grace made in him. When
Jonas felt himself cast out of Gods sight he remembred Jehovah
(even out of the belly of Hell, when his Soul fainted in him) and
looked again to his holy Temple, which was the type of Christ.
Jonah 2.4.7. Doubtless we live by faith and not by sight (2 Corinthians 5.7.) and of faith we read (not of Sanctification) that it is the
evidence of things not seen, Hebrews 11.1. And therefore when
Sanctification, and all the comforts and blessings thereof may be
hid, yet faith may be evident, for it giveth evidence to them all,
even then when they are out of Sight.

Touching your 3d doubt (Whether the sight of faith will give
any setled comfort till the Spirit witness Gods thoughts of peace to
the Soul) you object, If the Lord give a setled constant sight of a
lively faith, together with a setled Sight of the promise made to

faith, the Lord Jesus may (if he please) give setled comfort to the Soul by speaking and breathing words of peace as well as by witnessing imediately thoughts of peace, unless we should think his words are different from his thoughts.

Answ. 1. Be not offended at the phrase (thoughts of peace) it is a Scripture phrase Jeremiah 29.11, which when God revealeth in his word (as there) the words are words of peace. For I put no difference between thoughts of peace and words of peace, save only this, that Gods Spirit breathing in words of peace maketh his thoughts of peace towards us, evidently to appear, which before lay hid in him. But your objection seemeth to imply a contradiction: For if you speak of the sight of faith in sad hours when faith may be discerned, and yet suspected to be dead; how can you then suppose that God should give us a setled constant sight of a lively faith, and that together with a setled sight of the promise made to faith? A setled constant sight of a lively faith, and yet a faith suspected to be dead cannot stand together.

2ly. When the Lord giveth (as you put the case) a setled constant faith together with a setled sight of the promise made to faith; I easily beleeve the Lord Jesus may be pleased to give setled comfort to the Soul, by speaking and breathing words of peace to it. But I deny that this is the first comfort the Lord hath spoken to that Soul. I do not find that ever God wrought in any, a setled constant faith, much less a setled constant sight of it, with a setled sight of the promise made to it, before he revealed his gracious acceptance of him in Christ Jesus, in a promise of free grace imediately; I mean, without the mediation of faith or works already præ existent or fore wrought in the Soul, but to be wrought by the Spirit breathing in the promise.

Furthermore concerning this doubt, you propound three things to my consideration. 1. How it will stand with my answer to your 9th Question where faith is put into Sanctification, and here is made contradistinct from it.

Answ. You know it is no new thing, When faith is spoken of in the case of Effectual Calling or of Justification, it is then considered not as a part of Sanctification, not as a quality acting holiness in us; but as in relation to Christ the object of it. (See Ames *Me-*

dull. lib. 1. c. 29. §. 8.)[14] but yet as a quality inherent in us and deriving holiness from Christ in all our Christian duties, it is a part of Sanctification.

2. You pray me to consider, "whether it be *ad idem*[15] to argue from primitive comfort to setled comfort."

Answ. The Argument is *ad idem,* though all primitive comfort and setled comfort be not the same; because the Argument holdeth *a pari,*[16] that if the sight of the gift or work of faith, or of any other gift or work of Sanctification will not give setled comfort to the Soul touching his sanctified estate, unless the Lord reveal by his Spirit his gracious acceptance of him and his work, in a promise of grace made to the Soul in that way; then neither can Sanctification or any work of it give primitive comfort to the Soul, unless the Lord reveal by his Spirit his gracious acceptance of his person, unto a justified estate, without any work at all; because there is no promise at all of Justification made unto works, or to the sight of them.

3ly. You wish me to consider, Whether if it be a prejudice to free grace to receive primitive comfort from the witness of the Spirit to or by a work, why not the like in after comforts, which must be still as much of free grace as the first?

Answ. Because our first comforts spring from such blessings as go before all our works, as from Effectual calling, Adoption, Justification; and therefore as they are wrought together without works, so they are revealed without works. It is the glory of grace to conceal all mention of works there; and the free and gracious revelation of them without works begetteth those works which flow from them, and which afterward bear witness to them. But the following comforts in which God beareth witness to our Sanctification they are often dispensed upon works, because it is the glory of grace to encourage and reward the gifts and fruits of grace. Hence are those frequent speeches to the Churches, I know thy works, etc. And to him that overcometh will I give etc. And yet this let me add here also, that when God acknowledgeth a good

14. Cotton cites this same passage in his reply to Peter Bulkeley.
15. To the same.
16. Equally.

work and speaketh comfort to it, as he did to Abraham Genesis
22.12. yet he directeth him to look for the blessing both of his
work and of his comfort, not in the things themselves but in
Christ. In thy seed (saith he) shalt thou and all the nations of the
Earth be blessed, v. 18. The blessing lieth not in the deed, but in
the Seed.

To 12.

To your 12th Question (Whether a man may prove himselfe
in a state of Grace by his Sanctification when his Justification lyeth prostrate) I answered, If my Justification lyeth prostrate (that
is, altogether down, dark and hidden from me) I cannot prove
myself in a state of grace by my Sanctification. For whilst that I
cannot beleeve that my person is accepted in Justification, I cannot beleeve that my works are accepted of God as any true Sanctification.

In your reply you confesse "it is difficult but not impossible.
For supposing a man savingly sanctified, you lay down three
things. (1) That though Justification be hid from the eye yet Sanctification and faith are still in the heart and oftentimes effectually
working, as in Jonah and others. (2) When Sanctification is working it may be seen, because others may see it and the Lord may so
bless their speeches that the party cannot but acknowledg Gods
work and from thence may behold Gods love. (3) That when God
hideth his face most there is oft in a justified Soul very deep and
unfeigned sorrow, very lively faith of dependance upon the Lord,
and oftimes very close and humble walking before him. Therefore Grace being thus now in a very special manner operative, if
search be made it may through Gods help be plainly discerned,
James 2.22."

Answ. 1. There is a difference between a man that never saw
his Justification by any light of Gods spirit and him that hath
sometimes seen it by the witness of the Spirit in a promise of free
grace, though now it be hidden from him. This latter may sooner
be convinced of his justification by the fruits of his faith in his
Sanctification than the former. For he that never saw his Justification did never see his Sanctification nor can not be persuaded that
his Sanctification is such as God accepteth. But he that hath seen
God accepting his person in justification he hath learned more

clearly to discerne of the nature and truth of Sanctification and may sooner be convinced of the work of God in him self than the other either will or can be.

2. The way of Grace and of the Gospel of Grace for the comforting such as being truly justified are savingly sanctified, and that have now lost the sight of it which sometimes they had. The way, I say, is not so much to stand to shew them the working of their own Sanctification within them, as to discover the face of God in Christ which is now hid from them. To publish the glad tidings of faith and salvation to such a Soul in Jesus Christ will sooner revive him than all the arguments you can fetch from Gods works in himselfe. When the two Disciples had so much lost the sight of their Justification by Christ as that they doubted whether it was he that should save Israel or no, Luke 24.21. Christ recovered their cold and dead hearts, not by recounting what great change he had sometimes wrought in them, nor by telling them what a good fruit of the life of Christ in them it was that they took the death of Christ so sadly (as sad indeed they were ver. 17.) but by expounding to them all the Scriptures concerning the necessity and use of his sufferings, v. 25.26. and that set their hearts into a glowing and burning warmth, v.32. When my Spirit is in a swoon the Aqua vitae bottle hangeth not at my girdle but standeth at the right hand of the grace of Christ.

3. Suppose by chaffing the Soul in a swoon you might revive the same heat and life that was in him, still you will find this to be true: He will never be convinced to see life in his Sanctification, till he see life in his justifying faith, which is that that putteth life and truth into his Sanctification: He will ever fear that without faith his best works of Sanctification are but *splendida peccata*, goodly glistering beautifull sins.

To prevent this, you cast in a threefold objection. "(1.) Though it be true that my person is accepted before my work, yet it is not necessary that what first is should be first seen, for then Election should be first seen. (2ly) I may know my work to be accepted by knowing it to be sound (Isaiah 56.6.7.) Except any will say that the difference between a sound work and unsound lyeth not in the being of the work but in the acceptation of it. (3ly) You see not how this will stand with my answer to the 7th Question, to

wit, that a weak beleever before the witness of the Spirit itself may
see his work of waiting and the promise made thereto, and conclude from thence his safe estate; And therefore you infer that he
must see his waiting to be a work accepted. And yet here, I say, a
man can see no work accepted till he see his person accepted; and
that by the imediate witness of the Spirit itself, without respect to
a work; as you conceive me to mean in my answer to the 5th
question."

Answ. Your two former objections may be answered together.
We do not therefore account it necessary that Justification should
be first seen because it first is, but because that faith whereby we
are justified must first be seen, looking upon Christ (in whom our
person is accepted) and from him deriving that power and vertue
whereby our Sanctification is quickened; or else we cannot see our
Sanctification accepted as hath been shewed above. And therefore though the soundness and unsoundness of a work in itself
doth not depend upon Gods accceptance (which is a thing without)
but upon the being of the work, yet faith in Christ is required not
only to the acceptance of the work, but even to the Soundness and
being of the work, wherein if faith be not lively the work is a dead
work. As for that place in Isaiah 56.6.7, I would ask whether any
man can joyn himself to the Lord without faith; or whether he can
see himself to joyn to the Lord and not see the faith by which he is
joyned. If the Argument depend on the words following, I demand whether any man can serve the Lord or love the name of the
Lord, to be his servant or keep his Sabbath and take hold of his
Covenant, not only without the presence of faith, but also without
the efficacy and life of it? As the Apostle saith neither circumcision
availeth any thing nor uncircumcision but faith that worketh in
love Galatians 5.6. So surely, neither doth the service of God, nor
the love of Gods name, nor of his service, nor any of the rest avail
any thing, unless faith be working in them all. And how can we see
them availing any thing to our comfort, unless we see faith working in them? As we cannot love the name of the Lord unless he
first love us, 1 John 4.19, so neither can we see that we love the
Lord unless we see him first loving us.

To your 3d objection, My answer is (passing by the variation

of my words in your rehearsing of them) that though a weak beleever may see his waiting on the Lord (or rather the Lord helping
him to wait) and may thence conclude that he on whom he waiteth will not absent himselfe for ever; yet I said before and expresly
presupposed it that he had first a promise given him of God before, though not by the Spirit itself working his own proper work
yet revealing the fathers work drawing such a Soul freely (without
respect to work) to wait on Christ, or else revealing the Sons work
giving ease and refreshing and liberty to the Soul. For you know
the Scripture maketh three witnesses of Christ and of our estate in
him, (aswell 3 in Heaven as three on Earth) the Father the Son
and the Holy Ghost; and all these three as they have their distinct
work about our estate in Christ, so do they bear a distinct witness
unto it; and yet all of them by the Spirit (as I shewed above) and
therefore it is said for them all, that it is the Spirit that beareth
witness because the Spirit is truth 1 John 5.6. And therefore as
the Father draweth us to Christ (John 6.44.) So the Spirit of the
father witnesseth to our Souls that the Father doth draw us: And
as the son maketh us free (John 8.36.) so the Spirit of the Son doth
witness some ease and freedome and refreshing to the Soul; and
all before he work and witness his own work in us, and thereby
seal up all with full Assurance and power. And all these works of
the Father and of the Son, of the Spirit the Spirit witnesseth in
promises of free grace without respect to work.

So that if you compare my former Answers which you alledge
(whether to the 7th Question or to the 5th or to this 12th) You will
find a variety of the witnesses of the Spirit but no contradiction or
variation of my speech thereof in the one place or in the other. In
one place I say, A weak beleever may see the Lord drawing or
helping of him to wait, before he have received the witness of the
Spirit itself, to wit, revealing his own work. In this other place
I say, no man can see his work accepted till he see his person accepted. But when you add, you conceive me to mean, by the witness of the Spirit itself; if you mean revealing his own work, so indeed you make up a contradiction, but not out of my words but
your own. For I do hold that a man may see his person accepted
by the witness of the Spirit of Christ applying Christs works of

ease and refreshing and child like liberty to the Soul, before he have received the witness of the Spirit itself revealing his own proper work in us.

To 13th.

To your thirteenth Question (Whether the evidencing of Justification by Sanctification be a building my Justification upon my Sanctification, or a going on in a Covenant of Works) After some explication and distinction of the terms I gave you mine Answer in 6 or 7 propositions.

In the First whereof you consent with me, and in the Second; and partly in the Third: only in the latter part thereof you consent not, which was this. "That to give a man no other ground of his Justification but only the evidence of his Sanctification, may be a building of his Justification upon his Sanctification." My Meaning is, that if a man neither give nor can give any other ground (as having indeed no other ground to give) of his Justification but only the evidence of his Sanctification (which I fear is the case of too too many professors) their faith is not builded nor grounded at all upon the righteousnes of Christ nor upon the free promise of grace wherein that righteousnes is applied to us, but only upon their own works: and so their faith beleeveth not on him that justifieth the ungodly (which is the faith of the Gospel Romans 4.5) but on him which justifieth the Godly; which is such a faith as Adam might have, and so belongeth to the Covenant of Works.

To this you say you may not consent; and why not? "because (say you) to give no other evidence of my Justification but Sanctification, is at the most but to build the Assurance of my Justification upon my Sanctification whereas the being of Justification is much different from the seeing of it etc."

Answ. 1. I pray you consider; You change my words, and therein alter my meaning. For I do not say, to give no other evidence, but to give no other ground of my Justification. And besides, you turn my speech as if I had said, to give no other ground of my seeing or knowing my Justification whereas I said, to give no other ground of my Justification. But take my speech and meaning according to my own words, and your exception against it will appear to be groundless. For, to give no other ground of my

Justification but only the evidence of my Sanctification is not only, at the most, to build the Assurance of my Justification upon my Sanctification but it is also to build and ground my Justification upon my Sanctification for I have no other ground to give for the being of it.

2. Besides, Take my words as you turn them, and yet so your exception will not hold. For if I give no other evidence of Justification but Sanctification I do not only build the sight or assurance of knowledg of my Justification but also the Assurance of faith of my Justification upon my Sanctification. Now I conceive there is a real difference betwixt them two. For, Knowledg is a distinct gift from faith and superadded to it 2 Peter 1.5. when assurance of justifying faith is once obtained, which only springeth from the clear apprehension of the free love of God giving the righteousnes of Christ in a promise of free grace. Assurance of knowledg may be had (as you say right) from other arguments, from our own Sanctification and Works, as from the Effects or Adjuncts etc. But Assurance of faith, Calvin knoweth not how to fasten the grounding of that upon our own righteousnes or works, which is our Sanctification, as we have shewed above. He still maketh the Assurance of faith not to arise from our Works or to be founded thereon, but maketh Works as a *posterior probatio accedere instar signi*.[17] When therefore a man can give no other Argument of the Assurance of his faith whereby he is justified but his Sanctification he buildeth his Justification either upon no foundation at all, or only upon such an one as Works, which can have no place but if any where in a Covenant of Works.

To shew the danger of giving no other ground of Justification but only the evidence of Sanctification I alledged the example of the Publican (Luke 18) who saw no evidence of his Sanctification but rather of his corruption, and yet went home justified; implying thence that if a teacher shall give no ground of Justification but evidence of Sanctification then either the Publican went home unjustified (which is contrary to the text) or his Justification was groundless, which is not to be beleeved. The mercy of

---

17. A later proof added like a sign. The reference is probably to the *Institutes,* III.xv.

* See new note p. xix.

God on him a Sinner (of which the Lord set home unto his Soul the great need, and which therefore he cryed so earnestly for) is a sufficient ground of his Justification.

To this example of his you reply, "you cannot reach whereto it tendeth; for, (1) The Scripture saith not that he saw himself justified at all." Answ. Nor do I say he did: but I said, that to give evidence of Sanctification for the only ground of Justification is against the Scripture, which reckoneth the Publican for a justified person who had no such evidence.

(2.) "Nor doth the Scripture say (say you) that our Saviour gave the Publican rather the sight of his sinfull corruption than the sight of his Sanctification for an evidence of his Justification." Answ. Nor do I say, he did. But I say he gave him to go home justified, when yet he rather saw the evidence of his sinfull corruption than of his Sanctification.

(3.) "Nor do you see How any more can be concluded thence in your apprehension, but that a man without sight of Sanctification may be justified." Answ. Nor do I conclude any more from thence; and therefore I said, if a man can give no other ground of his Justification but only the evidence of his Sanctification he giveth such a ground as the Publican could not give, who yet was justified: And therefore it is not the evidence of Sanctification that may be given as a ground of Justification but something before it.

(4) You say "you know not how this instance can prove that he which giveth a man no other ground to evidence his Justification but from the evidence of his Sanctification doth build his Justification upon his Sanctification and so goeth on in a Covenant of Works." Answ. Nor do I know how this instance can prove that conclusion; Nor did I alledge it to prove that, but this, That therefore he which giveth a man no other ground of his Justification but only the evidence of his Sanctification He doth not build his Justification upon such grounds as Evangelical Justification is grounded upon; witness that of the Publican: but upon such as the Law holdeth forth in a Covenant of Works.

(5) And lastly. "Suppose (say you) he saw himself justified, whilst he saw no Sanctification but only sinful corruption; surely he might have been much more assured if he had seen himself

sanctified." Answ. (1.) Still you work upon this mistake; as if I had argued from the Publicans sight or Assurance of Justification which came not into my heart, nor is it intimated much less expressed in any of my words. But by this I discern, whence it cometh to pass, that I am thought to speak so obscurely; for if men that hear me, do instead of my words take up words of their own, and carry them to infer other conclusions than I aime at; I do not wonder if they cannot well understand, how that which I speak at one time, and that which they take me to speak at another can agree together. Words uttered in the Pulpit are transient, and may more easily be mistaken and forgotten, when I see even words written and extant, and abiding extant and obvious to the sight are so much mistaken and by mistake turned upside down. (2) Yet thus much let me add, that whereas you say, "that if the Publican saw himself justified when he saw no Sanctification surely he might have been much more assured if he had seen himself sanctified." With your favour I conceive, that if we speak of the assurance of Justifying faith, the sight of my Sanctification alone addeth nothing to the Assurance thereof: for that only which cleareth the promise of free grace more and more to my soul (which only the manifestation of Gods free love can do by the witness of his Spirit) that only is it which addeth more and more strength to the assurance of justifying faith. The sight of Sanctification may add more and more strength to the assurance of Knowledge, or of historical faith of my justified estate; but not any strength to the Assurance of justifying faith, unless it be so far forth as the Lord doth reveal in my Sanctification a clearer manifestation of his fatherly love by the witness of his Spirit and then it is not the sight of Sanctification simply considered in itself, but the sight of Gods free love revealed in it by his Spirit that strengtheneth my justifying faith in my quiet and assured resting upon Christ for my justification.

Touching the testimony of our dear and Reverend Brethren, I conceive it giveth clear witness to my Proposition (though you think otherwise) whether you take it as I write it, or as you repeat it; For if a man do not or cannot give any ground of his Justification but only from his Sanctification it is a sign he can give no evidence how he came by his Sanctification and then (its one of their pithie expressions) if a man holds forth rich treasure and cannot give account how he came by it, it is a shrewd sign either the treasure is counterfeit, or else he stole it. So in this case. For seeing there are saving graces which are not sanctifying, and those so necessary as without which going before, no true Sanctification can be had; then they that cannot evidence their Justification from those former saving graces, but hold forth only their Sanctification for a full evidence, they do not only give fewer evidences than the truth affordeth (which is the only fault you find in it) but do also give such an Evidence, and that alone, as is either counterfeit or very suspicious; more like to be legal than Evangelical; especially when it is so fully and securely rested in.

To the 4th Proposition. For a fourth Proposition I said, That if a Soul truly justified and not seeing it, do betake himself to his works, to hasten his Assurance (to wit, his Assurance of finding Christ, in finding joy and peace in his works) in so doing, though he be not under a Covenant of Works (as being justified before) yet he goeth aside to a Covenant of Works, as Abraham went aside to Hagar (who was a type of a Covenant of Works Galatians 4) for the hastening of the sight and fruition of the promised seed, by fellowship with her etc.

To this in your Reply you object two things

"1. If by betaking himself to Works, I do understand, to works as a way whereby a man may after attain to the sight of his Justification; you argue that if this be to go aside to a Covenant of Works then five evill consequences will follow. (1.) That David did ill to confesse his sins, to humble himself for them, (when Gods face was hid from him) that he might again see Gods face, and favour in his Justification Psalms 32.1. to 6. etc. (2) That the Lord did ill to command his people to humble themselves and seek his face and to turn from their evil waies that he might forgive their sins 2 Chronicles 7.14. 1 John 1.9. (3) That the Apostle hath sent us aside to a Covenant of Works when he exhorted to use all dilligence adding one grace to another thereby to make our calling and Election sure, 2 Peter 1.5. to 10. (4) That Christ hath done ill to command us to pray for the Spirit (prayer being an act of Sanctification wherein many graces are acted) and when we have so done, to beleeve the promise of receiving of it. (5.) That to seek

Assurance from a divine witness (which the water of Sanctification is made to be 1 John 5.6.8.) is a going aside to Hagar."

Answ. To all these ill consequences I answer at once, God forbid (even the God of all grace forbid) that by betaking a mans self to his works I should understand, or you should conceive me to understand the use of prayer and other holy duties, whereby we may after come to the sight of our Sanctification. No, no, (beloved brethren) it was not Abrahams use of Hagar as a servant to Sarah to do the household duties of a Servant in the family, that was a betaking himself to Hagar, but his marriage fellowship with her, and expecting the promised seed by vertue of the promise in her loynes. My meaning therefore was not to beat men off from the use of holy duties or from seeking the face of God and sight of Justification by Christ in the use of them, (it being part of that way wherein himself hath appointed us to seek him in Christ) but it was my true intent to prevent a twofold and frequent abuse of the use of holy duties even in honest minds.

1. Such a devoting or betaking of the Soul to them as seeking the right of the promised blessing in them; whereas indeed the right of the blessing is neither promised to them nor dependeth on them. It is a sound and profound truth, and a part of the mysterie of the Covenant of Grace which Calvins testimonies formerly alledged do hold forth; *Nec ab operibus oritur, nec inde pendet vel Dei gratia, vel salutis et fidei certitudo;*[18] For (as I said before) the right of all the promises dependeth not upon the performance of duties, (which are the qualifications mentioned in those kind of promises) but it dependeth wholly upon our union with Christ for to Christ (as I said) are all the promises made Galatians 3.16. 2 Corinthians 1.20. Our right therefore to them dependeth on our union with him; as the right of a wife to all her husbands goods dependeth not upon her good conditions or qualifications or good duties about him; but upon her marriage union with him. And therfore (as hath been said above) when Christ promiseth to mourners that they shall be comforted, and to them that hunger and thirst after him, that they shall be satisfied: he doth not bid

---

18. The grace of God and the certainty of salvation and faith neither arise from works nor depend on them.

them comfort themselves in this, that they do mourn, or to satisfie
themselves with this, that they do thirst, (which were as if we
should bid a thirsty man to satisfie his thirst, not by coming in to
drink, but in this that he is thirsty, which is a sign of life.) but he
calleth them to come to him (unto him I say) and drink: If any
man be athirst (saith he) let him come to me and drink, and that
which shall satisfie him, is not to drink refreshing out of his thirst,
but from the Spirit of life which he shall give him. This he spake
(saith the Text) of the water of life, to wit, of the Spirit which they
that beleeved in him should receive John 7.37.38.39. But alas,
how many be there that satisfie their souls in this, that they are
thirsty, and so think they have right to the promise made to men
in their condition, and there take up their stand and rest.

A 2d abuse of holy duties is when the Soul resteth satisfied,
though not so much with the right of the blessings which he con-
ceiveth to be promised to his duties, yet with the sight and sense of
the comforts and fruits which he receiveth and enjoyeth from his
dayly conversing with his duties. For certain it is that in the frequent and conscionable use of good duties, not only Gods children but also even hypocrites may find many great and sweet enlargments and comforts, as in prayer and preaching etc.   And if
hereupon a man shall bless himself as having found Christ in such
duties (when yet God did not manifest Christ to him therein, but
only comfort in the work done) his case (in that respect) may be no
better than is the estate of many an hypocrite now in Hell.   And
yet how many professors be there that herein sit down fully satisfied and look for no other Christ nor any other Heaven upon
Earth than such comforts and enlargments. As Abraham for a
while looked for no other blessed seed than in the face of Ishmael.
You know it is not the mantle of Elijah, it is not ordinances and
duties (though they be mighty and blessed in their lawfull use)
but the Lord God of them all, whom we ought to seek for in them.
And yet not him, either in the right or in the vertue or sweetness
of them, but in the free grace of God giving Christ himself unto
the Soul in a promise of Grace.

I need not apply this, to avoid the five ill consequences which
you conceive will follow upon the disallowance of betaking a
mans self to holy duties, thereby as by a way to hasten the sight of

Christ in his Justification. For the clearing of two words will clear all. 1. What I mean by betaking. 2. What you mean by way.

For the 1st. By betaking I do not mean the frequent and dilligent use of good duties, by them to seek the face of God, manifesting his free grace to me in Christ but such an use of them whereby I either seek to attaine right of the promised blessings by doing the duty which the promise calleth for, or else do satisfie myself in the comforts and enlargments I find in the duties, though I have not yet found Christ in them revealing himself in a free promise.

For the 2d. What you mean by way. If you mean by the way, part of the way, as if having gone through your duties you then have a further way to goe, after all is done, still to wait for Christ to witness to your Souls his acceptance of you, by his Spirit sealing a promise of free grace to you; I consent with you, this is not a going aside to a Covenant of Works. But if you mean by way, the whole way; as if when a man had done his duties and found his qualifications and comforts and enlargment in both, he had then gone his whole way, and might then sit down as at the end of his way, as having attained what he sought for. If this be your meaning, I dare not excuse this way from being a way of the Covenant of Works: and yet in so doing I shall not need to fear to rush upon the rocks of such ill consequences as you gather from my Speech.

For the 1. David did not seek Gods face and favour in the right of his duties of Humiliation, nor in the meltings he might find in them, but in Gods pardoning his sin out of his free grace and not imputing wickedness to him, as the Apostle expoundeth it Romans 4.6.7.8. and therefore he did not rest in his duties or works therein as at the end of his way: but still looked for free grace without works till he had attained it in the face of Christ.

For the 2d. God did not command his people to humble themselves and pray and seek his face and turne from their evil waies, and there to rest, as in the end of their way. For he that in all these duties commanded them to seek his face, did not command them there to take up their stand, when they had found these duties; but still to seek his face, till they had found his face lifted up on them in Christ, pardoning their sins, not for their sakes, not for their duties sake, but only for his own holy names sake.

For the 3d. Peter did not exhort them to make their calling

and Election sure neither first nor last by getting those gifts of grace, and abounding in them, and so resting. But they having first obtained like precious faith with the Apostles through the righteousness of God and of our Saviour Jesus Christ (2 Peter 1.1.) he exhorteth them to add those other gifts of grace, and to be fruit-full in them, and to abound in that fruitfulness; not thereby, as by Effectual means, nor thereby as by the full end of their way to make their calling and Election sure: but in all these, and after all these, and above all these still to look for the making of their call-ing and Election sure from the only means thereof which he had set before them in the second verse, Grace (saith he) and peace be multiplied unto you: how? by the knowledge of your faith, and vertue, and temperance and patience and Godliness, and broth-erly kindness and love? No, but by the knowledge of God and Jesus Christ our Lord.   Let no man say, If it be so, that all the multiplying of our grace and peace, and so all the Assurance of our calling and Election springeth from the knowledg of God in Christ Jesus, then what needed Peter urge them to give such great dilligence to make up such a train of these spirituall gifts and du-ties, carrying them all along as it were in a dance (as the word sig-nifieth) and all to this end to make their calling and Election sure. I answer; Because they be part of that way that leadeth to that end, even as the Lord comanded the Israelites to march, and (as it were) to trayl their weapons about the walls of Jericho, and at length to blow with their trumpets and shout (Joshua 6.) and yet not there-fore to think, that by any such means the walls of Jericho should fall down, nor that they having walked in all these marches (as in a way) should sit down at length, and rest in the work done: but they were after all and above all to wait by faith on the mighty power and free grace of God unto his people, that he would for his own names sake by the might of his glorious arm, cast down these walls before them; and therefore it is said, by faith (not by the weapons of war, nor by marches of Souldiers, nor by sound of trumpets, nor by shoutings of the people, but by faith) the walls of Jericho fell down, after they had been encompassed seven daies, Hebrews 11.30.   So here, not by the chain of these graces, nor by the march of these duties, but even by faith looking up to Christ the author and finisher of our faith, the walls of Assurance are built up, out of his free grace. The Assurance of our Estates Calvin (on the place)[19] would not have to be gathered from these graces and duties, as from the cause, but as from the signs and effects thereof. Neither doth he refer this Assurance to the Conscience, but either to other men, or to the thing itself. So loath he is to allow the Assurance of faith of our good estates to arise from our Sanctification. Yet I willingly grant it in the sense that I have spoken.

For the 4th. When Christ comanded us to pray for the Spirit and beleeve the promise of receiving it when we have done (as you express it) he did not bid us expect the Spirit by right of our prayers, nor when we have done our prayers to sit down now, as at the end of our way, but (as your selves confesse) even then still to beleeve, that is, by faith to wait for the answer of our prayers out of his free Grace.

For the 5th. Though we do confess it to be a turning aside to a Covenant of Works, to seek the Assurance of faith from the water of Sanctification if we seek it from thence as the ground of our right, or therein as the end of our way: yet we readily accept the witness of our Sanctification as a *posterior probatio*[20] (as Calvin calls it) when the witness of the Spirit in a promise of free grace hath gone before it. Yea, I beseech you let us consider and search without prejudice in the fear of God, Whether our Sanctification in itself may be called a divine testimony, but only as it shall please the Spirit of God to bear witness in it. For as it seemeth to me, it is not every supernatural work that can give a divine testimony (though it do give a true testimony) of a divine truth. Else the Heavens and the Earth might be said to give a divine testimony of Gods eternal power and Godhead, which yet no man is wont to say, though they do give a true and certain testimony thereof. The Apostle John telleth us of 6 witnesses that give testimony to Christ and to our life in him, 3 in Heaven and 3 in Earth; and yet I think upon true search it will be found that none of the 3 in Heaven do bear witness but by the Spirit and none of the 3 in

19. John Calvin, *A Commentarie on the Whole Epistle to the Hebrewes* (London, 1605), 276.
20. A "latter, or secondary proofe": Cotton's translation, p. 183.

Earth do bear divine testimony, but by the Spirit clearing them all unto our Consciences; and therefore when John speaketh of the water and blood (1 John 5.6) he maketh it the Spirit which beareth witness even in them, aswell as by himself. Which if it be true, then how shall we discern the witness of our Sanctification but by the light of the Spirit breathing in it? or how shall we discern the divine power of that testimony but in the divine revelation of the Spirit testifying his acceptance of our Sanctification and the duties thereof, as his own work in Christ out of his free grace? The duties of Sanctification though they are the works of God in us, yet still they are but Works; and works have no power at all to beget faith (for they are the fruits of faith, faith is before them) nor have they any greater power to increase faith, or the assurance of faith, than the Word of God hath, which is the principal organ sanctified of God for that end. Now the word of God it self hath no power in it-self or from it self to encrease faith or the assurance of faith, but as the Spirit of God revealeth and applyeth Gods free grace in it. And therefore neither have the Works of Sanctification power in themselves or from themselves to strengthen faith or the Assurance of faith in us; but as the Spirit of God shall breathe in them and testifie Gods acceptance both of us and of them of his free grace. If therefore we had both works and word of God to testifie of our estates, yet we are not come to the end of our way for the attainment of Assurance, but must still wait for the Spirit of God to make both of them effectual for that end.

To the 2d Objection which you make to my 4th Proposition, "That if by betaking a mans self to Works I do understand Evangelical saving Works wherein together with the promise and Spirit of grace as in a glass I do behold the Lords love, yet still you say it is no going aside to Hagar. For to settle our Assurance on Christ or his faithfulness in a free promise revealed by the Spirit towards us who have such a work, is no going aside to Hagar, but rather a resting upon Christ. We confess (say you) if a justified Soul in such an estate do feel the Lord sanctifying his heart and find peace, so he ought to do; as being a sensible expression of the Lords great love in removing sin, so great an evil by the Spirit of his Son. We confess also that some Christians when they feel it not, fall to doubting; which yet is their weakness ignorance and sin, as being an act of unbelief. And therefore such are to be better in-

structed in the Covenant of Gods free grace, not to be condemned
of going aside to a Covenant of Works."

Answ. First I must settle my Assurance of faith on Christ, and
take it home to me as God giveth it and declareth it to me. Now he
doth not declare his righteousness to me but as he doth give it sitting upon a throne of righteousnes and grace, to glorifie both
those attributes together; That he doth then hold forth and declare his justice the Apostle teacheth us (Romans 3.26.) to declare
(saith he) his righteousnes that he might be just and a justifier of
him that is of the faith of Jesus. If God then declare his righteousnes that himself is just when he justifieth us, then where shall our
imperfect righteousnes appear? God shall not declare himself to
be just if he declare himself to justifie us upon sight of any good
works in us (they being imperfect) or any promise made thereunto. And therefore in the Court of Justification when God pronounceth or declareth us to be just, he declareth not any righteousnes of our own, but of Christ only, which (being perfect)
declareth the Lord to be perfectly righteous and just in accepting
of Christs righteousnes, and his only, to our justification. Again,
in pronouncing and declaring the righteousness of Christ to be
ours (which is our Justification) the Lord sitteth upon the throne
of his grace (Romans 3.23.24). If God will then declare his righteousnes to be ours out of his Grace, then he will not declare it to
us in the holiness of our works, nor in the promises made thereto.
Grace and Works in this case are not subordinate, but opposite.
When you speak of a free promise revealed by the Spirit unto us
who have such a work, you do imply a contradiction, if you look
no further. For the promise which is made to works or workers is
not revealed nor performed of Grace but of debt, (Romans 4.4)
It is the glory of Grace to dash all works out of countenance when
the Lord sitteth upon a throne of Grace to pronounce and declare
a Sinner to be righteous in Christ Jesus. When the Lord declareth
himself pacified to the Soul (as he doth in Assurance of Justification) he doth not bring our Sanctification but our Sins to remembrance, that we might be ashamed and confounded and never
open our mouthes any more, Ezekiel 16.63. Nor will it stand with
the glory of grace to bring us to rest or assurance of peace in
Christ, in the mediation of our Works.

When you confess that a justified Soul feeling the Lord to

sanctifie his heart, may find peace therein and ought so to do: I would say thus much; There is a two fold peace 1. A peace of Justification, opposite to the war and disturbance which our conscience hath from the guilt of sin. 2ly. A peace of Sanctification opposite to the war and disturbance which the Conscience hath from the rebellion of sin. If we feel the Lord sanctifying our hearts, we may find peace of Sanctification from thence; but the peace of Justification springeth only from the righteousnes of Christ imputed to us of free grace, whence being justified by faith we have peace with God, Romans 5.1. The Soule doth not find it self justified nor at peace with God from the guilt of former sins by any present removal of the evil of Sin.

You confess also that "when some Christians feel not the Lord sanctifying their hearts they fall to doubting, which you conceive to be their ignorance and weakness and sin, and an act of unbelief; who should therefore be better instructed in the Covenant of Grace, but not condemned of going aside to a Covenant of Works."

Answ. If such doubting be their sin, and a sin of unbelief, is it not because their faith is not setled upon the free grace of God in Christ, but upon their own works? And what sin is that I pray you but a turning from the grace of the Gospell, to settle their justification upon the works of the Law? And what is that else but a turning aside to a Covenant of Works? I consent unto you that such Christians are to be better instructed in the Covenant of Grace, and I would grant you further that all that so do, are not forthwith to bee condemned of lying under a Covenant of Works, because some truly justified Christians through ignorance and misinstruction may fail herein. But why they should not be blamed of going aside to a Covenant of Works, I see no reason, unless it be a fault to call a sin by its proper name.   When I said, such Christians ground not their faith of Assurance on Christ, nor on the free promise of Gods grace, nor on the witness of the Spirit herein, You reply

"1 That they clearing up their Sanctification as the way, they come to see the face of Christ as the end and bottom on which their peace is setled and grounded. 2ly. Although Christ ought to be the cheif matter of our consolation, yet a Christian ought to seek to see his interest in Christ not only in beholding the face

and hearing the voice, but also in feeling the gracious work of
Christ (1 John 2.3. and 3.14.19.) and therefore thus to do is no
more a building of hay and stubble upon a golden foundation
than to seek to see and be assured of our interest in him in an absolute promise, or in beholding his face. And if Christians in this
case are put to sad doubts of their own estates, it is not because
they sought to see Christ in clearing up their Sanctification, but
because they are not abundantly exercised in that way (2 Peter
1.9.11) or if they be, it hath been their ignorance and weakness to
be so doubtful; which sin of theirs ought not to make us more
negligent in seeking to behold Christ in this glass, and to find him
in his own way."

Answ. 1. To the first reply. The clearing up of Sanctification
I dare not say as you say that it is the way wherein to come to see
Christ as the end and bottom on whom the peace of our justification is setled and grounded. Calvin certainly knew no such way,
when in expounding those Scriptures, he writeth as you have
heard above, and especially in that 1 John 3.19. *Semper autem
meminerimus non habere nos ex charitate notitiam quam dicit
Apostolus, quasi inde petenda sit salutis certitudo. Et certe non
aliunde cognoscimus nos esse Dei filios nisi quia gratuitam suam
adoptionem cordibus nostris per spiritum suum obsignat.*[21] The
way to find the God of Israel declaring himself a merciful God
unto our Souls in the pardon of our Sins, is rather to come with
halters about our necks (as the Embassadors of Syria came to the
King of Israel) than with golden chains of righteousnes and holiness. To clear up our Sanctification as the way wherein to find
Christ justifying of us, is to make Sanctification the door whereby
to open the way to the sight of Christ; and so Christ is not the door
to open both the light of Gods countenance and all the gracious
work of Sanctification to us. We cannot find Christ the end and
bottom of our peace, unless we find him first, aswell as last; the
first ground of our peace as well as the chief top and end of it. To
clear Sanctification before we clear Christ the author and finisher
of it, and faith in him by which all such Sanctification is wrought
as doth accompany Salvation (Acts 15.9) will clear up a righteous-

---

21. Cotton had previously quoted this passage in English; see p. 106.

ness without the life of Righteousnes, and will also clear up our own righteousness before the righteousnes of Christ.

Answ. 2d. To your 2d Reply thus far I consent with you that a Christian ought to seek to see Christ not only in beholding his face and hearing his voice, but also in feeling his gracious work: But that he ought to seek to see his interest in Christ justifying him from Sin in feeling his gracious work (and by this work you mean Sanctification) that I dare not consent to. For so, a Christian should seek to see his interest in Christ justifying him from sin where neither his interest doth lye, nor the sight by faith of his Interest. Yea so he should seek to see his faith in his feeling, to which the life of faith is opposed 2 Corinthians 5.7. The places you quote out of John do neither speak of our first knowledg of Christ and fellowship with him, nor of our knowledg by faith of our Interest in him; as we have seen out of Calvin above. And therefore thus to build our Assurance of faith on Christ, upon the feeling of our Sanctification, is at the best a building of hay and stubble upon a golden foundation; yea it may be feared lest it be not a building of a golden foundation upon hay and stubble. If Calvins building be solid and firm (and he was counted a Master builder in his time) *Hoc fixum lectoribus manet* (saith he) *primus ad pietatem gradus sit, agnoscere Deum esse nobis patrem etc. Instit.* l.2.c.6.§4.[22] If this ought to be firmly fixed in the hearts of Christians, that the first step to Godliness is to acknowledg God in Christ to be our Father, then surely to make the feeling of Sanctification the way to the acknowledgment or assurance that God is our Father in Christ, is to make a former step to the first step, and a way out of the way, and a stubble building. If Christians be often put (as you grant) to sad doubts of their own estates in this way of building, I verily fear it is because they lay not Christ in his proper place, which is the foundation both in our Justification of Grace, and in our true peace. But in stead of Him they lay the feeling of their Sanctification as the corner stone of their peace, and the first light of their comfort.

The place you quote in Peter doth not argue it to be a way of

---

22. "Only let the readers agree on this point: let the first step toward godliness be to recognize that God is our Father to watch over us, govern and nourish us, until he gather us into the eternal inheritance of his Kingdom."

God, for men to seek to see Christ in their Justification by clearing up their Sanctification and by abundant exercise in that way. The 9th verse which you send me to, maketh plainly against it: For if they that have not this clearing of Sanctification by encrease of Grace do forget that they were purged from their old sins, then it is plain that before they walked in this way of growth in grace they knew that they were purged from their sins; for no man can be said to forget that which he never knew before. And for the 11th verse which you also quote, it only holdeth forth that which no man denieth, to wit, that the way of faith and of the fruits thereof is the Royal way (Gods high way) to his Heavenly kingdom: and so Piscator[23] maketh it a fifth Argument used by the Apostle to persuade to grow in faith, and the fruits of it, taken from the benefit of such a way; that way (saith he) which leadeth us without stumbling into Gods heavenly kingdom, that way ought we to walk in: but the way of the above named vertues, faith and the fruits thereof leadeth us without stumbling, into Gods heavenly kingdom: Therefore that way ought we to walk in. Which we all willingly grant. But how it toucheth this cause, to wit, that in the way of feeling our Sanctification wrought, to seek the Assurance of faith of our justification this I discern not.

You conclude your Reply to this point with an Advertisement touching the Allegory of Abraham and Hagar; which you say "will only prove, that for a man to go aside to a Covenant of Works (whereof I make Hagar to be a type) to seek to see the promised seed there, is to go aside to a Covenant of Works; But to seek to see the Lords face by seeking to feel the Lords own work in us is no going aside to Hagar. For all doing and use-making of Works implyeth not straightway a Covenant of Works. Whereupon you express your disrelish; That in these points of evidencing Justification by Sanctification there should be such frequent using and urging of Works, and of our own works: which though a fair construction might be made of it, yet to some it might seem to savour more strongly of Popish leaven than Protestant doctrine doth imply."

Answ. Not I but the Apostle saith, Hagar was a type of the Law

---

23. Johannes Piscator, *Analysis Logica Septem Epistolarum Apostolicarum* (Herborn, 1593), 175–179.

or Covenant of Works Galatians 4.24.25. But when you say that to go aside to a Covenant of Works to seek to see the promised seed is a going aside to a Covenant of Works, it seemeth to me an empty tautologie. To go aside to a Covenant of Works (for what end so-ever) is doubtless a going aside to a Covenant of Works, if *idem* be *idem*. But this I say, That to seek our first Assurance of our Justification by Christ, or to seek the Assurance of Faith of our Justification in Christ by our works of Sanctification is to make such an use of Works as for which the Lord hath not sanctified them in the Covenant of Grace, but is peculiar to the Covenant of Works. For if the Covenant of Grace do hold forth Justification and the Assurance of Justification not out of Works but out of Grace, and out of Grace not to works, but without works, to him that worketh not, then to make use of Works and of Grace to works to gather the Assurance of my Justification is not the way of the Covenant of Grace but of the Covenant of Works rather. But the former proposition is true in all the parts of it. Of the first part there is no question amongst us, nor any Protestants; That the Covenant of Grace doth hold forth Justification neither out of Works, nor out of Grace to works. And of the latter part there need be little question; for if the Assurance of Justification be of Works or of Grace to works, then the promise is not sure of grace to faith, contrary to the Apostle Romans 4.16. As Christ was seen of Abraham to the rejoycing of his heart so he is seen of all the children of Abraham; For the Apostle sets him, and his Justification and his faith and the grounds of it, as a pattern to us all, Romans 4.23.24. Now certain it is that Christ was seen of Abraham in a free promise of Grace without works; For this is a word of free promise, so shall thy seed be, upon which Abraham beleeved Genesis 15.6. And this was a like free promise I will give thee a son of Sarah (Genesis 17.6.) Upon which Abraham beleeved and rejoyced v.17. as seeing Christ in the promise to the evident assurance and comfort of his faith. And if this be the way of the Covenant of Grace, to give Assurance of faith, and comfort of our Justification out of grace without mention of works; then, to seek the Assurance of faith and comfort of our justification out of Works, is not the way of the Covenant of Grace. But in the Covenant of Works, I find a clear promise (yea many promises to this purpose) that such as keep the commandments of the Lord their God and walk in his wayes, the Lord will establish them (that is, confirm and assure them) to be an holy people unto himself, Deuteronomy 28.9. If you therefore disrellish so much of the name of works, and of our owne works in this point of evidencing and assuring to our faith our Justification from our Sanctification then you must be entreated (as I do entreat you heartily in the Lord) to disrellish the thing itself; to wit, all mention of Sanctification and all works of Sanctification and of promises made to such works as the grounds and means and waies of obtaining our first Assurance of Justification. And seeing we all professe (according to the intentions of our hearts) to hold forth Protestant doctrin, let us hold it forth in the language of Calvin and others our best Protestants, who speak of purity of life and growth in grace and all the works of Sanctification as the effects and consequents of our Assurance of Faith; as Bellarmine chargeth it upon Protestants, and Pareus acknowledgeth it to be true of our first Assurance. And therefore if we will speak as Protestants, we must not speak of good works as causes or waies of our first Assurance. For Effects and consequents are not so much as waies much less are they causes unto those things whereof they are effects and consequents. For waies, though they be not causes yet they are Antecedents to the things unto which they are waies. And though you deny good works to be the grounds and causes of our Assurance of Faith, yet indeed you carry it otherwise: For you maintain that a man may gather his first Assurance of his justified estate from his works of Sanctification. From whence it will unavoidably follow that our works are the grounds and causes of our first Assurance; For you know well that *Causa efficiens est a qua res est.*[24] Such things (*a quibus*) from which our first Assurance doth arise, and before which it was not, they are the causes of our Assurance. But you make good works such things (*a quibus*) from which our first Assurance ariseth, and before which it is not (at least in many good Christians) and therefore you make them causes of our Assurance. Which, seeing it is disallowed by the chief Protestant writers, if you contrary to them do hold it forth for Protestant doctrin, that we may gather our first

---

24. The efficient cause is that by which the thing is produced.

Assurance of Justification from our Sanctification it is not the change of Words that will change the matter. Call you our good works what you please, whether Sanctification or gifts of Grace or saving graces (or any such like) yet seeing our good works are indeed the same thing, the point is rather worse than better, to clothe unwholsome and Popish doctrin with Protestant and wholsome words.

To Proposition the 5th.

The summe of my fifth Proposition you make to be, That a justified Soul seeing and beholding by renewed knowledg, certain evidences of Justification (as Prayer brokenness of heart etc.) dare not, nay cannot take them as certain evidences of his Justification. Whereto you reply

"1. If he dare not take them as evidences of the Lords love, according to the promise of Love, it is his Sin and unbelief, for which he deserveth to be rebuked, as making God a lyar, 1 John 5.11.12. A poor beleeving soul dare say sometimes that which the word saith, But the Word saith That the poor and hungry etc. are blessed: Ergo."

Answ. 1. In that you say The poor beleeving soul dare say sometimes what the word saith, you grant (in a manner) as much as I in the Proposition hold forth: For if he dare say so sometimes, it argueth it is not alwaies that he dare say so. And I did not say, that he never durst say so, but that it is often so with him, that he dareth not. If you think I said, he cannot say so, it is your speech, not mine.

2. It is one thing to say, He is blessed as the word saith; another thing to take his brokenness of Spirit and prayer etc. and them as beheld by renewed knowledg as certain evidences of his Justification. For when I speak of certain evidences I speak as men are commonly wont to intend, as certain Assurances to Faith of a mans Justification. Now God is not wont to beget or build up certain Assurance or Plerophorye[25] of faith of a mans justification by the sight of his works, and the sight of them only, by renewed knowledg. For our best works are but creatures, and our renewed knowledg by which we see them is but a creature, and it is not two

_____

25. A seventeenth-century English word meaning "fullness of assurance."

creatures (no though the letter of the Word were joyned with them) that are able to beget a divine faith; which requireth the almighty power of God to beget and encrease it. A divine faith resteth only upon a divine testimony, and it witnessing the free love of God unto the Soul in Christ Jesus; And the free love of God in Christ Jesus justifying a Sinner God is not wont to witness upon the sight of our gracious dispositions, but upon the sight of our great ungodliness, that so the glory of Grace, and the vertue and value of Christs righteousnes may be the more magnified. Nevertheless, this I willingly grant you, that it is a sin in a Soul truly justified and assured through faith of his Justification by the witness of the Spirit in the promise of grace, if seeing and beholding such gracious dispositions wrought in it, though he see them only by renewed knowledg, yet it is his sin if he do not take them for good and sound secondary arguments to confirm his knowledg of his regenerate estate. Yea and I will not deny that it is the sin of unbelief that the Spirit of God doth not reveal to it the sight of Gods love that hath regenerated it in beholding such gracious fruits of Regeneration. For surely as Faith is the evidence of things hidden; so unbelief is the hiding of things evident. Nevertheless, though it was the sinfull blindness of Hagar, not to see the well that was before her, when she had so great need of it, yet may be the well was not so evident and obvious to her bodily sight, unless God had opened her eyes to see it (Genesis 21.19). So though it be the sinful blindness of Gods people many times not to see the fountain of Gods love regenerating them in such gracious dispositions (as like streams flow from it) yet still it may remain true that the love of God is not so obvious and evident to the sight of renewed knowledg unless the Lord by his Spirit open the eye of Faith to behold it.

The place which you quote out of John maketh indeed the sin of unbelief a great wickedness as making God a lyar. But it is not because a Christian doth not believe upon the testimony of his renewed knowledg but because many a beleever hath all the six witnesses in himself, and there is no beleever but hath the Spirit of God within him, and he hath at lest witnessed the work of the Father and of the Son to him, which it is sin not to believe.

Secondly, You say, "If he cannot take these as evidences he is to lament his unbelief, and to seek to the Lord to persuade his heart, as the man in the Gospel did, Mark 9.24."

Answ. We deny not he is to lament his unbelief if he cannot take these as evidences when the Spirit applieth them in the word. Neither do wee deny that it is his sin, if when the Word doth apply them to him, the Spirit doth not also concurr to apply them with the word. For it is our sins that withhold good things from us, Jeremiah 5.25. Neither do we deny that such a Soul ought to seek the Lord to persuade his heart to beleive: but it is because he is to crave light and strength from the declaration of the free love of God to him in Christ, in a promise of free grace, that so he may take those evidences upon evident grounds according to God in Gods own way.

Thirdly, You object, "The Lord never maketh promises whereby to comfort a man in a poor drooping condition, but they can and shall comfort him in that condition: otherwise the Lord should provide means for an end out of his infinite love to his people, and yet they should never attain to that end."

Answ. We willingly grant you that the means which the Lord provideth for any end, do ever attain to that end according to his purpose and will. And we grant further, that God hath provided such promises to be in part as means (or waies) of comfort to a man in a poor drooping condition. But how? There be two things in such promises which tend to comfort (1.) That for the present the promise pronounceth their blessed estate. (2) For the future, that he promiseth comfort and satisfaction shall be ministred unto them.

For the 1st. The pronouncing of their estate for the present blessed, is fit to comfort if the promises be received by faith, otherwise the word profitteth not, Hebrews 4.2. And if by faith it be received it is then applied and set home to the Soul, not by the light of renewed knowledg but by the witness of the Spirit who hath also revealed Christ to the same poor soul before and given Christ to him in a promise; or else he would never have found himself poor for want of him, or have come to hunger and thirst after him, nor seen his right to the promises by such qualifications without him.

For the 2d. When Christ promiseth comfort and satisfaction to such souls for the future, his meaning is not to direct them to seek their comfort and satisfaction in themselves, or in their own mourning or thirsty condition, but in coming to him, and in drinking the water that he will give them. For so he expoundeth himself John 7.37.38.39. If any man (saith he) be athirst let him come to me and drink, he that beleeveth on me out of his belly shall flow rivers of water; this he spake of the Spirit etc. And therefore it was I said, Such hungry and thirsty Souls will still seek and wait for further and clearer fellowship with Christ, till the Spirit of God reveal Gods thoughts of love to him in a free promise of grace. Whereto you reply

"We say the same, if by a free promise, you understand a conditional aswell as an absolute promise; which kind of promises if they be not free should rather abolish than make parts of the Covenant of Grace."

Answ. This is still to keep such souls in suspense and dependance upon a work, or else to comfort them in a work, where the Lord hath not laid up the comfort of peace of their justification for them. If the Soul be hungry and thirsty and rest not in his hunger and thirst but go to Christ for satisfaction, and then take Christ not in a free promise of grace but in another conditional promise, then the Soul must either rest in the promise made to that condition (but that he saw he could not do so before, nor was it the will of Christ he should) or else he must go again to Christ that for his sake (not for his own good conditions sake) God would speak comfort to him. If you say, God may give a man comfort in one condition for his Christs sake when he hath not done in another. It is true, if you speak of the comfort of Sanctification, but if you speak of the comfort of Justification he declareth not his grace in justifying a godly man, in any work of his righteousness; but in justifying a Sinner without any condition or work of his righteousnes. Neither doth this abolish such conditional promises from being parts of the Covenant of Grace, as if they were not free. For free they be, not because blessings are freely promised to such conditions (for so it is in a Covenant of Works) but because both the conditions are perfectly fulfilled in Christ, and the blessings and promises are laid up in him; and therefore we go to him for all, for his names sake.

When I said that such a poor Soul will still wait for further and clearer fellowship with Christ, to wit, because he cannot gather comfort from his poverty or hungerings: you reply further

"So he ought, not only till he once receive the witness of the Spirit but for clearer and clearer light till he see the face of God in Heaven."

Answ. It is true: But it is one thing to seek assurance to Justifying faith, another thing to seek the end of my faith the Salvation and glorification of my Soul with him in his presence. The words which you quote out of our learned Country-man, do not cross the words which were quoted by me out of him, Especially within so few lines as in the next page. It is true, when the Sun is set, starr light may yet appear; and so may the graces of Gods Spirit appear in us, when the sunshine light of Gods countenance may be hid from us: but yet, as he that should only see starrs in the skie and had never seen or known the Sun rising could neither conclude there was a Sun in the other Hemisphere, nor that it will arise in this: But if he do conclude there is a Sun in the other Hemisphere, it is because he hath seen it arising in our Hemisphere heretofore; And though it hath for a night season departed, yet it hath been wont to rise again every morning. So it is here; If a poor Soul seeing his graces do believe that God will again arise unto him, though now he hide his face from him, surely it is because he hath formerly seen Gods favour rising upon him in the face of Christ in a free promise of Grace, which though the sense of it may be withdrawn for a season yet the same favour and love of God ever liveth, and will return to him again when Gods appointed time is come.

To Proposition the 6th.

You conceive me that What I here hold forth amounteth in summe to this conclusion; "that in a Covenant of Grace no man seeth any thing to evidence his good estate, or seeth what he doth see but by the imediate witness of the Spirit itself."

Answ. When I read such a vast conclusion, I revised my script again to see what words might fall from me that might give ground for such a conclusion. My words I find to be these; "That when the Spirit of God doth shed abroad his light into the Soul and giveth him a clear sight of his estate in a free promise of grace in Christ, such an one clearly discerneth both his Justification and Sanctification the one of them giving good evidence to the other, the blood to the water and the water to the blood and the Spirit to them both, 1 John 5.6.8. And thus in evidencing his Justification by his Sanctification he doth not build his justification upon his Sanctification nor hereby go in a Covenant of Works nor go aside to it."

How these words give any ground for such a conclusion I do not understand. You might as well conclude that he that saith, He seeth any thing evidently and clearly by day light, he seeth nothing by starr light or candle light. Or because Christ telleth his disciples that hitherto he hath spoken to them in parables, but the time would come (to wit when the Holy Ghost should come upon them in power) when he would shew them plainly of his Father (John 16.25) that therefore he had told them of nothing plainly before. But plain it is, that the Apostles made account he had spoken in good measure plainly to them before, so as they were grown up both to faith and the Assurance of faith (John 6.69). And Christ himself telleth them that to them it was given to know the mysteries of the Kingdom of God, but to others it was not given, (Matthew 13.11.) My plain meaning is as I have above expressed, that it is neither the word of God nor any work of grace wrought by the soul that can give clear evidence unto faith, either of our Justification or Sanctification unless the Spirit of God do give him a clear sight of his Justification in a free promise of grace in Christ, and a clear sight of his Sanctification in any promise whether absolute or conditionall; so that the Condition be lookt at as fulfilled in Christ and the promise fulfilled for his sake.   Sound proofs which you call for, to convince That all our clear sight of our estates is from the Spirit of God, may be these,

1. From the Office of the Spirit which is to teach us all things and to clear up all things pertaining to Spiritual sight. For as there go three things to the clearing of the bodily sight (1) The clearing of the eye (to wit of the organe and visive faculty in it.) (2) The clearing of the object to be seen. (3) The clearing of the medium (the Air) through which the object seen is brought to the eye. So there are three things in like sort required to the clearing of spiritual sight. (1) The opening of the eyes of the understanding

(Ephesians 1.18)   (2) The opening of the mysteries of Gods kingdome, Ephesians 3.5.   (3) The opening of the Scriptures, and
works of God in us. (Luke 24.27.45. Genesis 22.12)   Now there is
no means given by God under Heaven for the opening and declaring of all these evidently unto the Soul but only the Spirit of
God. It is He that openeth the eyes of our Understanding Ephesians 1.17.18. It is he that openeth all the mysteries of grace and of
Christs kingdom to us, 1 Corinthians 2.10. It is he that openeth
the Scriptures John 14.26. and 16.13. and declareth to us all the
works of God in us, and about us. 1 Corinthians 2.12. 1 John 3.24.
Yea Calvin is so clear in this point, That he professeth the Scriptures themselves cannot find faith to acknowledg them to be the
word of God till they be sealed and confirmed to the hearts of men
by the inward testimony of the Spirit *Instit.* l.1. Cap. 7. §. 4.

A second proof may be from the nature of our spiritual estate.
It is a Spiritual thing doubtless, and consequently to be discerned
Spiritually, only by Spiritual light and by Spiritual understanding
and by comparing Spirituall things with Spirituall things. And
therefore it is the Spirit of God that must of necessity help our infirmities here, or else we shall not see these things clearly, as we
ought to see and as we had need to see them for our setled comfort.

If it be said, There is no regenerate Christian but hath his
Mind and Conscience enlightened with Spiritual knowledg, and
thereby may clearly enough see his Spiritual estate.

I Answer: Though every regenerate man have his Mind and
Conscience enlightned in some measure, yet there is more required to clear spirituall sight than a mind and conscience enlightned, even the clearing of the object (our spiritual estate) and
the clearing of the Scripture that concerneth it; and the clearing
of the works of God in us. And it is not any discourse of a mind or
Conscience enlightned that can clearly evidence these unto the
Soul, unless the Spirit of God set in and clear them to us. The
Disciples of Christ had their mind and Conscience enlightned
when they were first regenerate, but yet having eyes, they did not
see sundry things pertaining unto God and to themselves, Mark
8.17.18. And when they saw any thing by the reasoning of their
own Spirits, what could they find more than the Souls of Christians do find by hearing Godly Ministers reasoning and discours-

ing in their Sermons out of the Scriptures? And yet you know, and all Christians know that unless the Spirit of God set in and clear up the truth and power and grace of God in all those reasonings, their souls will not be able to gather clear evidences of their estates from all they hear.

A Third proof may be from the nature of Faith. This faith cannot rest upon any object but upon the Lord and his free grace and mercy to us in Christ Jesus; and this revealed to us in some Divine testimony. Now the Word of God, though it be a Divine testimony in regard of the truths taught in it, and in regard that God delivered them; yet the application of them (as was said before) is not of Divine force, as a divine testimony unless the Spirit breathe in them and apply them to me. And the works of Sanctification in me, though they be the works of God (the fruits of the Spirit) in me, yet created things they be, and divine faith they cannot work to assure me of the Lords acceptance of such Sanctification; unless the Spirit of God before witness to them that they are wrought in him and accepted by him of his free grace in Christ. For faith is the operation of God and not of any created power Colossians 2.12. and it is the Spirit that begetteth and encreaseth it not any creature. Nevertheless when I thus speak of the necessary concourse of the Spirit of God to clear up our spiritual estate, by imediate light from himself, by the clearing the grace of God and the word of his grace to my Justification and after both, the work of his grace to my Sanctification. Yet I do not mean only such a concourse of the Spirit wherein the Spirit himself beareth witness in his own proper work (though then indeed his witness is most clear, most certain and most powerfull) but I mean such a concourse of the Spirit as he doth more ordinarily put forth in every of those testimonies whether in Heaven or earth, whereof John speaketh 1 John 5.7.8. For as I said before, whether it be the Father or the Son that beareth witness to our spiritual and Eternal estate in Christ, they do it by the Spirit revealing their work to us: or whether it be the water and the blood that bear witness, it is the Spirit that beareth witness in them 1 John 5.6. or else the testimony would not be the witness of God in us.

If this one Conclusion thus opened and proved do clear up all other Questions and disputes among us (as you say they are all taken up in this, and indeed this cleared will reach far in clearing most of them) then let this Conclusion be in a special manner searched into, that (by the help of Christ) it may be cleared on all hands, and make more speedy way for the clearing of the rest.

One thing you object against this Conclusion, that it bringeth in a preposterous reasoning about Mens Estates. That whereas heretofore it hath been wont to be argued thus, He that beleeveth shall be saved, He that is justified shall be saved, He that is sanctified, shall be saved: Now it is thus, He that shall be saved is justified is sanctified, hath faith. viz. He first seeth his good estate in Gods thoughts of peace, or in Election testified to him, and therein readeth himself a beleever, justified, sanctified etc.

Answ: These two kind of arguings may both stand together (rightly understood) as much as ever they did before. It is true, a man must first see Gods thoughts of peace towards him (I do not say in his Election, but in his Effectual calling) saying to him, Thou art of my people, before I can beleeve or say, The Lord is my God Zechariah 13.9. Though I have the gift of Faith, given me in Christ, in my Effectual Calling in order of nature before I be justified; yet till the Lord say to my Soul, my sins are pardoned, I cannot beleeve, or see myself to be justified: nor can I see my self to be sanctified with that Sanctification which accompanieth Salvation till I see Christ made unto me of God my Wisedome Righteousnes Sanctification and Redemption.

If this kind of arguing seems uncouth and strange to us in these daies, surely it is because these latter daies are perillous times. In Elder times both the Scripture language and the language of our Soundest Divines were wont to express it; The Lord must prevent us in every work of Grace or else we shall not follow him. If we cannot love him but he must first love us, neither can we see our selves loving him, till we see him first loving us. And yet seeing the Lord preventing us with his grace first, as we have first argued from his grace to us, to conclude our good estates towards him; So afterwards from the Effects we may argue to the Cause, and from our faith and Sanctification argue to the Lords Justification of us, and to his Salvation reserved for us in the Heavens.

---

* See new note p. xix.

To 14th.

I said a Christian is more active after Regeneration than before: Before Regeneration we are not active at all; no, nor in *proxima potentia* passive, to receive help from God to do it. But after Regeneration *Acti agimus.* If we act or go forth in the strength of our own Spiritual gifts without looking up to Christ we fall as Peter did Matthew 26.33.35.

You reply: "The best men without Christ can do nothing, yet through Christ can do all things Philippians 4.13. And therefore after Conversion *Acti agimus.*" Well, thus far then we agree; Yet so, (say you) as that Christ hath given to his people more than *proximam potentiam* to receive help from him. If you mean, we have not only power to receive help from him; but we have power also by his help to use this help in bringing forth spiritual fruits, I consent with you: for so much I expressed when I said *Acti agimus.*[26] But if you mean that we have not only power to receive help from him, but by the power of the gift of grace received we are active without his renewed help, to fetch help from him; I confess I want power to put forth an act of Faith to beleeve it. For without Christ the Apostles could do nothing, John 15.5. no not then when they were in Christ then they could not put forth an act of any of those gifts of grace received, no not this act to fetch renewed help from Christ unless him self prevent them. And Paul to the Philippians telleth them, that it is God that worketh in us, not only the habits but the acts; he worketh not only the will and the deed, but τὸ θέλειν and τὸ ενεργεῖν to will and to do of his good pleasure Philippians 2.13. If we do not keep a spiritual gift, much less do we act it without the Holy Ghost (who stirreth us up to take all from Christ) 2 Timothy 1.14. And this is the dif-

---

26. Cotton and the ministers were using these scholastic terms to explain man's role in salvation. The power (*potentia*) here referred to is a power within the person to act once set in motion by an outside force: hence the phrase, acted upon, we act (*acti agimus*). In this context *potentia* was a "passive" power, and Cotton undoubtedly had the scholastic meaning in mind when he spoke of passive faith. It could also be defined as a material cause in the sense of "that from which something is produced." Cotton was afraid the other ministers were placing too great an emphasis upon the causative power or agency of the self.

ference between the life of Adam in innocency, and the life of faith; that Adam having received spiritual gifts and thereby a life in himself, was able to act them livelily, and where he needed any help, he was able to have fetched it from the tree of life. But the life of Faith giving us a root of life, not from the Spiritual gifts received but in Christ, Itself and all other gifts in us become active and lively not of themselves, but as Christ is active in them and putteth forth himself in them day by day. Hence it is that the Apostle describeth the life of faith, as that we so live by Faith that not we but Christ being said to live in us, it is not we that are first active in any duty of spiritual life, but he first stirreth up our faith that our faith might fetch in from him continual supply of spiritual life to all our holy actions.

But say you, "We have more than the nearest power to receive help from Christ, for the graces of Christ in his members are like Christ in part (John 1.16) spiritual and heavenly, and therefore active in their proper nature, sometimes more sometimes less; yet because sin in us is too strong for grace nakedly considered in itself, and the feebleness of grace received is such that it is subject to many alterations and changes; and the dispensation of God now having appointed us a life of faith (which standeth in receiving new supply by peecemeal, and not in being possessed of the whole portion at once, we therefore need a dayly assistance of the Spirit to help, and of faith to go out to Christ for dayly power and life."

Answ. Though the graces of Christ in his members be in part like to the graces of Christ in himself, that is (as you rightly say) spiritual and heavenly; yet are they not therefore in us as they are in him, active of themselves without further help. They are not active or putting forth themselves according to their proper nature, to act spiritually more or less without a renewed act of help from Christ to set them awork. It was to the Disciples after their Conversion to whom Christ spake, without me yee can do nothing. Which place Augustine well weighing, he doth not say (saith he) without me you can do no great thing, but without me you can do nothing; nor doth he say, without me you can hardly do any thing, but without me you can do nothing; nor doth he say, without me you can perfect nothing, but without me you can do nothing, not a good thought much less a good desire. To teach us (saith he) that we can do no good thing without him; It is written, his mercy shall prevent me (Psalms 59.10) to teach us that we cannot finish any good thing without him. It is written again, His mercy shall follow me (Psalms 23.6.) Thus Augustine *contra duas Epistol: Pelag: ad Bonifacium.* lib 2. Cap. 8. And the same Augustine in his book *de Corruptione et Gratia,*[27] Cap. 2. answering to an objection, Wherefore are we comanded to do good, if it be not we that do it, but it is God that worketh both to will and to do. Let such (saith he) understand if they be the children of God, *Spiritu Dei se agi, ut quod agendum Est agant. Et cum egerint illi a quo aguntur gratias agant. Aguntur enim ut agant, non ut ipsi nihil agant.*[28] Such another speech of his to the like purpose Calvin quoteth out of him, *Dices mihi ergo, agimur non agimus: Imo agis et ageris, et tunc bene agis si a bono agaris, Spiritus Dei qui in te agit agentibus adjutor est, nomen adjutoris præscribit quod et tu aliquid agas.*[29] Which last words lest they may be misapplied to foment some active power in us of ourselves through gifts received, Calvin in the next words thus expoundeth it; *Quod autem adjungit, Ex nomine auxilii colligi posse nos etiam aliquid agere, non convenit ita accipere, quasi seorsim aliquid nobis tribuat; Sed ne foveat in nobis ignaviam sit Dei actionem cum nostra conciliat, ut velle sit a natura, bene autem velle a gratia: nisi Deus nos adjuvet non modo non vincere sed neque pugnare poterimus.*[30] *Instit.* Lib. 2. Cap. 5.§.14.

----

27. Augustine, "A Treatise Against Two Letters of the Pelagians," *A Select Library of the Nicene and Post-Nicene Fathers of the Christian Church,* ed. P. Schaff (New York, 1887), 5, 374–434; "Treatise on Rebuke and Grace," ibid., 472–491.

28. They are acted upon by the Spirit of God, so that they are able to do what must be done. And when they have acted let them give thanks to Him by whom they have been acted upon. For they are acted upon in order that they might act, not in order that they themselves do nothing.

29. "You will say to me, 'Therefore we are acted upon and do not act ourselves.' Yes, you act and are acted upon. And if you are acted upon by one who is good, then you act well. The Spirit of God who acts upon you is the helper of those who act. The name 'helper' indicates that you also do something." *Institutes,* trans. Battles, II.v.14.

30. "(In the first part of the statement he indicates that man's action is not taken away by the movement of the Holy Spirit, because the will, which is directed to aspire to good, is of nature.) But when he directly adds that

To 15th.

In Answer to your Fifteenth Question I said, That it was not an unsafe but a lawful way to conclude a mans safe estate by way of a practical reasoning; so be it, the reasoning were not carnal but Spiritual: One Proposition being expressed in the word or safely deduced thence, the other being an experimental observation of a good Conscience enlightned by the Spirit of God and looking up to Christ to conclude the conclusion from both. Nevertheless I added, A good Conscience will not fully satisfie itself in this way, till it be established by the witness of the Spirit itself; Or if it should so satisfie and rest itself, God will in time awaken it to a sense of his further need of Christ.

Before I come to your Reply give me leave Somewhat to explaine my self more fully, lest this way of practical reasoning may be misconstrued by some or other. Four things are needful to be explained

1. When it is said a man may conclude his safe estate, what kind of Conclusion is meant, whether a Conclusion of Knowledge or of Faith?

2. What is the Safe estate to be concluded, whether of Justification or Sanctification?

3. What kind of proposition in the Word he should conclude upon, whether absolute or Conditional

4. What kind of enlightening by the Spirit is meant, Whether a created spiritual light abiding in the regenerate Conscience, or an immediate light of the Spirit of God above the light of the letter of the Word, and above the created light of the Conscience, even the divine testimony of the Spirit though not revealing his own proper and peculiar work, yet at lest the work of the Father or the Son. According to these differences of things I would explain myne Answer in different manner.

1. To make a Conclusion of Faith it will be needfull that as

---

from the word 'help' it can be inferred that we also do something, we must not so understand it as if something were to be attributed to each of us separately. But in order not to encourage indolence in us, he connects God's action with our own in these words: 'To will is of nature, but to will aright is of grace.' Therefore he had said a little earlier, 'Unless God helps, we shall be able neither to conquer nor even to fight.' " Ibid.

the one Proposition be contained in the Word (either expresly or by just consequence) So the other be witnessed to the Conscience by the Spirit itself, revealing the free grace of God to him either drawing him in the work of the Father, or easing him in the work of the Son.

2. To make a Conclusion of Knowledg, it will hold if the one Proposition be contained in the Word and the other observed by the experience of a good Conscience, enlightned with that created light which hath renewed it. Howbeit, this Conclusion of Knowledg must follow after the conclusion of Faith, not go before it. It is easier to add knowledg to our faith (according to the Counsel of the Apostle Peter (2 Peter 1.5.) than faith to our knowledge. And indeed unless Faith go before, which maketh hidden things (as all spiritual matters be) evident, knowledg will not be able to give a true discernment of them.

3. To make a Conclusion of faith of our justified estate, it will be requisite that the proposition contained in the Word be an absolute promise or some word of grace freely offering Christ and his righteousness without the condition of any works of ours to go before it; and instead of an Assumption there must be an effectual application not so much of that proposition, as of Christ in it. For as Dr. Ames well observeth (*Medull.* lib. 1. cap. 27. § 17.18.) "We are justified by faith no otherwise than as it revealeth Christs righteousness, for which we are justified. And Christs righteousness is not laid up in the truth of any proposition which we beleeve, but in Christ alone who is made unto us of God our righteousnes." Howbeit in the proposition or word of grace wherein Christ is graciously offered he poureth out the Spirit of his grace into the hearts of his chosen to beget both faith and Repentance. Acts 10.43.44. Zechariah 12.10.

4. To make a Conclusion of Knowledg of our Sanctified estate, it will suffice if one proposition contained in the Word be either absolute or conditional, and the other observed by the experience of a good conscience enlightned with the created light which hath renewed it. But if from thence we would infer a conclusion of our justified estate, it may be safely admitted (as Calvin speaketh) as a *posterior probatio* of that which was evident to faith before; which caution is necessarily to be attended to in this kind of rea-

soning that we build not the faith of our justified Estate, neither Faith of dependance nor faith of Assurance upon such a conclusion so gathered. For that Faith whereby we are justified (of what degree soever it be) cannot be begotten by any created light or power, nor can it rest upon any ground but Divine testimony nor upon any object but the grace of God freely giving Christ to be our righteousness.

If therefore it be demanded, Whether I may not conclude my Salvation and the Safe Estate thereof from such practical reasoning as this,

He that Repenteth and beleeveth the Gospel shall be saved

But I repent and beleeve the Gospel

Therefore I shall be saved, (and consequently am   justified) [margin: in this blank was the word [while]]
I would answer, The conclusion is safe if the minor proposition be true. And the minor is true, if the Gospel have been first published (or preached) and applied to that Soul, not only by the outward ministry of the Word but by the Spirit of God himself, revealing the grace of Christ to him therein. For it is from the Spirit of Grace, that Christ being set before us in the Gospel, we do by faith see him as crucified by us and for us, and upon sight of him do mourn over him and for him, Zechariah 12.10. But if before sight of Christ revealed and applied to us in the Gospel by the Spirit of Grace we find ourselves humbled for sin and then finding some promises made to humble and heavy laden sinners shall take them as belonging to ourselves in this condition (as our Spirits will be apt to do) and thereupon come to take up faith and belief that Christ is ours: In this way we now indeed take up no more than a legal humiliation and Repentance. And such a Repentance, and the faith raised up out of it, is not the Repentance and faith of the Gospel, and therefore will not safely infer or conclude a state of Salvation. For in the Gospel, Christ, and the promise of grace in him, is first offered and applied (or given) to the Soul by the Spirit of Grace, and so bringeth forth grace and Repentance in us. But in this other way we bring Repentance and faith to the Gospel, and so take hold of the promise of grace; which is a way not of the Gospel, from grace to produce Works: but of the Law, from Works to find grace, which cannot be safe for Christians to rest satisfied in.

Thus having cleared the meaning of mine own Answer to your Fifteenth Question, I come to your Reply.

"We also (say you) conceive it sinfull to rest satisfied in the witness of our own Spirit unless the Spirit itself bear witness with it that we are the sons of God: But we hear of some that think it an unsafe way to conclude a mans safe estate by way of practical Syllogisme; and so quench Gods Spirit in themselves by seeking a Spirit without any work of the Spirit in themselves, imagining that the Lords Spirit should bear witness without, and not with their Spirit which we take to be contrary to Romans 8.16."

Answ. When you say you do also conceive it sinfull to rest satisfied in the witness of our own Spirit: Though you seem therein to consent with mine answer to your Question, yet indeed I feared you mistook my true meaning therein. Which therefore I thought meet more plainly to unfold, according to what I have now expressed. For my part I do not only think it sinfull to rest satisfied in the testimony of our Spirit but utterly unsafe, unless the testimony of the Spirit of God have born witness to our estates before it or with it. For our Spirit of itself is but a creature, though a good creature. And though it might take in the word to bear witness with it: yet (as I have said) the word without the Spirit of God breathing in it is a dead letter and unable to beget faith. And therefore such a faith as hath noe other ground to rest upon but the testimony of our Spirits applying the word to our Estates, surely it is not gotten by divine power but by two creatures, and indeed by the word mistaken and our spirits mistaking. And so it is not only sinfull but utterly unsafe to rest satisfied with it: as it was utterly unsafe for the Prophets of Israel to walk in the light of their own Spirits when they had seen nothing (no answer from the Lord) Ezekiel 13.3. "And therefore if you hear there be some that think it an unsafe way to conclude a safe estate by way of such a practical Syllogisme" (wherein the minor is only the testimony of our Spirits) I am contented to be reckoned as one of them, as concurring herein with them in the same judgment. Neither do we hereby "quench Gods Spirit in our selves," by seeking a Spirit without any work of the Spirit in our selves. For we seek not a Spirit that worketh not, but that which witnesseth Gods free grace without works: and afterward confirmeth his witness (as he did his Gospel) by works following. And so I understand that place which you quote out of Romans 8.16. not that the Spirit itself when it beareth witness of our justification beareth witness upon some work in our Spirits: but that when the Spirit itself beareth witness of Gods free grace to our Souls in Christ without works, then cometh in our Spirit as a second testimony to witness and confirm the same by the works and fruits of the Spirit wrought in us. In which also the Spirit of God doth often concur to bear witness to our Spirits that the works of our Spirits are of God and accepted of him. And so the Spirit of God preventeth our Spiritt in witnessing Gods Fatherly Adopting love, justifying us from sin of his free grace in Christ without works. It worketh with our Spirits helping our infirmity to bring forth the fruits and works of the Spirit. It followeth our Spirit, in witnessing that both our Spirit and the works thereof are of God and accepted with him. Our Spirit cannot witness any divine testimony unless the Spirit of God bear witness with it and in it. But the Spirit of God may witness a divine testimony, not only to beget faith, but even full assurance of Faith, even then when our Spirit may keep silence, yea and be ashamed and confounded ever to open the mouth more, as convinced of sin against so much mercy, Ezekiel 16.63.

To the 16th.

My Answer was that a Christian soul is more usually wont to press the Lord for spiritual mercies by arguments drawn from his own spirituall miseries and infirmities rather than from the graces of Christ in himself. Nevertheless the Saints do also make use of arguments from those graces, but they are usually such whereby they go out of themselves and their own strength and worth, as Faith, Hope, desire, Seeking, waiting etc.; or such as do express the Spiritual bent and inclination or affection which they desire may be quickened and satisfied with their spiritual and proper object or End. But the force of their Arguments from their graces is fetched (still I mean usually) not from the force or fulness or power of them, but from the weakness or emptiness of them.

Whereto you reply, "That the Saints do use Arguments both from their own Spiritual miseries and infirmities, and from the graces of Christ in them: And both these may well stand together in the same prayer. And they make use of these not rarely but frequently, and of these not some sorts only, but all sorts, and that ordinarily. Which is easie to shew by induction of many places in Scripture."

Answ: When I see your Induction, I hope God will keep me from shutting mine eyes against light. All that I can say for the present is, That I have not usually observed the Saints in Scripture to urge the Lord in their prayers by arguments from their graces otherwise than I have spoken. Only I would be understood that it was not my meaning to speak of the graces or gracious dealings of the Saints towards men: For towards them they do often plead even before the Lord, their righteous and gracious dealings, the more to provoke the Lord to take their part against unjust and undeserved requitalls which they have found from man.

CHAPTER 6

John Wheelwright, A Fast-Day Sermon

ON January 19, 1637, the colony of Massachusetts Bay held a general fast,[1] the "occasion" being "the dissensions in our churches." But the fast failed to restore peace to the troubled colony, for the sermon John Wheelwright preached that day in the Boston Church raised the Antinomian Controversy to a higher pitch. John Wheelwright (1592?–1679) was a Puritan minister in England before emigrating to the colony in the spring of 1636. On his arrival, he received a warm welcome from the Boston Church, partly, no doubt, because he was married to Anne Hutchinson's sister-in-law, but also because he sympathized with the opinions of the congregation. In October, after the Boston congregation voted to add him to the church's ministry, John Winthrop stood up and opposed the vote on the grounds that Wheelwright took a "doubtful" stand on two points of theology. Wheelwright then had to settle for a position as preacher to a group of "Farmers" at Braintree.[2]

Wheelwright's fast-day sermon got him into further trouble. Though some nineteenth-century historians found the sermon innocuous,[3] the reaction of his contemporary audience was quite different. When the General Court met in March, it judged him guilty of "sedition" and "contempt,"[4] crimes for which, the following November, he was banished from the colony. Wheel-

---

1. New England fast-days (including this one) are described in William DeLoss Love, *The Fast and Thanksgiving Days of New England* (Boston, 1895).
2. Winthrop, *History, 1,* 254, 239–241.
3. This was James Savage's opinion; ibid., 257n.
4. *Massachusetts Records, 1,* 189.

wright's friends did not let the Court's action pass unchallenged. At the March session, the Boston Church presented a petition defending the minister, and sixty persons signed a "remonstrance" protesting his conviction. These protests set the stage for the bitterly contested election in May.

Wheelwright left Massachusetts in November, 1637, and settled at Exeter, New Hampshire. Subsequently he lived in various Maine and New Hampshire towns before finally returning to Massachusetts in 1662 as minister of Salisbury.

There are two manuscript versions of the fast-day sermon, neither of which has the greater claim to authority. One copy, which belongs to the Massachusetts Historical Society, has been printed in the *Proceedings of the Massachusetts Historical Society, 9*, 256–274. The other manuscript is in the Massachusetts State Archives, vol. 240, 21–28, and was printed in *John Wheelwright,* ed. Charles Bell (Boston, 1876). The text below follows this copy, with material in brackets supplied from the other version.

Matthew the 9. 15.

And Jesus said unto them, can the Children of the bridechamber mourne, as long as the Bridegroome is with them? but the dayes will come, when the Bridegroome shall be taken from them and then they shall fast.

Our blessed Lord and Saviour Jesus Christ, though he was the most innocent that ever was, so that they which hated him, hated him without a cause, yet notwithstanding the wicked world, they were ever taking exceptions, both against his sayings and doings.

In the beginning of this chapter, they brought unto him a man sicke of the palsey, lying upon a bedd, Jesus seeing their faith, said unto him, sonne be of good cheare, thy synnes be forgiven thee, the Scribes say within themselves that he blasphemeth, Christ perceiving their thoughts, answered for himselfe, and telleth them, he could as easily forgive synnes, as restore this man to health; Christ goeth from thence and goeth to the receipt of custome, and calleth Mathew the Publican, and he receaveth him into his house and maketh a feast, Christ sitteth downe with Publicans and synners, the Pharisees take exceptions, and tell his Disciples, that their

Master eateth with Publicans and synners, and Christ hearing of it, answereth for himselfe and telleth them, they were fit subjects to worke upon, he justifieth the ungodly. Those that are justified by Christ must not looke to be saved by sacrifice, but by the mercy of Christ. A little after the Disciples of John were instigated by the Scribes and Pharisees Mark 2.18, and they put this question unto him, Why they and the Pharisees fast often? and the Disciples of Christ fast not? And Christ answered in my text. And thus you see the coherence and dependance of these words.

The text consisteth of two arguments, whereby Christ did proove and shew, that it was not for his Disciples to fast. The first is taken from the remoovall of any just cause of fasting which they had for the present. The second argument is taken from a position or putting a just cause of fast they should have hereafter, and that was the remooving Christ from them.

I will not stand to shew the difference of fasts, which are either constrayned, civill, miraculous, dayly or religious: but the fast here spoken of in my text, is of the last sort, and mourning is added in my text, because fasting and mourning go together. Joel 2. and where it is here said, the children of the bridechamber cannot fast, it is to be understood an impossibility of seasonablenes, they cannot do it seasonably.

The text contayneth in it two poynts, but I wrap all up in one poynt of Doctrine, and that is this. That the only cause of the fasting of true beleevers is the absence of Christ.

Either Christ he is present with his people, or els absent from his people; if he be present with his people, then they have no cause to fast: therefore it must be his absence that is the true cause of fasting, when he is taken away then they must fast; If we take a view of all the fasts, that have beene kept either in the old or new-Testament, we shall find the fasts that have beene kept by true beleevers, have had this for the ground of them, the absence of the Lord. What was the reason why the people of Israell kept a fast, Judges the 20. and 1 Samuel 7 and Jehosephat and all Judah 2 Chronicles 20 and the people of Israell after they came out of captivity, Nehemiah 9. And the church of Antioch, Acts 13. and Paul and Barnabas, Acts 14. was it not because they wanted the Lord to protect, defend, pardon, and assist? Where there is mention made of fasting in the Scripture, you shall likewise find mention made of turning unto the Lord, and the Prophett Joel when he speaketh of a fast, he biddeth them turne to the Lord: whereby it is evident, that the reason why Gods people do fast, is because there is a distance betweene them and the Lord.

Reas: 1. The first reason is, when Jesus Christ is aboundantly present he doth make a supply of whatsoever the children of God can procure in this extraordinary way of fasting: Wee know that under the captivity the people of God they fasted exceedingly, they kept a fast in the fourth moneth .5.7.10. and now the Lord promiseth a restauration of Jerusalem, that is especially accomplished in the kingdome of Christ, when he shall raigne over his, and he saith, in this day he will turne the fast of the fourth moneth .5.7.10. into joyfull gladnes and chearefull feasts Zechariah 8.[5] There is a prophecy of a glorious Church, which the Lord will have under the new testament, and especially when the Jewes come to be converted unto God, and there is a promise that the Lord will dwell with them, and they shall be his people and he will be with them, and the effect of it is, all teares shall be wiped from their eyes: Revelation 21.4. and the same is prophecied in Isaiah 65.19. so farr as Christ is present he taketh away all cause of mourning and weeping, and in his presence is fulnes of joy, and at his right hand there is pleasures for evermore. Psalms 16.11.

Reas: 2. The second reason is, because when the Lord Jesus Christ cometh once to be absent, then cometh in matter of mourning and fasting, all misery followeth the absence of Christ, as you see darknes followeth the absence of the sunne, the Lord leaveth Hezekiah 2 Kings 20. 12. 13. and then what followeth upon it, he sinneth exceedingly in shewing the Ambassadors the treasure in his house. The Lord departeth from his Disciples, and his Disciples leave him and forsake him. John 16. so when it pleaseth the Lord to absent himselfe, then cometh in cause of mourning, and this hath beene the reason that the servants of God have wonderfully desired the presence of the Lord. Moses desired Gods presence, or els never to go up, and so David Psalms 27.9. because he

---

5. Zechariah 8.19: Thus saith the Lord of hosts; The fast of the fourth month, and the fast of the fifth, and the fast of the seventh, and the fast of the tenth, shall be to the house of Judah joy and gladness, and cheerful feasts.

knew very well, if God were absent from him, then misery would follow.

Use 1. The first use may serve to teach us a reason, why those that are the children of God upon their first acquaintance they get with the Lord, they are not much addicted unto fasting, the Lord doth not cary them that way; the time when Christ was upon the earth, he being present with his Disciples, he was ever and anon instructing of them, when they were in doubt of any thing he telleth them; and if they could not answere many doubts, then Christ came and answered for them, and if at any tyme they were in any danger, then Christ comforteth them, and was ever and anon with them. And thus the Lord dealeth with his children spiritually in regard of his spirituall presence, when Christ first cometh to breake into the soules of his, he is wonderfully pleasant unto them, and ever and anon instructing of them and comforting of them, yea, the Lord heareth them before they pray, or when they are a speaking and doth exceedingly solace them; but afterwards it may be the saynts of God may come to be left and forsaken of the Lord, either because the children of their mother is angry with them, and make them keepe the vyneyard, those under a covenant of works, maketh them travaile under the burthen of that Covenant, and so maketh the Lord absent himselfe from them, and then Christ cometh to depart from them, and then they fast; or els whilest they grow carnall and fall into a spirituall sleepe Christ leaves them. Canticles 5.6.

2. Secondly, from hence we are taught how to cary and behave ourselves now upon this day of humiliation, there are divers evills which wee may happily desire should be removed, both from forrayne Nations and from this place where we live, and divers good things we desire should be procured both for them and ourselves. What is the course we must take? Must we especially looke after the removing those evill things, and procuring those good things? This an hipocrite will do, see the example of Ahab. 1 Kings 21.27.28.29. and the Lord will grant the desire of hipocrites: in this case, see 78 Psalms 34. for there the hipocriticall people of the Jewes, in their misery sought the Lord, and the Lord being full of compassion, he forgiveth their iniquities and destroyeth them not, in the 38 verse of that psalme, must we then do as they did?

by no meanes: what must we do then? we must looke first, at the Lord Jesus Christ, and must desire now that Jesus Christ may be receaved in other Nations and other places, and may be more receaved amongst our selves, we must turne unto the Lord, and then he will turne all into a right frame; when many enimyes came against Jehosophat, what doth he? he goeth and seeketh the Lord and his eyes are towards the Lord. 2 Chronicles 20. 12. So the children of God are a company, a generation that seeke the Lord and his strength and face evermore, Psalms 105.4. they do not only seeke the gifts of his spiritt, but the Lord himselfe, they doe not seeke after strength to be received from the Lord only, but they seeke after the strength that is in the Lord, they do not seeke only to know the Lord by fruits and effects, but looke upon the Lord with a direct eye of faith they seeke his face, and this is the generation of seekers spoken of. Psalms 24.6. Therefore if we meane to procure good things and remoove evill things, this will be our course, seeing the absence of the Lord is the cause of fasting, and the end of our fasting must be our turning to the Lord, and he will turne to us, Joel 2. and thus the Lord will turne all things for the good of his, Romans 8.32. if we[6] get the Lord Jesus Christ, we shall have all things.

3. Thirdly from hence we are taught a reason, why those that do not know the Lord Jesus, they are usually given most unto fasting, not that I condemne fasting by any meanes; but this is it, many tymes those that are the least acquainted with the Lord Jesus are given [the] most of all to fasting, the Papists are given much to fasting and punish themselves by whipping, and the people in Captivity they weare not acquainted with the Lord, and so did not fast to the Lord. Zechariah 7.5.6. and yet appoynted more fasts then the Lord appoynted, the 4.5.8. 10 moneth, and the Pharisees fasted twice a weeke Luke 18.12. they want the Lord Jesus Christ, and they must have something to rest upon and must close with some thing, and because they want Christ they fast. This for the first use of instruction.

Use 2. The second use is of exhortation, it serveth to exhort us all in the feare of God to have a speciall care, that we part not with

---

6. To this point the text comes only from the Massachusetts State Archives copy, the other being incomplete.

the Lord Jesus Christ, if we part with Christ we part with our lives, for Christ is our life saith Paul, Colossians 3.4, the Lord Jesus Christ is not only the author of [our] life, but is the [very] seat of the life of Gods children, and all their life is derived from Christ, for he is the roote, and he convayeth life to the branches, and those that are the children of God, they live by the faith of the sonne of God: Galatians 2.20. they have faith to lay hold on the sonne of God, and the sonne of God convayeth life unto them; therefore if we part with Christ, we part with our lives, therefore it standeth us all in hand, to have a care Christ be not taken from us, if we belong to the election of grace, Christ cannot be taken wholy away from us, yet he may be taken away in some degree, therefore let us have a care to keepe the Lord Jesus Christ.

Object: It may be here demanded, what course shall we take to keepe the Lord Jesus Christ?

Answ: The way we must take, if so be we will not have the Lord Jesus Christ taken from us, is this, we must all prepare for a spirituall combate, we must put on the whole armour of God, Ephesians 6.[11], and must have our loynes girt and be redy to fight; behold the bed that is Solomons, there is threescore valient men about it, valient men of Israell, every one hath his sword in his hand and being expert in warre, and hath his sword girt on his thigh, because of feare in the night, if we will not fight for the Lord Jesus Christ, Christ may come to be surprised. Solomon lyeth in his bed, and there is such men about the bed of Solomon, and they watch over Solomon and will not suffer Solomon to be taken away, and who is this Solomon, but the Lord Jesus Christ, and what is the bed, but the Church of true beleevers, and who are those valient men of Israell, but all the children of God, they ought to shew themselves valient, they should have their swords redy, they must fight, and fight with spirituall weapons, for the weapons of our warfare are not carnall but spirituall 2 Corinthians 10. 4. and therefore wheresoever we live, if we would have the Lord Jesus Christ to be aboundantly present with us, we must all of us prepare for battell and come out against the enimyes of the Lord, and if we do not strive, those under a covenant of works will prevaile, Wee must have a speciall care therefore to shew our selves couragious, All the valient men of David and all the men of

Israell, Barak and Deborah and Jael, all must out and fight for
Christ, curse the Meroz, because they came not out to helpe the
Lord against the mighty. Judges 5.23. Therefore if we will keepe
the Lord Jesus Christ and his presence and power amongst us, we
must fight.

That these things may be the better cleared, we must understand and call to our considerations, that as soone as ever Christ
was borne into the world Herod and all Jerusalem was troubled
Matthew 2. and if the Lord had not prevented him, he sought to
destroy him, and when Christ Jesus came once to shew himselfe
and to declare himselfe and exercise his publike ministry, the
world setteth themselves against him to intrap him, and they labor to kill him, and never left till they had crucified the Lord of
glory, for this was done by Herod and Pontius Pilate: Acts 4. and
when they have crucified him, that would not serve the turne, but
he being buried, they came and made it sure and sealeth the stone,
and setteth watch and ward, and would have buried the Lord for
ever, and would have kept him eternally in the grave; but he
raysed himselfe by his power; and since Christs resurrection and
ascension all the enimyes of the Lord Jesus Christ, they [endeav-
our to doe] it spiritually, and as the[y] buried the Lord Jesus
Christ and labored to keepe him there, so spiritually they burie
Christ, and they do not only labor to do this, that are Pagonish,
but the Antichristian. Why do the heathen rage and the people
imagine a vayne thing: Psalms 2.1. what people are they, the people of God, the people of the Jewes, this people do imagine to take
away the Lord Jesus Christ, and what hath beene the practice of
all Antichristian spiritts, but only to take away the Christ, the
sonne of the living God, and put in false Christs, and to deceave
the elect, if it were possible, Matthew 24.24. for what is Antichrist,
but one being against Christ, and for Christ, his being for Christ,
is being against Christ, because he would put one in the roome
of Christ: therefore if we would keepe the Lord Jesus Christ
amongst us, we must stand upon our gard and watch over the
Lord Jesus Christ, as the valient men of Israell watched over Solomon.

Object: It may be demaunded what course must we take to
prevaile in this combate, for fight we must?

Answ: If we would prevayle thorough the strength of the Lord
(for of our selves we can do nothing) then we must first contend
for the faith once delivered to the saynts. Jude 3. That is the Gospell, it was but once delivered for the substance, though many
tymes in regard of the manner, we must therefore strive for the
faith of the Gospell, and strive together for the Gospell: Philippians 1.27. if that the Light once be taken away, and darknes come
upon the face of the Church, then we may be eaysily deluded, and
a false Christ put in true Christs roome.

Object: It may be demaunded, what is the Gospell?

Answ: It is the same glad tydings the Lord sent into the world
of a Saviour that is borne unto us, even Jesus Christ the Lord, this
same Gospell is that heavenly doctrine, that was prophecied of
before by the Prophet concerning Jesus Christ the Lord, to be
made of the seed of David. The Gospell is a divine heavenly supernaturall doctrine, contayning in it the revelation of Jesus Christ.
To preach the Gospell is to preach Christ, and the Apostle saith
Galatians 6.14. God forbidd that I should glory in any thing but
in the crosse of Christ: so that the Gospell is such a doctrine as
doth hold forth Jesus Christ and nothing but Christ, when such
a doctrine is holden forth as doth reveale Jesus Christ to be our
wisdome, our righteousnes, our sanctification and our redemption 1 Corinthians 1. 30. when all is taken away from the creature,
and all given to Christ, so that neither before our conversion nor
after, we are able to put forth one act of true saving spirituall wisdome, but we must have it put forth from the Lord Jesus Christ,
with whom we are made one; and such a doctrine holden forth as
declares, that we are not able to do any worke of sanctification,
further then we are acted by the Lord, nor able to procure our
justification, but it must be the Lord Jesus Christ that must apply
himselfe and his righteousnes to us; and we are not able to re-
deeme our selves from the least evill, but he is our redemption;
when Christ is thus holden forth to be all in all, all in the roote,
all in the branch, all in all, this is the Gospell, this is that fountayne open for the inhabitants of Judah and Jerusalem for sinne
and for uncleanenes: Zechariah 13. 1. and this is the well, of which
the wells under the old Testament were certayne types, this same
well must be kept open, if the Philistines fill it with earth, with

the earth of their owne inventions, those that are the servants of
Isaack, true beleevers, the servants of the Lord, must open the
wells agayne, this is the light that holdeth forth a great light [that
is Jesus Christ, for he is the greate light] that lighteneth every one,
that cometh into the world John 1.9. and if we meane to keepe
Christ, we must hold forth this light.

Object: It may be demaunded, is there nothing to be holden
forth in poynt of justification, but only the righteousnes of the
Lord Jesus Christ, may there not be a revelation of some worke of
sanctification, and from that, may not we be caried to Christ Jesus,
and so come to beleeve in the Lord Jesus Christ, must Christ be all
in poynt of justification?

Answ: Truly both in poynt of justification, and the knowledg
of this our justification by faith, there must be nothing in the
world revealed but Christ Jesus, none other doctrine under
heaven is able to justify any, but merely the revelation of the
Lord Jesus Christ, I am not ashamed of the Gospell saith Paul, for
it is the power of God to salvation, 1 Romans 16. How? For in it,
the righteousnes of God is revealed: so it could not be a doctrine
with power to convert a soule if the righteousnes of the Lord were
not revealed: therefore when the Lord is pleased to convert any
soule to him, he revealeth not to him some worke, and from that
worke, carieth him to Christ, but there is nothing revealed but
Christ, when Christ is lifted up, he draweth all to him, that belongeth to the election of grace; if men thinke to be saved, because
they see some worke of sanctification in them, as hungring and
thirsting and the like: if they be saved, they are saved without the
Gospell. Nc, no, this is a covenant of works, for in the covenant of
grace, nothing is revealed but Christ for our righteousnes; and so
for the knowledge of our justification by faith, nothing is revealed
to the soule but only Christ and his righteousnes freely given, it
was the very grace of God that appeared, that same apparition
whereby the soule cometh to know that he is justified, the object
of it is Christ freely given, when the loving kindnes of Christ appeared 3 Titus 5. not by the works of righteousnes, they are layd
aside, and the Lord revealeth only to them the righteousnes of
himselfe given freely to the soule; if men have revealed to them
some worke of righteousnes in them selves, as love to the brethren

and the like, and hereupon they come to be assured they are in a good estate, this is not the assurance of faith, for faith hath Christ revealed for the object, therefore [if] the assurance of ones justification be by faith as a worke, it is not Gospell.

Object: It may further be demaunded, must not any sanctification by the Gospell be pressed upon those that are the children of God, but only as it cometh from Jesus Christ the roote, and as he worketh it in those, that are true beleevers?

Answ: Not in the Gospell. Sanctification must be preached no other way, all dutyes of sanctification pressed upon the children of God must be [soe] urged, as with all it be declared that they grow from the roote Christ Jesus. Worke out your salvation with feare and trembling, Philippians 2.12. It is he that worketh in you both to will and do of his good pleasure; this is the covenant of grace, the Lord Jesus will be our sanctification, and worke sanctification in us and for us. A new hart will I give you, and a new spiritt, and they shall walke in my statutes and you shall keepe my judgments and do them. Ezekiel 36.26.27. I will forgive your sinnes, and write my Law in your harts and inward parts; [If works be soe pressed as] if a beleever had power in him selfe to worke, it killeth the spirit of Gods children, put any worke of sanctification in a legall frame and it killeth him, the Law killeth, but it is the spiritt that quickens, that is the Gospell in which the spiritt of God is convayed, when God speaketh he speaketh the words of eternall life: [and Peter saith to Christ, whether shal we goe, for with ye is the wordes of eternal life,] therefore ought no works of sanctification to be urged upon the servants of God, so as if they had a power to do them, it will kill the soule of a man, and it oppresseth the poore soules of the saynts of God: Christ saith, Matthew 11.28, come unto mee all ye that labor and are heavy laden, and as long as we are absent from Christ we are heavy laden; but when Christ pulleth us to himselfe and takes our burthen upon him, then we find ease; Learne of me for I am meeke and lowly, and you shall find rest to your soules, Christ was so meeke and lowly, as content to receave all from the father, and so must we be meeke and lowly, and content to receave all from Christ; if the dutyes be pressed any other way, they will be burthens, that neither wee, nor our fathers were[7] able to beare; therefore if we meane to keepe the Lord Jesus Christ, wee must keepe open this fountayne and hold forth this light, if there [be] a night of darknes, the feare (saith the Spirit of God) is in the night.

2. The second action we must performe and the second way we must take is, When enimyes to the truth oppose the wayes of God, we must lay load upon them, we must kill them with the word of the Lord, Hosea 6.5. The Lord hath given true beleevers power over the Nations, and they shall breake them in peeces as shivered with a rod of yron; and what rod of yron is this, but the word of the Lord, and such honor have all his saynts. Psalms 149.9. The Lord hath made us of threshing instruments with teeth and we must beate the hills as chaffe, Isaiah 41.15. Therefore in the feare of God, handle the sword of the spiritt, the word of God, for it is a two edged sword, and Hebrews 4.12, this word of God cutteth men to the hart.

Object: It may be objected that there will be little hope of victorie for the servants of God, because the children of God are but few, and those that are enimyes to the Lord and his truth are many?

Answ: True, I must confesse and acknowledge the saynts of God are few, they are but a little flocke, and those that are enimyes to the Lord, not onely Pagonish, but Antichristian, and those that run under a covenant of works are very strong: but be not afrayd, the battle is not yours but Gods, Yee know the speech rendred by the Prophet when so many came against Joshua. Joshua 23. 10. One of you shall chase a thousand; and if we should go in our owne strength we should be swallowed up many a time may Israel say, if it had not beene for the Lord, we had beene swallowed up, if it were not for the Lord of hoasts, there were little hope of prevayling by the saynts, but out of the mouthes of babes and sucklings, God ordayneth him prayse, to still the enimyes, the Lord will magnifie his name in the saynts, and though Gods people be but few, yet it is the Lord of hoasts, that God of heaven and earth, that layed the foundation upon the seas, and in comparison of

---

7. "Will be" in the other copy.

whom, all the Nations are nothing, Jehovah is his name that great God, it is Michaell that fighteth with the Angells; therefore though the people be few, yet it is all one for God to save with many or those that have no strength.

Object: It will be objected, that divers of those who are oposite to the wayes of grace and free covenant of grace, they are wondrous holy people, therefore it should seeme to be a very uncharitable thing in the servants of God to condemne such, as if so be they were enimyes to the Lord and his truth, whilest they are so exceeding holy and strict in their way.

Answ: Brethren, those under a covenant of works, [the] more holy they are, the greater enimyes they are to Christ, Paul acknowledgeth as much in Galatians [1] he saith he was zealous according to the Law and the more he went in a legall way, the more he persecuted the wayes of grace 13 [and 14] Acts. where all the devout people were such, as did expell Paul out of Antioch and out of all the coasts, It maketh no matter how seemingly holy men be, according to the Law; if they do not know the worke of grace and wayes of God, they are such as trust to their owne righteousnes, they shall dye sayth the Lord. Ezekiel 33.13. What a cursed righteousnes is that, that thrusteth out the righteousnes of Christ, the Apostle speaketh, they shall transforme themselves into an Angell of Light, 2 Corinthians 11.14. Therefore it maketh no matter how holy men be that have no acquaintance with Christ. Seest thou a man wise in his owne conceit, more hope their is of a foole then of him. Proverbs 26.12. We know (through the mercy of God) assoone as Christ cometh into the soule, he maketh the creature nothing: therefore if men be so holy and so strict and zealous, and trust to themselves and their righteousnes, and knoweth not the wayes of grace, but oppose free grace; such as these, have not the Lord Jesus Christ, therefore set upon such with the sword of the Spiritt, the word of God.

Object: It will be objected, that the children of God should be a meeke generation, it is an exhortation the Apostle giveth. James 3.13.

Answ: For to fight couragiously and in the cause of God, and to be meeke, they are divers, but not opposits, they may stand very well together: You know when Steven was of a meeke frame, for the Spirit of God was in him, and he was of a calme quiet frame

and disposition, and yet you see what a vehement speech Steven
made to the enimyes of God, Acts. 7.51. it cut them to the very
hart, yet Steven a meeke man, he prayed for his enimyes in a
meeke frame of spiritt, and yet vehement to those that oppose the
wayes of God. Christ was meeke, I am sure you will say, and he
saith, learne of mee for I am meeke and lowly, yet when he cometh
to those that did oppose the wayes of grace, you are the children of
the divell, John 8.44. and in the 23 Matthew 23. Woe be to you
Scribes Pharisees hipocrites, a vehement speech he useth, yet
Christ the meekest man that ever was, therefore you may easily
beate downe those holds, by the sword of the Spiritt, the word of
God.

Object: This will cause a combustion in the Church and
comon wealth, may be objected.

Answ: I must confesse and acknowledge it will do so, but what
then? did not Christ come to send fire upon the earth, Luke 12.49.
and what is it, that it were alredy kindled, he desireth it were
kindled, and it is the desire of the Spirit and of the saynts that this
fire were kindled; is not this that that is prophesied of, Isaiah 9.5.
This battle betweene Michaell and his Angells, the battle betweene Gods people and those that are not, those battles of Christians must be burning, and what is it, but the burning of the word
of God accompanied by the Holy Ghost, this is prophesied of in
Malachi 4.1. the day shall come that shall burne like an oven and
all that do wickedly shall be stubble, and this is the terrible day of
the Lord, when the gospell is thus held forth, this is a terrible day
to all those that do not obey the Gospell of Christ; Brethren, we
know that the whore must be burnt, Revelation 18.8. it is not
shaving of her head and paring her nayles and changing her ray-
ment, that will serve the turne, but this whore must be burnt.
Many speake of the externall burning of Rome, but I am sure
there must be a Spirituall burning, and that burning by the fire of
the Gospell; This way must Antichrist be consumed. 2 Thessalonians 2. why should we not further this fire, who knoweth not
how soone those Jewes may be converted? Revelation 18 and 19
chapters after the burning of the whore followes, Alleluia, a prays-
ing of the Lord in Hebrew; wee know not how soone the conversion of the Jewes may come, and if they come, they must come by
the downfall of Antichrist, and if we take him away, we must

---

* See new note p. xix.

burne him; therefore never feare combustions and burnings.

Object: Lastly it may be objected against those combats and fightings, if Ministers and christians be so downeright and so strive and contend, and holde forth the word of God with such violence and power, this will be a meanes to discourage those that are weake Christians, and do them a great deale of hurt.

Answ: Let the Gospell be never so cleerely held forth, it never hurteth the children of God, no, it doth them a great deale of good, that same very fire of the word, that burneth up all unbeleevers, and all under a Covenant of works, that Gospell doth exceedingly cleare Gods children. Malachi 4.2. then the sonne of righteousnes shall come with healing in his wings, and in the 3 Matthew Christ when he handleth the Gospell, he layeth the axe to the roote of the tree, and what followeth hereupon, he will purge his floare, [layeth the axe to the roote,] and cutteth downe all hipocrites, and those that build upon any thing besids Christ, and then he will purge the Church, and gather the wheate into the garner, true beleevers will come in, unbeleevers and hipocrites chaffe will be burnt up: so the same Gospell that is a word of terror to the wicked men, is a great comfort to all that beleeve in the Lord Jesus Christ.

3. Thirdly, if we meane to keepe the Lord Jesus Christ, we must be willing to suffer any thing, You know in the 12 Revelation 11. the saynts of God overcame, and over came by the blood of the Lambe, that is by the Lord Jesus Christ, and by the word of the testimony, that is the Gospell, and they loved not their lives unto the death, that is, if we will overcome we must not love our lives, but be willing to be killed like sheepe; it is impossible to hold out the truth of God with externall peace and quietnes, if we will prevaile, if we be called, we must be willing to lay downe our lives, and shall overcome by so doing; Sampson slew more at his death, then in his life, and so we may prevaile more by our deathes, then by our lives.

4. Fourthly, if we will keepe Christ, we must consider, that we cannot do any of this, by any strength that is in our selves, but we must consider that it is the Lord that must helpe us and act in us, and worke in us, and the Lord must do all; When as Zerobabell and Joshua and the people came out of captivity to build the tem-

ple, they all tooke their rest, and lett the temple alone, till the Lord came and stirred up the spiritt of Zerobabell and Joshua and the people, and then they fall a building: so (brethren) we may thinke to do great matters, and lye quietly and calmely, and let the enimyes of the Church do what they will, till the Lord stirr us up, the Judges stirred not, till the Spiritt of God came upon them, and then they did wonderfull things; so in some measure, we must looke for the Spirit of the Lord to come upon us, and then we shall do mighty things through the Lord, it is the Lord himselfe that must effect and do all: this for the first exhortation, not to suffer the Lord Jesus Christ to be taken violently away from us, wheresoever we live, we shall find some that go under a covenant of works, and these are enimyes to Christ, and the flesh will lust against the Spiritt. Galatians 5. 17, and so we shall find it in our spiritts, those that are after the flesh, do mind the things of the flesh, Romans 8.5. therefore wheresoever we are, we shall have Christ taken from us by violence, if the Lord be not pleased to give us to use these meanes.

The second use of exhortation, we that are under a Covenant of grace, let us all have a care so to carry our selves that we may have the presence of the Lord, that he may not depart from us; for if the Lord depart we shall have cause of mourning indeede: That we may carry and behave ourselves, as the Lord Jesus Christ, who is amongst us, that he may still be more and more present with us,

1. First we must have a speciall care, that as any of us are interested with the Gospell, so to deale faithfully in the dispencing of it, whether we be in place or not in place, whether brethren or sisters, being made pertakers of the grace of God, being made stewards wee are to be found faithfull, [therefore let us have a caire to deale faithfully,] and to hold forth the truth as it is in the Lord Jesus Christ, and then wee shall find the Lord to be present with us, Matthew 28. 20 Behold I am with you, if you teach that, that he hath comanded, he will be with them; therefore in the feare of God have a care, that we do renounce the hidden things of dishonestie, and that we do not use any deceit; Let us not be as some that corrupt the word, but in sinserity in the sight of God as in Jesus Christ, so let us speake, Let us all have a care to hold forth Christ, and not to runne into generalityes, lest Christ vanish away

in a cloud, while the saynts of God stand gazing and have sad harts, when we are to hold forth any truth, let us deale faithfully in this kind, and the Lord will be abundantly present, we shall find he shall be a saviour wheresoever he cometh either of life or death, and if we be faithfull in few things, he will make us rulers over many. Matthew 25. Therefore if we meane to injoy the presence of Christ, and still would have more of the Lord Jesus Christ, and would have Christ to come and say, good and faithfull servant, and bestow more of his presence amongst us, let us be faithfull in dispensing any word of truth.

2. Secondly let us have a care all of us, that we love one another, this is my comaundement that you love one another, as I have loved you. 1 John 3.23. The Lord Christ delighteth in a loving people, when the saynts of God love one another, and are willing to lay downe their lives one for another, the Lord delighteth in them, Christ was loving when he was upon the earth, if the Disciples were in danger at any tyme, he came and supported them, and helped them when they were poased by the Scribes and Pharisees, sometyme he came and answered for them. Acts 2.15. some mocked at them, then Peter steppeth up and saith, those are not drunken as ye suppose, he loved them and answered for them. Moses seeing an Egiptian striving with his brother, he came and killed him. Acts 7.24.25.26. So Christ putetth into his people a loving spiritt; therefore let us have a care, [that] we do not alienate our harts one from another, because of divers kind of expressions, but let us keepe the unity of the spiritt in the bond of peace, let us have a care to love one another, and then the Lord Jesus Christ will be still more and more present.

3. Thirdly, let us have a care that we shew our selves [holy] in all manner of good conversation. 1 Peter 1.5. both in private and publike and in all our cariages and conversations, let us have a care to be holy as the Lord is holy, let us not give an ocasion to those that are coming on, or manifestly opposite to the wayes of grace, to suspect the way of grace, let us cary our selves, that they may be ashamed to blame us, let us deale uprightly with those, with whom we have occasion to deale, and have a care to guide our familyes, and to performe duties that belong to us, and let us have a care that we give not ocasion to others to say we are libertines or

Antinomians, but Christians, let us expresse the vertue of him that hath called us, and then he will manifest his presence amongst us. John 14. if you love me I will manifest myselfe to you, he will crowne his owne worke with his presence, he will come into his garden and eate of the pleasant fruits; therefore let us carry our selves, so that we may have no cause of mourning, for if the Lord be absent, there is cause of mourning.

The third use is for reproofe. And first it serveth to condemne all such as in their fastings and dayes of humiliation, do principally and above all seeke for blessings to be procured and evills remooved, and this is that, they are first carryed unto, this is not the mayne matter, the mayne matter is the absence of the Lord; therefore if wee will do as we ought to do, and performe this duty a right way; We must first of all be carryed unto the Lord Jesus Christ: they may procure great blesseings from the Lord, and yet the Lord never accept of them, they may pray to the Lord and fast and humble themselves, and the Lord may heare them and pardon them, and turne away his wrath; and yet for all that, never save them; how did the Lord cary himselfe towards the people of the Jewes, you know the Lord gave them his presence in the wildernes, and gave them an extraordinary signe of his presence, they had a pillor of fire by night and a cloud by day, and the Lord did cause the Angell of his presence to go before them. 9 Nehemiah 12. and gave them his good spiritt to instruct them. Isaiah 63. and yet for all that, the body of them were hipocrites, and the Lord sware in his wrath, that they should never enter into his rest, what is the matter, they procure unto themselves things from God and the blessing of God; but they did not get the Lord himselfe, they had the Angell of Gods presence to go before them, but they had not the Lord Jesus Christ in them, they had the spiritt to instruct them, but they had not the spirit to dwell in them, they procure blessings to themselves from the Lord, but they never got the Lord of blesseings: therefore all those that turne unto these blessings in the first place, and do not first of all turne to the Lord, will never be made pertakers of the Lord.

2. The second sort that are to be condemned, are all such as do sett themselves against the Lord Jesus Christ, such are the greatest enimyes to the state that can be, if they can have there wills, you

shall see what a lamentable estate both the Church and comon wealth will be in, then we have neede of mourning, the Lord he cannot endure those that are enimyes to himselfe and people and unto the good of his Church, such shall never be able to prevaile against the Lord: What will be the end and issue do you thinke, if people do set them selves against the wayes of grace and the Lord Jesus Christ? this will be the issue of it, those that oppose the wayes of grace and resist the truth, they shall wax worse and worse. 2 Timothy 3. and they may happily proceede a great way, but the tyme will come that they shall go no further, and by reason of agitation of things it will come to passe, that the truth will be cleared and their folly will be manifested to all men, so saith the Apostle, it is hard to kicke against the pricks. Acts 9.5. whosoever striveth against the Lord cannot prosper; if men or women fall upon the Lord Jesus Christ they breake, but if the Lord Jesus Christ do fall upon them, he will breake them all to powder, if any fall upon Christ and they will not let Christ alone but fall upon them which hold him forth, and will abuse them, and be buffeting the Lord Jesus Christ, there is never a stroke they give, but maketh wounds in their consciences, but if they will be heaving out Christ, they shall find it the heaviest stone that ever was, it will fall and breake them all to powder; if people set themselves against the Lord, and the wayes of grace and his truth, this will be the issue of it on their part, either those that set themselves against the wayes of God, they will be put to silence by the light that cometh from Christ, that they will be so convinced, that they shall not be able to speake any more in their cause, as Christ put downe those that came against him, that they durst aske him no more questions, and there cometh such a power from the word held forth by the saynts of God, that it [will] strike a feare into their harts that oppose it. What aylest thou O Jordan that the floods go backe, tremble thou earth at the presence of the Lord, they that came to take Christ they fell backe, there cometh a divine power from the Lord and turneth them all backe, the Lord will strike with trembling those that come against Jerusalem, or if they be not put to silence, it will come to passe in tyme, they will fall into wonderfull strong passions and will quarrell with the saynts of God; it was the case of

Zedekiah and Michaih, the question was [which][8] of them had the spiritt of God, he came and smote the Prophet of God upon the cheeke, but Gods spirit is no smiting spirit: Steven convinced the Jewes, and did by the power of the Holy Ghost, evidence his cause to be the cause of God, and they were not able to resist the spirit by which he spake, and they all came and run upon him, Why do you resist the Holy Ghost? what maketh the sinne against the Holy Ghost, but inlightening, and setting themselves against the wayes of truth and persecuting it in malice and wrath: it is a feareful thing to fall into the hands of the living God. Hebrews 10.31. for our God is a consuming fire, Hebrews 12.29. let every one (in the feare of God) have a care, how they set themselves against the truth and wayes of God, and the wayes of Jesus Christ, for we must all apeare before the Judgment seat of Christ. 2 Corinthians 5. 10.

The last use shall be for consolation, (howsoever this be a day of humiliation yet the apprehension of Gods grace and mercy and goodnes, it worketh the kindliest humiliation, sinnes are to be considered and looked upon, but sinnes against the God of grace, may melt one: In that day I will power upon them the spiritt of grace, and they shall mourne, Zechariah 12. 10. Therefore the last use shall be for consolation,) and it may serve to comfort the children of God which do hold forth the Lord Jesus Christ and do disire that the Lord Jesus Christ may be received into Churches, into families, into the harts of the people of God. (Brethren) those that walke this way are the greatest freinds unto the Church and comon wealth, they intend and labor and indeavour to bring [in] the Lord Jesus Christ, and if Christ be present, there will be no cause of fasting and mourning: therefore let me (in the name of God) incourage all those that hold forth the wayes of grace, and do indeavour to make knowne the Lord Jesus Christ. (Brethren and Sisters) endeavour to bring Christ into the harts of people, and then you shall make the Church happie, and yourselves happy, lift up your heads O ye gates etc. Psalms 24.7. bring the Lord Jesus not only into thy house, but into thy chamber of him that did beget you, endeavor it, for this is Gods way, and it is

---

8. Whether: Massachusetts State Archives copy.

a way to bring peace and happines both to Church and Comon wealth.

Secondly, it may comfort the saynts of God in this respect, that seeing the Lord Jesus Christ his absence is the cause of fasting and mourning, this is a comfort to the children of God, that come what will come they shall be in a happy estate, they shall be blessed: suppose those that are Gods children should loose their houses and lands and wives and freinds, and loose the acting of the guifts of grace, and loose the ordinances, yet they can never loose the Lord Jesus Christ, this is a great comfort to Gods people: suppose the saynts of God should be banished and deprived of all the or- dinances of God, that were a hard case (in some respect) for we had better part with all, then the ordinances; but if the ordinances should be taken away, yet Christ cannot: for if John be banished into an Iland: Revelation 1.9. 10, and the spiritt come upon him on the Lords day, there is amends for the ordinances, amends for banishment, if we loose the ordinanses for God, he will be ordi- nances unto us: therefore let the saynts of God be incouraged though they should loose all they have, yet they being made one in Christ, and Christ dweling in their harts by faith, they may be persuaded nothing can seperate them from Christ: Romans 8.38.39. Therefore let the saynts of God rejoyce, that they have the Lord Jesus Christ, and their names written in the booke of life, be glad and rejoyce, for great is your reward in heaven.

CHAPTER 7

John Cotton, *A Conference . . . Held at Boston*

RECONCILIATION between Cotton and the other ministers became imperative once the Antinomian Controversy
threatened to destroy the colony. At the May, 1637 session of the
General Court, Thomas Shepard preached a sermon in which he
reduced the points at issue so greatly that "except men of good
understanding, and such as knew the bottom of the tenents of
those of the other party, few could see where the difference was;
and indeed it seemed so small, as . . . they might easily have come
to reconciliation." About the same time, Cotton also "stated
the differences in a very narrow scantling." Such gestures led Winthrop to believe that, "if men's affections had not been formerly
alienated," the quarrel could have been fully resolved. As it was
he could report that agreement had been reached on the issue of
sanctification.[1]

But further negotiations were necessary before the rest of the
issues were disposed of. Near the end of August, in "private meetings," the ministers persuaded Cotton and John Wilson to drop
the grievances each had against the other. At the synod that met
on August 30, the ministers agreed to condemn eighty-two errors.
Even so there remained "five points in question, between Mr.
Cotton and Mr. Wheelwright on the one part, and the rest of the
elders on the other part, which were after reduced to three, and
those after put into such expressions as Mr. Cotton and they
agreed, but Mr. Wheelwright did not."[2]

---

1. Winthrop, *History, 1,* 264.
2. Ibid., 282, 285–286. In his own review of the controversy, Cotton indicated that a final debate over five questions occurred *before* the synod began.
See p. 400.

In 1646 Cotton's answers to three questions were published in London as *A Conference Mr. John Cotton Held at Boston With the Elders of New-England.*[3] The same three questions recur on Winthrop's list of the "five points in question," and Cotton's answers clearly reflect a spirit of reconciliation. These facts suggest that Cotton's statements in *A Conference* are contemporaneous with the synod. But there are better reasons for dating them earlier. One is that Cotton does not yield his previous position unequivocally. Another is that this set of answers bears a direct relationship to the debate growing out of the *Sixteene Questions.* In *A Conference* Cotton twice refers to that debate and quotes again from the authorities he had previously cited. A further clue may be that in the copybook containing the emended version of the *Sixteene Questions* the text of *A Conference* follows immediately after Cotton's "Rejoynder." Finally, we know that Archbishop Laud received a copy of the answers on October 15, 1637, a date that leaves very little time for their transmission to England if they were written in early September.[4] It seems most likely, therefore, that the document grew out of the continuing discussions among the ministers between May and August.

The only printed version of *A Conference* presently available is the one published in London by an obscure English minister, Francis Cornwell.[5] Having somehow acquired a manuscript copy, Cornwell sent it to the press after giving up hope that "some learned and faithfull friends of his [Cotton] would . . . have

---

3. It was republished the same year as *Gospel Conversion.* The reason for the new edition was that the original contained a misbound signature (pages 36–48). *Gospel Conversion* is merely a correct binding of identical sheets.

4. The copy Laud received is calendered in *Calender of State Papers, Colonial Series, 1, 1574–1660,* ed. W. N. Sainsbury (London, 1860), 259; it is reproduced on Library of Congress Microfilm Ac. 10, 741, Reel 4. Along with Cotton's answers, Laud received a list of "3. Propositions which have devided Mr Hooker, and Mr Cotton in Newe England." The first two of these propositions correspond to questions 2 and 3 that Cotton answered. The third is, "Whither there be any saving preparation in a Christian soule before his unyon with Christ," to which is added the cryptic note: "This latter is only Hookers opinion, the rest of the Ministers do not concur with him: Cotton and the rest of the contrary opinion are against him and his party in all."

5. He may have been the Francis Cornwell who graduated A.B. at Cambridge in 1621/22.

* See new note p. xix.

Printed a larger, and an exacter Copy of it."[6] Fortunately an "exacter copy" can be reconstructed from two manuscript versions. One is the copy that Laud received, the other the copy at the Massachusetts Historical Society. As printed below, *A Conference* follows the 1646 edition, with material from the manuscripts added in brackets. Where the printed text is corrupt, rather than incomplete, changes have been made in the text itself on the authority of two other readings, and the original printed version appears in the footnotes. Apart from entire sentences, only those words and phrases that improve the sense of Cornwell's copy have been incorporated. Cornwell's preface has been omitted.

A Conference

A CONFERENCE that Mr. John Cotton had with the *Elders* of the Congregations in *New-England,* touching   [1] three Questions that are here discussed on:

[Upon Revisal of all that hath been written by our Brethren, only three things of weight are left controversal, if my hopes fail me not.]

1. *Touching gracious conditions, or qualifications, wrought in the soule before faith.*

2. *Touching the gathering of our first evident assurance of our faith from sanctification.*

3. *Touching the active power of faith, and other spirituall gifts of grace in a Christian conversation.*

[Touching the First; In the begining of your Reply to the 8th Question[7] you grant That God may and often doth work Faith of Dependance by absolute promises: which argueth your judgment to be, That sometimes God worketh Faith of Dependance by conditional promises. Then]

The first Question [is]

Quest. 1. *Whether there be any gracious conditions, or qualifications, in the soule before faith, of dependance unto which, such promises are made?*

---

6. *A Conference,* sig. (a) 3 verso.

7. Cotton here refers, as he does again later, to the "Reply" and "Rejoynder" growing out of the *Sixteene Questions.*

[You grant it.] Wee deny it, for these reasons.

Reas. 1. If there be any gracious conditions, or qualifications, wrought in us before faith of dependance;   [2]
then, before wee receive union with Christ: The reason
is,

For by faith of dependance it is, that wee first received union
with Jesus Christ, *Joh.* 1. 12.

But there be no gracious conditions wrought in us before wee
received union with Jesus Christ;

Therefore there bee no gracious conditions, or qualifications,
wrought in us before faith of dependance.

Minor.

If wee cannot bring forth good fruit, till wee be good trees; nor
become good trees, untill wee be grafted or united unto Jesus
Christ; then there can be no gracious conditions, or qualifications
wrought in us, before wee receive union with Christ.

But wee cannot bring forth good fruit, till wee become good trees; nor become trees of righteousnesse,   [3]
untill wee be grafted into Jesus Christ;

Therefore there bee no gracious conditions, or qualifications
wrought in us, before we received union with Jesus Christ.

The Proposition is cleare of it selfe [. The Assumption is as
clear], that wee cannot bring forth good fruit, untill we be good
trees: *Mat.* 7. 18. *A corrupt tree cannot bring forth good fruit.*
Nor can we become the good trees of righteousnesse, of the Lords
plantation, *Isai.* 61.3. untill wee be grafted into Christ. *Joh.* 15.4.
As the branch cannot beare fruit of it selfe, except it abide in the
vine, no more can yee, except yee abide in me. Verse 5. *I am the*
vine, yee are the branches; hee that abideth in me, and I in him,
the same bringeth forth much fruit: for without me ye can doe
nothing.

A second proofe of the Minor.

If there be any gracious conditions, or qualifications
wrought in us before union with Christ, then we may be   [4]
in a state of grace and salvation, before we be in Christ:
But that cannot be: *Acts* 4. 12. *Neither is there salvation in any*
other; for there is none other name under heaven given amongst
men, whereby wee may be saved.

Reas. 2. If there be any gracious condition or qualification in us before faith, then there may be something in us pleasing unto God before faith:

But there is nothing in us pleasing unto God before faith; [for without faith (and therefore before faith) it is impossible to please God] *Heb.* 11.6. *But without faith it is impossible for us to please him: for hee that cometh to God, must beleeve that hee is, and that hee is a rewarder of them that diligently seek him.*

Object. But there must be some saving preparatives wrought in the soule, to make way for faith, and our union with Christ. For wee must be cut off from the old *Adam,* before wee can be grafted into the new: Wee must be dead to the first [5] husband, before we can be married unto another.

Answ. 1. To works of creation there needeth no preparation; the almighty power of God calleth them to be his people, that were not his people, 1 *Pet.* 2.10. And by calling them to be so, hee maketh them to bee so. *Rom.* 9.25, 26. *As hee saith in* Hosea, *I will call them, My people, which were not my people; and her, Beloved, which was not beloved.* Verse 26. *And it shall come to passe that in the place where it is said unto them, Yee are not my people, there shall they be called, The children of the living God.*

2. While Satan, the strong man, keepeth the house, Christ the stronger cometh upon him, and bereaveth him of his armour, and divideth the spoyle, *Luke* 11.21, 22.

Wee are dead to our first husband the Law by the body of Christ, *Rom.* 7.4. and therefore it is by the vertue of Christs death we have fellowship with Christ; and that [6] giveth the deadly stroak unto our first husband.

The second Question.

Quest. 2. *Whether a man may evidence his justification by his sanctification?*

The state of the Question is thus unfolded. [It is granted of all hands.]

First, To take a mans sanctification, for an evident cause or ground of his justification, is flat Popery.

Secondly, To take a mans sanctification, for an evident cause or ground of that faith whereby hee is justified, is utterly unsafe;

for faith is built upon Jesus, the Christ, the head corner stone, *Ephes.* 2.20. *Mat.* 16.16. and not upon works: A good work floweth from faith not faith from them.

Thirdly, To take common sanctification, that is,   [7]
such a reformation and a change of life as floweth [only]
from a spirit of bondage, restraining from sin, and constraining unto duty, and sometimes accompanied with enlargement and comforts in duty; yet without the sense and feeling of the need of Christ, and before union with him, to take such a sanctification for an evident signe of justification, is to build upon a false and sandy foundation.

Fourthly, That when a man hath first attained assurance of faith, of his justification, by the witnesse of the Spirit of Christ, in a free promise of grace, made to him in the bloud of Christ, *Acts* 13.38, 39. hee may discern, and take his sanctification as a secondary witnesse, [f]or any evident signe or effect of his justification.

[Thus farr wee consent. There remaineth controverted this Question. Whether a man may gather his   [8]
first evidence or Assurance of faith of his Justification
from his Sanctification?[8]
You hold the Affirmative.] Wee hold in the Negative part.
The first Argument.

As *Abraham* came to the first assurance of his justification, so wee, and all that beleeve, as *Abraham* did; for hee is made a patterne to us in point of justification: *Rom.* 4.23. *Now it was not written for his sake alone, that it was imputed to him;* V. 24. *But for us also, to whom it shall be imputed, if we beleeve on him that raised up Jesus our Lord from the dead.* V. 25. *Who was delivered for our offences, and raised againe for our justification.*

But *Abraham* came to his first assurance of [Justification not from] his sanctification, not from any promise made thereunto, but from a free promise of grace; *Rom.* 4. 18. *Who against hope, beleeved in hope, that hee might become the father of many nations: according to that which was spoken, So shall thy seed be.*

---

8. "Whether a man may gather the first evidence or assurance of his faith, of his justification, by his sanctification?" Printed text.

V. 19. *And being not weak in faith, he considered not his own body now dead, when he was above an hundred yeares old; neither the deadnesse of* Sarahs *wombe.* Vers. 20. *He staggered not at the promise of God through unbeliefe, but was strong in faith, giving glory to God.* Vers. 21. *And being fully perswaded that what hee had promised hee was able to performe:* Vers. 22. *And therefore it was imputed unto him for righteousnesse.*   [9]

The promise was absolute, and free, So shall thy seed be as the stars of heaven: this hee beleeved with full assurance of faith, resting onely on the faithfulnesse and grace, and power of him that promised, *Rom.*21.

Therefore wee, and all the children of *Abraham,* come to our first assurance of our Justification, not from our Sanctification, or from any promise made thereunto; but from the free promise of grace.

The second Argument.

No man can take his assurance of faith[9] of the Justification: But as God will declare and pronounce him righteous in Christ Jesus.   [10]

But God will not declare, and pronounce us righteous in Christ, upon the sight and evidence of our sanctification.

Therefore we cannot take the assurance of faith of our Justification, from the sight and evidence of our sanctification.

[The Proposition is Evident.]

The Assumption is proved thus.

If [when] God justifieth us (that is) declareth, and pronounceth us to bee righteous, he doth then declare his owne righteousnesse, that he might be just; Then he doth not declare us to be righteous in Christ, upon the sight and evidence of our sanctification, which is a righteousnesse of our owne.

But when God justifieth us, that is, first declareth us, and pronounceth us to be righteous, he doth declare his owne righteousnesse; that he might be just.

----

9. Here, two sentences below, and on p. 14 the printed text reads, "of the faith."

Therefore he doth not first pronounce and declare   [11]
us righteous upon sight, and evidence of our sanctification, which is a righteousnesse of our owne.
                The proofe of the Proposition.
It will not stand with the righteousnesse of God to declare and
pronounce a man just, upon the sight of such an imperfect righteousnesse, as our best sanctification is: And therefore when God
declareth, and pronounceth us righteous; He doth it not upon
any sight of any sanctification, or righteousnesse of ours: But
onely upon the sight of the perfect righteousnesse of Christ imputed unto us.
                The proofe of the Assumption.
That when God justifieth us (that is, when he first declareth,
and pronounceth us to be righteous) he doth declare his own
righteousnesse, that he might be just, as *Paul* speaketh, *Rom.*3.26.
and the justifier of him, which beleeveth on Jesus.
And it is the speech of *David,* that when God declar-   [12]
eth himselfe to bee just; hee declareth onely the sinne-
fulnesse of the Creature, *Psal.*51.4.
                The third Argument.
If the promise be made sure of God unto faith out of grace;
Then it is not first made sure to faith out of works.
But the promise is made sure of God to faith out of grace,
*Rom.*4.5.[10] to him that worketh not, but beleeveth on him, that
justifieth the ungodly, his faith is accounted for righteousnesse.
Therefore the promise is not [first] made sure to faith out of
works.
                [Proofe of the Major.]
From the opposition of Grace, and Works, *Rom.*11.6. *And if
by grace then it is no more of workes; otherwise grace is no more
grace.*
Object. The opposition standeth not onely betweene grace
and workes, but betweene grace and the merits of works;
now no man ascribeth the assurance of faith in the   [13]
promise to the merits of works.

---

10. Both manuscripts specify Romans 4. 16, the text that fits with the
argument.

Answ. The opposition standeth not only betweene grace and the merits of works: but between grace and the debt due to workes; For so the Apostle *Paul* expresseth it, *Rom.4.4. Now to him that worketh is the reward not reckoned of grace, but of debt.*

If the assurance of faith of our justification, doe spring from sight of sanctification, it is by right of some promise made unto such a worke, and the right which a man hath by promise to a worke, maketh the assurance of the promise, but [due] debt unto him: and then the promise is not sure unto him out of grace.

The fourth Argument.

If when the Lord declareth himselfe pacified toward us, he utterly shames us, and confounds us, in the sight and sense of our unworthynesse, and unrighteousnesse; then he doth not give unto us our first assurance of the faith of our justifi-   [14] cation, upon the sight and sense of sanctification.

But when the Lord declareth himself pacified towards us, he doth utterly ashame us, and confound us, in the sight and sense of our unworthynesse, and unrighteousnesse.

Therefore he doth not first give us assurance of faith of our justification, upon the sight and sense of our sanctification.

The consequence is plaine from the Law of Contraries: For, if the Lord shame us with a sight and sense of sinne; hee doth not then, first comfort and incourage us, with the sight and sense of sanctification.

Minor is proved, *Ezek.16.63. Rom.4.5.*

Ezek.16.63. That thou maist remember and bee confounded, and never open thy mouth any more because of thy shame; when I am pacified toward thee, for all that thou hast done, saith the Lord God.

Rom.4.5. To him that worketh not, but beleeveth on   [15] *him that justifieth the ungodly, his faith is accounted for righteousnesse.*

The fifth Argument.

When sanctification is not evident, it cannot be an evidence of justification.

But when Justification is hidden, and doubtfull, Sanctification is not evident.

Therefore Sanctification cannot be our first evidence of Justification.

Minor.

When Faith is hidden and doubtfull, Sanctification is not evident:

But when Justification is hidden and doubtfull, Faith is hidden and doubtfull.

Therefore when Justification is hidden and doubtfull, Sanctification is not evident.

The first proofe of the Major.

If *Faith be the evidence of things not seene,* then
when Faith it selfe is hidden and doubtfull, which mak-   [16]
eth all things evident, what can be cleare unto us.

But *Faith is the evidence of things not seene, Hebr.*11.1.

Therefore when Faith it selfe is hidden and doubtfull, Sanctification cannot be evident.

The second proofe of the Major.

If no Sanctification be true and sincere, but when it is wrought in faith: then neither can it be evident [but]¹¹ when it evidently appeareth to bee wrought in Faith: Therefore when Faith is hidden, and doubtfull, Sanctification cannot be evident.

But no Sanctification is pure and sincere, but when it is wrought in Faith: nor [can it]¹² be evident, but when it evidently appeareth to bee wrought in Faith.

Therefore when Faith is hidden and doubtfull, Sanctification cannot be evident.

The sixth Argument.

Such a Faith as a practicall Sillogisme can make, is
not a Faith wrought by the Lords Almighty power: For   [17]
though *Sillogismus fidem facit;* yet such a faith is but
an humane faith; because the Conclusion followeth but from the strength of reasonings, or reason; not from the power of God, by which alone Divine things are wrought, *Ephes.*1.19.20. *Col.*2.12.

But the Faith which is wrought by a word, and a worke, and the light of a renewed Conscience without the witnesse of the spirit; and before it, is such a Faith as a practicall Sillogisme can make.

---

11. The printed text reads "evident. But."
12. Cannot: printed text.

Therefore such a Faith as is wrought by a word, and a worke, or by the light of a renewed Conscience, without the witnesse of the Spirit, and before it; is not a Faith wrought by the Lords Almighty power.

The proofe of the Minor.

From the condition of all these three; the Word, the Work, and the light of a renewed Conscience; they are [18] all but created blessings, and gifts [and] therefore[13] cannot produce of themselves a work of Almighty power. Because the Word without the Almighty power of the Spirit is but a dead Letter; and the Work hath no more power then the Word; nor so much neither. For Faith cometh rather by hearing of a Word, then by seeing of a Worke, *Rom.*10.17. And the light of a renewed Conscience, is [but] a created gift of spirituall knowledge in the conscience.

[Objections against the Truth removed.]

*Object.*1. 1 *John* 2.3. *Hereby we know that wee know him, that we keepe his Commandements.* 1 *John* 3.14. *Wee know wee have passed from death to life, because we love the Brethren.* *Vers.*19. *Hereby we know we are of the truth.*

Answ. 1. No better Answer need to be expected then what *Calvin* hath given in the exposition of these Scriptures; who thus expoundeth them.

'Though every beleever hath the testimony of his Faith from his Workes, yet that commeth in, *a posteriori* [19] *probatione,* a latter, or, secondary proofe, instead of a signe. Therefore the assurance of Faith (saith hee) doth wholly reside in the grace of Christ; and we must alwaies, saith he, remember, that it is not from our love to the Brethren, that we have the knowledge of our estate, which the Apostle speaketh of, as if from thence were fetched the assurance of salvation. For surely wee doe not know by any other meanes, that we are the Children of God: but because hee sealeth unto our heart by his Spirit, [his] adoption of us out of free-grace: and we by faith receive the assured pledge of him, given in [Christ, and love therefore is] an

---

13. In the printed text the sentence ends with "gifts," and "therefore" begins a new sentence.

addition, or inferiour helpe, for a prop unto faith, not for a foundation to leane on.'[14]

*Answ.*2. Certaine it is, that those which *John* writ unto, were three sorts of men: *Old men, Young men, and Babes:* Yet there was none of them but did know their good   [20] estate, by the knowledge of the Father; before they knew their good estat by their brotherly love: For even of Babes (he saith) *they knew the Father*, 1 *Joh.*2.13. And therefore by the rule of relation, they knew their Son-ship and adoption: And if it should bee asked, how they knew it; *John* telleth, *By the unction they had received from Christ*, 1 *Joh.* 2. [20.] 27. that is, *by the spirit it selfe, which taught them to know all things;* which no created gifts of Sanctification could doe. Even in nature, children doe not first come to know their parents, either by their love to their brethren, or by their obedience to their parents; but from their parents love descending on them: *So we loved him, because he first loved us*, 1 *John* 4.19. *Herein is love, not that we loved God, but that he loved us, and sent his Son to bee a propitiation for our sins*, 1 *Joh.*4.10.

Object. If *John* [should][15] give sanctification for an evidence of adoption, to such as knew their good estate   [21] before by the witnesse of the Spirit; this were but to light a Candle unto the Sunne?

Answ. 1. Whether were it more absurd to light a Candle unto the Sunne, or to light a Candle to [seek][16] a mans eyes; Now faith is instead of eyes unto the soule: *By Faith Abraham saw the day of Christ, and rejoyced, though it were a farre off, Joh.* 8.56.

Answ. 2. The same Apostle saith, that there bee six witnesses that give light and evidence unto our spirituall life in Christ: of which three be in heaven, and three on the earth; and the Spirit in both: yet he did not thinke it a vaine thing to give the water of [Sanctification],[17] (as out of the death and resurrection of Christ we receive the power *to walk in newnesse of life, Rom.* 6.3.4.) as a witnesse after foure of the greater lights.

---

14. The printed text reads, "our" and "Christs love. Therefore as." See note 13, p. 106.
15. Could: printed text.
16. See to: printed text.
17. Baptism: printed text.

Answ. 3. If you take Sanctification for a created gift [(as it is distinguished from the witness of the Spirit itself)] it is indeed but a Candle to the Sunne. But when *John* maketh it, but [a witnesse] to confirme faith, he meaneth then, the [22] Spirit of God beareth witnesse in it: or else the testimony of sanctification, though it be a divine gift or work, yet it would not give a divine testimony, nor increase divine faith; for the heavens and earth are divine and supernaturall works, yet they doe not give [a] divine testimony of the Godhead, [nor can beget divine faith of the Godhead] unlesse the Spirit of God himselfe doe beare witnesse in them.

Therefore John[s] giving sanctification for an evidence of a good estate, to such as already knew it, by the witnesse of the Spirit, is not a lighting of a candle to the Sunne; but as the setting up of another window, though a lesser, to convay the same Sun light into the house[18] another way.

Object. 2. In 2 *Pet. chap.* 1. from *verse* 5. to 10. the Apostle exhorteth us, by adding one gift of sanctification to another, to *make our calling and election sure.*

Answ. Let *Calvin* answer for me: This assurance [23] (saith he) whereof *Peter* speaketh, by adding grace to grace, is not in my judgement to be referred unto conscience, as if the faithfull did thereby before God [come to] know themselves called, and chosen; but if any man will understand [it by making][19] it sure before men, there will be no absurdity in this sense: Neverthelesse it might be extended further, that every one may be confirmed in their calling, by their godly and holy life. But that is a proofe, not from the cause; but from a signe, and effect.[20] [I say noe more of this text, because you have it further Cleered in the answer to your Reply.]

Object. 3. There be many conditionall promises in the Gospel, which are made to the gifts and duties of sanctification; which are all in vaine, if poore drooping soules, finding such gifts, and du-

---

18. "Soul" in Massachusetts Historical Society copy.

19. It, of making of: printed text.

20. John Calvin, *Commentarius in Petri Apostoli Epistolam Posteriorem,* in *Opera Quae Supersunt Omnia* (Brunswick, 1896), 55, cols. 447–450. Calvin is cited again on this passage, p. 406.

ties of sanctification in themselves, may not take comfort from them, according to the promise.

Answ. 1. The conditionall promises are made to poore drooping soules, not in respect of such conditions,   [24] or as they are qualified with such gifts and duties of sanc- tification; but in respect of their union with Christ, to whom the promises belong, *Gal.*3.26, 28, 29. The fruits of such an union with Christ, such duties and gifts of sanctification be, when they be sincere: otherwise, if the promises were made to such soules, in respect of such conditions, then the reward promised would be- long unto them, not of grace, but of debt, *Rom.*4.4. A promise made to any condition, after it be made, it becometh due debt to him, in whomsoever such condition is to be found: But therefore that such promises might be of grace, they are made to us, not as wee are indued with such and such conditions; but as wee who have such and such conditions are united unto Christ. Whence it is, that such blessings offered in such promises, as they are ten- dered to us in Christ, so are they fulfilled to us in Christ.

Whereupon, we look for the blessing, not in our gifts   [25] and duties; but in going still unto Christ, for a clearer and fuller manifestation of him to us, and of comfort in him. As for example, A thirsty soule, to whom promise is made that hee shall be satisfied; hee looketh not presently to be satisfied from his thirsting, nor from any right his thirsting might give him in the promise; but hee looketh to be satisfied by going unto Christ, in drinking more abundantly of him by his Spirit, as Christ himself directeth such drooping soules to doe: and so we are to make use of such kind of promises; *Joh.* 7.37, 38, 39.

Answ. 2. No man can see his gifts and duties of sanctification in himselfe, but hee must first have seen Christ by faith, the Spirit of Christ enlightening his understanding in the knowledge of him. As in case of mourning, to which many promises are made, No man can (with Evangelicall repentance)   [26] mourne over Christ, and for [him], untill the Spirit [working] faith, and by faith beholding Christ, hee hath seen him crucified [by him and for him][21] *Zech.*12.10. So then these condi-

---

21. The printed text reads, "himselfe . . . work . . . crucified, and by him."

tions, and the promises made to them, doe not give us our first
sight of Christ, nor the first glympse of light and comfort from
him; but rather our sight of Christ, and some glympses of light
and comfort from him, doth beget such conditions in us.

Answ. 3. Such conditionall promises are not in vain, though
poore drooping soules have found [some comfort before][22] them,
and though they cannot suck present comfort from them, and
from their good conditions accordingly to them.

Reas. 1. Because these promises being [dispensed][23] in a Covenant of free-grace made in Christ, by them doe work (if they were
not wrought before) or at least confirme such conditions
in the soule. As when God promised them to send a Re-   [27]
deemer out of Sion, *unto them which turne from trans-*
gression in Jacob, Isai. 59.20. the Apostle expoundeth it, *That*
Christ shall come out of Sion, and shall turne away transgression
from Jacob: which is as much as if hee should say, He shall work
that condition which the promise was made unto. And this the
Apostle maketh to be the meaning, and the blessing of the promise, according to the Covenant of grace, *Rom.*11.26, 27.

*Reas.*2. The promises are not in vain to such soules, in whom
such good conditions are wrought; because they direct them
where they may find comfort, and satisfying to their hearts desire:
to wit, not by clearing their good conditions in themselves; but by
coming unto Christ, and drinking a more full draught of his
Spirit; as Christ directeth thirsty soules to doe, [in the place even
now alledged] *Joh.* 7.37. *If any man thirst, let him come*
to me, and drink. V. 38. *Hee that beleeveth on me, (as*   [28]
the Scripture saith) out of his belly shall flow rivers of
living water. V. 39. *But this hee spake of the Spirit, that they*
which beleeve on him, shall receive.

Object. But why may not the holy Spirit breathe his first comforts into our soules, even on such conditions? Is not this to limit
the Spirit, who is [most] free, *and bloweth where hee listeth?*
Joh.3.8.

Answ. He doth not breathe his first comforts in such conditions, because he listeth not: it is not his good pleasure to give us

___

22. No comfort by: printed text.
23. Discerned: printed text.

our first comfort (which is the comfort of our Justification) from our owne righteousnesse, before hee give us comfort in the right-eousnesse of Christ. The holy Spirit in all his dispensations to us ward, delighteth to receive all [first] from Christ, rather then from us; that so hee might glorifie Christ in us. *The Comforter whom I shall send to you, hee shall glorifie me; for hee shall re-ceive of mine, and shew it unto you*, Joh. 16.14. Nor will   [29] he so much dishonour the righteousnesse and grace of the Father of glory, as first to pronounce and declare us justified in the sight of our owne righteousnesse.

Object. 4. In *Mat*.7. from *verse* 16. to 20. The tree is knowne by his fruit.

Answ. True, to others; but not unto himselfe. If a tree could know it selfe, it would first come to know it selfe, by seeing upon what root it grew, before it came to see what fruit it did beare; *Job.* 15. 1,2,3,4,5.

Object. 5. But this Doctrine is new, it is not ancient, nor gray-headed.

Answ. The Doctrines of the Covenant of free-grace are ever new; because they are the Doctrines of the New-Covenant, which can never waxe old: should it once waxe old, it would soone van-ish away, *Heb.* 8. from *vers.* 8. to 13. though it be as ancient as *Abraham*, yea, as *Adam;* for hee had his first comfort and assurance, in an absolute promise of free-grace,   [30] *Gen.*3.15. yet it hath ever seemed new in every age.

Augustines Doctrine of Conversion, that is of grace, and not of free-will.

Luthers Doctrine of Justification, that is of [grace],[24] not of works.

Calvins Doctrine of Predestination, that is of grace, not of faith and works fore-seen: were all of them thought new Doc-trines in their times; and yet all of them the ancient truths of the everlasting Covenant of grace.

And surely, for this Doctrine in hand, *Calvin* is as clear, as my hearts desire to God is wee all might be; his words have been partly rehearsed before, in the answer of some Objections; and partly in my large Answer to your Reply.

---

24. Faith: printed text.

Bellarmine taketh it to be the generall Doctrine of the *Lu-therans*, That, Assurance of faith goeth before works, and doth not follow after, *Institut. lib.3. cap. 9.* And   [31] *Pareus* in answer unto him, saith, That though there be an assurance that followeth good works, yet the former assurance from the witnesse of the Spirit goeth before.[25]

And seeing they that are the chief Reformers of the Protestant Assemblies, doe generally make sanctification a fruit of faith, and doe define faith to be, A [assurance of speciall mercy][26] in Christ; it must needs be out of controversie their judgement, That a man receiveth his first assurance, not from his sanctification, which they make to be an effect flowing from it; but from an higher principle, even from the grace of the Father, and the righteousnesse of the Sonne, the Lord Jesus Christ; and witnessed by the holy Spirit.

Bilney, in the Book of Martyrs, in his Epistle to B. *Tunstall*, relating the manner of his conversion, protested, That when hee had wearied himself in many superstitious   [32] works of fasting, and Popish pennance, hee received at last his first assurance, from that place in *Timothy*, 1 *Tim.*1.15. hee calleth it a most sweet word unto him, *This is a true saying, and worthy of all men to be received, Jesus Christ came into the world to save sinners, of whom I am the chiefe.* A word from an absolute promise, set home unto him by the holy Spirit, without respect of any sanctification formerly wrought or seene in him.

Alas, how farre are they mistaken, that thinke the contrary Doctrine hath beene sealed with the bloud of Martyrs?

Zancheus his judgement, though he was a godly and an eminent learned man, yet I would not have named him, but that Mr. *Perkins* highly approved his discourse, and translated it, as a choyce piece, into his owne Volume, which maketh it obvious to every godly Reader, that studieth *Perkins*   [33] learned Workes; Page 429.[27] the first testimony, saith

---

25. Pareus, *Roberti Bellarmini . . . De justificatione,* the same passage as cited on p. 93.

26. Special assurance of mercy: printed text.

27. Girolamo Zanchy (1516–1590), a Reformed theologian; Cotton cites *A Briefe Discourse Taken Out of the Writings of H. Zanchivs,* in Perkins, *The Workes of That Famous and Worthy Minister of Christ in the Vniuersitye of Cambridge, Mr. William Perkins* ([London], 1612), *1,* 429–438.

Zanchey [and Perkins from him][28] by which God assureth us of
our election, is that inward testimony of the Spirit, of which the
Apostle *Paul* speaketh, *Rom.* 8.16. *The Spirit witnesseth to our
spirits, that wee are the sonnes of God;* And afterward comming
to give some direction how a man may know, whether this testimony be true, and proceedeth from the holy Spirit, or no.

Hee answereth, *Page* 433. three waies.

1. First, A man may know it, first, by the perswasion it selfe.
2. Secondly, By the manner of its perswasion.
3. Thirdly, By the effects.
1. For the first, the holy Spirit doth not simply say it, but doth perswade with us; that we are the sonnes of God: And no flesh can doe
it.
2. [Again][29] By reasons drawne not from our worke, or   [34]
from any worthinesse in us; but from the alone goodnesse
of God the Father, and the grace of Christ freely bestowed, and in
this manner the Devill will never perswade any man.
3. The perswasion of the holy Spirit is full of power; for they
which are perswaded that they are the sons of God, cannot, but
must needs call him Father, and in regard of love to him do hate
sinne; and on the contrary, they have a sound hearty desire to do
his Word and Will revealed.

Answ. 2. For the second Answer to the imputation of Novelty;
'Either (saith *John Cotton*) I am exceedingly deceived, or it justly
falleth upon the contrary Doctrine, and they are much mistaken
that think otherwise; I never read it to my best remembrance, in
any Author olde or new: that ever a man received his first evidence of the faith of his Justification, from his Sanctification; unlesse it be one, (whom I met within these two   [35]
dayes) Printed within these two yeares, that maintaineth
our first comfort of Justification from Sanctification. But generally all our English Orthodox Teachers doe oppose it.'

Amongst the English Teachers none, for ought I know, did
more advance the Doctrine of Marks and Signes, then Master

---

28. The printed text reads, "Porcius, for him."
29. Misplaced in the printed text at the end of the preceding sentence.

Nicholas Byfield,[30] and yet he himselfe professeth, that humane reason cannot beleeve such great things from God, [for] any thing that is in us: But onely because we [see][31] the Word of God assuring such happinesse unto such as lay hold upon the promises contained in it. So that which[32] breedeth Faith, or as he calleth it, the perswasion of our good estates, [is the revelation of Gods promises by his word and Spirit:] Yet notwithstanding, saith he, the assurance of Faith is much increased, and confirmed by Signes; the former part of which speech, touching the first be-gettings of the assurance of Faith, consenteth with me;   [36] the latter, concerning the increasing and confirming of the assurance, argueth plainely his consent, thus farre also, that he meant not that the assurance of the Faith of Justification should spring from Sanctification: But when he would have the assurance of Faith to bee increased and confirmed by the [sight][33] of Signes, I would not refuse it; If by the assurance of Faith, hee meanes onely assurance of Knowledge; or if he meaneth onely assurance of Faith, properly so called, I would then put in this caution.

That then the Spirit of God himselfe had need, by his owne testimony, to reveale our [sanctification] unto us, and Gods free grace in accepting [it][34] in Christ: or else it is not Word, nor Worke, nor the light of a renewed conscience, that can increase, or confirme, the assurance of Faith of our Justification: But only the manifestation of Gods Free-grace, in a Di-   [37] vine testimony, satisfied by his owne good Spirit.

[I come now to the Third and last Controversie, if indeed it be a Controversie, and not some mistake, as I would gladly hope it is.

If our Brethren do conceive that gifts of Sanctification though they be living and active, yet they are not active of themselves to

---

30. Nicholas Byfield (1579–1622), an English minister; Cotton bases his statement on Byfield, *The Signes, or, An Essay Concerning the Assurance of Gods love and mans salvation* (London, 1637).
31. The printed text reads, "from ... having."
32. The printed text has "it is that" following "so that."
33. Light: printed text.
34. The printed text reads, "justification ... us."

any spiritual holy duty acceptable to God but as faith is active in them: and if they conceive that Faith though it be living, yet is not active to go out of itself to Christ, but as it is stirred up and helped of Christ by his Spirit then there is no controversie left in this case.

In hope that your judgment is no otherwise I will not proceed to further needless disputation about it, till I hear further. Only because in this part concerning the activeness of faith, this controversie remaineth;]

The third Question is concerning the activenesse of Faith:

THE Controversie is

Quest. 3. Whether Faith concurre as an active instrumentall cause to our Justification?

In the explicating of it, I must first speake what it is that [satisfieth][35] mee.

1. First, we doe beleeve, that in our effectuall calling, *God draweth us to union with Christ, Joh. 6. 44. Shedding abroad his Spirit in our hearts, Rom.5. 5.* And *working Faith in us to receive Christ, Joh.* 1.12.13. And *to live by Faith upon him, Gal.2.20.*

2. Secondly, we are no sooner alive in *Christ,* but we are accounted of God as his *adopted children in Christ, Gal.*
3. 26. *Ephes.* 1.5. *and so are made heires of righteous-*   [38]
nesse, Galat. 3. 29. *God imputing the righteousnesse of his Sonne Jesus to us for our justification, Rom.* 4.23.24.25.

As we were no sooner alive in the first *Adam,* but we became his children, and heires of his transgression; God imputing the guilt of it to our condemnation.

Now in this we all consent; that in receiving the gift of Faith we are meerely passive.

But yet a double Question heere ariseth.

Quest. 1. Whether in receiving of *Christ* (or the Spirit, who commeth into our hearts in his name) we be meerly passive?

Quest. 2. Whether our Faith bee active to lay hold upon the righteousnesse of Christ, before the Lord doe first impute the righteousnesse of Christ unto us.

-----

35. Justifieth: printed text.

[For the 1st. We beleeve That as in receiving the gift of faith we are passive, so in receiving Christ or the Spirit of Christ we be passive also.]

Our Reasons are.

Reas. 1. If it be the spirit of Grace shed abroad in our hearts, that doth beget Faith in us: then if wee were [39] Passive in receiving Faith, wee are much more passive in receiving Christ, or the Spirit of Christ, that begetteth Faith: for if we have no life to be Active untill Faith come; we have much lesse life to be Active before the Cause, and root of Faith come.

But it is the spirit of Grace, shed abroad in our hearts, that begetteth Faith in us, *Zech.* 12. 10.

Therefore if we be Passive in receiving Faith; we are much more Passive, in receiving the spirit that begetteth Faith.

Reas. 2. If we bee active in laying hold on Christ, before he hath given us his Spirit: then we apprehend him, before he apprehend us: then wee should doe a good act, and so bring forth good fruites, before wee become good trees; yea, and bee good trees before we be in Christ.

But these are all contrary to the Gospell, *Philip.* 3. [40] 12.13. *Matth.* 7. 18. *John* 15.4.5.

Therefore wee bee not active in laying hold on Christ, before hee hath given us his Spirit.

Quest. 2. Whether our Faith bee active to lay hold upon Christ for his righteousnesse, before the Lord do first impute the righteousnesse of Christ to us; we conceive no.

For these Reasons.

Reason 1. If the sinne of *Adam* were imputed unto us for our condemnation, assoone as we were alive by naturall life before we had done any act of life, good or evill: then the righteousnesse of Jesus Christ is imputed unto us to our Justification, as soon as we be alive unto God by Faith, before wee have done any act of Faith.

But the former is plaine, *Rom.* 5. 18. 19.

Therefore the latter also.

Reas. 2. If our Faith be first active, to lay hold upon Christ for his righteousnesse, before God imputeth it [41] unto us; Then wee take Christs righteousnesse to our selves, before it bee given unto us.

But that wee cannot doe, for in the order of nature, giving is the cause of taking; unlesse wee take a thing by stealth.

Reas. 3. If our Faith be first active in laying hold on Christ for his righteousnesse, before God impute it unto us; then we doe justifie God, before he doth justifie us.

For hee [that] receiveth the testimony which God hath given of his Son: that God hath given us life in his Sonne, he hath set to his seale *that God is true, John* 3. 33. And so he which justifieth God, as others that doe not receive the testimony, condemne God of lying, 1 *Joh.* 5. 10.

But we cannot Justifie God before he justifie us; no more then we can love him *before hee first loved us,* 1 *Joh.* 4. 19.

Reas. 4. If our Faith be first active to lay hold on *Christ* for his righteousnes, before God impute his right-   [42] eousnes unto us: Then wee are righteous [in an act and work of][36] our own righteousnesse, before we be righteous, by the imputed righteousnes of *Christ.*

But we be to our best acts and workes of righteousnesse, unrighteous, till our sinnes bee pardoned, which is not untill the righteousnesse of *Christ* be imputed to us.

Reason 5. In the order of nature, the object is before the act that is conversant about it: [but the imputation of Christs righteousness is the object of faith: and] Therefore it is in the order of nature, before the act of our Faith.

Object. 1. To beleeve on the name of Christ is an act of Faith; To beleeve on the name of *Christ,* is to receive *Christ, John* 1. 12.

Therefore the receiving of *Christ* is by an act of Faith.

Answ. The place in *John,* upon which the weight of this Argument lieth, saith no more, but that they which received *Christ* in the second *Aorist* in the time past, doe beleeve   [43] on his name in the time present. Which we willingly grant; that they who receive *Christ,* their faith becommeth active through him to beleeve in his name. [But this we deny, that they did first beleeve on his name] that so they might receive him, and his righteousnesse.

---

36. The printed text reads, "righteous men to act, and work out our."

Object. 2. We are justified by Faith, Rom. 3.28. [Therefore faith is an active cause of our Justification.]

Answ. When we are said to bee justified by Faith; It is [not meant by the work of faith, but] by the [object of faith which is the] righteousnesse of *Christ* imputed unto us.

Object. 3. Abrahams To credere, his act of beleeving, *was imputed unto him for righteousnesse,* Rom. 4. 3.

Answ. It is taken generally amongst the Learned, for a singular opinion of Master *Wotton,*[37] that *To credere,* the act of beleeving should be imputed for righteousnesse.

For, indeed, the act of beleeving is neither a righteousnesse according unto the Law; For *the Law is perfect,* Psal. 19.7. Nor a righteousnesse according unto the Gospell; For the act of beleeving is an act of our owne, though given of grace: [44] But the righteousnesse of the Gospell is not an act of our own. And therefore *Paul desireth that he may be found in Christ, not having his owne righteousnesse which is of the Law, but that which is through the Faith of Christ, the righteousnesse which is of God by faith,* Phil. 3.9. to wit, *the righteousnesse of Christ imputed.*

Object. 4. But this Doctrine is opposite unto the streame of all the Learned; a passive Faith is not heard of amongst men, and they doe generally make Faith an instrumentall cause of [our][38] Justification.

Answ. A passive Faith is rarely hard of out of my mouth, but yet the thing meant by it, is [neither][39] rare in the writings of the learned, nor sometimes the word passive Faith.

Two things are meant by the [word. Faith][40] may be said to be passive in our Justification, in a double respect.

1. Because a habite of Faith may be called passive, be-   [45] fore it putteth forth any act, and we are justified assoone as by an habit of faith we are alive in *Christ;* in the first moment of our conversion, before Faith hath put forth any act: [as chil-

_____

37. Anthony Wotton (1561–1626), a Puritan theologian who was accused of Socinianism.

38. Their: printed text.

39. Never: printed text.

40. Word of Faith, and: printed text.

dren also are justified by the habit of faith; and] as we were all guilty of *Adams* sinne, before we were active to reach forth any consent unto it.

2. Faith may be said to bee passive in our justification, because it doth not lay hold on *Christ,* to fetch Justification from him, till *Christ* have first laid hold on us, and imputed his righteousnesse to us; and declared it unto us by his Spirit, in a free promise of Grace: And then Faith becommeth active, actually to receive *Christs righteousnesse;* and actually to beleeve on it, either by way of dependance, or assurance.

For the truth is, seeing wee are not justified [by faith], neither as it is a gift in us; nor as it is an acting and working from us; but in regard of his object, the righteousnesse of   [46] *Christ* which it receiveth.

Therefore which way soever Faith may receive *Christ* first or last, by the same way we may be justified by it.

Now Faith of it selfe, even the habit of Faith is an emptying grace, and so is as an empty vessell, fit to receive *Christ* and his righteousnes.

And both the act of Faith, whether of dependance on *Christ,* or of our assurance in *Christ,* carrieth us out of our selves unto him, and so maketh us fit to receive *Christ,* and his righteousnesse.

Thus I have explained what I meane by a passive Faith.

Let me shew you, that neither the Word, nor the [meaning] of it, is [uncouth to][41] our best learned men of eminent worth for parts and abilities.

Calvine in his Institutions, *Lib.*3. *cap.*[1]3. *Sec.* 5. *Quoad Justificationem* [*res est mene passiva fides, nihil affereus nostrum ad conciliandam Dei gratiam, sed a Christo accipieus quod nobis deest*].[42]

Ursinus in his Catechisme, *Quest.* 60, *Sect.* 5. *Potius*   [47] *Deum primum.*[43]

---

41. Nor the naming of it, is an untruth from: printed text.

42. "For, as regards justification, faith is something merely passive, bringing nothing of ours to the recovering of God's favor but receiving from Christ that which we lack." *Institutes,* trans. Battles, III.xiii.5.

43. Zacharias Ursinus (1534–1583), a Reformed theologian; Cotton cites *The Summe of Christian Religion . . . Lectures upon the Catechism Authorised by . . . Prince Frederick* (Oxford, 1587).

Chemierius de fide, lib. 13. Chap. 6 Verissimum esse [*dico fidem justificantem si non tempore saltem ratione sequi Justificationem: Et mox, Fidem esse causam Justificationis nego, tunc enim Justificatio non esset gratuita, sed ex nobis* etc.][44]

Doctor *Amesius in Medullam Theologie, lib.1. Cap.26. Recepti Christi* [*respectu hominis est vel passiva vel activa Philippians* 3.12. *Apprehendam, Apprehensus sui* (that I may apprehend I was apprehended) *Passiva receptio Christi est qua Spirituale principium gratiae ingeneratur nominis voluntati Ephesians* 2.5. *Vivificavit,* he hath quickened us. Since][45] he acknowledge a passive receiving of Christ, he must acknowledge a passive Faith: for there is no receiving of Christ, but by Faith.

In a Booke of choice *English Sermons,* [called the Saints Cordialls][46] that goeth under the name of Doctor *Sybbs,* and our Brother *Hooker,* and master *Davenport,* there [is] one stiled the Witnesse of Salvation, on *Rom.* 8.15. 16. where in *Page* 185. are these words: *In Justification, Faith is a sufferer onely; But in Sanctification, it worketh, and purgeth the whole man.*

[That some of][47] our Learned men that doe generally make Faith an instrumentall cause of their Justification. I confesse it is true; But I doe not understand them (as *Chemerius* doth in the like case) to meane no other kinde of cause; then [48] *Causa sine qua non,* or, *Causa removens,* or *prohibens.* For Faith keepeth the Soule empty of confidence in it selfe, and maketh a way for the receiving of the righteousnesse of Christ.

---

44. Daniel Chamier (1565–1621), a Reformed theologian; the reference is to *Panstratiae Catholicae* (Geneva, 1626), *3,* 960. "I say it is most true that faith is justifying when it follows justification, if not in time, at least in reason. And moreover, I deny faith to be the cause of justification when justification is not free but rather from ourselves."

45. Cotton cites the same passage from Ames in his answer to Bulkeley. As translated in *The Marrow of Sacred Divinity,* the quotation reads, "Receiving in respect of man is either passive, or active," and "Passive receiving of Christ is that whereby a spirituall principle of grace is begotten in the will of man." The printed text inserts a reference to "Paul Baynes on the Ephesians" before Ephesians 2, but the Latin edition of *The Marrow* makes it clear that the Scriptural reference is from Ames.

46. *The Saints Cordialls; Delivered in Sundry Sermons at Graies-Inne, and in the Citie of London* (London, 1629). This is primarily a collection of the sermons of Richard Sibbes (1577–1635).

47. As for: printed text.

* See new note p. xix.

Even as the poore Widdowes empty vessells made a way for the [running][48] of the oyle out of the Cruse; whereas the fulnesse of the Vessell caused the stay.

The good Lord empty us more and more of our selves, that we may be filled with him, *Out of whose fulnesse wee receive grace for grace,* John 1. 16.

Gloria sit soli Deo.

---

48. Receiving: printed text.

CHAPTER 8

John Winthrop, *A Short Story of the Rise,*
reign, and ruine of the Antinomians,
Familists & Libertines

A *Short Story of the Rise, reign, and ruine of the Antinomians, Familists & Libertines, that infected the Churches of New-England* is the official history of the Antinomian Controversy, written (for the most part) by the man who was not only "an eye and eare-wittnesse of the carriage of matters," as the title page declared, but also chiefly responsible for the "ruin" of the Antinomians. John Winthrop had ample opportunity to observe Mrs. Hutchinson at close range (her house in Boston was across the street from his) and disliked what he saw from the start.[1] The feeling was reciprocated. During the "reign" of the Antinomians in the Boston Church, the members came close to censuring Winthrop for his attack upon John Wheelwright. But Winthrop could conclude the *Short Story* with the remark that the "Justice of God" had prevailed, since in the end it was Mrs. Hutchinson who fell "under that censure, which (not long before) she had endeavoured and expected to have brought upon some other, who opposed her proceedings."

The *Short Story* is essentially a collection of documents: the "Catalogue of . . . erroneous opinions" drawn up by the synod of 1637; the "Remonstrance or Petition" presented to the General Court in March, 1637 by John Wheelwright's supporters; an ac-

---

1. For Winthrop's role in the Controversy see Edmund S. Morgan, *The Puritan Dilemma, The Story of John Winthrop* (Boston, 1958).

count of the proceedings of the Court against them, and of Mrs. Hutchinson's examination before the Court; a description of a foetus miscarried by Mary Dyer, one of the Antinomians; a justification of the Court's censure of Wheelwright; and finally, a summary of Mrs. Hutchinson's trial before the Boston Church. Though Winthrop's name does not appear upon the title page, all but the first two of these documents are clearly of his authorship.[2] His commentary upon them was so cursory, and the documents themselves were arranged in such a discontinuous way, that Thomas Weld, who was in England acting as an agent for Massachusetts[3] when the first edition of the *Short Story* appeared in 1644, determined to add a preface "laying downe the order and sense of this story." Weld's preface and a new title[4] were the only differences between the first and second editions. The two books seem, in fact, to be composed of identical sheets. A third edition, reset, was published in 1644, and a fourth in 1692.

The circumstances of the book's transmission to England remain a mystery. Like other documents in this collection, it was published because of its relevance to the ongoing controversies in England about church government and the nature of the spiritual life. In the early 1640s, "Antinomian" sects were beginning to appear in England. Meanwhile, the Westminster Assembly, which first met in July, 1643, was deliberating the reconstruction of the English Church. From the colonists' point of view, the *Short Story* testified to the triumph of Congregationalism over the dangers of Antinomianism. But to an English audience, and especially to English Presbyterians, it provided ammunition for the attack on the New England Way.

The following text follows the third edition of the *Short Story,* the same previously reprinted in Adams.

---

2. The accounts of the Court's proceedings and of Mrs. Hutchinson's church trial are, of course, based on other records.

3. Thomas Weld (1595–1661) emigrated to New England in 1632, and returned to England in 1641.

4. The title of the first edition was *Antinomians and Familists Condemned By the Synod of Elders in New-England: with the Proceedings of the Magistrates against them, And their Apology for the same.*

* See new note p. xix.

A Short Story

To the Reader.

I Meeting with this Book, newly come forth of the Presse, and being earnestly pressed by diverse to perfect it, by laying downe the order and sense of this story, (which in the Book is omitted) Though for mine owne part, I was more slow unto it; not as if I thinke it containes any thing but truth; but because the names of some parties, that acted in our troubles, that have, since that time, (I hope) repented, and so God having pardoned their sins in Heaven, I should have beene loath to have revived them on earth; But considering that their names are already in Print without any act of mine, and that the necessity of the times call for it, and it's requisite that Gods great works should be made knowne; I therefore, in a straight of time, not having had many houres, have drawne up this following Preface, and prefixed hereunto, with some additions to the conclusion of the Book. I commend thy selfe and this to the blessing of God.

T. W.

The Preface.

After we had escaped the cruell hands of persecuting Prelates, and the dangers at Sea, and had prettily well outgrowne our wildernes troubles in our first plantings in New-England; And when our Common-wealth began to be founded, and our Churches sweetely settled in Peace, (God abounding to us in more happy enjoyments then we could have expected:) Lest we should, now, grow secure, our wise God (who seldome suffers his owne, in this their weary-some Pilgrimage to be long without trouble) sent a new storme after us, which proved the sorest tryall that ever befell us since we left our Native soyle.

Which was this, that some going thither from hence full fraught with many unsound and loose opinions, after a time, began to open their packs, and freely vent their wares to any that would be their customers; Multitudes of men and women, Church-members and others, having tasted of their Commodities, were eager after them, and were streight infected before they were aware, and some being tainted conveyed the infection to others: and thus that Plague first began amongst us, that had not the wisedome and faithfulnesse of him, that watcheth over his vineyard night and day, by the beames of his Light and Grace cleared and purged the ayre, certainely, we had not beene able to have breathed there comfortably much longer.

Our discourse of them shall tend to shew,

1. *What these opinions were.*

2. *How they spread so fast and prevailed so suddainely.*

3. *How they did rage and raigne when they had once gotten head.*

4. *How they fell and were ruined, when they were at highest.*

The opinions, (some of them) were such as these; I say, some of them, to give but a tast, for afterwards you shall see a litter of fourescore and eleven of their brats hung up against the Sunne, besides many new ones of Mistris Hutchinsons, *all which they hatched and dandled; As*

1. *That the Law, and the Preaching of it is of no use at all, to drive a man to Christ.*

2. *That a man is united to Christ, and justified without faith: yea from eternity.*

3. *That faith is not a receiving of Christ, but a mans discerning that he hath received him already.*

4. *That a man is united to Christ onely, by the worke of the Spirit upon him, without any act of his.*

5. *That a man is never effectually Christs, till he hath assurance.*

6. *This assurance is onely from the witnesse of the Spirit.*

7. *This witnesse of the Spirit is meerly immediate without any respect to the word, or any concurrence with it.*

8. *When a man hath once this witnesse he never doubts more.*

9. *To question my assurance, though I fall into Murther or Adultery, proves that I never had true assurance.*

10. *Sanctification can be no evidence of a mans good estate.*

11. *No comfort can be had from any conditionall promise.*

12. *Poverty in spirit (to which Christ pronounceth blessednesse, Mat. 5. 3.) is onely this, to see I have no grace at all.*

13. *To see I have no grace in me, will give me comfort; but to take comfort from sight of grace, is legall.*

14. *An hypocrite may have* Adams *graces that he had in Innocency.*

15. *The graces of Saints and Hypocrites differ not.*

16. *All graces are in Christ as in the Subject, and none in us, so that Christ beleeves, Christ loves, &c.*

17. *Christ is the new Creature.*

18. *God loves a man never the better for any holinesse in him, and never the lesse, be he never so unholy.*

19. *Sinne in a childe of God must never trouble him.*

20. *Trouble in conscience for sins of commission, or for neglect of duties, shewes a man to be under a Covenant of workes.*

21. *All Covenants to God expressed in words are legall workes.*

22. *A Christian is not bound to the Law as a rule of his conversation.*

23. *A Christian is not bound to pray except the Spirit moves him.*

24. *A Minister that hath not this (new) light is not able to edifie others that have it.*

25. *The whole letter of the Scripture is a covenant of works.*

26. *No Christian must be prest to duties of holinesse.*

27. *No Christian must be exhorted to faith, love, and prayer, &c. except we know he hath the Spirit.*

28. *A man may have all graces, and yet want Christ.*

29. *All a beleevers activity is onely to act sinne.*

Now these, most of them, being so grosse, one would wonder how they should spread so fast and suddenly amongst a people so religious and well taught.

For declaring of this, be pleased to attend two things.

1. *The nature of the Opinions themselves, which open such a faire and easie way to Heaven, that men may passe without difficulty. For, if a man need not be troubled by the Law, before faith, but may step to Christ so easily; and then, if his faith be no going out of himselfe to take Christ, but onely a discerning that Christ is his owne already, and is onely an act of the Spirit upon him, no act of his owne done by him; and if he, for his part, must see noth-*

*ing in himselfe, have nothing, doe nothing, onely he is to stand
still and waite for Christ to doe all for him. And then if after faith,
the Law no rule to walke by, no sorrow or repentance for sinne;
he must not be pressed to duties, and need never pray, unlesse
moved by the Spirit: And if he fals into sinne, he is never the more
disliked of God, nor his condition never the worse. And for his
assurance, it being given him by the Spirit, he must never let it
goe, but abide in the height of comfort, though he fals into the
grossest sinnes that he can. Then their way to life was made easie,
if so, no marvell so many like of it.*

*And this is the very reason, besides the novelty of it, that this
kind of doctrine takes so well here in* London, *and other parts of
the Kingdome, and that you see so many dance after this pipe, running after such and such, crowding the Churches and filling the
doores and windowes, even such carnall and vile persons (many of
them) as care not to heare any other godly Ministers, but onely
their Leaders. Oh, it pleaseth nature well to have Heaven, and
their lusts too.*

2. *Consider their sleights they used in fomenting their Opinions, some of which I will set downe: as*

1. *They laboured much to acquaint themselves with as many,
as possibly they could, that so they might have the better opportunity to communicate their new light unto them.*

2. *Being once acquainted with them, they would strangely
labour to insinuate themselves into their affections, by loving sa-
lutes, humble carriage, kind invitements, friendly visits, and so
they would winne upon men, and steale into their bosomes before
they were aware. Yea, assoone as any new-commers (especially,
men of note, worth, and activity, fit instruments to advance their
designe) were landed, they would be sure to welcome them, shew
them all courtesie, and offer them roome in their owne houses, or
of some of their owne Sect, and so having gotten them into their
Web, they could easily poyson them by degrees; It was rare for any
man thus hooked in, to escape their Leaven.*

3. (*Because such men as would seduce others, had need be
some way eminent) they would appeare very humble, holy, and
spirituall Christians, and full of Christ; they would deny them-*

selves farre, speake excellently, pray with such soule-ravishing expressions and affections, that a stranger that loved goodnesse, could not but love and admire them, and so be the more easily drawne after them; looking upon them as men and women as likely to know the secrets of Christ, and bosome-counsels of his Spirit, as any other.

And this opinion of them was the more lifted up through the simplicitie and weaknesse of their followers, who would, in admiration of them, tell others, that, since the Apostles times, they were perswaded, none ever received so much light from God, as such and such had done, naming their Leaders.

4. As they would lift up themselves, so also their Opinions, by guilding them over with specious termes of Free Grace, glorious light, Gospel truths, as holding forth naked Christ: and this tooke much with simple honest hearts that loved Christ, especially with new converts, who were lately in bondage under sinne and wrath, and had newly tasted the sweetnesse of Free Grace; being now in their first love to Christ, they were exceeding glad to imbrace any thing, that might further advance Christ and Free Grace; and so drank them in readily.

5. If they met with Christians that were full of doubts and feares about their conditions, (as many tender and godly hearts there were) they would tell them, they had never taken a right course for comfort, but had gone on (as they were led) in a legall way of evidencing their good estate by Sanctification, and gazing after qualifications in themselves; and would shew them from their owne experience, that themselves for a long time were befooled even as they are now, in poring upon graces in themselves, and while they did so they never prospered, but were driven to pull all that building downe, and lay better and safer foundations in Free Grace; and then would tell them of this Gospel-way we speake of, how they might come to such a setled peace that they might never doubt more, though they should see no grace at all in themselves: and so (as it is said of the Harlots dealing with the young man, Prov. 7. 21.) with much faire speech they caused them to yeeld, with the flattering of their lips they forced them.

6. They commonly laboured to worke first upon women, be-

ing (as they conceived) the weaker to resist; the more flexible, ten-
der, and ready to yeeld: and if once they could winde in them, they
hoped by them, as by an Eve, *to catch their husbands also, which*
indeed often proved too true amongst us there.

7. *As soone as they had thus wrought in themselves, and a*
good conceit of their Opinions, by all these wayes of subtilty, into
the hearts of people; nextly they strongly endeavored with all the
craft they could, to undermine the good Opinion of their Minis-
ters, and their doctrine, and to worke them cleane out of their
affections, telling them they were sorry that their Teachers had so
mis-led them, and trained them up under a Covenant of workes,
and that themselves never having beene taught of God, it is no
wonder they did no better teach them the truth, and how they may
sit till doomes day under their legall Sermons, and never see light;
and withall sometimes casting aspersions on their persons, and
practise, as well as their doctrine, to bring them quite out of es-
teeme with them. And this they did so effectually, that many de-
clined the hearing of them, though they were members of their
Churches, and others that did heare, were so filled with prejudice
that they profited not, but studied how to object against them, and
censure their doctrine, which (whiles they stood right) was wont
to make their hearts to melt and tremble.

Yea, some that had beene begotten to Christ by some of their
faithfull labours in this Land, for whom they could have laid
downe their lives, and not being able to beare their absence, fol-
lowed after them thither to New-England *to injoy their labours;*
yet these falling acquainted with those Seducers, were suddenly so
altered in their affections towards those their spirituall fathers,
that they would neither heare them, nor willingly come in their
company, professing they had never received any good from them.

8. *They would not, till they knew men well, open the whole*
mystery of their new Religion to them, but this was ever their
method, to drop a little at once into their followers as they were
capable, and never would administer their Physicke, till they had
first given good preparatives to make it worke, and then stronger
& stronger potions, as they found the Patient able to beare.

9. *They would in company now and then let fall some of their*
most plausible errors, as a bait let downe to catch withall; now if

any began to nibble at the baite, they would angle still, and never give over till they had caught them; but if any should espie the naked hooke, and so see their danger, and professe against the opinions, then you should have them fairely retreat, & say, Nay, mistake me not, for I doe meane even as you doe, you and I are both of one minde in substance, and differ onely in words: By this kinde of Jesuiticall dealing, they did not onely keepe their credit with them, as men that held nothing but the truth; but gained this also, viz. that when, afterwards, they should heare those men taxed for holding errors, they would be ready to defend them, and say, (out of their simplicity of heart) Such men hold nothing but truth, for I my selfe once judged of them, even as you doe, but when I heard them explaine themselves, they and I were both one: By this Machivilian policy, these deluders were reputed sound in their judgements, and so were able to doe the more hurt, and were longer undetected.

10. What men they saw eminent in the Country, and of most esteeme in the hearts of the People, they would be sure still, to father their opinions upon them, and say, I hold nothing but what I had from such and such a man, whereas their judgements and expressions also were in truth, farre differing from theirs upon point of tryall, but if it came to passe, that they were brought face to face to make it good, (as sometimes they have beene) they would winde out with some evasion or other, or else say, I understood him so: for it was so frequent with them to have many darke shadowes and colours to cover their opinions and expressions withall, that it was a wonderfull hard matter to take them tardy, or to know the bottome of what they said or sealed.

11. But the last and worst of all, which most suddainly diffused the venome of these opinions into the very veines and vitalls of the People in the Country, was Mistris Hutchinsons *double weekly-lecture, which she kept under a pretence of repeating Sermons, to which resorted sundry of* Boston, *and other Townes about, to the number of fifty, sixty, or eighty at once; where, after she had repeated the Sermon, she would make her comment upon it, vent her mischievous opinions as she pleased, and wreathed the Scriptures to her owne purpose; where the custome was for her Scholars to propound questions, and she (gravely sitting in the chaire) did make answers thereunto.*[5] *The great respect she had at first in the hearts of all, and her profitable and sober carriage of matters, for a time, made this her practise lesse suspected by the godly Magistrates, and Elders of the Church there, so that it was winked at, for a time, (though afterward reproved by the Assembly and called into Court) but it held so long, untill she had spread her leavin so farre, that had not providence prevented, it had proved the Canker of our Peace, and ruine of our comforts.*

By all these meanes and cunning sleights they used, it came about that those errors were so soone conveyed, before we were aware, not onely into the Church of Boston, *where most of these Seducers lived, but also into almost all the parts of the Country, round about.*

These Opinions being thus spread, and growne to their full ripenesse and latitude, through the nimblenesse and activity of their fomenters, began now to lift up their heads full high, to stare us in the face, and to confront all that opposed them.

And that which added vigour and boldnesse to them was this, that now by this time they had some of all sorts, and quality, in all places to defend and Patronise them; Some of the Magistrates, some Gentlemen, some Scholars, and men of learning, some Burgesses of our Generall Court, some of our Captaines and Souldiers, some chiefe men in Townes, and some men eminent for Religion, parts and wit.[6] *So that wheresoever the case of the Opinions came in agitation, there wanted not Patrons to stand up to plead for them; and if any of the Opinionists were complained of in the Courts for their misdemeaners, or brought before the Churches for conviction or censure, still, some or other of that*

---

5. Though meetings to review the week's sermons were a common and respected practice among Puritans, the synod of 1637 condemned as "disorderly, and without rule" "such a set assembly . . . where sixty or more did meet every week, and one woman (in a propheticall way, by resolving questions of doctrine, and expounding scripture) took upon her the whole exercise." Winthrop, *History, 1,* 286.

6. Bernard Bailyn has pointed out that support for Mrs. Hutchinson and John Wheelwright came "predominantly" from the merchants who made Boston the center for trade in New England. *The New England Merchants in the Seventeenth Century* (Cambridge, 1955), 40. The social and economic characteristics of the Antinomian party are defined more elaborately in Battis, *Saints and Sectaries.*

party would not onely suspend giving their vote against them, but would labour to justifie them, side with them, and protest against any sentence that should passe upon them, and so be ready, not onely to harden the Delinquent against all meanes of conviction, but to raise a mutinie, if the major part should carry it against them; So in Towne-meetings, Military-trainings, and all other societies, yea almost in every family, it was hard if that some or other were not ready to rise up in defence of them, even as of the apple of their owne eye.

Now, oh their boldnesse, pride, insolency, alienations from their old and dearest friends, the disturbances, divisions, contentions they raised amongst us, both in Church and State, and in families, setting division betwixt husband and wife!

Oh the sore censures against all sorts that opposed them, and the contempt they cast upon our godly Magistrates, Churches, Ministers, and all that were set over them, when they stood in their way!

Now the faithfull Ministers of Christ must have dung cast on their faces, and be no better then Legall Preachers, Baals Priests, *Popish Factors, Scribes, Pharisees, and Opposers of Christ himselfe.*

Now they must be pointed at, as it were with the finger, and reproached by name, Such a Church officer is an ignorant man, and knowes not Christ; such an one is under a Covenant of workes; such a Pastor is a proud man, and would make a good persecutor; such a Teacher is grossely Popish; so that through these reproaches occasion was given to men to abhorre the offerings of the Lord.

Now, one of them in a solemne convention of Ministers dared to say to their faces, that they did not preach the Covenant of Free Grace, *and that they themselves had not the seale of the Spirit, &c.*

Now, after our Sermons were ended at our publike Lectures, you might have seene halfe a dozen Pistols discharged at the face of the Preacher, (I meane) so many objections made by the opinionists in the open Assembly against our doctrine delivered, if it suited not their new fancies, to the marvellous weakning of holy truths delivered (what in them lay) in the hearts of all the weaker sort; and this done not once and away, but from day to day after our Sermons; yea, they would come when they heard a Minister was upon such a point as was like to strike at their opinions, with a purpose to oppose him to his face.[7]

Now, you might have seene many of the Opinionists rising up, and contemptuously turning their backs upon the faithfull Pastor of that Church, and going forth from the Assembly when he began to pray or preach.[8]

Now, you might have read Epistles of defiance and challenge, written to some Ministers after their Sermons, to crosse and contradict truths by them delivered, and to maintaine their owne way.

Now, might one have frequently heard, both in Court and Church-meetings, where they were dealt withall, about their Opinions, and exorbitant carriages, such bold and menacing expressions as these.

This I hold, and will hold to my death, and will maintaine it with my bloud. And if I cannot be heard here, I must be forced to take some other course.

They said moreover what they would doe against us (biting their words in) when such and such opportunities should be offered to them, as they daily expected. Insomuch that we had great cause to have feared the extremity of danger from them, in case power had beene in their hands.

Now, you might have heard one of them preaching a most dangerous Sermon in a great Assembly;[9] *when he divided the whole Country into two ranks, some (that were of his Opinion) under a Covenant of Grace, and those were friends to Christ; others under a Covenant of Workes, whom they might know by this, if they*

---

7. When the emigrants were experimenting with freer forms of worship in the mid 1630s, they welcomed the idea of questions from church members during the service; but in the aftermath of the controversy the synod of 1637 frowned upon the practice and it was gradually abandoned. [Richard Mather], *Church-Government and Church-Covenant Discussed* (London, 1643), 78–79; Winthrop, *History, 1,* 287.

8. The reference is to the Antinomians' treatment of John Wilson (1588–1667), pastor of the Boston Church. Wilson came over with Winthrop in 1630, and thus had been a minister of the church for a longer period than Cotton.

9. John Wheelwright.

evidence their good estate by their Sanctification: those were (said he) enemies to Christ, Herods, Pilates, Scribes and Pharisees, yea, Antichrists; and advised all under a Covenant of Grace, to looke upon them as such, and did, with great Zeale, stimulate them to deale with them as they would with such: And withall alleadging the Story of Moses that killed the Egyptian, barely left it so: I mention not this or any thing, in the least degree, to reflect upon this man, or any other; for God hath long since opened his eyes (I hope.) But to shew what racket these Opinions did make there, and will any where else where they get an head.

Now, might you have seene open contempt cast upon the face of the whole generall Court in subtile words to this very effect. That the Magistrates were Ahabs, Amaziahs, Scribes and Pharisees, enemies to Christ, led by Satan, that old enemy of Free Grace, and that it were better that a Milstone were hung about their necks, and they were drowned in the Sea, then they should censure one of their judgement, which they were now about to doe.

Another of them you might have seene so audaciously insolent, and high-flowne in spirit and speech, that she bade the Court of Magistrats (when they were about to censure her for her pernicious carriages) Take heed what they did to her, for she knew by an infallible revelation, that for this act which they were about to passe against her, God would ruine them, their Posterity, and that whole Common-wealth.

By a little tast of a few passages in stead of multitudes here presented, you may see what an height they were growne unto, in a short time; and what a spirit of pride, insolency, contempt of authority, division, sedition they were acted by: It was a wonder of mercy that they had not set our Common-wealth and Churches on a fire, and consumed us all therein.

They being mounted to this height, and carried with such a strong hand (as you have heard,) and seeing a spirit of pride, subtilty, malice, and contempt of all men, that were not of their minds, breathing in them (our hearts sadded, and our spirits, tyred) wee sighed and groaned to Heaven, we humbled our soules by prayer and fasting, that the Lord would find out and blesse some meanes and wayes for the cure of this sore, and deliver his truth and our selves from this heavie bondage. Which (when his owne time was come) he hearkened unto, and in infinite mercy looked upon our sorrowes, and did, in a wonderfull manner, beyond all expectation free us by these meanes following.

1. *He stirred up all the Ministers spirits in the Countrey to preach against those errors, and practises that so much pestered the Countrey, to informe, to confute, to rebuke, &c. thereby to cure those that were diseased already, and to give Antidotes to the rest, to preserve them from infection. And though this ordinance went not without its appointed effect, in the latter respect, yet we found it not so effectuall for the driving away of this infection, as we desired, for they (most of them) hardned their faces, and bent their wits how to oppose and confirme themselves in their way.*

2. *We spent much time and strength in conference with them, sometimes in private before the Elders onely, sometimes in our publike Congregation for all comers; many, very many houres and halfe dayes together we spent therein to see if any meanes might prevaile; we gave them free leave, with all lenity and patience, to lay downe what they could say for their Opinions, and answered them, from point to point, and then brought cleare arguments from evident Scriptures against them, and put them to answer us even untill they were oftentimes brought to be either silent, or driven to deny common principles, or shuffle off plaine Scripture; and yet (such was their pride and hardnesse of heart that) they would not yeeld to the truth, but did tell us they would take time to consider of our arguments, and in meane space meeting with some of their abetters, strengthened themselves againe in their old way, that when we dealt with them next time, we found them further off then before, so that our hopes began to languish of reducing them by private meanes.*

3. *Then we had an Assembly of all the Ministers and learned men in the whole Countrey, which held for three weekes together, at* Cambridge *(then called* New-Towne) *Mr.* Hooker *and Mr.* Bulkley *(alias* Buckley) *being chosen Moderatours, or Proloquutors, the Magistrates sitting present all that time, as hearers, and speakers also when they saw fit: a liberty also was given to any of the Countrey to come in and heare, (it being appointed, in great part, for the satisfaction of the people) and a place was appointed for all the Opinionists to come in, and take liberty of speech,*

(onely due order observed) as much as any of our selves had, and as freely.

The first weeke we spent in confuting the loose opinions that we gathered up in the Country, the summe of which is set downe, pag. 1. &c. The other fortnight we spent in a plaine Syllogisticall dispute, (ad vulgus *as much as might be*) *gathering up nine of the chiefest points, (on which the rest depended) and disputed of them all in order, pro and con. In the forenoones we framed our arguments, and in the afternoones produced them in publick, and next day the Adversary gave in their answers, and produced also their arguments on the same questions; then we answered them, and replyed also upon them the next day. These disputes are not mentioned at all in the following discourse, happily, because of the swelling of the booke. God was much present with his Servants, truth beganne to get ground, and the adverse party to be at a stand, but after discourse amongst themselves, still they hardened one another, yet the worke of the Assembly (through Gods blessing) gained much on the hearers, that were indifferent, to strengthen them, and on many wavering, to settle them: the error of the opinions and wilfulnesse of their maintainers laid starke naked.*

4. Then after this meane was tryed, and the Magistrates saw that neither our Preaching, Conference, nor yet our Assembly meeting did effect the cure, but that, still, after conference had together, the Leaders put such life into the rest, that they all went on in their former course, not onely to disturbe the Churches, but miserably interrupt the civill Peace, and that they threw contempt both upon Courts, and Churches, and began now to raise sedition amongst us, to the indangering the Common-wealth; Hereupon for these grounds named, (and not for their opinions, as themselves falsely reported, and as our godly Magistrates have beene much traduced here in England) for these reasons (I say) being civill disturbances,[10] the Magistrate convents them, (as it plaine

---

10. English critics of the New England Way seized upon the punishment of the Antinomians to argue that the colonists were treating matters of conscience as civil crimes. Cf. Perry Miller, *Orthodoxy in Massachusetts* (Cambridge, 1933), Chapter 8.

appeares, pag. 28, 29. *of this booke) and censures them; some were disfranchised, others fined, the incurable amongst them banished.*

This was an other meane of their subduing, some of the leaders being downe, and others gone, the rest were weaked, but yet they (for all this) strongly held up their heads many a day after.

5. *Then God himselfe was pleased to step in with his casting voice, and bring in his owne vote and suffrage from heaven, by testifying his displeasure against their opinions and practises, as clearely as if he had pointed with his finger, in causing the two fomenting women in the time of the height of the Opinions to produce out of their wombs, as before they had out of their braines, such monstrous births as no Chronicle (I thinke) hardly ever recorded the like. Mistris* Dier *brought forth her birth of a woman child, a fish, a beast, and a fowle, all woven together in one, and without an head, as* pag. 44. *describes, to which I referre the reader.*

Mistris Hutchison *being big with child, and growing towards the time of her labour, as other women doe, she brought forth not one, (as Mistris* Dier *did) but (which was more strange to amazement)* 30. *monstrous births or thereabouts, at once; some of them bigger, some lesser, some of one shape, some of another; few of any perfect shape, none at all of them (as farre as I could ever learne) of humane shape.*[11]

These things are so strange, that I am almost loath to be the reporter of them, lest I should seeme to feigne a new story, and not to relate an old one, but I have learned otherwise (blessed be his name) then to delude the world with untruths.

And these things are so well knowne in New England, *that they have beene made use of in publike, by the reverend Teacher of* Boston, *and testified by so many letters to friends here, that the things are past question.*

And see how the wisdome of God fitted this judgement to her sinne every way, for looke as she had vented mishapen opinions, so she must bring forth deformed monsters; and as about 30. *Opinions in number, so many monsters; and as those were publike, and not in a corner mentioned, so this is now come to be*

---

11. Cf. Winthrop, *History, 1,* 326–328. A modern medical diagnosis is included in Battis, *Saints and Sectaries,* 248n, 346–348.

* See new note p. xix.

knowne and famous over all these Churches, and a great part of the world.

And though he that runnes may read their sinne in these judgements; yet, behold the desperate and stupendious hardnesse of heart in these persons and their followers, who were so farre from seeing the finger of God in all these dreadfull passages, that they turned all from themselves upon the faithfull servants of God that laboured to reclaime them, saying:

This is for you, yee legalists, that your eyes might be further blinded, by Gods hand upon us, in your legall wayes, and stumble and fall, and in the end breake your necks into Hell, if yee imbrace not the truth.

Now I am upon Mistris Hutchisons *story, I will digresse a little to give you a further tast of her spirit, viz. After she was gone from us to the Iland, the Church of* Boston *sent unto her foure of their members, (men of a lovely and winning spirit, as most likely to prevaile) to see if they could convince and reduce her, according to 2* Thes. 3. 13. *When they came first unto her, she asked from whom they came, and what was their businesse; They answered, We are come in the name of the Lord Jesus, from the Church of Christ at* Boston, *to labour to convince you of &c. ——— At that word she (being filled with as much disdaine in her countenance, as bitternesse in her spirit) replied, What, from the* Church *at* Boston? *I know no such* Church, *neither will I owne it, call it the* Whore and Strumpet *of* Boston, *no Church of Christ; so they said no more, seeing her so desperate, but returned.*[12] *Behold the spirit of errour, to what a passe it drives a man!*

This loud-speaking providence from Heaven in the monsters, did much awaken many of their followers (especially the tenderer sort) to attend Gods meaning therein; and made them at such a stand, that they dared not sleight so manifest a signe from Heaven, that from that time we found many of their eares boared (as they had good cause) to attend to counsell, but others yet followed them.

6. *The last stroke that slew the Opinions, was the falling away of their Leaders.*

---

12. This episode is reported more fully in the notebook of Robert Keayne, as reprinted in this collection.

1. *Into more hideous and soule-destroying delusions, which ruine (indeed) all Religion; as, that the soules of men are mortall like the beasts.*

That there is no such thing as inherent righteousnesse.

That these bodies of ours shall not rise againe.

That their owne revelations of particular events were as infallible as the Scripture, &c.

2. *They also grew (many of them) very loose and degenerate in their practises (for these Opinions will certainly produce a filthy life by degrees) As no prayer in their families, no Sabbath, insufferable pride, frequent and hideous lying; diverse of them being proved guilty, some of five, other of ten grosse lies; another falling into a lie, God smote him in the very act, that he sunke downe into a deepe swoune, and being by hot waters recovered, and comming to himselfe, said, Oh God, thou mightst have strucke me dead, as* Ananias *and* Saphira, *for I have maintained a lie.* Mistris Hutchison *and others cast out of the Church for lying, and some guilty of fouler sinnes then all these, which I here name not.*[13]

These things exceedingly amazed their followers, (especially such as were led after them in the simplicity of their hearts, as many were) and now they began to see that they were deluded by them.

A great while they did not beleeve that Mistris Hutchison *and some others did hold such things as they were taxed for, but when themselves heard her defending her twenty nine cursed opinions in* Boston *Church, and there falling into fearfull lying, with an impudent fore-head in the open Assembly, then they beleeved what before they could not, and were ashamed before God and men, that ever they were so led aside from the Lord and his truth, and the godly Counsell of their faithfull Ministers, by such an Imposter as she was.*

Now no man could lay more upon them, then they would upon themselves, in their acknowledgment.

---

13. The reference is to Captain John Underhill, for whose involvement in the Controversy see Adams, *Three Episodes of Massachusetts History*, 2, 551–558.

Many after this came unto us, who before flew from us, with such desires as those in Act. 2. Men and brethren what shall we doe? and did willingly take shame to themselves in the open Assemblies by confessing (some of them with many teares) how they had given offence to the Lord and his people, by departing from the truth, and being led by a spirit of error, their alienation from their brethren in their affections, and their crooked and perverse walking in contempt of authority, slighting the Churches, and despising the counsell of their godly Teachers.

Now they would freely discover the sleights the Adversaries had used to undermine them by, and steale away their eyes from the truth and their brethren, which before (whiles their hearts were sieled) they could not see. And the fruit of this was, great praise to the Lord, who had thus wonderfully wrought matters about; gladnesse in all our hearts and faces, and expressions of our renued affections by receiving them againe into our bosomes, and from that time untill now have walked (according to their renued Covenants) humbly and lovingly amongst us, holding forth Truth and Peace with power.

But for the rest, which (notwithstanding all these meanes of conviction from heaven and earth, and the example of their seduced brethrens returne) yet stood obdurate, yea more hardned (as we had cause to feare) then before; we convented those of them that were members before the Churches, and yet, laboured once and againe to convince them, not onely of their errors, but also of sundry exorbitant practises which they had fallen into; as manifest Pride, contempt of authority, neglecting to feare the Church, and lying, &c. but after no meanes prevailed, we were driven with sad hearts to give them up to Satan: Yet not simply for their Opinions (for which I find we have beene slanderously traduced) but the chiefest cause of their censure was their miscarriages (as have beene said) persisted in with great obstinacy.

The persons cast out of the Churches, were about nine or ten, as farre as I can remember; who, for a space, continued very hard and impenitent, but afterward some of them were received into fellowship againe, upon their repentance.

These persons cast out, and the rest of the Ringleaders that had received sentence of banishment, with many others infected by them, that were neither censured in Court, nor in Churches, went all together out of our jurisdiction and precinct into an Iland, called Read-*Iland, (surnamed by some, the Iland of errors) and there they live to this day, most of them, but in great strife and contention in the civill estate and otherwise, hatching and multiplying new Opinions, and cannot agree, but are miserably divided into sundry sects and factions.*

But Mistris Hutchison *being weary of the Iland, or rather the Iland weary of her, departed from thence with all her family, her daughter, and her children, to live under the Dutch, neare a place called by Sea-men, and in the Map, Hell-gate. (And now I am come to the last act of her Tragedy, a most heavie stroake upon herselfe and hers, as I received it very lately from a godly hand in* New-England) *There the Indians set upon them, and slew her and all her family, her daughter, and her daughters husband, and all their children, save one that escaped;*[14] *(her owne husband being dead before) a dreadfull blow. Some write that the Indians did burne her to death with fire, her house and all the rest named that belonged to her; but I am not able to affirme by what kind of death they slew her, but slaine it seemes she is, according to all reports. I never heard that the Indians in those parts did ever before this, commit the like outrage upon any one family, or families, and therefore Gods hand is the more apparently seene herein, to pick out this wofull woman, to make her and those belonging to her, an unheard of heavie example of their cruelty above al others.*

Thus the Lord heard our groanes to heaven, and freed us from this great and sore affliction, which first was small like Elias *cloud, but after spread the heavens, and hath (through great mercy) given the Churches rest from this disturbance ever since, that we know none that lifts up his head to disturbe our sweet peace in any of the Churches of Christ amongst us, blessed for ever be his name.*

I bow my knees to the God of truth and peace, to grant these Churches as full a riddance from the same or like Opinions, which doe destroy his truth, and disturbe their peace.

---

14. This event occurred in 1643.

A POSTSCRIPT.

I Thinke it fit to adde a comfortable passage of newes from those parts written to me very lately by a faithfull hand, which as it affected mine owne heart, so it may doe many others, viz. That two Sagamores (or Indian Princes) with all their men, women and children, have voluntarily submitted themselves to the will and law of our God, with expressed desires to be taught the same; and have for that end put themselves under our government and protection, even in the same manner, as any of the English are: which morning-peepe of mercy to them (saith he) is a great meane to awaken the spirit of prayer and faith for them in all the Churches.

T. Welde.

A Catalogue of such erroneous opinions as were found to have beene brought into *New-England,* [1] and spread under-hand there, as they were condemned by an Assembly of the Churches, at *New Town, Aug.* 30.1637.

The Errors

1. In the conversion of a sinner, which is saving and gracious, the faculties of the soule, and workings thereof, in things partaining to God, are destroyed and made to cease.

The Confutation.

1. This is contrary to the Scripture, which speaketh of the faculties of the soule, (as the understanding and the will) not as destroyed in conversion, but as changed, *Luk.* 24. 45. Christ is said to have opened their understandings: *Joh.* 21. 18. *Peter* is said to be led whither he would not, therefore he had a will. Againe, to destroy the faculties of the soule, is to destroy the immortality of the soule.[15]

---

15. "God made man an understanding creature, indued with rational faculties, the understanding to be the leading faculty, and the will to be the appetite of the soul, according to reason.": John Davenport, *The Saints Anchor-Hold, In All Storms and Tempests* (London, 1661), 66. Perry Miller has described the relationship between the "faculty" psychology and the conversion process in *The New England Mind: The Seventeenth Century* (Cambridge, 1954), Chs. 9–10.

* See new note p. xix.

Error 2. In stead of them, the Holy Ghost doth come and take place, and doth all the works of those natures, as the faculties of the human nature of Christ do.

Confutation 2. This is contrary to Scripture which speaketh of God, as sanctifying our soules and spirits; 1 *Thess.* 5. 23. purging our consciences, *Heb.* 9. 14. refreshing our memories, *Joh.* 14. 26.

Error 3. That the love which is said to remain, when faith and hope cease, is the Holy Ghost.

Confutation 3. This is contrary to the Scriptures, which put an expresse difference betweene the Holy Ghost and love, 2 *Cor.* 6. 6. And if our love were the Holy Ghost, we cannot bee said to love God at all, or if wee did, it was, because we were personally united to the Holy Ghost.

Error 4, 5. That those that bee in Christ are not under the Law, and commands of the word, as the rule of life. *Alias,* that the will of God in the Word, or directions thereof, are not the rule whereunto Christians are bound to conforme themselves, to live thereafter.

Confutation 4, 5. This is contrary to the Scriptures, which direct us to the Law and to the Testimony, *Esay* 8. 20. which also speaks of Christians, as not being without Law to God, but under the Law to Christ, 1 *Cor.* 9. 22.

Error 6. The example of Christs life, is not a patterne according to which men ought to act.

Confutation 6. This position (those actions of Christ   [2]
excepted which hee did as God, or as Mediatour, God
and Man, or on speciall occasions, which concerne not us,) is unsound, being contrary to the Scripture, wherein the example of Christs life is propounded to Christians as a patterne of imitation, both by Christ and his Apostles. *Mat.* 11. 29. Learne of mee, for I am meek, &c. 1 *Cor.* 11. 1. Bee yee followers of mee, as I am of Christ, *Ephes.* 5. 2. Walk in love as Christ hath loved us, 1 *Pet.* 2. 21. Christ also suffered for us, leaving us an example, that yee should follow his steps, 1 *Joh.* 2. 26. Hee that saith hee abideth in him, ought so to walke, even as hee hath walked.

Error 7. The new creature, or the new man mentioned in the Gospell, is not meant of grace, but of Christ.

Confutation 7. The false-hood of this proposition appeareth from the Scriptures, which first propound Christ and the new creature as distinct one from another, 2 *Cor.* 5. 17. If any man bee in Christ, hee is a new creature. Secondly, The new man is opposed to the old man, the old man is meant of lusts and vices, and not of *Adams* person, *Ephes.* 2. 22. 24. Therefore the new man is meant of graces and vertues, and not of the person of Christ, *Col.* 3. 9. 10. Thirdly, The new man is expressely said to consist in righteousnesse and true holinesse, *Ephes.* 4. 25. and to bee renewed in knowledge, *Col.* 3. 10. which are graces, and not Christ.

Error 8. By love, 1 *Cor.* 13. 13. and by the armour mentioned *Ephes.* 6. are meant Christ.

Confutation 8. This position is neere of kin to the former, but secondly, the opposite, 1 *Cor.* 13. meaneth that love which hee exhorteth Christians to beare one towards another, which if it were meant of Christ, hee might bee said to exhort them to beare Christ one to another, as well as to love one another, 2. Faith and hope there mentioned, have Christ for their object, and if by love bee meant Christ, hee had put no more in the latter word, then in the two former. 3. And besides, it may as well bee said, Faith in love, as Faith in Christ, and hope in love, as hope in Christ, if that were the meaning. And by armour, *Ephes.* 6. cannot bee meant Christ. First, because two parts of that armour are Faith and Hope, whereof the Scriptures make Christ the object: *Col.* 1. 5. Beholding the stedfastnesse of your Faith in Christ, 1 *Cor.* 15. 19. If in this life only wee had hope in Christ, &c. now these graces, and the object of them cannot bee the same. Secondly, a person armed with that armour, may bee said to bee a sincere righteous patient Christian, but if by the armour bee meant Christ, sweete predication should have been destroyed, and you might more properly say, a Christifyed Christian.

Error 9. The whole letter of the Scripture holds for a covenant of workes.

Confutation 9. This position is unsound, and contrary to the constant tenor of the Gospel, a maine part of the Scriptures which in the letter thereof holds not forth a covenant of works, but of grace, as appeareth, *Joh.* 3. 16. 1 *Tim.* 1. 15. *Mat.* 11. 28. *Heb.* 8. 10, 11, 12.

Error 10. That God the Father, Son, and Holy   [3]
Ghost, may give themselves to the soule, and the soule
may have true union with Christ, true remission of sins, true marriage and fellowship, true sanctification from the blood of Christ,
and yet bee an hypocrite.[16]

Confutation 10. The word [true] being taken in the sense of
the Scriptures, this also crosseth the doctrine of *Ephes.* 4. 24.
where righteousnesse and true holinesse are made proper to him,
that hath heard and learned the truth, as it is in Jesus.

Error 11. As Christ was once made flesh, so hee is now first
made flesh in us, ere wee bee carryed to perfection.

Confutation 11. Christ was once made flesh, *Joh.* 1. 14. no
other incarnation is recorded, and therefore not to bee believed.

Error 12. Now in the covenant of workes, a legalist may attaine
the same righteousnesse for truth, which *Adam* had in innocency
before the fall.[17]

Confutation 12. Hee that can attaine *Adams* righteousnesse in
sincerity, hath his sin truely mortifyed, but that no legalist can
have, because true mortification is wrought by the covenant of
grace, *Rom.* 6. 14. Sin shall not have dominion over you, for you
are not under the Law, but under Grace.

Error 13. That there is a new birth under the covenant of
workes, to such a kind of righteousnesse, as before is mentioned,
from which the soule must bee againe converted, before it can bee
made partaker of Gods Kingdome.

Confutation 13. This is contrary to *Titus* 3. 4. where the new
birth is made a fruit of Gods love towards man in Christ; of any
new birth besides this, the Scripture speaketh not. It is also contrary to 2 *Cor.* 3. where it is made the worke of the Spirit, (that is,
the Gospel) opposed to the letter (that is, the Law) to give life;
the new birth brings forth the new creature, and the new creature
argueth our being in Christ, 2 *Cor.* 5. 17. It is true indeed Gods
children that are borne againe, must be converted againe, as *Mat.*
18. 3. but that conversion is not from that grace which they have
received, but from the corruption that still remaines.

---

16. Cf. errors 16, 18 and 73.

17. This question came up in the correspondence between Shepard and
Cotton, with Cotton expressing the "error" here condemned.

Error 14. That Christ workes in the regenerate, as in those that are dead, and not as in those that are alive, or, the regenerate after conversion, are altogether dead to spirituall acts.

Confutation 14. This is contrary to *Rom.* 6. 11. Yee are alive unto God, in Jesus Christ, *Ephes.* 2. 1. 5. Hee hath quickned us, 1 *Pet.* 2. 5. Living stones, *Gal.* 2. 20. The life that I now live.

Error 15. There is no inherent righteousnesse in the Saints, or grace, and graces are not in the soules of beleevers, but in Christ only.

Confutation 15. This is contrary to 2 *Tim.* 1. 5. The unfained faith that dwelt in thee, and dwelt first in thy Grandmother, 2 *Pet.* 1. 4. partakers of the divine nature; which cannot bee, but by inherent righteousnesse, 2. *Tim.* 1. 6. Stirre up the grace of God which is in thee, *John* 1. 16. Of his fulnesse wee all receive grace for grace: but if there be no grace in us, wee   [4] receive nothing from his fulnesse, 2 *Cor.* 4. 16. Our inward man is renewed day by day, *Rom.* 12. 2. with *Ephes.* 4. 23. wee are changed or renewed.

Error 16. There is no difference betweene the graces of hypocrites and beleevers, in the kinds of them.

Confutation 16. If this be true, then hypocrites are wise, humble, mercifull, pure, &c. and so shall see God, *Mat.* 5. 8. but they are called fooles, *Mat.* 7. 26. *Mat.* 25. 1, 2, 3. neither shall they see God, *Mat.* 24. 51. *Mat.* 13. 20, 21, 22, 23. *Heb.* 6. 7, 8, 9. the difference of the grounds, argueth the difference in the kinds of graces.

Error 17. True poverty of spirit doth kill and take away the sight of grace.[18]

Confutation 17. This is contrary to *Mark.* 9. 24. Lord, I beleeve, help my unbeleefe: if this were so, then poverty of spirit should hinder thankfulnesse, and so one grace should hinder another, and the graces of the Spirit should hinder the worke of the Spirit, and crosse the end why hee is given to us, 1 *Cor.* 2. 12.

Error 18. The Spirit doth worke in Hypocrites, by gifts and graces, but in Gods children immediately.

Confutation 18. This is contrary to *Nehem.* 5. 15. So did I because of the feare of the Lord: *Heb.* 11. 17. *Noah* moved with feare, prepared an Arke.

---

18. Cf. error 50.

Error 19. That all graces, even in the truely regenerate, are mortall and fading.

Confutation 19. This is contrary to *John* 4. 14. they are graces which flow from a fountaine which springeth up to eternall life, and therefore not fading, *Jer.* 31. 39. 40.

Error 20. That to call into question whether God be my deare Father, after or upon the commission of some hainous sinnnes, (as Murther, Incest, &c.) doth prove a man to be in the Covenant of workes.[19]

Confutation 20. It being supposed that the doubting here spoken of, is not that of finall despaire, or the like, but onely that the position denyeth a possibility of all doubting to a man under a Covenant of grace, this is contrary to Scripture, which speaketh of Gods people under a Covenant of grace, in these or other cases, exercised with sweete doubtings and questions: *David* was a justified man, (for his sinnes were pardoned, 2 *Sam.* 12. 12, 13.) yet his bones waxed old through his roaring all the day long, and the heavinesse of Gods hand was upon him night and day, and the turning of his moysture into the drought of Summer, *Psal.* 32. 3, 4. And Gods breaking his bones by with-holding from him the joy of his Salvation; *Psal.* 51. 8. shew that he was exercised with sweete doubts, and questions at least, as this position speaketh of: and the like may be gathered out of *Psal.* 77. 3, 4. where the holy man *Asaph,* mentioneth himselfe, being troubled when he remembred God, and that he was so troubled, he could not speake nor sleepe, and expostulateth with God, Will the Lord cast off for ever? and will he be favourable no more? and   [5] *vers.* 6, 7, 8, 9. These shew that he had at least sweete doubts, as the position mentioneth, and yet he was not thereby proved to be under a Covenant of workes, for he doth afterward confesse this to bee his infirmity, *vers.* 10. and receiveth the comfort of former experiences, in former dayes, and his songs in the nights, and of Gods former workes, *vers.* 5, 6. 10, 11, 12. and he resumeth his claime of his right in God by vertue of his Covenant, *vers.* 13.

Errour 21. To be justified by faith is to be justified by workes.

---

19. Cf. error 32, and question 5 in the Shepard-Cotton correspondence.

Confutation 21. If faith, in this position be considered not simply as a worke, but in relation to its object, this is contrary to the Scripture, that so appropriateth Justification to faith, as it denieth it to workes, setting faith and workes in opposition one against another in the point of Justification, as *Rom.* 3. 27. Where is boasting then? It is excluded. By what Law? by the Law of workes. no, but by the Law of faith, and *vers.* 28. We conclude, that a man is justified by faith, without the workes of the Law, and *chap.* 4. 16. Therefore it is by faith, that it may be by grace, compared with *vers.* 4. To him that worketh is the reward reckoned not of grace, but of debt.[20]

Errour 22. None are to be exhorted to beleeve, but such whom we know to be the elect of God, or to have his Spirit in them effectually.

Confutation 22. This is contrary to the Scriptures, which maketh the commission which Christ gave his Disciples in these words, Go preach the Gospel to every creature, he that beleeveth and is baptized shall be saved, *Mar.* 16. 15. 16. where the latter words imply an exhortation to beleeve, and the former words direct that this should not onely be spoken to men knowne to be elected, or onely to men effectually called, but to every creature; The Scripture also telleth us, that the Apostles in all places called upon men to repent, and beleeve the Gospel, which they might not have done, had this position beene true.

Errour 23. We must not pray for gifts and graces, but onely for Christ.

Confutation 23. This is contrary to Scripture which teacheth us to pray for wisdome, *Jam.* 1. 5. and for every grace bestowed by vertue of the new Covenant, *Ezech.* 36. 37. as acknowledging every good gift, and every perfect giving is from above, and commeth downe from the Father of lights. The whole 119. Psalme, besides innumerable texts of Scripture, doth abundantly confute this, by shewing that the servants of God have beene taught by the Spirit

---

20. Cf. errors 26–28, 37, 55 and the first "unsavoury" speech. The role of faith in the process of salvation was one of the major questions in the debate between Cotton and his fellow ministers. The latter argued that faith was the instrument or means God had appointed for receiving grace. For Cotton's interpretation of Romans 4.4, see p. 98.

of God to pray for every gift and grace needfull for them, and not onely for Christ.

Errour 24. He that hath the seale of the Spirit may certainely judge of any person, whether he be elected or no.[21]

Confutation 24. This is contrary to *Deut.* 29. 29. Secret things belong to God; and such is election of men not yet called.

Errour 25. A man may have all graces and poverty of spirit, and yet want Christ.

Confutation 25. This is contrary to *Matth.* 5. 3. Blessed are the poore in spirit: but without Christ none can be blessed, *Ephes.* 4. 22. 24. he that hath righteousnesse and true holinesse, hath learned the truth, as it is in Jesus, and therefore hath Christ.

Errour 26. The faith that justifieth us is in Christ, and never had any actuall being out of Christ.   [6]

Confutation 26. This is contrary to Scripture, *Luke* 17. 5. Lord encrease our faith, *Ergo,* faith was in them, 2 *Tim.* 1. 6. faith is said to dwell in such and such persons, therefore faith was in them, *Esay* 64. 7. No man stirres up himselfe to lay hold upon thee.

Errour 27. It is incompatible to the Covenant of grace to joyne faith thereunto.

Confutation 27. This is contrary to *Marke* 16. 16. Preach the Gospel, hee that beleeveth shall be saved, *Rom.* 4. 3. *Abraham* beleeved, and it was counted to him for righteousnesse, and *Abraham* is a patterne to all under the Covenant of grace, *Rom.* 4. 24.

Errour 28. To affirme there must be faith on mans part to receive the Covenant; is to undermine Christ.

Confutation 28. First, Faith is required on mans part to receive the Covenant of grace, according to these Scriptures, *John* 1. 12. To as many as received him, even to them that beleeved on his name, *Marke* 16. 16. He that beleeveth shall be saved. Secondly, to affirme there must be faith on mans part to receive Christ, is not to undermine Christ, but to exalt him, according to these Scriptures, *John* 3. 33. He that beleeveth hath put to his seale that God is true; and so honours Gods truth, which cannot

---

21. Cf. errors 31 and 65. All three errors are clues to the ecclesiastical significance of the controversy. In effect, the Antinomians were insisting on more rigorous methods of passing on candidates for church membership.

    * See new note p. xx.

undermine Christ; *Rom.* 4. 20. but was strong in the faith, giving glory to God, &c.

Errour 29. An hypocrite may have these two witnesses, 1 *John* 5. 5. that is to say, the water and bloud.

Confutation 29. No hypocrite can have these two witnesses, water and bloud, that is, true justification and sanctification, for then he should be saved, according to these Scriptures, *Rom.* 8. 30. 2 *Thess.* 2. 13. *Acts* 26. 18.

Errour 30. If any thing may be concluded from the water and bloud, it is rather damnation, then salvation.

Confutation 30. This is contrary to the Scriptures last mentioned.

Errour 31. Such as see any grace of God in themselves, before they have the assurance of Gods love sealed to them are not to be received members of Churches.

Confutation 31. This is contrary to *Acts* 8. 37. 38. where the Eunuch saw his faith only, and yet was presently baptized, and therfore by the same ground might be admitted.

Errour 32. After the revelation of the spirit, neither Devill nor sinne can make the soule to doubt.

Confutation 32. This position savours of errour, else *Asaph* had not the revelation of the Spirit, seeing he doubted, (*Psal.* 73. 13) whether he had not clensed his heart in vaine, and that God had forgotten to be gracious; then also faith should be perfect which was never found, no not in our father *Abraham.*

Errour 33. To act by vertue of, or in obedience to a command, is legall.

Confutation 33. So is it also Evangelicall, the mystery [7] of the Gospel is said to be revealed for the obedience of faith, *Rom.* 16. 25. Also the Lord Jesus is said to be the author of salvation to all that obey him, *Hebr.* 5. 9. If we love Christ we are to keep his Commandements, *John* 14. 29.

Errour 34. We are not to pray against all sinne, because the old man is in us, and must be, and why should we pray against that which cannot be avoyded?[22]

Confutation 34. This is contrary to 1 *Thess.* 5, 23. 1 *Cor.* 13. 7.

---

22. Cf. error 49.

Errour 35. The efficacy of Christs death is to kill all activity of graces in his members, that he might act all in all.[23]

Confutation 35. This is contrary to *Rom.* 6. 4. Our old man is crucified with him, that the body of sinne might be destroyed, that we should not serve sinne: contrary also to *Hebr.* 4. 14. that he might through death destroy him, &c. and 1 *John* 3. 8. whence we infer, that if Christ came to destroy the body of sin, to destroy the Devill, to dissolve the workes of the Devill, then not to kill his owne graces, which are the workes of his owne Spirit.

Errour 36. All the activity of a beleever is to act to sinne.

Confutation 36. Contrary to *Rom.* 7. 15. as also to *Gal.* 5. 17. the spirit lusteth against the flesh.

Errour 37. We are compleatly united to Christ, before, or without any faith wrought in us by the Spirit.[24]

Confutation 37. The terme [united] being understood of that spirituall relation of men unto Christ, whereby they come to have life and right to all other blessings in Christ, 1 *John* 5. 12. He that hath the Son hath life: And the terme [compleatly] implying a presence of all those bands and ligaments and meanes as are required in the word, or are any wayes necessary to the making up of the union, we now conceive this assertion to be erroneous, contrary to Scripture, that either expressely mentioneth faith when it speaketh of this union, *Ephes.* 3. 17. that Christ may dwell in your hearts by faith, *Gal.* 2. 20. Christ liveth in me by faith; or ever implyeth it in those phrases that doe expresse union; as comming to Christ, *John* 6. 35. and eating and drinking Christ, *vers.* 47 compared with *vers.* 54. having the Sonne, 1 *John* 5. 12. and receiving Christ, *John* 1. 12. and marriage unto Christ, *Ephes.* 5. 32. if there

---

23. Cf. errors 36 and 43. These errors were the basis of the accusation that the ministers were preaching a covenant of works. The ministers countered the accusation by insisting that the works or activity they spoke of were "workes of his [Christ's] owne Spirit." In *The Parable of the Ten Virgins Opened & Applied,* Shepard argued that activity on man's part was essential. "It is true the Spirit only can do it; but yet the same Spirit that seals the elect, the same Spirit commands the elect not to sit idle and dream of the Spirit, but to use all diligence to make it sure." *Works, 2, 78.*

24. This error recalls the debate between Bulkeley and Cotton over "union" with Christ, as well as the ensuing arguments pursued throughout the "Reply" and the "Rejoynder."

be no dwelling of Christ in us, no comming to him, no receiving him, no eating nor drinking him, no being married to him before and without faith; but the former is true, therefore also the latter.

Errour 38. There can be no true closing with Christ in a promise that hath a qualification or condition expressed.

Confutation 38. This opinion we conceive erroneous, contrary to *Esay* 55. 1, 2. Ho! every one that thirsteth come yee to the waters, *Matth.* 11. 28. Come to me all yee that are weary and heavy laden, *John* 7. 37. If any man thirst, let him come to me and drinke, *Revel.* 22. 17. Let him that is athirst come, *Marke* 1. 15. Repent and beleeve the Gospel: if the word   [8] indefinitely be sanctified, for the begetting of faith, if the Gospel it selfe be laid downe in a conditionall promise, if the Apostles and Prophets, and Christ himselfe, have laid hold upon such promises to help to union, and closing with himselfe, then there may be a true closing with Christ in a promise that hath a qualification or condition expressed.[25]

Errour 39. The due search and knowledge of the holy Scripture, is not a safe and sure way of searching and finding Christ.

Confutation 39. This is contrary to expresse words of Scripture, *John* 5. 39. Search the Scriptures, for they testifie of me, *Acts* 10. 43. To him give all the Prophets witnesse, *Rom.* 3. 21. the righteousnesse of God witnessed by the Law and the Prophets, *Isa.* 8. 20. To the Law and to the Testimony, *Acts* 17. 11. The Bereans were more noble, in that they searched the Scriptures daily. If the Prophets give witnesse to Christ, if his righteousnesse bee witnessed by Law and Prophets, and that they bee noble that daily search the Scriptures, and that Christ so farre alloweth their testimony of him, that the Scripture saith, there is no light but in

---

25. Cf. errors 48 and 81. The distinction between absolute and conditional promises was another of the ministers' devices for explaining man's activity. Bulkeley explained the conditional promise in this fashion: "First, That there is a condition of the Covenant: The Lord doth not absolutely promise life unto any; he doth not say to any soule, I will save you and bring you to life, though you continew impenitent and unbelieving, but commands and works us to repent and believe, and then promises that in the way of faith and repentance, he will save us. He prescribes a way of life for us to walk in, that so wee may obtaine the salvation which he hath promised; he brings us first through the doore of faith, *Act.*14." *The Gospel-Covenant,* 280.

and according to them, then the due searching and knowledg of Scriptures, is a safe way to search Christ; but the former is true, therefore also the latter.

Error 40. There is a testimony of the Spirit, and voyce unto the Soule, meerely immediate, without any respect unto, or concurrence with the word.

Confutation 40. This immediate revelation without concurrence with the word, doth not onely countenance but confirme that opinion of Enthusianisme, justly refused by all the Churches, as being contrary to the perfection of the Scriptures, and perfection of Gods wisedome therein: That which is not revealed in the Scripture, (which is *objectum adæquatum fidei*)[26] is not to be beleeved: but that there is any such revelation, without concurrence with the word, is no where revealed in the Scripture, *Ergo.* 1 *Cor.* 4. 16. Presume not above that which is written. Againe, if there be any immediate Revelation without concurrence of the word, then it cannot be tryed by the word, but wee are bid to try the spirits. To the law and Testimony, *Esay* 8. 20. to try all things, 1 *Thess.* 5. 21. So the Bereans, *Acts* 17. 11. and the rule of tryall is the word, *Joh.* 5. 39.

Error 41. There bee distinct seasons of the workings of the severall Persons, so the soule may bee said to bee so long under the Fathers, and not the Sons, and so long under the Sons work, and not the Spirits.

Confutation 41. This expression is not according to the patterne of wholesome words, which teacheth a joynt concurrence of all the Persons, working in every worke that is wrought, so that wee cannot say, the Father works so long and the Son works not, because the same worke at the same time is common to them both, and to all the three Persons, as the Father drawes, *Joh.* 6. 44. so the Son sends his Spirit to convince, and thereby draws, *Joh.* 16. 7, 8.

Error 42. There is no assurance true or right, unlesse it bee without feare and doubting.[27]

---

26. An object equal to faith.

27. Cf. errors 56, 58 and 32. The Antinomian position on assurance explains their appeal to "Christians that were full of doubts and feares about their conditions," as Weld noted in his preface to the *Short Story*. The ortho-

Confutation 42. This is contrary to Scripture; the [9]
penman of *Psal.* 77. had true assurance, *ver.* 6. and yet
hee had doubts and feares of Gods eternall mercy, *ver.* 7, 8, 9. The
best Faith is imperfect and admits infirmity, *ver.* 10. 1 *Cor.* 13. 10,
11, 12. Where there is flesh that doth fight against every grace, and
act thereof, and is contrary to it, there can bee no grace perfect,
Ergo, doubting may stand with assurance, *Gal.* 5. 17.

Error 43. The Spirit acts most in the Saints, when they indevour least.

Confutation 43. Reserving the speciall seasons of Gods preventing grace to his owne pleasure, In the ordinary constant
course of his dispensation, the more wee indevour, the more assistance and helpe wee find from him, *Prov.* 2. 3, 4, 5. Hee that
seeks and digs for wisdome as for treasure shall find it, *Hos.* 6. 3.
2 *Chron.* 15. 2. The Lord is with you, while you are with him; If
by indevour be meant the use of lawfull meanes and Ordinances
commanded by God, to seeke and find him in, then is it contrary
to *Mat.* 7. 7. Aske, seeke, knock, &c.

Error 44. No created worke can bee a manifest signe of Gods
love.

Confutation 44. If created workes flowing from union with
Christ bee included, it's against *Johns* Epistles, and many Scriptures, which make keeping the Commandements, love to the
Brethren, &c. evidences of a good estate, so consequently of Gods
love.

Error 45. Nothing but Christ is an evidence of my good estate.

Confutation 45. If here Christ manifesting himselfe in workes
of holinesse, bee excluded, and nothing but Christ nakedly revealing himselfe to faith, bee made an evidence, it is against the
former Scriptures.

Error 46. It is no sinne in a beleever not to see his grace, except he be wilfully blinde.

---

dox position was that the saints frequently experienced doubts. "True believers may have the assurance of their salvation divers ways shaken, diminished and intermitted, as by negligence in preserving of it, by falling into
some special sin, . . . by some sudden or vehement temptation, by Gods with-
drawing the light of his countenance." Westminster Confession, Ch. 18, sect.
IV.

Confutation 46. This is contrary to the Scripture, which makes every transgression of the Law sinne, though wilfulnesse be not annexed; and this crosseth the worke of the Spirit which sheweth us the things that are given us of God; 1 *Cor.* 2. 12. and crosseth also that command, 2 *Cor.* 13. 5. Prove your faith, and therefore we ought to see it.

Error 47. The Seale of the Spirit is limited onely to the immediate witnesse of the Spirit, and doth never witnesse to any worke of grace, or to any conclusion by a Syllogisme.[28]

Confutation 47. This is contrary to *Rom.* 8. 16. to that which our Spirit beares witnesse, to that the Spirit of God beares witnesse, for they beare a joynt witnesse, as the words will have it: but our Spirits beare witnesse to a worke of grace, namely that beleevers are the children of God, *Ergo.*

Error 48. That conditionall promises are legall.

Confutation 48. Contrary to *John* 3. 16. *Matthew* 5. 3. &c.

Error 49. We are not bound to keepe a constant course of Prayer in our Families, or privately, unlesse the Spirit stirre us up thereunto.

Confutation 49. This is contrary to *Ephes.* 6. 18. 1 *Thes.* 5. 17.

Error 50. It is poverty of spirit, when wee have grace,   [10] yet to see wee have no grace in our selves.

Confutation 50. The weake beleever *Mark.* 9. 24. was poore in spirit, yet saw his own Faith weak though it were. *Peter* when hee was brought to poverty of spirit by the bitter experience of his pride, hee saw the true love hee had unto Christ, and appealed to him therein, *Joh.* 21. 15. *Paul* was lesse then the least of all Saints in his owne eyes, therefore poore in spirit, yet saw the grace of God, by which hee was that he was, and did what hee did, and was truly nothing in his own eyes, when hee had spoken of the best things hee had received and done, *Ephes.* 3. 18. If it bee poverty of the spirit to see no grace in our selves, then should poverty of spirit crosse the office of the Spirit, which is to reveale unto us, and make us to see what God gives us, 1 *Cor.* 2. 9. 10, 11, 12. then

---

28. Cf. question 15 of the *Sixteene Questions* and the debate thereon.

it should make us sinne, or crosse the will of God, which is, that wee should not bee ignorant of the gracious workings of Christ in us from the power of his death and resurrection, *Rom.* 6. 3. Know yee not, &c. then would it destroy a great duty of Christian thankfulnesse, in, and for all the good things which God vouchsafeth us, 1 *Thes.* 5. 18.

Error 51. The soule need not to goe out to Christ for fresh supply, but it is acted by the Spirit inhabiting.

Confutation 51. Though wee have the Spirit acting and inhabiting us, this hinders not, but I may and need goe out to Christ for fresh supply of Grace, *Joh.* 1. 16. Of whose fulnesse wee have all received, and grace for grace; 2 *Cor.* 12. 8. *Paul* sought thrice to Christ for fresh supply; *Heb.* 12. 2. Looke unto Christ the Authour and finisher of our faith.

Wee must looke up to the hils from whence commeth our helpe, *Ephes.* 4. 16. by whom all the body receiveth increase, and to the edifying of it self.

Error 52. It is legal to say, wee act in the strength of Christ.

Confutation 52. This is contrary to the Scriptures, the Gospel bids us bee strong in the Lord, and in the power of his might, *Ephes.* 6. 10 and bee strong in the grace that is in Christ Jesus, 2 *Tim.* 2. 1. and *Paul* saith, I can do all things through Christ that strengtheneth me, *Phil.* 4. 13. and that was not legall strength.

Error 53. No Minister can teach one that is anoynted by the Spirit of Christ, more then hee knowes already unlesse it be in some circumstances.[29]

Confutation 53. This is also contrary to Scripture, 2 *Cor.* 1. It is God that stablisheth us with you, &c. *Ephes.* 1. 13. and 4. 12. 14. The *Corinthians* and *Ephesians,* were anoynted and sealed, and yet were taught more of *Paul* in his Epistles then only in some circumstances.

Error 54. No Minister can bee an instrument to convey more

---

29. Errors 53 and 54 suggest that the Antinomians were moving toward the conception of the ministry that the Quakers would later espouse. Cf. Geoffrey Nuttall, *The Holy Spirit in Puritan Faith and Experience* (Oxford, 1946). According to the traditional Puritan conception of the ministry, its validity depended on the will of God, not on the minister's personal fitness.

of Christ unto another, then hee by his own experience hath come unto.

Confutation 54. This is contrary to *Ephes.* 4. 11, 12. the weakest Minister may edify the strongest Christian which hath more experience then himselfe.

Error 55. A man may have true Faith of dependance,   [11] and yet not bee justifyed.

Confutation 55. This is contrary to the Scripture, *Acts* 13. 39. Al believers are justifyed, but they that have true faith of dependance are believers, therefore justifyed.

Error 56. A man is not effectually converted till hee hath full assurance.

Confutation 56. This is crosse to the Scripture, *Isa.* 5. 10. wherein wee see that a man may truely feare God (therefore truely converted) and yet walke in darknesse, without cleare evidence or full assurance.

Error 57. To take delight in the holy service of God, is to go a whoring from God.

Confutation 57. No Scripture commands us to go a whoring from God, but first, the Scripture commands us to delight in the service of God, *Psal.* 100. 2. Serve the Lord with gladnesse, *Isa.* 58. 13. Thou shalt call the Sabbath thy delight, *Ergo.* Secondly, God loves not such as go a whoring from him, *Psal.* 73. *ult.* but God loves a cheerful server of God, 2 *Cor.* 8. Therefore, such as serve him cheerfully, do not thereby go a whoring from him.

Error 58. To help my faith, and comfort my conscience in evill houres, from former experience of Gods grace in mee, is not a way of grace.

Confutation 58. What the Saints have done and found true comfort in, that is a way of grace; but they did help their faith, and comfort their conscience from former evidences of Gods grace in them: *Psal.* 77. 5, 6, 11. I considered the dayes of old, and called to remembrance my songs in the night; and by this raised hee up his faith, as the latter part of the *Psalm* sheweth; and this was in evil houres, *ver.* 2, 3. 2 *Cor.* 1. 12. This is our rejoycing, that in simplicity and godly purenesse, wee have had our conversation, and this was in sad houres *ver.* 4, 5, 8, 9, 10. *Job* 35. 10. None saith, Where is God that made mee, which giveth songs in the night?

here the not attending to former consolation, is counted a sinful neglect.[30]

Error 59. A man may not bee exhorted to any duty, because hee hath no power to do it.

Confutation 59. This is contrary to *Phil.* 2. 12, 13.[31] Work out your salvation &c. For it is God that worketh in you both the will and the deed, *Ephes.* 5. 14. Awake thou that sleepest, so 1 *Cor.* 15. *ult.*

Error 60. A man may not prove his election by his vocation, but his vocation by his election.[32]

Confutation 60. This is contrary to 1 *Thes.* 2. 4. knowing your election, because our Gospel came unto you, not in word only, but in power, 2 *Thess.* 2. 13, 14. God hath elected you to life, through sanctification of the Spirit, whereunto hee hath called you by our Gospel.

Error 61. All Doctrines, Revelations and Spirits, must be tried by Christ the word, rather then by the Word of Christ.

Confutation 61. This assertion of it intends to exclude the word, we conceive it contrary to *Esay* 8. 20. *John* 5. 39. *Acts* 17. 11. also to 2 *John* 4. 1, 2. Trye the spirits, every spirit that confesseth that Jesus Christ is come in the flesh, &c. whcre Spirits and Doctrines confessing that Christ is come in the flesh,   [12] are made distinct from Christ.

Error 62. It is a dangerous thing to close with Christ in a promise.

Confutation 62. This is contrary to *Joh.* 3. 16. *Act.* 10. 43. *Isa.* 55. 1, 2. *Matth.* 11. 28. *Joh.* 7. 37. If Christ in these places invite men to come unto him, and bids them incline and hearken, and tells them their Soules shall live, and they shall drinke and be refreshed by him, and by these promises encourageth them to close with him, then it is no dangerous thing to close with him in

---

30. This "confutation" contains, in brief, the position of Shepard, Bulkeley, and the orthodox ministers on assurance. If the saint began to doubt his estate, he could take comfort from his "conversation," his constant walk in the ways of God.

31. In his fast-day sermon, Wheelwright proposed another interpretation of the verses from Philippians; see p. 162.

32. See note 5, p. 69.

a promise, it is no danger to obey a Command of God: but we are commanded to beleeve the Gospell, *Mar.* 1. 15, 1. the promise being a part of the Gospell.

Error 63. No better is the evidence from the two witnesses of water and blood, mentioned 1 *John.* 5. 6, 7, 8. then mount *Calvary,* and the Souldiers that shed Christs bloud, and these might have drunke of it; poore evidences.

Confutation 63. Then what God hath ordained or made an evidence, is no better then what he hath not made, then Christ loseth his end in comming by water and blood, *vers.* 6. then the Spirit should agree no better with the witnesse of water and bloud, then it doth with Mount *Calvary,* and the Souldiers: but the Spirit doth agree with the water and the bloud, and not with the other, 1 *Joh.* 5. 7. These three agree in one.

Error 64. A man must take no notice of his sinne, nor of his repentance for his sinne.

Confutation 64. This is contrary to *David,* whose sinnes were ever before him, *Psal.* 51. hee considered his wayes (and the evill of them) that he might turne his feete to Gods Testimonies, *Psal.* 119. 59. If we confesse our sinnes, he is faithfull and just, &c. If we say we have not sinned we make him a lyar, 1 *Joh.* 1. 8, 9, 10. *Job* tooke notice of sinne and of his repentance, I abhorre my selfe and repent in dust and ashes, *Job* 42. 6. *David* seeth, and saith, I am sorry for my sinnes, *Psal.* 38. 28. *Solomons* penitent must know the Plague in his heart, that is, his sinne and the punishment thereof, 1 *Kings* 8. 38.

Error 65. The Church in admitting members is not to looke to holinesse of life, or Testimony of the same.

Confutation 65. This is contrary to *Rom.* 1. 7. and the inscriptions of divers Epistles, being directed to Saints, and Saints by calling, and 1 *Cor.* 14. 33. Churches of the Saints, *Acts* 2. the members there, were said to repent before they were admitted, and 1 *Cor.* 5. the incestuous person should not then have beene cast out for want of holinesse, and *Paul* could not be received into communion without Testimony, *Acts* 9. 26.

Error 66. To lay the brethren under a Covenant of works, hurts not, but tends to much good to make men looke the better to their evidences.

Confutation 66. If that bee done ungroundedly, it is contrary to *Isa.* 5. 20. where woe is pronounced to such as call good evill, &c. and *Ezek.* 13. 22. that make such hearts [13] sad, as the Lord would not have sadded; and it is against the rule of the Covenant, 1 *Cor.* 13. besides, it may trench upon the devils office in accusing the Brethren, and then it will be good to tell untruth, good to breake house and Church Communion, then good to break nearest relations, then good to bite one another, and good to offend the little ones, *Matth.* 18.

Errour 67. A man cannot evidence his justification by his sanctification, but he must needs build upon his sanctification, and trust to it.

Confutation 67. First, this is contrary to 1 *John* 3. 18, 19. where the holy Ghost saith, that by unfained and hearty love we may have assurance, and yet neither there nor any where else would have us trust to our sanctification, so *vers.* 7. He that doth righteousnesse is righteous, as he is righteous. Secondly, if poverty of spirit, which emptieth us of all confidence in our selves, may evidence a mans justification without trusting to it, then may sanctification without trusting to it; but the former is true, therefore also the latter. Thirdly, if it be an ordinance of God to evidence our justification by our sanctification, then we may doe this without trusting to it: but that is apparent from, 2 *Pet.* 1. 10.[33] *Ergo.*

Errour 68. Faith justifies an unbeleever, that is, that faith that is in Christ, justifieth me that have no faith in my selfe.

Confutation 68. This is contrary to *Hab.* 2. 4. For if the just shall live by his faith, then that faith that justifies is not in Christ. So *John* 3. *ult.* He that beleeveth not, the wrath of God abideth on him: it is not anothers faith will save me.

Errour 69. Though a man can prove a gracious worke in himselfe, and Christ to be the authour of it, if thereby he will prove Christ to be his, this is but a sandy foundation.

---

33. Error 67 is the gist of Cotton's warning in the "Rejoynder" that the ministers' distinctions will lead only to making sanctification the first ground of justification. The texts from 1 John and 2 Peter, cited here and in confutation 69, figure throughout the debate. In the "Rejoynder" and *A Conference* Cotton relied on Calvin's explication to sustain his position.

Confutation 69. This is contrary to these Scriptures, *John* 14.
21. and 28. He that keepeth my commandements, is he that loveth
me, and he that loveth me, shall be loved of my Father, and I will
love him, and will shew my selfe unto him, 1 *John* 3. 14. We know
that we have passed from death to life, because we love the brethren, and 1 *John* 5. 12. He that hath the Sonne hath life: therefore
he that can prove that he hath spirituall life, may assure himselfe
that hee hath Christ.

Errour 70. Frequency or length of holy duties or trouble of
conscience for neglect thereof, are all signes of one under a Covenant of workes.

Confutation 70. This is contrary to these Scriptures, 1 *Cor.* 15.
58. Be abundant alwayes in the worke of the Lord: if the faithfull
in Christ Jesus be commanded to abound alwayes in the worke of
the Lord, that is, holy duties, then frequency in holy duties is no
signe of one under a Covenant of workes: but the former is true,
therefore also the latter; as also 1 *Thes.* 4. 17. 18. *Psal.* 55. 17. Evening and morning and noone will I pray and make a noyse, and he
will heare me; and elsewhere, Seven times a day doe I praise thee,
Psal. 119. 146. *Psal.* 1. 2. So also contrary is the third
branch to these Scriptures, 2 *Cor.* 7. 8. 11. the Corin-   [14]
thians were troubled in conscience, and sorrowed that
they had neglected the holy duties of Church censure towards the
incestuous person, and *Isa.* 64. 7. and 8. *Cant.* 5. 2. *Rom.* 7. 19. I
doe not the good I would, which he lamenteth and complaineth
of.

Errour 71. The immediate revelation of my good estate, without any respect to the Scriptures, is as cleare to me, as the voyce of
God from Heaven to *Paul*.

Confutation 71. This is contrary to *John* 14. 26. He shall teach
you all things, and bring all things to your remembrance, &c.
whence we reason thus. If the Spirit reveale nothing without concurrence of the Word, then this revelation of the Spirit without
respect to the Word is not cleare, nor to be trusted: but the Spirit
doth reveale nothing, but with respect to the Word, for *John* 14.
26. If the office of the Spirit be to teach and to bring to remembrance the things that Christ hath taught us, *Esay* 8. 20. what ever

spirit speakes not according to this Word, there is no light there.

Errour 72. It is a fundamentall and soule-damning errour to make sanctification an evidence of justification.

Confutation 72. This is contrary to these Scriptures, *Rom.* 8. 1. They that walke after the Spirit, are freed from condemnation, and are in Christ, and so justified: so 1 *John* 3. 10. In this are the children of God knowne, &c.

Errour 73. Christs worke of grace can no more distinguish betweene a Hypocrite and a Saint, then the raine that fals from Heaven betweene the just and the unjust.

Confutation 73. This proposition being generall includes all gracious works, and being so taken is contradicted in the parable of the sower, *Matth.* 13. 20. 21, 22. where the good ground is distinguished from the stony by this, that it brings forth fruit with patience, so *Hebr.* 6. 9. there is something better in the Saints then those common gifts which are found in Hypocrites.[34]

Errour 74. All verball Covenants, or Covenants expressed in words, as Church Couenants, vowes, &c. are Covenants of workes, and such as strike men off from Christ.

Confutation 74. First, this is contrary to Scripture, *Esay* 44. 5. One shall say, I am the Lords, another shall call himselfe by the name of the God of *Jacob: Rom.* 10. 10. With the mouth confession is made to salvation. Secondly, contrary to reason, for then the Covenant of grace is made a Covenant of workes, by the writing, reading, and preaching of the same, for they are verball expressions of the Covenant on Gods part, as Church Covenants verbally expresse our closing herewith.

Errour 75. The Spirit giveth such full and cleare evidence of my good estate, that I have no need to be tried by the fruits of sanctification, this were to light a candle to the Sun.

Confutation 75. This opinion taken in this sense, that after

---

34. Shepard's *The Parable of the Ten Virgins Opened & Applied* is largely taken up with defending the orthodox view, that "there is a certain plenitude, fullness, or full measure of the Spirit of grace in the hearts of the faithful, which the most glorious, yet unsound professors of virgin churches want, and have not in their vessels, but fall short of.": *Works, 2,* 295, and cf. 332–337.

the Spirit hath testified a mans good estate, the person
need not to be tried by the fruit of sanctification, is con-   [15]
trary to the scope of the whole first Epistle of Saint *John,*
where variety of arguments are propounded to all beleevers in
common, 1 *John* 5. 13. to distinguish the persons of beleevers from
unbeleevers; the water is annexed to the Spirit and bloud, 1 *Iohn*
5. 8.

  Errour 76. The Devill and nature may be cause of a gracious
worke.

  Confutation 76. The words are unsavoury, and the position
unsound, for taking [gracious] according to the language of the
Scripture, gracious words, *Luke* 4. 22. Let your speech be gracious, gracious words are such as issue from the saving grace of
Christs Spirit indwelling in the soule, which neither the Devill,
nor nature is able to produce, for Christ professeth, *Iohn* 15. 3, 4.
Without me yee can doe nothing, nothing truly gracious, *Iohn* 3.
What ever is borne of the flesh is flesh, and *Rom.* 7. 18. In my flesh
dwels no good, (truly spirituall and gracious) *Gen.* 6. 5. Every im-
agination of the thoughts of a mans heart, are evill, and that continually; Besides, the Devill is that evill and wicked one, onely
wickednesse, an adversary to Gods grace and glory, that which is
contrary to corrupt nature, and the hellish nature of Satan, and
above the power of both, they cannot be the causes of gracious
works.

  Errour 77. Sanctification is so farre from evidencing a good
estate that it darkens it rather, and a man may more clearly see
Christ, when he seeth no sanctification then when he doth, the
darker my sanctification is, the brighter is my justification.

  Confutation 77. This is contrary to the Scripture of truth,
which rather giveth the name of light to sanctification and holinesse, and even for this use, to cleare our justification, 1 *Iohn* 1.
6, 7. For the holy Ghost concludes as from a cleare and infallible
promise, and proposition, that if we walke in the light, as he is in
the light, then doth the bloud of Christ cleanse us from all sinne;
meaning, that then and thereby it appeareth that it is done: as by
the contrary unholinesse, and unholy walking is like darknesse,
which obscureth all the goodly presumption flourishes and hopes
of an unregenerate man, *vers.* 6. For this purpose, 1 *Iohn* 5. 8. the

water of sanctification is made a witnesse, now the nature of a witnesse is not to darken and obscure matters in question, but to cleare them, and *Psal.* 51. 10, 11, 12. when *David* saw his heart so uncleane, and his spirit so altogether out of order, his justification was not then brighter, for then he should have had the joy of his salvation more full, and not so to sinke as that he begs it might be restored to him, as implying, that his joy for the present was wanting to him.

Errour 78. God hath given sixe witnesses, three in Heaven and three in earth, to beget and build justifying faith upon.

Confutation 78. This expression answers not the patterne of wholesome words, for if this position be taken thus, God hath given all these sixe witnesses both to beget and also to build justifying faith upon, it is contrary to Scripture, for God hath not given all these sixe witnesses to beget justifying faith, because the water of sanctification, which is one of the sixe, doth
not goe before justifying faith, but followeth after it; for   [16]
our hearts are justified by faith, *Acts* 15. 9.

Errour 79. If a member of a Church be unsatisfied with any thing in the Church, if he expresse his offence, whether he hath used all meanes to convince the Church or no, he may depart.

Confutation 79. Contrary to the rule of our Saviour, *Matth.* 18. If thy brother offend (convictingly) admonish; whence it is evident, that in our carriage towards a private brother we must convince him, before admonish him, much lesse separate from him. Therefore our carriage towards the whole Church must upon greater reason be with like prudence, and tendernesse; whence the argument followes thus. An offence taken before conviction will not beare an admonition, much lesse separation from a brother or Church: but the offence in the question propounded is such, *Ergo*.[35]

Errour 80. If a man thinke he may edifie better in another con-

---

35. The conclusion of the synod of 1637 was "that a member, differing from the rest of the church in any opinion, which was not fundamental, ought not for that to forsake the ordinances there; and if such did desire dismission to any other church, which was of his opinion, and did it for that end, the church whereof he was ought to deny it for the same end.": Winthrop, *History, 1,* 287.

gregation then in his owne, that is ground enough to depart ordinarily, from word, seales, fastings, feastings, and all administrations in his owne Church, notwithstanding the offence of the
Church, often manifested to him for so doing.

Confutation 80. It is contrary to the condition and station of
a member of the body in which he stands, 1 *Cor.* 12. 27. A member
must not put it selfe from the body upon its owne thoughts; as the
admission of a member was by the consent of the whole, so likewise must his dismission be. It is contrary also to the duty of a
member, *Ephes.* 4. 16. there must be an effectuall working in every part for the edification of the whole which this departure from
the administration of all the holy ordinances in the Church will
necessarily hinder. It is contrary also to the good of the whole
Church, and the rule which the Lord hath appointed for the pres-
ervation thereof, 1 *Cor.* 14. 33. God is not the author of confusion,
and therefore not of this practise which will certainly bring it, for
if one member upon these his imaginations may depart, why may
not ten, yea twenty, yea an hundred? Why may not the Pastor
upon such grounds leave his people, as well as they him, considering the tye is equall on both parts?

Error 81. Where faith is held forth by the Ministery, as the
condition of the covenant of grace on mans part, as also evidencing justification by sanctification, and the activity of faith, in that
Church there is not sufficient bread.

Confutation 81. This position seemeth to deny faith to be a
condition at all, or at all active, and so if condition in this place
signifie a qualification in man wrought by the holy Ghost, without which the promises doe not belong to men, this is contrary to
Scripture, for *John* 6. 48. Christ is the bread of life, and yet in the
same chapter faith is held out as a condition of the covenant by
the Ministery of Christ himselfe; and the activity of it is held forth
in these words, Verily I say unto you, unlesse yee eate the flesh,
and drinke the bloud of the Sonne of man, you have no life in
you, and who so eateth, &c. As for the lawfulnesse of evidencing justification by sanctification (if it be under-   [17]
stood of that sanctification which is by faith in Christ)
it is contrary to the intent of the whole Epistle of *John,* besides
many other places of Scripture which yet hold forth bread suffi-

cient (if by sufficient is meant that doctrine, which in its right use is wholsome and good food) for it was written that their joy might be full; yet the evidencing of justification by sanctification is expressely held forth *chap.* 1. *vers.* 7. where he saith, If we walke in the light, as Christ is in the light, we have fellowship one with another, and the bloud of Jesus Christ cleanseth us from all sinne; by walking in the light, in opposition to walking in darknesse spoken of before, *verse* 6. Sanctification is evidently meant, and this is expressely noted to be an evidence of our good condition, when it is said, if we so walke, the bloud of Christ cleanseth us from all sinne.

Errour 82. A Minister must not pray nor preach against any errour, unlesse he declare in the open Congregation, upon any members enquiry, the names of them that hold them.

Confutation 82. This is contrary to Scriptures, which teach Ministers to pray and preach against all errours by whom soever they be held, when it calleth them Watchmen and Stewards, in whom faithfulnesse is required in all administrations: yet withall it enjoyneth them if a brother sinne not openly, to admonish him in secret, first betweene them two alone, and afterwards in the presence of two or three witnesses, and after that (and not before) to bring the matter to the Church, *Matth.* 18. 15, 16, 17.

Vnsavoury speeches confuted.

These that follow were judged by the Assembly aforesaid, as unsafe speeches.

1. *To say that we are justified by faith is an unsafe speech, we must say we are justified by Christ.*

Answer 1. False, for the constant language of the Scripture is not unsafe; but we are justified by faith, is the constant language of the Scripture, *Rom.* 5. 1. being justified by faith; the righteousnesse of faith, *Rom.* 10. 31, 32. Righteousnesse by faith, *Phil.* 3. 9, 10.

2. The distinct phrase of the Scripture used in distinguishing Legall and Evangelicall righteousnesse is no unsafe speech, but such is this, *Rom.* 9. 31, 32. *Israel* found not righteousnesse, because they sought it of the Law, and not of, or by faith, so *Rom.*

10. 5, 6. The righteousnesse of faith, saith thus, &c. The Apostle makes these two so directly opposite, as *membra dividentia,* or contrary species, that there is no danger one should be taken for another, but that it's so safe, as that he that affirmes the one denies the other: yea in the most exact expression that ever *Paul* made, to exclude whatsoever might be unsafe to- [18] wards a mans justification, you have this phrase, yea twice in the same verse, *Phil.* 3. 9. not having mine owne right-eousnesse, which is of the Law, but that which is through the faith of Christ; And againe, The righteousnesse which is of God by faith (ἐπὶ τῇ πίσει) *Ergo,* it is no unsafe speech, yea it must be said on the contrary from those grounds, that is to say a man is justified before faith, or without faith is unsafe, as contrary to the lan-guage of the Scriptures.

And for the second part, that we must say, we are justified by Christ, it is true so farre, as that it cannot be denyed, nor is it un-sound or unsafe at all so to speake, but if it meane a must of neces-sity alwayes, or onely so to speake as it is here set in opposition to the phrase of being justified by faith, then it is utterly false, for as much as the Scripture leades us along in the way of other expres-sions ordinarily, and the Apostle gives us the truth of doctrine and soundnesse of phrase together, *Rom.* 10. 3. Christ is the end of the Law for righteousnesse to every one that beleeveth.

2. *To evidence justification by sanctification, or graces, sa-vours of Rome.*

Answer. Not so. 1. *Rome* acknowledgeth not justification in our common sense, *Scil.* by righteousnesse imputed. 2. *Rome* de-nies evidencing of our justification and peace with God, and teacheth a doctrine of doubting, and professeth that a man can-not know what God will doe with him for life or death, unlesse by speciall revelation, which is not ordinary. But if they meane old *Rome,* or *Pauls Rome,* to which he wrote, it's true, that it savours of the doctrine that they received, as appeareth, *Rom.* 8. 28. All things co-worke for good (the evill of every evill being taken away, which is a point of justification, and this is propounded under the evidence of the love of God) to them that love him, because *Rom.* 8. 2. 9. 13. 14. the evidencing of our being in Christ, freedome from condemnation, and adoption is prosecuted by arguments from sanctification, as by having the spirit, being led by the spirit, walking after the spirit, mortifying the deeds of the flesh by the spirit: and if hereto were added the doctrine of Saint *John* so abundant this way in his first Epistle (whereof I have already made mention) I doubt not, but it was the faith of the Church of *Rome* that then was, so that the speech is unsavoury, and casting a foule aspersion upon a good thing expressed in the Scriptures, but as for the point it selfe, that is included, we referre it to its place, to be discussed, when it is rightly stated.

3. *If I be holy I am never the better accepted of God, if I be unholy I am never the worse, this I am sure of, he that hath elected me must save me.*

Answ. These words savour very ill, and relish of a carelesse and ungracious spirit, for howsoever we grant that our acceptation unto justification is alwayes in and through Christ the same in Gods account, yet this expression imports, that though a mans conversation be never so holy and gracious, yet hee can expect never the more manifestation of Gods kindnesse and love to him, contrary to *Psal.* 50. *ult.* To him that orders his conversation aright I will shew the salvation of God, and *John* 14. 21. It implies secondly, that though a mans conversation be never so vile and sensuall, yet he neede not feare nor expect any   [19] further expression of Gods displeasure and anger to breake forth against him, or withdrawings of his favour from him, contrary to *Psal.* 51. 8. 11, 12. where God breakes *Davids* bones for his sinne, and *Jonah* 2. 4. *Jonah* was as one cast out of Gods presence, and 2 *Chron.* 15. 2. If you forsake him hee will forsake you: And in a word it imports, as if God neither loved righteousnesse, nor hated wickednesse, contrary to *Psal.* 45. 6. 7. and did take no delight in the obedience of his people, contrary to *Psal.* 147. 11. The Lord delighteth in those that feare him, &c. As concerning the last clause, he that hath elected me must save me: it is true, the foundation of Gods election remaineth sure, yet it is as true, that whom he chooseth, he purposeth to bring to Salvation, through sanctification of the Spirit, 2 *Thes.* 2. 13.

4. *If Christ will let me sinne, let him looke to it, upon his honour be it.*

Answ. This retorts the Lords words upon himselfe, *Prov.* 4.

23, 24. Keepe thine heart, &c. Ponder thy paths, &c. and therefore no lesse blasphemous, and is contrary to the professed practise of *David, Psal.* 18. 23. I was upright before him, and kept my selfe from mine iniquity: The latter clause puts the cause of Gods dishonour upon himselfe, no lesse blasphemous then the former, and contrary to *Rom.* 2. 23. where the dishonouring of God is laid upon themselves.

5. *Here is a great stirre about graces and looking to hearts, but give me Christ, I seeke not for graces, but for Christ, I seeke not for promises, but for Christ, I seeke not for sanctification, but for Christ, tell not me of meditation and duties, but tell me of Christ.*

Answ. 1. This speech seemeth to make a flat opposition betweene Christ and his graces, contrary to that in *Joh.* 1. 16. Of his fulnesse we all received, and grace for grace; and betweene Christ and his promises, contrary to *Gal.* 3. 13, 14. Christ was made a curse that wee might receive the promise of the Spirit, and *Luke* 1. 70. with 74. And betwixt Christ and all holy duties, contrary to Tit. 2. 14. and therefore hold forth expressions not agreeing to wholesome doctrine.

6. *A living faith, that hath living fruits, may grow from the living Law.*

Answ. This whole speech is utterly crosse to the sound forme of words required, 2 *Tim.* 1. 13. Hold fast the forme of sound words. 1. That a Hypocrite may have a living Law, is contrary to *James* 2. 17. where the hypocrites faith is called a dead faith. 2. That a hypocrite may bring forth living fruite, is contrary to that, *Heb.* 9. 14. 3. That all this growes from a living law, contrary to 2 *Cor.* 3. 6. where the law is called a killing letter, and to *Gal.* 3. 21. If there had beene a law which could have given life, &c.

7. *I may know I am Christs, not because I doe crucifie the lusts of the flesh, but because I doe not crucifie them, but beleeve in Christ that crucified my lusts for me.*

Answ. 1. The phrase is contrary to the Scripture language, *Gal.* 5. 24. They that are Christs, have crucified the flesh with the affections and lusts. 2. It savours of the flesh,   [20] for these three things may seeme to be expressed in it.

1. If Scripture makes not opposite, but subordinate, *Rom.* 8. 13.

I through the Spirit crucifie the flesh. 2. That if I doe not crucifie my lusts, then there is an open and free way of looking to Christ, contrary to the Scripture, *Mat.* 5. 8. Blessed are the pure in heart, for they shall see God, both in boldnesse of faith here, and fruition hereafter, 2 *Tim.* 2. 19. Let every one that names the Lord Jesus, depart from iniquity. 3. That beleeving in Christ, may ease me from endeavouring to crucifie my lusts in my owne person; which is so grosse, that it needes no more confutation then to name it. 4. The safe sense that may be possibly intended in such a speech is this, If I crucifie the flesh in my own strength, it is no safe evidence of my being in Christ, but if renouncing my selfe, I crucifie the flesh in the strength of Christ, applying his death by faith, it is a safe evidence of my being in Christ: but this sense conveighed in these words, is to conveigh wholesome doctrine in an unwholesome Channell, and a darkening and losing the truth in an unsavoury expression.

8. Peter *more leaned to a Covenant of workes then* Paul, Pauls *doctrine was more for free grace then* Peters.[36]

Answ. To oppose these persons and the doctrine of these two Apostles of Christ, who were guided by one and the same Spirit in preaching and penning thereof, (2 *Pet.* 1. 21. Holy men of God spake as they were moved by the holy Ghost, 2 *Tim.* 3. 16. All Scripture is given by inspiration of God) in such a point as the Covenant of workes and grace, is little lesse then blasphemy.

9. *If Christ be my Sanctification, what neede I looke to any thing in my selfe, to evidence my justification?*

Answ. This position is therefore unsound, because it holds forth Christ to be my sanctification, so as that I neede not looke to any inherent holinesse in my selfe; whereas Christ is therefore said to be our sanctification, because he workes sanctification in us, and we daily ought to grow up in him, by receiving new supply and increase of grace from his fulnesse, according to 2 *Pet.* 3. 18. Grow in grace and in the knowledge of our Lord Jesus Christ.

---

36. This distinction no·doubt stems from the ministers' reliance upon a verse in 2 Peter to support their case for man's activity: "Wherefore the rather, brethren, give diligence to make your calling and election sure: for if ye do these things, ye shall never fall" (2 Peter 1.10).

* See new note p. xx.

The proceedings of the Generall Court holden at
New Towne in the Massachusets in New England,   [21]
Octob.[37] 2. 1637. Against Mr. *Wheelwright* and
other erroneous and seditious persons for their disturbances
of the publick peace.

Although the Assembly of the Churches had confuted and
condemned most of those new opinions which were sprung up
amongst us, and Mr. *Cotton* had in publique view consented with
the rest, yet the leaders in those erroneous wayes would not give
in, but stood still to maintain their new light, which they had
boasted of, and that the difference was still as wide as before, *viz.*
as great as between heaven and hell: Mr. *Wheelwright* also continued his preaching after his former manner, and Mistris *Hutchison* her wonted meetings and exercises, and much offence was
still given by her, and others in going out of the ordinary assemblies, when Mr. *Wil.*[38] began any exercise; and some of the messengers of the Church of *Boston,* had contemptuously withdrawn
themselves from the generall Assembly, with professed dislike of
their proceedings, and many evidences brake forth of their dis-
contented and turbulent spirits; it was conceived by the Magistrates, and others of the Countrey, that the means which had been
used, proving uneffectuall, the case was now desperate, and the
last remedy was to bee applyed, and that without further delay,
lest it should bee attempted too late, when fitter opportunity
might bee offered for their advantage, as they had boasted, and did
certainly expect upon the returne of some of their chiefe supporters, who by a speciall providence were now absent from them:
And for this end the generall Court being assembled in the ordinary course, it was determined to begin with these troublers of
our peace, and to suppresse them by the civill authority, whereunto there was a faire occasion offered upon a seditious writing,
which had been delivered into the Court in *March,* when Mr.
Wheel. was convict of sedition, &c. under the hands of more than
threescore of them, and intitled *A Remonstrance or Petition,* the
Contents whereof were as followeth:

---

37. The correct date is November 2.
38. John Wilson.

Wee whose names are under written (have diligently observed this honoured Courts proceedings against our deare and reverend brother in Christ, Mr. *Wheel.* now under censure of the Court, for the truth of Christ) wee do humbly beseech this honourable Court to accept this Remonstrance and Petition of ours, in all due submission tendred to your Worships.

For first, whereas our beloved Brother Mr. *Wheel.* is censured for contempt, by the greater part of this honoured Court, wee desire your Worships to consider the sincere intention of our Brother to promote your end in the day of Fast, for whereas wee do perceive your principal intention the [22] day of Fast looked chiefely at the publick peace of the Churches, our Reverend Brother did to his best strength, and as the Lord assisted him, labour to promote your end, and therefore indevoured to draw us neerer unto Christ, the head of our union, that so wee might bee established in peace, which wee conceive to bee the true way, sanctifyed of God, to obtaine your end, and therfore deserves no such censure as wee conceive.

Secondly, Whereas our deare Brother is censured of sedition; wee beseech your Worships to consider, that either the person condemned must bee culpable of some seditious fact, or his doctrine must bee seditious, or must breed sedition in the hearts of his hearers or else wee know not upon what grounds hee should bee censured. Now to the first, wee have not heard any that have witnessed against our brother for any seditious fact. Secondly, neither was the doctrine it selfe, being no other but the very expressions of the Holy Ghost himselfe, and therefore cannot justly be branded with sedition. Thirdly, if you look at the effects of his Doctrine upon the hearers, it hath not stirred up sedition in us, not so much as by accident; wee have not drawn the sword, as sometimes *Peter* did, rashly, neither have wee rescued our innocent Brother, as sometimes the *Israelites* did *Jonathan,* and yet they did not seditiously. The Covenant of free Grace held forth by our Brother, hath taught us rather to become humble suppliants to your Worships, and if wee should not prevaile, wee would rather with patience give our cheekes to the smiters. Since therefore the Teacher, the Doctrine, and the hearers bee most free from sedition (as wee conceive) wee humbly beseech you in the

name of the Lord Jesus Christ, your Judge and ours, and for the
honour of this Court, and the proceedings thereof, that you will
bee pleased either to make it appeare to us, and to all the world, to
whom the knowledge of all these things will come, wherein the
sedition lies, or else acquit our Brother of such a censure.

Further, wee beseech you remember the old method of Satan,
the ancient enemy of Free Grace, in all ages of the Churches, who
hath raised up such calumnies against the faithfull Prophets of
God, *Eliah* was called the troubler of *Israel, 1 King.* 18. 17, 18.
Amos was charged for conspiracy, *Amos* 7. 10. *Paul* was counted a
pestilent fellow, or moover of sedition, and a ring-leader of a Sect,
Acts 24. 5. and Christ himselfe, as well as *Paul,* was charged to bee
a Teacher of New Doctrine, *Mark.* 1. 27. *Acts* 17. 19. Now wee beseech you consider, whether that old serpent work not after his
old method, even in our daies.

Further, wee beseech you consider the danger of medling
against the Prophets of God, *Psal.* 105. 14. 15. for what yee do unto
them, the Lord Jesus takes as done unto himselfe; if you hurt any
of his members, the head is very sensible of it: for so saith the Lord
of Hosts, Hee that toucheth you toucheth the apple of mine eye,
Zach. 2. 8. And better a mill-stone were hanged about
our necks, and that wee were cast into the sea, then that   [23]
wee should offend any of these little ones, which beleeve
on him, *Matthew* 18. 6.

And lastly, wee beseech you consider, how you should stand
in relation to us, as nursing Fathers, which gives us encouragement to promote our humble requests to you, or else wee would
say with the Prophet, *Isa.* 22. 4. Look from mee that I may weep
bitterly, Labour not to comfort mee, &c. or as *Jer.* 9. 2. O that I
had in the wildernesse a lodging place of a wayfaring man. And
thus have wee made known our griefes and desires to your Worships, and leave them upon record with the Lord and with you,
knowing that if wee should receive repulse from you, with the
Lord wee shall find grace.

Amongst others who had subscribed to this writing, *William
Aspinwall*[39] was one, and being returned for one of the Deputies

39. William Aspinwall, like the following two Antinomians, John Cogshall and William Coddington, was a prominent merchant in Boston. All
three went to Rhode Island.

of *Boston,* it was propounded in the Court, whether hee was fit to bee received a member of the Court, having subscribed to the said writing, which was so much to the dishonour and contempt thereof, &c. Whereupon hee was demanded if hee would justifie the matter contained in the said writing: which when hee had peremptorily affirmed, by the vote of the Court hee was presently dismissed: Whereupon Mr. *Cogshall,* another of the Deputies of *Boston,* who had not subscribed to the said writing, being then a Deputy of the Court, spake very boldly to the Court, and told them, that seeing they had put out Mr. *Aspinwall* for that matter, they were best make one work of all, for as for himselfe, though his hand were not to the Petition, yet hee did approve of it, and his hand was to a Protestation, which was to the same effect; Whereupon the Court dismissed him also, and sent word to *Boston* to chuse two new Deputies: then Mr. *Coddington* the third Deputy, moved the Court (by Order from the Town of *Boston*) that the former censure against Mr. *Wheel.* might bee reversed, and that the Order made against receiving such as should not bee allowed by the Magistrates might bee repealed; whereby the Court perceived their obstinate resolution in maintaining this faction, and thereupon gave Order hee should be sent for; and for the Law, the answer was, that whereas a Declaration had been made of the equity of that Law, and that specially for the satisfaction of those of *Boston,* and an Answer had been published by some of them, wherein much reproach and slander had been cast upon the Court, to which a reply had been made above six weeks since, but was kept in upon expectation that the late Assembly would have had some good effect, in clearing the points in controversie, and reconciling the minds of the adverse party, but they continuing obstinate and irreconciliable, it was thought fit the whole proceedings about the law should bee brought forth, and accordingly the next day, the Declaration, the Answer and the Reply[40] were all brought to the Court, and there openly read; which

---

40. In May, 1637, the General Court passed an order forbidding any colonist to receive "such persons as might be dangerous to the commonwealth" for a period of longer than three weeks without the permission of the magistrates (*Massachusetts Records, 1,* 196). As Winthrop explained in the *History,* the intent of the law was to forestall additions to the Antinomian party through emigration from England. The law aroused such discontent that Winthrop

gave such satisfaction to those which were present as no man ought to object, and some that were of the adverse party, and had taken offence at the Law, did openly acknowledge themselves fully satisfyed.

When the Warrant came to the Town of *Boston*, they assembled together and agreed (the greater part of them) to send the same Deputies which the Court have rejected,   [24] pretending that it was their liberty, and those were the ablest men, &c. but Mr. *Cotton* comming amongst them, and perceiving their rash and contemptuous behaviour, by his wisdome diverted them from that course: so they chose two other, but one of them they knew would bee rejected, because his hand was also to the seditious writing, as it fell out, for hee refusing to acknowledge his fault in it, was also dismissed, and a new Warrant sent for another to bee chosen, which they never made any return of, but that contempt the Court let passe.

When Mr. *Wheelwright* appeared, it was declared to him, that whereas hee was long since[41] convict of sedition and contempt of authority, and time had been given him from Court to Court, to come to the knowledge of his offence, the Court thought it now time to know how his mind stood, whether he would acknowledge his offence, or abide the sentence of the Court? His Answer was to this effect, that hee had committed no sedition nor contempt, hee had delivered nothing but the truth of Christ, and for the application of his doctrin it was by others, and not by him, &c.

To which it was answered by the Court, that they had not censured his doctrine, but left it as it was; but his application, by which hee laid the Magistrates, and the Ministers, and most of the people of God in these Churches, under a Covenant of works, and

---

wrote "A Declaration of the Intent and Equitye of the Order," which Henry Vane then attacked in "A briefe Answer to a certaine declaration." Winthrop came back with "A Reply to an Answer," a document he apparently made public at the November session of the Court. *History, 1,* 267; Thomas Hutchinson, ed., *A Collection of Original Papers Relative to the History of the Colony of Massachusetts-Bay* (Boston, 1769), 67–100.

41. At the General Court session in March. His sentencing had been delayed in the hope that he would recant.

thereupon declared them to bee enemies to Christ, and Anti-christs, and such enemies as *Herod* and *Pilate,* and the Scribes and Pharisees, &c. perswading the people to look at them, and deale with them as such, and that hee described them so, as all men might know who hee meant, as well as if hee had named the parties; for he was present in the Court[42] a little before, when both Magistrates and Ministers did openly professe their judgement in that point, and that they did walk in such a way of evidencing justification by sanctification, &c. as hee held forth to bee a Covenant of works.

Secondly, the fruits of that Sermon of Mr. *Wheelwright,* together with the Declaration of his judgement in that point both before and since, have declared it to tend to sedition: for whereas before hee broached his opinions, there was a peaceable and comely order in all affaires in the Churches, and civill state, &c. now the difference which hee hath raised amongst men, by a false distinction of a Covenant of grace and a Covenant of works; whereby one party is looked at as friends to Christ, and the other as his enemies, &c. All things are turned upside down among us: As first, in the Church, hee that will not renounce his sanctification, and waite for an immediate revelation of the Spirit, cannot bee admitted, bee hee never so godly; hee that is already in the Church, that will not do the same, and acknowledge this new light, and say as they say, is presently noted, and under-esteemed, as savouring of a Covenant of works: thence it spreads into the families, and sets divisions between husband and wife, and other relations there, till the weaker give place to the stronger, otherwise it turnes to open contention: it is come also   [25] into Civill and publike affaires, and hath bred great disturbance there, as appeared in the late expedition against the Pequeds; for whereas in former expeditions the Towne of *Boston* was as forward as any others to send of their choyce members, and a greater number then other Townes in the time of the former Governour; now in this last service they sent not a member, but one or two whom they cared not to be rid of, and but a few others, and those of the most refuse sort, and that in such a carelesse man-

---

42. Cf. Winthrop, *History, 1,* 256–257.

ner, as gave great discouragement to the service, not one man of
that side accompanying their Pastour, when he was sent by the
joynt consent of the Court, and all the Elders upon that expedition, nor so much as bidding him farewell[43]; what was the reason
of this difference? Why, nothing but this, Mr. *Wheelwright* had
taught them that the former Governour and some of the Magistrates then were friends of Christ and Free-grace, but the present
were enemies, &c. Antichrists, persecutors: What was the reason
that the former Governour never stirred out, but attended by the
Serjeants, with Halberts or Carbines, but this present Governour
neglected?[44] Why, the people were taught to looke at this, as an
enemy to Christ, &c. The same difference hath beene observed in
Towne lots, rates, and in neighbour meetings, and almost in all
affaires, whereby it is apparent what disturbance the seditious application of Mr. *Wheelwright* hath wrought among us; therefore
as the Apostle saith, I would they were cut off that trouble you;
and as *Cain, Hagar,* and *Ismael,* were expelled as troublers of the
families, (which were then as commonwealths) so justice requires,
and the necessity of the peace cals for it, that such disturbers
should be put out from among us, seeing it is one of their tenents,
that it is not possible their opinions, and externall peace, can
stand together; and that the difference betweene them and us is
(as they say) as wide as between Heaven and Hell.

Further the Court declared what meanes had beene used, to
convince him and to reduce him into the right way, as first at the
Court, when he was convict of his offence, the Ministers being
called together did labour by many sound arguments, both in
publike and private to convince him of his errour and sinne, but
he contemptuously slighted whatsoever they or the Magistrates
said to him in that behalfe; and since that much paines had beene
taken with him, both by conference and writing, not onely privately, but also by the late Assembly of the Churches, wherein his

---

43. In the midst of the Antinomian Controversy, Massachusetts and Connecticut joined forces to fight a war against the Pequot Indians. John Wilson
went along as chaplain to the expedition. Ibid., 265–266.

44. When Winthrop replaced Vane as governor in May, 1637, the "serjeants," who were "Boston men," refused to escort him. Ibid., 263.

erroneous opinions, which were the groundworke of his seditious Sermon, were clearely confuted, and himselfe put to silence, yet he obstinately persisted in justification of his erroneous opinions; and besides there was an Apologie[45] written in defence of the proceedings of the Court against him, which though it were kept in for a time in expectation of a Remonstrance, which some of his party were in hand with, for justification of his Sermon, yet it was long since published, and without question he hath seene it: besides the Court hath used much patience towards him from time to time, admonishing him of his danger, and waiting for his repentance, in stead whereof he hath threatned us with an appeale, and urged us to proceed: To this Mr. *Wheel-*   [26] *wright* replyed, that he would, by the helpe of God, make good his doctrines, and free them from all the arguments which had beene brought against them in the late Assembly, and denyed that he had seene the Apology, but confessed that he might have seene it if he would. This was observed as an argument of the pride of his spirit, and wilfull neglect of all the meanes of light in that he would not vouchsafe to read a very briefe writing, and such as so much concerned him.

Although the cause was now ready for sentence, yet night being come, the Court arose, and enjoyned him to appeare the next morning.

The next morning he appeared, but long after the houre appointed; the Court demanded what he had to alleadge, why sentence should not proceed against him; He answered, that there was no sedition or contempt proved against him, and whereas he was charged to have set forth the Magistrates and Ministers, as enemies to Christ, &c. he desired it might be shewed him in what page or leafe of his Sermon he had so said of them; The Court answered, that he who designes a man by such circumstances, as doe note him out to common intendments, doth as much as if he named the party: when *Paul* spake of those of the circumcision, it was as certaine whom he meant as if he named the Jewes; when in *Bohemia* they spake of differences betweene men, *sub una & sub*

---

45. This "Apologie" follows as part of the *Short Story*.

  * See new note p. xx.

utraque, it was all one as to have said Papists and Protestants; so of the Monstrants and Remonstrants:[46] for by the meanes of him and his followers, all the people of God in this Countrey were under the distinction of men under the Covenant of grace, and men under a Covenant of workes. Mr. *Wheelwright* alleadged a place in *Matth.* 21. where Christ speaking against the Scribes and Pharisees, no advantage could they take against him because he did not name them, but it was answered they did not spare him for that cause, for then they would have taken their advantage at other times, when he did name them. One or two of the Deputies spake in his defence, but it was to so little purpose (being onely more out of affection to the party, then true judgement of the state of the cause) that the Court had little regard of it. Mr. *Wheelwright* being demanded if he had ought else to speake, said that there was a double Pharisee in the charge laid upon them. 1. In that the troubles of the Civill State were imputed to him, but as it was by accident, as it is usuall in preaching of the Gospel. 2. That it was not his Sermon that was the cause of them, but the Lord Jesus Christ. To which the Court answered, that it was apparent he was the instrument of our troubles, he must prove them to be by such accident, and till then the blame must rest upon himselfe, for we know Christ would not owne them, being out of his way. After these and many other speeches had passed, the Court declaring him guilty for troubling the civill peace, both for his seditious Sermon, and for his corrupt and dangerous opinions, and for his contemptuous behaviour in divers Courts formerly, and now obstinately maintaining and justifying his said errours and offences, and for that he refused to depart voluntarily   [27] from us, which the Court had now offered him, and in a manner perswaded him unto; Seeing it was apparent unto him, from that of our Saviour, *Matth.*   that we could not continue together without the ruine of the whole, he was sentenced to be disfranchised and banished our jurisdiction, and to be put in safe custody, except he should give sufficient security to depart before the end of March: Upon this he appealed to the Kings Majesty,

---

46. Theological parties in the Netherlands in the early seventeenth century.

but the Court told him an appeale did not lie in this case, for the King having given us an authority by his graunt under his great Seale of *England* to heare and determine all causes without any reservation, we were not to admit of any such appeales for any such subordinate state, either in *Ireland,* or *Scotland,* or other places; and if an appeale should lie in one case, it might be challenged in all, and then there would be no use of government amongst us: neither did an appeale lie from any Court in any County or Corporation in *England,* but if a party will remove his cause to any of the Kings higher Courts, he must bring the Kings Writ for it; neither did he tender any appeale, nor call any witnesses, nor desired any Act to be entered of it: then he was demanded if he would give security for his quiet departure, which he refusing to doe, he was committed to the custody of the Marshall. The next morning he bethought himselfe better, and offered to give security, alleadging that he did not conceive the day before that a sentence of banishment was pronounced against him, he also suffered to relinquish his appeale, and said he would accept of a simple banishment; The Court answered him, that for his appeale, he might doe as he pleased, and for his departure, he should have the liberty the Court had offered him, provided he should not preach in the meane time; but that he would not yeeld unto; so in the end the Court gave him leave to goe home, upon his promise, that if he were not departed out of his jurisdiction within foureteene dayes, he would render himselfe at the house of Mr. *Stanton,*[47] one of the Magistrates, there to abide as a prisoner, till the Court should dispose of him.

Mr. Cogshall.

The next who was called, was Mr. *John Cogshall,* one of the Deacons of *Boston,* upon his appearance the Court declared that the cause why they had sent for him, was partly by occasion of his speeches and behaviour in this Court the other day, and partly for some light miscarriages at other times, and that they did looke at him as one that had a principall hand in all our late disturbances of our publike peace. The first thing we doe charge you with, is your justifying a writing called a Remonstrance or Petition, but

---

47. Israel Stoughton of Dorchester.

indeed a seditious Libell, and that when Mr. *Asp.* was questioned
by the Court about it, you stood up uncalled, and justified the
same, saying to this effect, that if the Court meant to dismisse him
for that, it was best to make but one worke of all, for though your
selfe had not your hand to the Petition, yet you did approve
thereof, and your hand was to the Protestation, which was to the
same effect; whereupon you being also dismissed, used clamorous
and unbeseeming speeches to the Court at your departure, whereby we take you to be of the same minde with   [28]
those who made the Petition, and therefore liable to the
same punishment; upon this the Petition was openly read, and
liberty was granted to him to answer for himselfe. His first answer
was, that what he then spake, he spake as a member of the Court:
to which it was answered againe, that 1. hee was no member of the
Court standing upon tryall whether to be allowed or rejected, at
such time as he uttered most of those speeches. 2. Admit he were,
yet it is no privilege of a member to reproach or affront the whole
Court, it is licentiousnesse, and not liberty, when a man may
speake what he list; for he was reminded of some words he uttered
at his going forth of the Court, to this effect, that we had censured
the truth of Christ, and that it was the greatest stroke that ever
was given to Free-grace.

To which he answered, that his words were mistaken; for he
said that he would pray that our eyes might be opened to see what
we did, for he thought it the greatest stroke that ever was given
to *N. E.* for he did beleeve that Master *Wheelwright* did hold
forth the truth. He was further charged, that at the Court, after
the day of elections, he complained of injury, that the Petition
which was tendered, was not presently read before they went to
election.[48]

To which being answered, that it was not then seasonable, and
against the order of that day, but the Court were then ready to
heare it, if it were tendered; whereupon he turned his backe upon
the Court, and used menacing speeches to this effect. That since
they could not be heard then, they would take another course. To
which he answered (confessing he spake over hastily at that time)

---

48. At the election in May, the party sympathetic to Wheelwright "would
not proceed to election" before a petition in his behalf was read. Winthrop,
History, 1, 261–262.

that his words were onely these, then we must doe what God shall
direct us. He was further charged that he should say, that halfe the
people that were in Church-covenant in *N. E*, were under a Covenant of workes, this he did not deny, but said he proved it by the
parable of the ten Virgins, *Mat.* 15. After these and many other
speeches had passed betweene the Court and himselfe, by which
it plainely appeared that he had beene a very busie instrument, in
occasioning of our publike disturbances, and his justifying of Mr.
Wheelewrights Sermon; and the Petition or Remonstrance being
seditious writings, a motion was made for his banishment, but he
pretended that there was nothing could be laid to his charge, but
matter of different opinion, and that he knew not one example in
Scripture, that a man was banished for his judgement; it was answered, that if he had kept his judgement to himselfe, so as the
publike peace had not beene troubled or endangered by it, we
should have left him to himselfe, for we doe not challenge power
over mens consciences, but when seditious speeches and practises
discover such a corrupt conscience, it is our duty to use authority
to reforme both. But though a great part of the Court did encline
to a motion for his banishment, yet because his speech and behaviour at present were more modest and submisse, then formerly
they had beene, and for that he excused his former intemperances
by his much employment and publike businesses, it was thought
fit to deliver him from that temptation; so he was onely
sentenced to be disfranchized, with admonition no more   [29]
to occasion any disturbance of the publike peace, either
by speech or otherwise, upon paine of banishment and further
censure.

Mr. *Aspin.*

The next who was called was Mr. *William Aspin,* to whom the
Court said that his case was in a manner the same with Master
Cogshalls, his hand was to the Petition, he had justified Master
Wheelwright his Sermon, and had condemned the Court, and
therefore what could he say, why the Court should not proceede
to sentence? For he had beene present and heard what was said to
Master *Cogshall,* to have convinced him of his fault, and therefore it would be needlesse to repeate any thing. To this he answered and confessed the Petition, and that his heart was to it as
well as his hand, and that that for which Master *Wheelwright* was

censured was for nothing but the truth of Christ, and desired to know what we could lay to his charge therein. The Court told him that he being a member of this civill Body, and going contrary to his relation and oath, to stop the course of Justice in countenancing seditious persons and practises against the face of authority, this made him a seditious person. He answered he did but preferre a humble Petition, which he could not doe but he must intimate some cause why, and that *Mephibosheth* in his Petition did imply as much of *Davids* unjust sentence against him as was in this Petition. The Court replyed that he was ill advised to bring that example for his Justification which makes clearly against him, for *Mephibosheth* doth not charge *David* with any injustice not so much as by implication, but excuseth himselfe and layeth all the blame upon his servant. Then he alledged the Petition of *Esther* to *Ahasuerus;* but neither would that serve his turne, for she petitioned for her life, &c. without charging the King with injustice. Hee still fled to this plea, that it is lawfull for Subjects to Petition; the Court answered that this was no Petition, but a seditious Libell, the mis-naming of a thing doth not alter the nature of it: besides they called it in the first place a Remonstrance, which implies that they pretended interest, and is in the nature of it a plea, which challengeth a right of a party: besides they give peremptory Judgement in the cause, and that directly opposite to the judgement of the Court; the Court declared Mr. *Wheelwright* guilty, they proclaime him innocent, the Court judged his speech to be false and seditious, they affirmed it to be the truth of Christ, and the very words of the holy Ghost, which is apparently untrue if not blasphemous. Further in pretending their moderation, they put arguments in the peoples mindes to invite them to violence, by bringing the example of *Peter* drawing his Sword, wherein they blame not his fact, but his rashnesse. And that of the People rescuing *Jonathan,* which to make the more effectuall, they say that it was not seditious.

Lastly, it was great arrogance of any private man thus openly to advance his owne judgement of the Court, therefore it will appeare to their Posterity as a brand of infamy, upon these erroneous opinions, that those who maintained them were not censured for their judgement, but for seditious practises: He further pleaded, that no Petition can be made   [30]

in such a case, but something may bee mistaken through mis-
prision as trenching upon authority, the Court answered, that if
they had onely petitioned the Court to remit his censure, or had
desired respite for further considerations, or leave to propound
their doubts, there could have beene no danger of being mistaken.
Besides there was no neede of such haste in Petitioning, seeing the
sentence was not given, but deferring till the next Court, Master
Wheelwright enjoyned onely to appeare there. The Court then
being about to give sentence, Master *Aspin* desired the Court to
shew a rule in Scripture for banishment; the Court answered as
before, that *Hagar* and *Ismael* were banished for disturbance: hee
replied that if a Father give a child a portion and sent him forth, it
was not banishment: but it was answered, the Scripture calls it a
casting out, not a sending forth; and one said further that he was
a childe worthy of such a portion.

Then the sentence of the Court was for his dis-franchisement
and banishment, and time given him to the last of *March* upon
security for his departure then, which hee presently tendered, and
so was dismissed. The Court intended onely to have dis-franchised
him, as they had done Mr. *Cogshall,* but his behaviour was so contemptuous, and his speeches so peremptory, that occasioned a further aggravation, and it appeared afterward to bee by an over-
ruling hand of God, for the next day it was discovered, that hee
was the man that did frame the Petition, and drew many to subscribe to it, and some had their names put to it without their
knowledge, and in his first draught there was other passages so
foule, as hee was forced to put them out, and yet many had not
subscribed, but upon his promise that it should not bee delivered
without advice of Mr. *Cotton,* which was never done.

William Baulston, Ed. Hutchison.

After these, two of the Serjeants of *Boston* were called, *William Baulston,*[49] & *Ed. Hutchison,* these both had their hands to
the Petition, and justifyed the same, *William Baulston* told the
Court, that hee knew that if such a petition had been made in any
other place in the world, there would have been no fault found
with it. The other told the Court, (turning himselfe in a scornfull

---

49. The remaining signers of the petition are identified in Battis, *Saints
and Sectaries,* and in Adams's notes to the *Short Story.*

manner) that if they took away his estate, they must keep his wife
and children; for which hee was presently committed to the Officer. The Court reasoned a good while with them both, but they
were peremptory, and would acknowledge no failing, and because
of their contemptuous speeches, and for that they were known to
bee very busie persons, and such as had offered contempt to the
Magistrates, for that they were not of their opinion, they were
dis-franchised and fined, *William Baulston* twenty pounds, *Ed.
Hutchison* forty pounds.

The next morning *Ed. Hutchison* acknowledged his fault in
his mis-behaviour in the face of the Court, and so was
released of his imprisonment, but both were disabled   [31]
from bearing any publick Office.

Tho. Marshal, Dynely, Dier, Rich. Gridly.

Another day were called foure more of the principall stirring
men, who had subscribed to the Petition, *Thomas Marshal* the
Ferry-man, who justifyed the Petition so farre, that hee would not
acknowledge any fault; yet hee answered more modestly then the
former, therefore hee was not fined, but dis-franchised, and put
out of his place. *Dynely,* and *Dier,* had little to say for themselves,
but persisting in their justification, they were also dis-franchised:
likewise *Rich. Gridly,* an honest poore man, but very apt to med-
dle in publick affaires, beyond his calling or skill, (which indeed
was the fault of them all, and of many others in the Country)
meane condition, and weake parts, having nothing to say, but
that he could find no fault, &c. was dis-franchised.

Mistris Hutchison.

All these (except Mr. *Wheelwright*) were but young branches,
sprung out of an old root, the Court had now to do with the head
of all this faction, (*Dux fœmina facti*[50]) a woman had been the
breeder and nourisher of all these distempers, one Mistris *Hutchison,* the wife of Mr. *William Hutchison* of *Boston* (a very honest
and peaceable man of good estate) and the daughter of Mr. *Marbury,* sometimes a Preacher in *Lincolnshire,* after of *London,*[51]

---

50. Aeneid, Bk. 1, linc 364: the woman the leader in the act.
51. For Anne Hutchinson's life in England, see Battis, *Saints and Sectaries,* 7–15.

a woman of a haughty and fierce carriage, of a nimble wit and active spirit, and a very voluble tongue, more bold then a man, though in understanding and judgement, inferiour to many women. This woman had learned her skil in *England*, and had discovered some of her opinions in the Ship,[52] as shee came over, which had caused some jealousie of her, which gave occasion of some delay of her admission, when shee first desired fellowship with the Church of *Boston*, but shee cunningly dissembled and coloured her opinions, as shee soon got over that block, and was admitted into the Church, then shee began to go to work, and being a woman very helpfull in the times of child-birth, and other occasions of bodily infirmities, and well furnished with means for those purposes, shee easily insinuated her selfe into the affections of many, and the rather, because shee was much inquisitive of them about their spiritual estates, and in discovering to them the danger they were in, by trusting to common gifts and graces, without any such witnesse of the Spirit, as the Scripture holds out for a full evidence; whereby many were convinced that they had gone on in a Covenant of works, and were much humbled thereby, and brought to inquire more after the Lord Jesus Christ, without whom all their gifts and graces, all their contributions, &c. would prove but legall, and would vanish: all this was well, and suited with the publick Ministery, which went along in the same way, and all the faithful imbraced it, and blessed God for the good successe that appeared from this discovery. But when shee had thus prepared the way by such wholesome truths, then shee begins to set forth her own stuffe, and taught that no sanctification was any evidence of a good estate, except their justifica-   [32] tion were first cleared up to them by the immediate witnesse of the Spirit, and that to see any work of grace, (either faith or repentance, &c.) before this immediate witnesse, was a Covenant of works: whereupon many good soules, that had been of long approved godlinesse, were brought to renounce all the work of grace in them, and to wait for this immediate revelation: then sprung up also that opinion of the in-dwelling of the person of the Holy Ghost, and of union with Christ, and Justification before

52. See p. 322.

faith, and a denying of any gifts or graces, or inherent qualifications, and that Christ was all, did all, and that the soule remained
alwayes as a dead Organ: and other of those grosse errours, which
were condemned in the late Assembly, and whereof diverse had
been quashed, by the publick Ministery; but the maine and bottom of all, which tended to quench all indevour, and to bring to
a dependance upon an immediate witnesse of the Spirit, without
sight of any gift or grace, this stuck fast, and prevailed so, as it began to bee opposed, and shee being questioned by some, who marvelled that such opinions should spread so fast, shee made answer,
that where ever shee came they must and they should spread, and
indeed it was a wonder upon what a sudden the whole Church of
Boston (some few excepted) were become her new converts, and
infected with her opinions, and many also out of the Church, and
of other Churches also, yea, many prophane persons became of
her opinion, for it was a very easie, and acceptable way to heaven,
to see nothing, to have nothing, but waite for Christ to do all; so
that after shee had thus prevailed, and had drawn some of eminent place and parts to her party (whereof some profited so well,
as in a few moneths they outwent their teacher) then shee kept
open house for all commers, and set up two Lecture dayes in the
week, when they usually met at her house, threescore or fourescore persons, the pretence was to repeate Sermons, but when that
was done, shee would comment upon the Doctrines, and interpret
all passages at her pleasure, and expound dark places of Scripture,
so as whatsoever the Letter held forth (for this was one of her
tenents, that the whole Scripture in the Letter of it held forth
nothing but a Covenant of works) shee would bee sure to make it
serve her turn, for the confirming of her maine principles,
whereof this was another, That the darker our sanctification is,
the cleerer is our justification; And indeed most of her new tenents tended to slothfulnesse, and quench all indevour in the creature: and now was there no speech so much in use, as of vilifying
sanctification, and all for advancing Christ and free grace, and the
whole pedegree of the Covenant of works was set forth with all its
Complements, beginning at *Cain*, If thou dost well shalt thou not
bee accepted? then it is explained and ratifyed at Mount *Sinai*,
and delivered in the two Tables, and after sprinkled with the
blood of Christ, *Exod.* 24. and so carryed on in the Letter of the

Scripture, till it bee compleat, as the Covenant of Grace by the Spirit, seales, forgivenesse of sins, one of the venters whereon Christ begets children, &c. and in the end wherefore is all this adoe, but that having a more cleanly way, to lay [33] all that opposed her, (being neere all the Elders and most of the faithfull Christians in this Countrey) under a Covenant of workes, shee might with the more credit, disclose and advance her master-piece of immediate revelations, under the faire pretence of the Covenant of free Grace; wherein shee had not failed of her ayme, to the utter subversion both of Churches and civill state, if the most wise and mercifull providence of the Lord had not prevented it by keeping so many of the Magistrates, and Elders, free from the infection: for upon the countenance which it took from some eminent persons, her opinions began to hold up their heads, in Church Assemblies, and in the Court of Justice, so as it was held a matter of offence to speak any thing against them in either Assembly: thence sprang all that trouble to the Pastour of *Boston,* for his free and faithfull speech in the Court,[53] though required and approved: thence took Mr. *Wheelwright* courage to inveigh in his sermon against men in a Covenant of works (as hee placed them) and to proclaim them all enemies to Christ, Scribes and Pharisees, &c. whereas before hee was wont to teach in a plaine and gentle stile, and though hee would sometimes glaunce upon these opinions, yet it was modestly and reservedly, not in such a peremptory and censorious manner, as hee did then and after; for they made full account the day had been theirs, But blessed bee the Lord, the snare is broken, and wee are delivered, and this woman who was the root of all these troubles, stands now before the seat of Justice, to bee rooted out of her station, by the hand of authority, guided by the finger of divine providence, as the sequell will show.

When shee appeared, the Court spake to her to this effect.[54]

Mistris *Hutchison.* You are called hither as one of those who

---

53. At the December, 1636 session of the Court, John Wilson "made a very sad speech of the condition of our churches," a speech Cotton and the members of the Boston Church took "very ill." Winthrop, *History, 1,* 249–250.

54. This summary of Mrs. Hutchinson's examination should be compared with the fuller report that follows the *Short Story.*

have had a great share in the causes of our publick disturbances, partly by those erroneous opinions which you have broached and divulged amongst us, and maintaining them, partly by countenancing and incouraging such as have sowed seditions amongst us, partly by casting reproach upon the faithfull Ministers of this Countrey, and upon their Ministery, and so weakning their hands in the work of the Lord, and raising prejudice against them, in the hearts of their people, and partly by maintaining weekly and publick meetings in your house, to the offence of all the Countrey, and the detriment of many families, and still upholding the same, since such meetings were clearly condemned in the late generall Assembly.

Now the end of your sending for, is, that either upon sight of your errors, and other offences, you may bee brought to acknowledge, and reforme the same, or otherwise that wee may take such course with you as you may trouble us no further.

Wee do desire therefore to know of you, whether you will Justifie and maintaine what is laid to your charge or not?

Mistris *Hutchison*. I am called here to answer to such things as are laid to my charge, name one of them.

Court Have you countenanced, or will you justifie those seditious practises which have been censured here   [34] in this Court?

Hutch. Do you ask mee upon point of conscience?

Court No, your conscience you may keep to your self, but if in this cause you shall countenance and incourage those that thus transgresse the Law, you must bee called in question for it, and that is not for your conscience, but for your practise.

Hutch. What Law have they transgressed? the Law of God?

Court Yes, the fifth Commandement, which commands us to honour Father and Mother, which includes all in authority, but these seditious practises of theirs, have cast reproach and dishonour upon the Fathers of the Commonwealth.

Hutch. Do I intertaine, or maintaine them in their actions, wherein they stand against any thing that God hath appointed?

Court Yes, you have justified Mr. *Wheelwright* his Sermon, for which you know hee was convict of sedition, and you have likewise countenanced and encouraged those that had their hands to the Petition.

Hutch. I deny it, I am to obey you only in the Lord.

Court You cannot deny but you had your hand in the Petition.

Hutch. Put case, I do feare the Lord, and my Parent doe not, may not I entertain one that feares the Lord, because my Father will not let mee? I may put honour upon him as a childe of God.

Court That's nothing to the purpose, but wee cannot stand to dispute causes with you now, what say you to your weekly publick meetings? can you shew a warrant for them?

Hutch. I will shew you how I took it up, there were such meetings in use before I came, and because I went to none of them, this was the speciall reason of my taking up this course, wee began it but with five or six, and though it grew to more in future time, yet being tolerated at the first, I knew not why it might not continue.

Court There were private meetings indeed, and are still in many places, of some few neighbours, but not so publick and frequent as yours, and are of use for increase of love, and mutuall edification, but yours are of another nature, if they had been such as yours they had been evill, and therfore no good warrant to justifie yours; but answer by what authority, or rule, you uphold them.

Hutch. By *Tit*. 2. where the elder women are to teach the younger.

Court So wee allow you to do, as the Apostle there meanes, privately, and upon occasion, but that gives no warrant of such set meetings for that purpose; and besides, you take upon you to teach many that are elder than your selfe, neither do you teach them that which the Apostle commands, *viz*. to keep at home.

Hutch. Will you please to give mee a rule against it, and I will yeeld?

Court You must have a rule for it, or else you can- [35] not do it in faith, yet you have a plaine rule against it; I permit not a woman to teach.[55]

---

55. 1 Timothy 2.12.

Hutch. That is meant of teaching men.

Court If a man in distresse of conscience or other temptation, &c. should come and ask your counsell in private, might you not teach him?

Hutch. Yes.

Court Then it is cleare, that it is not meant of teaching men, but of teaching in publick.

Hutch. It is said, I will poure my Spirit upon your Daughters, and they shall prophesie, &c. If God give mee a gift of Prophecy, I may use it.

Court First, the Apostle applies that prophecy unto those extraordinary times, and the gifts of miracles and tongues were common to many as well as the gift of Prophecy. Secondly, in teaching your children, you exercise your gift of prophecy, and that within your calling.

Hutch. I teach not in a publick congregation: The men of *Berea* are commended for examining *Pauls* Doctrine; wee do no more but read the notes of our teachers Sermons, and then reason of them by searching the Scriptures.

Court You are gone from the nature of your meeting, to the kind of exercise, wee will follow you in this, and shew you your offence in them, for you do not as the *Bereans* search the Scriptures for their confirming in the truths delivered, but you open your teachers points, and declare his meaning, and correct wherein you think he hath failed, &c. and by this meanes you abase the honour and authority of the publick Ministery, and advance your own gifts, as if hee could not deliver his matter so clearly to the hearers capacity as your self.

Hutch. Prove that, that any body doth that.

Court Yes, you are the woman of most note, and of best abilities, and if some other take upon them the like, it is by your teaching and example, but you shew not in all this, by what authority you take upon you to bee such a publick instructer: (after shee had stood a short time, the Court gave her leave to sit downe, for her countenance discovered some bodily infirmity.)

Hutch. Here is my authority, *Aquila* and *Priscilla*, tooke upon them to instruct *Apollo*, more perfectly, yet he was a man of good parts, but they being better instructed might teach him.

---

* See new note p. xx.

Court See how your argument stands, *Priscilla* with her husband, tooke *Apollo* home to instruct him privately, therefore Mistris *Hutchison* without her husband may teach sixty or eighty.

Hutch. I call them not, but if they come to me, I may instruct them.

Court Yet you shew us not a rule.

Hutch. I have given you two places of Scripture.

Court But neither of them will sute your practise.

Hutch. Must I shew my name written therein?

Court You must shew that which must be æquivalent, seeing your Ministry is publicke, you would have   [36] them receive your instruction, as comming from such an Ordinance.

Hutch. They must not take it as it comes from me, but as it comes from the Lord Jesus Christ, and if I tooke upon me a publick Ministery, I should breake a rule, but not in exercising a gift of Prophecy, and I would see a rule to turne away them that come to me.

Court, It is your exercise which drawes them, and by occasion thereof, many families are neglected, and much time lost, and a great damage comes to the Common-wealth thereby, which wee that are betrusted with, as the Fathers of the Common-wealth, are not to suffer. Divers other speeches passed to and fro about this matter, the issue was, that not being able to bring any rule to justifie this her disordered course, she said she walked by the rule of the Apostle, *Gal.* which she called the rule of the new creature, but what rule that was, she would not, or she could not tell, neither would she consent to lay downe her meetings, except authority did put them downe, and then she might be subject to authority.

Then the Court laid to her charge, the reproach she had cast upon the Ministers, and Ministery in this Country, saying that none of them did preach the Covenant of free Grace, but Master *Cotton,* and that they have not the Seale of the Spirit, and so were not able Ministers of the New Testament: she denyed the words, but they were affirmed by divers of the Ministers, being desired by the Court to be present for that end. The matter was thus, It being reported abroad that Mistris *Hutchison* did slight them and their

Ministery in their common talke, as if they did preach nothing but a Covenant of workes, because they pressed much for faith and love, &c. without holding forth such an immediate witnesse of the Spirit as she pretended, they advised with Master *Cotton* about it, and a meeting was appointed at his house, and she being sent for, and demanded the reason why she had used such speeches, at first she would not acknowledge them, but being told that they could prove them by witnesses, and perswaded to deale freely and truely therein, she said that the feare of man was a snare, and therefore she was glad she had this opportunity to open her minde, and thereupon she told them, that there was a wide difference betweene Master *Cottons* Ministery and theirs, and that they could not hold forth a Covenant of free Grace, because they had not the Seale of the Spirit, and that they were not able Ministers of the New Testament.

It was neare night, so the Court brake up, and she was enjoyned to appeare againe the next morning. When she appeared the next day, she objected that the Ministers had spoken in their owne cause, and that they ought not to be informers and witnesses both, and required that they might be sworne to what they had spoken: to which the Court answered, that if it were needfull, an oath should be given them: but because the whole Court (in a manner man by man) did declare themselves to be fully satisfied of the truth of their testimones, they being 6. or 7. men of long approved godlinesse, and sincerity in their course,   [37] and for that it was also generally observed, that those of her party did looke at their ministery (for the most part) as a way of the Covenant of workes, and one had beene punished about halfe a yeere before,[56] for reporting the like of them. The Court did pause a while at it, whereupon she said that she had Mr. *Wilsons* notes of that conference, which were otherwise then they had

---

56. "Steven Greensmyth, for affirming that all of the ministers (except Mr. Cotton, Mr. Wheelwright, & he thought Mr. Hooker) did teach a covenant of works, was for a time committed to the marshal, & after enjoined to make acknowledgment to the satisfaction of every congregation, & was fined 40 pounds, & standeth bound in 100 pounds till this be done." *Massachusetts Records, 1,* 189.

related: the Court willed her to shew them, but her answer was shee had left them at home: whereupon Mr. *Wilson* (with the leave of the Court) said, that if she brought forth his notes, they should finde written at the foote of them, that he had not written downe all that was spoken, but being often interrupted, he had omitted divers passages; then she appealed to Mr. *Cotton,* who being called, and desired to declare what he remembred of her speeches, said, that he remembred onely that which tooke impression on him, for he was much grieved that she should make such comparison betweene him and his brethren, but yet he tooke her meaning to be onely of a graduall difference, when she said that they did not hold forth a Covenant of Free-grace, as he did, for she likened them to Christs Disciples, and their ministery, before his ascension, and before the holy Ghost was come downe upon them; and when she was asked by some of them, why they could not preach a Covenant of Free-grace, she made answer, because they had not the Seale of the Spirit: upon this the Court wished her to consider, that Mr. *Cotton* did in a manner agree with the testimony of the rest of the Elders: and as he remembred onely so much as at present tooke most impression in him, so the rest of the Elders had reason to remember some other passages, which he might not heare, or not so much observe as they whom it so neerely and properly concerned; All this would not satisfie Mistris *Hutchison,* but she still called to have them sworne, whereupon the Court being weary of the clamour, and that all mouths might be stopped, required three of the Ministers to take an oath, and thereupon they confirmed their former testimony.

Upon this she began to speake her mind, and to tell of the manner of Gods dealing with her, and how he revealed himselfe to her, and made her know what she had to doe; The Governour perceiving whereabout she went, interrupted her, and would have kept her to the matter in hand, but seeing her very unwilling to be taken off, he permitted her to proceed. Her speech was to this effect.

Mistris *Hutchison.*

When I was in old *England,* I was much troubled at the constitution of the Churches there, so farre, as I was ready to have joyned to the Separation, whereupon I set apart a day for humiliation by my selfe, to seeke direction from God, and then did God discover unto me the unfaithfulnesse of the Churches, and the danger of them, and that none of those Ministers could preach the Lord Jesus aright, for he had brought to my mind, that in the 1 *John* 4. 3. Every spirit that confesseth not, that Jesus Christ is come in the flesh, is the spirit of Antichrist; I marvelled what this should meane, for I knew that neither Protes-   [38] tants nor Papists did deny that Christ was come in the flesh; and are the Turkes then the onely Antichrists? now I had none to open the Scripture to me, but the Lord, he must be the Prophet, then he brought to my mind another Scripture, He that denies the Testament, denies the death of the Testator; from whence the Lord did let me see, that every one that did not preach the New Covenant, denies the death of the Testator; then it was revealed to me that the Ministers of *England* were these Antichrists, but I knew not how to beare this, I did in my heart rise up against it, then I begged of the Lord that this Atheisme might not be in my heart: after I had begged this light, a twelve moneth together, at last he let me see how I did oppose Christ Jesus, and he revealed to mee that place in *Esay* 46. 12, 13. and from thence shewed me the Atheisme of my owne heart, and how I did turne in upon a Covenant of works, and did oppose Christ Jesus; from which time the Lord did discover to me all sorts of Ministers, and how they taught, and to know what voyce I heard, which was the voyce of *Moses*, which of *John Baptist,* and which of Christ; the voyce of my beloved, from the voyce of strangers; and thenceforth I was the more carefull whom I heard, for after our teacher Mr. *Cotton,* and my brother *Wheelwright* were put downe, there was none in *England* that I durst heare. Then it pleased God to reveale himselfe to me in that of *Esay* 30. 20. Though the Lord give thee the bread of adversity, &c. yet thine eyes shall see thy teachers; after this the Lord carrying Mr. *Cotton* to *New England* (at which I was much troubled) it was revealed to me, that I must go thither also, and that there I should be persecuted and suffer much trouble. I will give you another Scripture, *Jer.* 46. Feare not *Jacob* my servant, for I am with thee, I will make a full end of all the Nations, &c. then the Lord did reveale himselfe to me, sitting upon a Throne of Justice, and all the world appearing before him, and though I must come to *New England,* yet I must not feare nor be dismaied. The Lord brought another Scripture to me, *Esay* 8. 9. The Lord spake this to me with a strong hand, and instructed me that I should not walke in the way of this people, &c. I wil give you one place more which the Lord brought to me by immediate revelations, and that doth concerne you all, it is in *Dan.* 6. When the Presidents and Princes could find nothing against him, because he was faithfull, they sought matter against him concerning the Law of his God, to cast him into the Lions denne; so it was revealed to me that they should plot against me, but the Lord bid me not to feare, for he that delivered *Daniel,* and the three children, his hand was not shortened. And see this Scripture fulfilled this day in mine eyes, therefore take heed what yee goe about to doe unto me, for you have no power over my body, neither can you do me any harme, for I am in the hands of the eternall Jehovah my Saviour, I am at his appointment, the bounds of my habitation are cast in Heaven, no further doe I esteeme of any mortall man, then creatures in his hand, I feare none but the great Jehovah, which hath foretold me of these things, and I doe verily beleeve that he will deliver me out of our hands, therefore take heed how you proceed against me; for I know   [39] that for this you goe about to doe to me, God will ruine you and your posterity, and this whole State.

When she had thus vented her mind, the Court demanded of her, how she expected to be delivered, whether by miracle as *Daniel* was, to which she answered, yes, by miracle as *Daniel* was. Being further demanded how shee did know that it was God that did reveale these things to her, and not Satan? She answered, how did *Abraham* know that it was the voyce of God, when he commanded him to sacrifice his sonne?

Mr. *Cotton* being present, and desired by the Court to deliver his judgement about Mistris *Hutchison* her Revelations, answered, there be two sorts of Revelations, some are without or besides Scripture, those I looke at as Satanicall, and tending to much danger, other are such as the Apostle speakes of, *Ephes.* 1. where he praieth for a spirit of revelation to be given them, those are never dispensed but according to the word of God, though the word revelation be uncouth, yet in Scripture sense I thinke it not

lawfull so to expresse it, and when ever it comes, it comes with the ministery of the word. Being againe desired to expresse himselfe particularly concerning her revelations, he demanded of her (by the leave of the Court) whether by a miracle she doth meane a worke beyond the power of nature, or onely above common providence? for if (as you say) you expect deliverance from this Court beyond the power of nature, then I should suspect such a revelation to be false. To this she answered, you know when it comes, God doth not describe the way. Mr. *Cotton* asked her againe, whether (when shee said shee should be delivered) she meant a deliverance from the sentence of the Court, or from the calamity of it? She answered, yes, from the calamity of it. Mistris *Hutchison* having thus freely and fully discovered her selfe, the Court and all the rest of the Assembly (except those of her owne party) did observe a speciall providence of God, that (while shee went about to cover such offences as were laid to her charge, by putting matters upon proofe, and then quarrelling with the evidence) her owne mouth should deliver her into the power of the Court, as guilty of that which all suspected her for, but were not furnished with proofe sufficient to proceed against her, for here she hath manifested, that her opinions and practise have been the cause of al our disturbances, & that she walked by such a rule as cannot stand with the peace of any State; for such bottomlesse revelations, as either came without any word, or without the sense of the word, (which was framed to humane capacity) if they be allowed in one thing, must be admitted a rule in all things; for they being above reason and Scripture, they are not subject to controll: Againe, she hath given a reason why she hath so much slighted the faithfull Ministers of Christ here, why? it was revealed to her long since in *England,* that all the packe of them were Antichristians, so as she durst heare none of them, after Mr. *Cotton* and Mr. *Wheelwright* were once gone; for they could not preach Christ and the new Covenant (as she affirmes), why, but they did preach somewhat, and if they could not hold forth Christ in a Covenant of Free-grace, then must they needs hold him forth in a Cove-   [40]
nant of workes, then are they not able Ministers of the
New Testament, nor sealed by the Spirit; for the servants of God, who are come over into *New England,* do not thinke themselves

more spirituall then other of their brethren whom they have left behind, nor that they can or doe hold forth the Lord Jesus Christ in their ministery, more truly then he was held forth in *England,* and seeing their ministery was a most precious sweete savour to all the Saints before she came hither, it is easie to discerne from what sinke that ill vapour hath risen, which hath made so many of her seduced party to loath now the smell of those flowers which they were wont to find sweetnesse in: yet this is not all (though it be too too vile) she can fetch a revelation that shall reach the Magistrates and the whole Court, and the succeeding generations, and she hath Scripture for it also, *Daniel* must be a type of Mistris *Hutchison,* the Lions denne of the Court of justice, and the Presidents and Princes of the reverend Elders here, and all must sort to this conclusion, she must be delivered by miracle, and all we must be ruined; See the impudent boldnesse of a proud dame, that *Athaliah*-like makes havocke of all that stand in the way of her ambitious spirit; she had boasted before that her opinions must prevaile, neither could she endure a stop in her way, as appeared once upon a slight occasion when her reputation being a little touch'd upon a mistake, yet so carried as she could not get the party upon that advantage which she expected, she vented her impatience with so fierce speech and countenance, as one would hardly have guessed her to have been an Antitype of *Daniel,* but rather of the Lions after they were let loose. The like appeared in her, when she could not have her will against her faithfull Pastor for his opposing her opinions, as she apprehended, so as neither reason, nor Scripture, nor the judgement and example of such as she reverenced could appease her displeasure. So that the Court did clearely discerne, where the fountaine was of all our distempers, and the Tragedy of *Munster*[57] (to such as had read it) gave just occasion to feare the danger we were in, seeing (by the judgement of *Luther* writing of those troublous times) we had not to doe with so simple a Devill, as managed that businesse, and therefore he had the lesse feare of him; but Satan seemed to have com-

---

57. Munster was the German city taken over in 1534 by radical Anabaptists who subsequently were beseiged and slaughtered by orthodox Protestant forces.

mission now to use his utmost cunning to undermine the Kingdome of Christ here (as the same *Luther* foretold, he would doe,
when he should enterprize any such innovation under the cleare
light of the Gospel) so as the like hath not beene knowne in former ages, that ever so many wise, sober, and well grounded Christians, should so suddenly be seduced by the meanes of a woman, to
sticke so fast to her, even in some things wherein the whole cur-
rent of Scripture goeth against them, and that notwithstanding
that her opinions and practise have beene so grosse in some particulars, as their knowledge and sincerity would not suffer them to
approve, yet such interest hath she gotten in their hearts, as they
seeke cloakes to cover the nakednesse of such deformities, as in the
meane time they are ashamed to behold.

The Court saw now an inevitable necessity to rid her   [41]
away, except wee would bee guilty, not only of our own
ruine, but also of the Gospel, so in the end the sentence of banishment was pronounced against her, and shee was committed to the
Marshall, till the Court should dispose of her.

Another day, Captaine *John Underhill* was sent for, and being
charged with joyning in the said Petition, acknowledged the same,
professing that hee could see no fault in it: being demanded a rule
by which hee might take so much upon him, as publickly to contradict the sentence of the Court, &c. hee alledged the example of
Joab his rough speech to *David*, when hee retired himself for
Absaloms death, and that *David* did not reprove him for it. To
this the Court answered.

First, That *Joab* was then in the matters of his own calling,
and being Generall of the Army, had liberty by his place to give
advice to the King in causes of that nature, but when hee failed in
the manner of his speech, therein hee is not to bee excused, and
therefore not to bee followed.

Secondly, *Joab* did not contradict or reprove any Judiciall
sentence of the King, but only an inordinate passion.

Thirdly, Hee was occasioned by an urgent necessity of the
safety of the King and State.

Fourthly, That which hee spake was in private, for the King
had withdrawn himself.

Fifthly, It appeares that *David* did take it as a great miscarriage, for hee presently displaced him.

Againe, in our cause, the Captain was but a private man, and
had no calling to deale in the affaires of the Court, therefore no
warrant from hence. Hee insisted much upon the liberty which
all States do allow to *Military* Officers, for free speech, *&c.* and that
himself had spoken sometimes as freely to Count *Nassaw.*[58]

But it was answered, wee are not to look at what some do tolerate, but what is lawfull, and there may bee a reason of State, to
connive at that disorder at some season, which may not with honour and safety bee permitted at another.

Being further demanded, how they came so many of them, to
bee so suddenly agreed in so weighty and doubtfull a case, hee answered, that many of them being present when Mr. *Wheelwright*
was convict of sedition, they were sore grieved at it, and suddenly
rushing out of the Court, a strange motion came into all their
mindes, so as they said (in a manner all together) Come let us petition; and for his part, from that time to this, his conscience which
then led him to it, will not suffer him to retract it.

The Court pityed him much, and were grieved at his obstinacy, that when all his arguments were taken away, hee had no defence left, hee would yet maintaine a bad cause by the light of a
deluded conscience, and withall they tooke notice how these ungrounded revelations began to work, and what dangerous consequences were like to follow of them, when so many
persons upon such a sudden motion had no scruple to   [42]
enterprize such a seditious action, nor can bee brought
by any light of reason or Scripture, to see their error: so the Court
(when they saw no other remedy) dis-franchised him, and discharged him of his place, but allowed him his quarters means.

There were diverse who were not present when that sudden
motion or revelation first set the Petition on foot, but were drawn
in after, who soon found their error, and did as freely acknowledge it, and desired to have their names put out of it, which was

---

58. Stadtholder of Holland from 1584 to 1625. Underhill, a professional
soldier, may have fought in the Netherlands in the wars against Spain.

easily granted, and their offence with a loving admonition remitted.

It had been observed a good time since, that some of the leaders of this faction (by occasion of new Disciples, being inquisitive about their tenents) would let fall these answers, I have many things to tell you, but you cannot beare them now; and there is a great light to break forth, if men do not resist it, and you shall see the bottom hereafter; and one of them reproved the rest, telling them that they had spoyled their cause, by being over hasty and too open, &c. And now it began to appeare, what their meanings were, for after Mistris *Hutchison* had discovered the secret by her speech in the Court, then others opened their minds, and professedly maintained these Enthusiasmes as the Oracles of God. And that such revelations as *Abraham* had to kill his Son, and as *Paul* had in the Ship, and when hee was caught up into the third heaven, &c. were ordinary, so that Mr. *Cotton* took notice of the danger of them, and publickly confuted them in diverse Sermons. Among other like passages there was one that fell out, at Mr. *Wheel* his farewell to those whom hee used to Preach unto at the Mount.

One of his own Scholars told him openly, that hee had Preached Antichristianisme, and had set up a Christ against a Christ; the same party maintained immediate revelations without any word at all, saying, that the free promises were only for those under the Law, but wee are to look for all our assurance by immediate Revelation, and that in the New Testament there are no signes, no not our baptisme, for the baptisme of water is of no use to us, when once wee are baptized with the Holy Ghost: hee said also that a man might bee adopted and not justified, and that every new creature is as a dead lump, not acting at all, but as Christ acts in him, and denyed all inherent righteousnesse, and that the commandements were a dead Letter. These things were so grosse, as Mr. *Wheelwright* could not but contradict him, yet hee did it so tenderly, as might well discover his neere agreement in the points, though his wisdome served him to bee more reserved till a fitter season; for that poore man being newly come on to the profession of Religion, must needs learn those points of Mr. *Wheel.* or draw them as necessary consequences from some of his tenents: And it is frequently found to bee an effect of all unsound and unsafe doctrines, that still the Scholar goeth a step further then his Teacher. So it hath proved in former times, *Luther,* and no doubt many of those who did imbrace his errors, in the first edition of them, yet lived and dyed in the true faith of Christ, but the succeeding generations (inheriting those   [43] erroneous tenents, which they had drawn from their godly forefathers, but not their godlinesse) proved hereticks and schismaticks to this day. So it hath been in the Churches of *Rome,* and others, and so wee may justly feare in these Churches in *New England,* howsoever that many that now adhere to these Familisticall opinions, are indeed truely godly, and (no doubt) shall persevere so to the end, yet the next generation, which shall bee trained up under such doctrines, will bee in great danger to prove plain Familists and Schismaticks. This discovery of a new rule of practise by immediate revelations, and the consideration of such dangerous consequences, which have and might follow thereof, occasioned the Court to disarm all such of that party, as had their hands to the Petition, and some others, who had openly defended the same, except they should give satisfaction to the Magistrates therein; which some presently did, others made a great question about it, for bringing in their armes, but they were too weake to stand it out.[59]

Thus it pleased the Lord to heare the prayers of his afflicted people (whose soules had wept in secret, for the reproach which was cast upon the Churches of the Lord Jesus in this Countrey, by occasion of the divisions which were grown amongst us, though the vanity of some weake minds, which cannot seriously affect any thing long, except it bee offered them under some renewed shape) and by the care and indevour of the wise and faithfull Ministers of the Churches, assisted by the Civill authority, to discover this Master-piece of the old Serpent, and to break the brood by scattering the Leaders, under whose conduct hee had prepared such Ambushment, as in all reason would soon have driven Christ and

---

59. The order of the Court, and the names of those who were thus disarmed (including fifty-nine from Boston) appear in *Massachusetts Records, 1,* 207–208.

Gospel out of *New England,* (though to the ruine of the instruments themselves, as well as others) and to the repossessing of Satan in his ancient Kingdom; It is the Lords work, and it is marvellous in our eyes. Mr. *Wheel.* is now gone to *Pascal,*[60] Mistris *Hutchison* is confined in a private house, till the season of the yeer shall bee fit for her departure, some of those whom God hath left to bee most strongly deluded, are preparing to follow them, and wee hope the Lord will open the eyes of the rest, and perswade them to joyn again with their sometime deare and most beloved brethren, that peace and truth may again flourish in *New England, Amen.*

After the Court had thus proceeded, some of the Churches dealt with such of their members as were found guilty of these erroneous and seditious practises, the Church of *Roxbury* (after much pains and patience to reduce them) excommunicated five or six;[61] and the Church of *Boston,* by the solicitation of some of the Elders of the other Churches, proceeded against Mistris *Hutchison,* the manner and issue whereof is set down in the next.

AT *Boston* in *New England,* upon the 17. day of *October* 1637. the wife of one *William Dyer,* sometimes a Citizen & Millener of *London,* a very proper and comely young   [44] woman, was delivered of a large woman childe, it was stilborn, about two moneths before her time, the childe having life a few houres before the delivery, but so monstrous and misshapen, as the like hath scarce been heard of: it had no head but a face, which stood so low upon the brest, as the eares (which were like an Apes) grew upon the shoulders.

The eyes stood farre out, so did the mouth, the nose was hooking upward, the brest and back was full of sharp prickles, like a Thornback, the navell and all the belly with the distinction of the sex, were, where the lower part of the back and hips should have been, and those back parts were on the side the face stood.

The arms and hands, with the thighs and legges, were as other

---

60. Pascataqua or Piscataqua, the area around the Piscataqua River in New Hampshire.

61. Cf. *Sixth Report of the Boston Record Commissioners* (Boston, 1881), 79, 81.

* See new note p. xx.

childrens, but in stead of toes, it had upon each foot three claws, with talons like a young fowle.

Upon the back above the belly it had two great holes, like mouthes, and in each of them stuck out a piece of flesh.

It had no forehead, but in the place thereof, above the eyes, foure hornes, whereof two were above an inch long, hard, and sharpe, the other two were somewhat shorter.

Many things were observable in the birth and discovery of this Monster.

1. The Father and Mother were of the highest forme of our refined Familists, and very active in maintaining their party, and in reproaching some of the Elders, and others, who did oppose those errors.

2. The Midwife, one *Hawkins* wife of St. *Ives,* was notorious for familiarity with the devill, and now a prime Familist.[62]

3. This Monster was concealed by three persons above five moneths.

4. The occasion of concealing it was very strange, for most of the women who were present at the womans travaile, were suddenly taken with such a violent vomiting, and purging, without eating or drinking of any thing, as they were forced to goe home, others had their children taken with convulsions, (which they had not before, nor since) and so were sent for home, so as none were left at the time of the birth, but the Midwife and two other, whereof one fell asleepe.

5. At such time as the child dyed (which was about two houres before the birth) the bed wherein the mother lay shook so violently, as all which were in the roome perceived it.

6. The after birth wherein the childe was, had prickles on the inside like those on the childes brest.

7. The manner of the discovery was very strange also, for it was that very day Mistris *Hutchison* was cast out of the Church for her monstrous errours, and notorious falsehood; for being commanded to depart the Assembly, Mistris *Dyer* accompanied her, which a stranger observing, asked another what woman that was, the other answered, it was the woman who had the Monster, which one of the Church of *Bos-*   [45]

---

62. Cf. Winthrop, *History,* 2, 10–11.

ton hearing, enquired about it from one to another, and at length came to Mistris *Hutchison,* with one of the Elders of the Church, to whom shee revealed the truth of the thing in generall onely; this comming to the Governours eare, hee called another of the Magistrates and sent for the Midwife, and (in the presence of the Elder, to whom Mistris *Hutchison* had revealed it) they examined her, who at first confessed it was a monstrous birth, but concealed the horns and claws, and some other parts, till being straitly charged, and told it should bee taken up, and viewed, then shee confessed all, yet for further assurance, the childe was taken up, and though it were much corrupted, yet the horns, and claws, and holes in the back, and some scales, &c. were found and seen of above a hundred persons.

8. The Father of this Monster, having been forth of the Town, about a Moneth, and comming home just at this time, was upon the Lords day (by an unexpected occasion) called before the Church for some of his monstrous opinions, as that Christ and the Church together, are the new creature, there is no inherent right-eousnesse in Christians, *Adam* was not made after Gods Image, &c. which hee openly maintained, yet with such shuffling, and equivo-cating, as hee came under admonition, &c.

A briefe Apologie in defence of the generall proceedings of the Court, holden at *Boston* the ninth   [46]
day of the first moneth, 1636,[63] against Mr. *J.*
VVheelwright a member there, by occasion of a Sermon delivered there in the same Congregation.

Forasmuch as some of the Members of the Court (both of the Magistrates and Deputies) did dissent from the major part, in the judgement of the cause of Mr. *Wheelwright,* and divers others have since censured the proceedings against him as unjust, or (at best) over hasty, for maintaining of which censures, many un-truths are like to be spread abroad, whereby the most equall Judges may be in danger of prejudice; and so the honour not of

---

63. I.e. March (the first month of the year, by the Puritans' reckoning), 1637.

the Court onely, but also of the tryall and justice it selfe may be blemished: It is thought needfull to make this publike Declaration of all the proceedings, with the reasons and grounds thereof, so farre as concerneth the clearing of the justice of the Court. As for such passages as fell by occasion, and are too large to be here inserted, such as desire to know them, may receive satisfaction from three or foure of *Boston* (being Mr. *Wheelwright* his speciall friends) who tooke all by Characters (we doubt not) will give a true report thereof; As for such as have taken offence, that the cause was not first referred to the Church, we desire them to consider these reasons.

1. This case was not matter of conscience, but of a civill nature, and therefore most proper for this Court, to take Cognizance of, and the rather for the speciall contempt which had beene offered to the Court therein, and which the Church could not judge of. 2. In some cases of religious nature, as manifest heresie, notorious blasphemy, &c. the Civill power may proceed, *Ecclesia inconsulta,* and that by the judgement of all the Ministers. 3. It had beene a vaine thing to referre a cause to the judgement of those who had openly declared their prejudice therein, both in the Court and otherwise, as by two Petitions under the hands of most of them, delivered into the Court on his behalfe, did plainely appeare. 4. The heat of contention and uncharitable censures which began to over-spread the Countrey, and that chiefely by occasion of that Sermon, and the like miscarriages, did require that the Civill power should speedily allay that heat, and   [47] beare witnesse against all seditious courses, tending to the overthrow of truth and peace amongst us: this onely by way of entrance, to the matter which now followeth.

In the beginning of the Court, the Deputies upon the fame of a Sermon delivered by Mr. *Wheelwright* (upon the fast day) which was supposed to tend to sedition, and disturbance of the publike peace, desired that he might be sent for, which the Court assenting unto, one of the Magistrates (his speciall friend) undertooke to give him notice thereof, and accordingly at the next meeting he was in the Towne, ready to appeare, when he should be called for, which was not till two or three dayes after, and then he was sent for (not by the Marshall, as the usuall manner is; but) by one of the Deputies his intimate friend upon his appearance he was made acquainted with the cause why he was sent for, *viz.* To satisfie the Court about some passages in his Sermon, which seemed to be offensive, and therewith a copy of it was produced, and he was demanded whether he would owne it: whereupon he drew forth another copy which he delivered into the Court, as a true copy, (for the substance of it) so he was dismissed very gently, and desired to be ready when he should be called for againe.

The next day he was againe sent for by the former messenger: About this time a Petition was delivered into the Court, under the hands of above forty persons, being most of the Church of *Boston* (being none of the Petitions before mentioned, which were delivered after) to this effect, that as free-men they might be admitted to be present in the Court in causes of judicature, and that the Court would declare whether they might proceed in cases of conscience, without referring them first to the Church.[64] To this the Court answered on the backside of the Petition, that they did conceive the Petition was without just ground, for the first part of it, the Court had never used privacie in Judiciall proceedings, but in preparation thereto by way of examination of the party, &c. they might and would use their liberty, as they should see cause; and for the other part of the Petition, when any matter of conscience should come before them, they would advise what were fit to be done in it.

When Mr. *Wheelwright* came in, the Court was private, and then they told him they had considered of his Sermon, and were desirous to aske him some questions which might tend to cleare his meaning, about such passages therein as seemed offensive; he demanded whether he were sent for as an innocent person, or as guilty? It was answered neither, but as suspected onely; Then he

---

64. The petitioners raised a sensitive question about the relationship between church and state: was the disturbance caused by Wheelwright's sermon simply a religious affair? If so, it was only the church that could censure him, for the colonists held to the separation of church and state in matters of discipline. The issue had previously arisen when the Boston Church wanted to censure Wilson for his "speech" to the General Court. Cf. John Winthrop, "Essay Against the Power of the Church to Sit in Judgment on the Civil Magistracy," *Winthrop Papers, 3,* 505–507.

demanded, who were his accusers? It was answered, his Sermon; (which was there in Court) being acknowledged by himselfe they might thereupon proceed, *ex officio:* at this word great exception was taken, as if the Court intended the course of the High Commission, &c.[65] It was answered that the word *ex officio* was very safe and proper, signifying no more but the authority or duty of the Court, and that there was no cause of offence, seeing the Court did not examine him by any compulsory meanes, as by oath, imprisonment, or the like, but onely desired him   [48] for better satisfaction to answer some questions, but he still refused, yet at last through perswasion of some of his friends, he seemed content; The question then put to him was, whether before his Sermon he did not know, that most of the Ministers in this jurisdiction did teach that doctrine which he in his Sermon called a Covenant of works; to this he said, he did not desire to answer, and hereupon some cried out, that the Court went about to ensnare him, and to make him to accuse himselfe, and that this question was not about the matter of his Sermon, &c. Upon this he refused to answer any further, so he was dismissed till the afternoone; The reason why the Court demanded that question of him, was not to draw matter from himselfe whereupon to proceed against him, neither was there any need, for upon a conference of the Ministers not long before there had beene large dispute betweene some of them and himselfe about that point of evidencing Justification by Sanctification, so as the court might soone have convinced him by witnesses, if they had intended to proceed against him upon that ground.

In the afternoone he was sent for againe in the same manner as before, and the Ministers also being in the Towne, and come thither to conferre together for further discovery of the ground of the differences which were in the Countrey about the Covenant of Grace, &c. they were desired to be present also in the Court, to beare witnesse of the proceedings in the case, and to give their advice as the Court (upon occasion) should require: so the doores

---

65. The Court of High Commission was the court before which nonconformist ministers in the Church of England were haled; hence its pejorative significance for the colonists, a significance attached in particular to the form of oath ("ex officio") required of those being questioned.

being set open for all that would to come in (and there was a great Assembly) and Mr. *Wheelwright* being willed to sit downe by the Ministers, his Sermon was produced, and many passages thereof was read to him, which for the better understanding we have digested into this order following.

He therein describeth two Covenants, the Covenant of Grace and the Covenant of Works; the Covenant of Grace he describeth to be, when in the point of Justification and the knowledge of this our Justification by Faith, there is nothing revealed but Christ Jesus; but if men thinke to be saved, because they see some worke of Sanctification in themselves, as hungring and thirsting, &c. this is a Covenant of Works; if men have revealed to them some work of righteousnesse, as love to the brethren, &c. and hereupon come to be assured that they are in a good estate, this is not the assurance of Faith, for Faith hath Christ revealed for the object, therefore if the assurance of a mans Justification be by Faith, as a Work, it is not Gospel.

Having thus described those who goe under a Covenant of Works, he pronounceth them to be enemies to Christ, to be Antichrists, to be flesh opposed to spirit; such as will certainly persecute those who hold forth the truth, and the wayes of Grace; he resembleth them to the Philistins, who stop up with the earth of their owne inventions, the Wels of true beleevers; he resembleth them also to *Herod,* who would have killed Christ so soone as he was borne, and to *Herod* and *Pilate* who did kill Christ when he came once to shew forth himselfe, and would   [49] have kept him eternally in the grave; he further describeth them out of the second Psalme, to be the people of God as the Jewes were, and such as would take away the true Christ and put in false Christs, to deceive if it were possible the very elect; he also describeth them by that in *Cant.* 10. 6. they make the children of Grace keepers of the Vineyard, they make them travell under the burden of the Covenant of Works, which doth cause Christ many times from them. He commeth after to a use of exhortation, wherein he stirreth up all those of his side to a spirituall combate, to prepare for battel, and come out and fight against the enemies of the Lord; (those under a Covenant of Works) he shewes whom he meaneth thus to excite, alluding to *Davids* valiant men, to

Baruch, Deborah, Jael, and all the men of *Jsrael,* and bind them hereunto under the curse of *Meroz;* He further exhorteth them to stand upon their guard, &c. by alluding to the 600. valiant men, who kept watch about the bed of *Solomon,* a type of Christ; then he encourageth those of his side against such difficulties as might be objected, as 1. If the enemies shall oppose the way of God, they must lay the more load on them, and kill them with the Word of the Lord; and there he alludeth to those places which speak of giving the Saints power over nations, binding Kings in chaines, and of threshing instruments with teeth, and foretels their flight by that in *Esay* 21. 15. They shall flee from the sword, &c.

2. Though the enemies under a Covenant of Works be many and strong, (as he confesseth they are) yet they ought not to fear, for the battel is the Lords, this he enforceth by that in *Josh.* 23. 10. One of you shall chase a thousand, and that of *Jonathan* and his armour-bearer.

3. Against tendernesse of heart, which they might have towards such under a Covenant of Works, as are exceeding holy and strict in their way, he animateth his party by perswading them, that such are the greatest enemies to Christ; this he seekes to illustrate by resembling such in their zeale to *Paul* when he was a persecutor, and in their devotion to those who expelled *Paul* and *Barnabas* out of *Antioch.* He taketh it for granted that these holy men trust in their righteousnesse, and that it thrusteth out the righteousnesse of Christ, and so concludes and foretels from *Ezech.* 33. They shall die, and that their righteousnesse is accursed, yet they transforme themselves (saith he) into Angels of light.

4. That his party might not feare lest he should breake the rule of meekenesse, &c. he bringeth in the example of *Stephen, Act.* 7. 58. and the example of Christ, *Joh.* 8. 44. and *Matth.* 23. 23.

5. To those who might feare, lest this strife should cause a combustion in Church and Common-wealth, he answers and tells them plainely it will doe so, but yet to uphold their hearts, he armes them with the prediction of Christ, *Luk.* 12. 49. and tells them that it is the desire of the Saints, that that fire were kindled, and with that in *Esa.* 9. 5. which he interprets of *Michael* and the

Angells, and with that in *Mal.* 4. 2. and by that in the Revelation, the whore must be burnt.

6. Hee armes them against persecution by exhorting   [50]
them not to love their lives unto the death, but be will-
ing to be killed like sheepe, seeing it is impossible to hold forth the truth of God with externall peace and quietnesse: This he en-forceth by the example of *Sampson,* who slew more at his death then in his life.

These passages of his Sermon being openly read, Master *Wheelwright* did acknowledge and justifie the same, and being demanded (either then or before) whether by those under a Cov-enant of workes hee did meane any of the Ministers and other Christians in those Churches, he answered, that if he were shewed any that walked in such a way, as he had described to be a Cove-nant of workes, them he did meane. Here divers speeches passed up and downe, whereof there was no speciall notice taken, as not materiall to the purpose in hand.

The Court proceeded also to examine some witnesses about another Sermon of his, whereat much offence had also beene taken, and not without cause, (as appeared to the Court) for in that he seemed to scare men not onely from legall righteousnesse, but even from faith and repentance, as if that also were a way of the Covenant of workes; but this being matter of Doctrine, the Court passed it by for the present, onely they (and the Ministers present, divers of them) declared their griefe to see such opinions risen in the Country of so dangerous consequence, and so directly crossing the scope of the Gospell, (as was conceived) and it was re-torted upon him which he in his Sermon chargeth his adverse party with, (though uncharitably and untruly) when he saith they would take away the true Christ, that to make good such a doc-trine as he held forth (to common intendment) must needes call for a new Christ and a new Gospell, for sure the old would not owne or justifie it.

Then the Court propounded a question to the Ministers, which (because they desired time of consideration to make answer unto) was given them in writing upon the outside of Master *Wheelwrights* Sermon, in these words; *Whether by that which you have heard concerning Master* Wheelwrights *Sermon, and that which was witnessed concerning him, yee doe conceive that the Ministers in this Country doe walke in and teach such a way of Salvation and evidencing thereof, as he describeth, and accounteth to be a Covenant of workes?* To this question (being againe called for into the Court the next morning) they returned an affirmative answer, in the very words of the question, adding withall, that they would not be understood, that their doctrine and Master *Wheelwrights* about Justification, and Salvation, and evidencing thereof, did differ in all things, but onely in the point presented, and debated now in Court, and that of this their answer they were ready to give reasons when the Court should demand them, and that to this they all consented, except their brother the teacher of *Boston:* After this (by leave of the Court) the Ministers all spake one by one in order, some more largely, laying open by solid arguments and notorious examples, the great dangers that the Churches and Civill State were falne into, by the differences which were growne amongst us in matters of Religion, offering themselves withall to employ all their studies to   [51] effect a reconciliation, shewing also their desires that Mr. *Wheelwright* would be with them, when they should meete for this purpose, and blaming his former strangenesse as a possible occasion of these differences of judgement. Others spake more briefely, but consented with the former; and all of them (as they had occasion to speake to Mr. *Wheelwright,* or to make mention of him) used him with all humanity and respect; what his carriage was towards them againe, those who were present may judge, as they saw cause.

The matters objected against Mr. *Wheel.* being recollected, and put to the vote, the opinion of the Court was, that he had run into sedition and contempt of the Civill authority, which accordingly was recorded to the same effect, and he was enjoyned to appeare at the next generall Court to abide their further sentence herein. And whereas motion was made of enjoyning him silence in the meane time, the Ministers were desired to deliver their advice what the Court might doe in such a case: Their answer was, that they could not give a cleare resolution of the question at the present, but for Mr. *Wheel.* they desired that the Court would rather referre him to the Church of *B.* to deale with him for that matter; which accordingly was done, and so he was dismissed: such of the Magistrates and Deputies, as had not concurred with the major part in the vote, (some of them) moved that the dissent might be recorded, (but it was denyed) as a course never used in this or any such Court. Afterward they tendered a Protestation, which was also refused, because therein they had justified Mr. *Wheel.* as a faithfull Minister of the Lord Jesus, and condemned the Court for undue proceeding; but this was offered them, that if they would write downe the words of the record, and subscribe their dissent without laying such aspersion upon the Court, it should be received.

Although the simple narration of these proceedings might be sufficient to justifie the Court in what they have done especially with these of this jurisdiction, who have taken notice of the passages in the generall Court in *Decem.* last, yet for satisfaction of others to whom this case may be otherwise presented by fame or misreport, we will set downe some grounds and reasons thereof, some whereof were expressed in the Court, and others (though not publickly insisted upon, yet) well conceived by some, as further motives to leade their judgments to doe as they did.

And, 1. It is to be observed, that the noted differences in point of Religion in the Churches here, are about the Covenant of workes, in opposition to the Covenant of grace; in clearing whereof much dispute hath beene, whether sanctification be any evidence of justification.

2. That before Mr. *Wheel.* came into this country (which is not yet two yeares since) there was no strife (at least in publick observation) about that point.

3. That he did know (as himselfe confessed) that divers of the Ministers here were not of his Judgement in those points, and that the publishing of them, would cause   [52] disturbance in the Country, and yet he would never conferre with the Ministers about them, that thereby he might have gained them to his opinion, (if it had beene the truth) or at least have manifested some care of the publick peace, which he rather seemed to slight, when being demanded in the Court a reason of such his failing, hee answered that he ought not to consult with

flesh and bloud, about the publishing of that truth which he had received from God.

4. It was well knowne to him that the Magistrates and Deputies were very sensible of those differences, and studious of pacifying such mindes as began to be warme and apt to contention about them, and for this end at the said Court in *December,* (where these differences and alienations of minde through rash censures, &c. were sadly complained of) they had called in the Ministers, and (Mr. *Wheel.* being present) had desired their advice for discovery of such dangers, as did threaten us hereby, and their helpe for preventing thereof; and it was then thought needefull, to appoint a solemne day of humiliation (as for other occasions more remote, so especially) for this which more neerely concerned us, and at this time this very point of evidencing justification by sanctification set into some debate, and Mr. *Wheel.* being present spake nothing, though he well discerned that the judgement of most of the Magistrates and neere all the Ministers closed with the affirmative.

5. That upon the said fast (Mr. *Wheel.* being desired by the Church to exercise as a private brother, by way of Prophecy) when Mr. *Cotton* teaching in the afternoon out of *Esa.* 58. 4. had shewed that it was not a fit worke for a day of Fast, to move strife & debate, to provoke to contention, &c. but by all means to labour pacification and reconciliation, and therein had bestowed much time, and many forcible arguments, yet Mr. *Wheel.* speaking after him, taught as is here before mentioned, wholly omitting those particular occasions which the Court intended, nay rather reproving them, in teaching that the onely cause of Fasting, was the absence of Christ, &c. and so notwithstanding the occasion of the day, Mr. *Cottons* example, the intent of the Court for procuring peace, he stirred up the people to contention, and that with more then ordinary vehemency. Now if any man will equally weigh the proceedings of the Court and these observations together, we hope it will appeare that Mr. *Wheelwright* was justly convict of sedition and contempt of authority, and such as have not leisure or will to compare them together, may onely reade that which here followeth, and receive satisfaction thereby, carrying this along with them, that the acts of authority holding forth the face, and stampe of a

divine sentence should not be lesse regarded then the actions of
any private brother, which a good man will view on all foure sides
before he judge them to be evill.

   Sedition and contempt are laid to his charge.

   Sedition doth properly signifie a going aside to make a party,
and is rightly described by the Poet, (for it is lawfull to
fetch the meaning of words from humane authority) *In*   [53]
*magno populo cum sæpe coorta est seditio sævitque ani-
mis,*[66] &c. whence it doth appeare that when the minds of the people being assembled are kindled or made fierce upon some sud-
daine occasion, so as they fall to take part one against another, this
is sedition; for when that *furor,* which doth *arma ministrare,* is
once kindled, the sedition is begun, though it come not to its perfection, till *faces et saxa volant: Tully* saith, *Seditionem, esse dis-
sensionem omnium inter se, cum eunt alii in aliud,*[67] when the
people dissent in opinion and goe severall wayes.

   Isidore saith, *Seditiosus est, qui dissentionem animorum facit
& discordias gignit,*[68] He that sets mens minds at difference, and
begets strife: And if we look into the Scripture we shall find examples of sedition agreeing to these descriptions. The uproare
moved by *Demetrius, Acts* 19. was sedition, yet he neither took up
armes, nor perswaded others so to doe, but onely induced the
minds of the people, and made them fierce against the Apostles,
by telling them they were enemies to *Diana* of the *Ephesians.
Korah* and his company moved a most dangerous sedition, yet
they did not stirre up the people to fight, onely they went apart
and drew others to them against *Moses* and *Aaron;* here was nothing but words, and that by a Levite, who might speake by his
place, but it cost more then words before it was pacified. Now in
our present case, did not Mr. *Wheel.* make sides when he proclaimed all to be under a Covenant of works, who did not follow
him (step by step) in his description of the Covenant of Grace? did

---

   66. *Aeneid,* Bk. 1, line 148: When often in a great people sedition has
broken out and it rages in their spirits.
   67. (Till) they throw firebrands and rocks: Tully saith, Sedition is the
disagreement of the people among themselves when each goes his own way.
   68. He is seditious who creates dissension of minds and gives birth to dis-
cord.

he not make himselfe a party on the other side, by often using these and the like words, We, us? Did he not labour to heat the minds of the people, and to make them fierce against those of that side, which he opposed (and whereof he knew that most of the Magistrates and Ministers had declared themselves) when with the greatest fervency of spirit and voyce, he proclaimes them Antichrists, enemies, Philistims, *Herod, Pilate,* persecuting Jewes, and stirred up them on his part to fight with them, to lay load on them, to burne them, to thresh them, to bind them in chaines and fetters, to kill them and vexe their hearts, and that under the paine of the curse of *Meroz? Tantæne animis cælestibus iræ?*[69] would one thinke that any heavenly spirit could have breathed so much anger, when an Angel would have given milder language to the Devill himselfe? and all this without vouchsafing one argument to convince these enemies of their evil way, or one word of admonition or advice to themselves, to draw them out of danger. But it is objected, that he expressed his meaning to be of a spirituall fighting and killing, &c. with the sword of the spirit onely. It is granted he did so, yet his instances of illustration, or rather enforcement, were of another nature, as of *Moses* killing the Egyptian in defence of his brother, *Sampson* losing his life with the Philistims, the fight of *Jonathan* and his armour-bearer, and of *Davids* worthies, *Baruc* and *Jael,* &c. these obtained their victories with swords and hammers, &c. And such are no spirituall weapons, so that if his intent were not to stirre up to open force and armes (neither doe we suspect him of any such purpose, otherwise then by consequent) yet his reading and experience   [54] might have told him, how dangerous it is to heat peoples affections against their opposites, a mind inflamed with indignation (among some people) would have beene more apt to have drawne their swords by the authority of the examples he held forth for the encouragement, then to have beene kept to spirituall weapons, by the restraining without cautions, such as cannot dispute for Christ with *Steven,* will be ready to draw their swords for him, like *Peter;* for *furor arma ministrat,*[70] like him who when he

---

69. *Aeneid,* Bk. 1, line 11: Is there such wrath in divine breasts?
70. Ibid., Bk. 1, line 150: for madness provides weapons.

could not by any sentence in the Bible confute an Heretick, could make use of the whole booke to break his head; we might hold forth instances more then enough. The warres in *Germany* for these hundred yeeres arose from dissentions in Religion, and though in the beginning of the contention, they drew out onely the sword of the Spirit, yet it was soone changed into a sword of steele; so was it among the confederate Cantons of *Helvetia*, which were so many Townes as neerely combined together, as ours here; so was it also in the *Netherlands* betweene the Orthodox and the *Arminians;* so hath it beene betweene the *Calvinists* and *Lutherans:* In every place we find that the contentions began first by disputations and Sermons, and when the minds of the people were once set on fire by reproachfull termes of incendiary spirits, they soone set to blowes, and had alwayes a tragicall and bloudy issue; And to cleare this objection, Mr. *Wheel.* professed before hand, what he looked for, *viz.* that his doctrine would cause combustions even in the Common-wealth, as well as in the Churches, which he could not have feared if he had supposed (as in charity he well might) that those who were set over the people here in both States were indeed true Christians; yea he not onely confesseth his expectation, but his earnest desire also of such combustions and disturbances, when he saith that it is the Saints desire to have the fire kindled, as if hee were come among Turks or Papists, and not among the Churches of Christ, amongst whom *Paul* laboured to quench all fire of contention, but with the *Corinthians, Romans,* and *Galatians,* and wished that those were cut off who troubled them, setting a mark upon such as made division, and a note of a carnall mind: therefore this objection will not save him, his offence is yet without excuse, hee did intend to trouble our peace, and hee hath effected it; therefore it was a contempt of that authority which required every man to study Peace and Truth, and therefore it was a seditious contempt, in that hee stirred up others, to joyn in the disturbance of that peace, which hee was bound by solemn Oath to preserve.

But here hee puts in a plea, that hee did take the only right way for Peace, by holding out the Lord Jesus Christ in the Covenant of free Grace, for without Christ there is no peace, but get Christ and wee have all.

To this wee reply, first, Wee would demand of him what hee accounts a holding forth a Covenant of Grace? for saving that hee saith, this is a Covenant of Grace, that is a Covenant of Works, no man can discerne any such thing by his proofes, for there is not any one argument in his Sermon to convince the judgement that so it is, and if wee search the Scripture, wee find in   [55] the Old Testament, *Jer.* 31. the Covenant of Grace to bee this, I will write my Law in their hearts, or, I will bee their God, &c. and in the New Testament, wee find, Hee that beleeves in the Lord Jesus Christ, shall bee saved, and that it is of Faith, that it might bee of grace; but other Covenant of Grace then these, or to the same effect, are not in our Bibles.

Again, Though it bee true, that get Christ and wee have all in some respect, yet wee must remember him of what hee said with the same breath, that Truth and externall Peace cannot possibly stand together, how then would hee have us beleeve, that such a holding forth Christ should bring the desired peace? This is somewhat like the Jewish *Corban,* I will give to God, and hee shall help my Parents, or as when a poore man stands in need of such reliefe, as I might give him, instead there of I pray to God to blesse him, and tell him that the blessing of God maketh rich; or, as I give a Lawyer a Fee to plead my cause, and to procure mee Justice, and when the day of hearing comes, hee makes a long speech in commending the justice of the King, and perswading mee to get his favour, because hee is the fountain of Justice; This is to reprove the wisdome of God, by looking that the supreme and first cause should produce all effects, without the use of subordinate and neerer causes and means; so a man should live out his full time by Gods decree only, without meat or medicine; this plea therefore will not hold, let us heare another.

It is objected, that the Magistrates may not appoint a messenger of God, what hee should teach: admit so much, yet hee may limit him what hee may not teach, if hee forbid him to teach heresy or sedition, &c. hee incurres as well a contempt in teaching that which hee was forbidden, as sins in teaching that which is evill. Besides, every truth is not seasonable at all times. Christ tels his Disciples that hee had many things to teach them, but they could not beare them then, *Joh.* 16. 12. and God giveth his Prophets the tongue of the learned, that they may know how to speak a word in season, *Isa.* 50, 40. and if for every thing there bee a season, then for every Doctrine, *Eccles.* 3. 1. The abolishing of the ceremoniall Law was a Truth which the Apostles were to teach, yet there was a season when *Paul* did refrain it, *Acts* 21. 24. and the same *Paul* would not circumcise *Titus,* though hee did *Timothy,* so the difference of persons and places, made a difference in the season of the doctrine: and if Mr. *Wheelwright* had looked upon the words which followed in his Text, *Matth.* 9. 16, 17. hee might have learned that such a Sermon would as ill suite the season, as old bottles doe new Wine, and by that in *Esay* before mentioned, hee might have known that the Spirit of God doth teach his servants to discern of seasons, as well as of truths; for if there be such a point in wisdom, as men call discretion, sure, Religion (which maketh truely wise) doth not deprive the servants of God of the right use thereof. When *Paul* was to deale with the sorcerer, who did oppose his doctrine, *Act.* 13. hee cals him the childe of the devill, &c. but when hee answered *Festus,* (who told him hee was madde, and rejected his doctrine also) hee useth him gently, and with termes of honourable respect. Though   [56] *Steven* cals the Jews stiffenecked, and of uncircumcised hearts, &c, as knowing them to bee malitious and obstinate enemies to Christ, yet *Paul* directs *Timothy* (being to deale with such as were not past hope, though they did oppose his Doctrine for the present) not to strive, but to use all gentlenesse, instructing them with meeknesse, &c. 2 *Tim.* 2. The Prophet *Elisha* when hee speaks to *Jehoram* very roughly, as one not worthy to bee looked at, yet hee shews a different respect of *Jehosaphat,* though hee were then out of his way, and under a sin, for which hee had been formerly reproved, 2 *King.* 3. Christ himselfe (though hee sharply reproveth the Pharisees, &c. yet hee instructeth *Nicodemus* gently, when hee objected against his doctrine, and that somewhat rudely, *Joh.* 3. The Apostles would not forbeare to Preach Christ, though Rulers forbad them, *Act.* 3. yet another Prophet forbare at another season at the command of King *Amasia,* 2 *Chron.* 25. so wee see that this plea of Mr. *Wheelwright* is as weak as the former, and will not excuse him from contempt.

If it bee yet objected, that his Sermon was not all for contention, seeing hee raised and pressed an use of brotherly love, wee grant hee did so, but it was *ejusdem farinæ*, a loafe of the same leaven with the other, for hee applyeth it to those of his own party, to perswade them to hold together, and help one another against those of the other party, whom hee setteth forth as their opposites and encourageth them thereto by the example of *Moses*, who in love to his brother, killed the *Ægyptian*.

A further objection hath been made against the proceedings of the Court, as if Mr. *Wheelwright* had not a lawfull tryall, as not being put upon a Jury of freemen. But the answer to this is easie, it being wel known to all such as have understanding of matters of this nature, that such Courts as have power to make and abrogate Laws, are tyed to no other Orders, but their own, and to no other rule but Truth and Justice, and why thrice twelve men sitting as Judges in a Court, should bee more subject to partiality then twelve such called as a Jury to the barre, let others judge.

Now if some shall gather from that which is here before mentioned, *viz.* that every truth is not seasonable at all times, if wee shall grant that what Master *Wheelwright* delivered was the truth, wee must desire him to take onely so much as wee granted, *viz.* by way of supposition onely; for letting passe (as wee said) such points as were meerly doctrinall, and not ripe for the Court (depending as yet in examination among the Elders) wee may safely deny that those speeches were truths, which the Court censured for contempt and sedition, for a brother may fall so farre into disobedience to the Gospel, as there may bee cause to separate from him, and to put him to shame, and yet hee is not to bee accounted an enemy, 2 *Thess.* 3. Therefore when Mr. *Wheelwright* pronounced such (taking them at the worst hee could make them) to bee enemies, &c. it was not according to the truth of the Gospell. Againe, to incense and heate mens minds against their Brethren, before hee had convinced or admonished [57] them, as being in an estate of enmity, &c. is not to bee termed in any truth of the Gospel; so likewise to bring extraordinary examples for ordinary rules, as of *Joh.* 8. 44. to incite his party to the like practise against such whose hearts they cannot judge of, as Christ could of theirs to whom hee spake, is as farre from the rule prescribed to ordinary Ministers, 2 *Tim.* 2. 25. and

to all Christians, *Gal.* 6. 1. and *Jam.* 3. 17. as that example of
Elijah (by which the Apostles would have called for fire from
heaven upon the Samaritans) was different from the Spirit
whereof they were: so to resemble such among us, as professe their
faith in Christ only, &c. and are in Church fellowship, and walk
inoffensively, submitting to all the Lords Ordinances in Church
and Common wealth, to resemble such to branded Reprobates,
and arch-enemies of Christ, such as *Herod,* &c. wee suppose hath
no warrant of Truth. Wee might instance in other like passages,
as his ordinary inciting to spirituall combates, by examples of
bodily fight and bloody victories, (being very unsutable) but these
may suffice to prove that all hee spake was not true, and by this is
the offence more aggravated, for if it were seditious only in the
manner, it must needs bee much worse, when the matter it selfe
also was untrue.

But if any shall yet pretend want of satisfaction, by all that
hath been produced, (for indeed it is beyond reason, how farre
prejudice hath prevailed to captivate some judgements, otherwise
godly and wise) and shal object further, that his doctrines, &c.
were generall, and so could not bee intended of any particular
persons, wee desire such, first to remember what application Mr.
Wh. made of the same in the open Court, *viz.* that hee did intend
all such as walked in such a way. Then again, let the case bee put
in a reversed frame, some other had then taught, that all such as
deny that sanctification (as it is held by the other party) is a good
evidence of justification, and that say or have their assurance by
faith, as a work of God in them, have it in the way of the Gospel,
that these were enemies to Christ, &c. Persecutors of the way of
grace, &c. and should have stirred up others against them, with
like arguments, and vehemency as Mr. *Wheelwright* did, there is
no doubt but Mr. *Wheel.* and others of his opinion, would soone
have pointed out those who must necessarily have been intended
by it: for it is well known that some proper adjunct, or some noted
circumstance may design a particular person or company, as well
as names, so Christ points out *Judas* by the sop, *Paul* the Jews, by
those of the circumcision, and the Antichrist, by That man of sin,
&c.

But wee meet yet with another objection, *viz.* that disturbance
of unity is not sedition, except it also lead to the hurt of utility.

To this wee answer, first, that if it tend immediately to such hurt, wee deny the truth of the proposition; for if in the time of famine, a man should stir up the people to fetch corn out of the houses of such as had it to spare, this were to an immediate pub-lick good, yet it were sedition. If *Jeremy* (when he taught the Jews, that they ought to set free their Hebrew servants) had also incited the servants to free themselves, this had   [58] not been free from sedition, yet it had not been against publick utility: But they alledge the examples of *Jehojadah,* who caused a disturbance, yet without sedition; wee answer, that case was very unlike to ours, for *Jehojadah* being High Priest, was also protector of the true King, and so chiefe Governour of the Civill State, and *Athaliah* being a meere usurper, hee did no other, then if a lawfull King should assemble his Subjects to apprehend a Rebell; and though a Prince or Governour may raise a party to suppresse or withstand publick enemies or other evils, yet it doth not follow that a private man, or a Minister of the Gospel may do the like: we read *Nehem.* 5. 7. that hee raised a great assembly against those who did oppresse their brethren, but wee read not that *Ezra* did so, upon the disorders which hee complained of, and yet that which hee did in assembling of the people, for redresse, &c. was by authority and counsell of the Nobles, *Ezra* 10. 8.

2. That this course of Mr. *Wheel.* did tend directly to the great hinderance of publike utility, for when brethren shall looke one at another as enemies and persecutors, &c. and when people shall looke at their Rulers and Ministers as such, and as those who goe about to take Christ and salvation from them, how shall they joyne together in any publike service? how shall they cohabite and trade together? how hardly will they submit to such Over-seers? how will it hinder all affaires in Courts, in Townes, in Families, in Vessels at Sea, &c. and what can more threaten the dissolution and ruine of Church and Commonwealth? Lastly, if it be al-leadged that such warlike termes are used by Christ and his Apos-tles in a spirituall sense, we deny it not, but we desire that the usuall manner of their applying them may be also considered, for *Paul* saith, 1 *Cor.* 9. So fight I, &c. I beate downe my body, &c. 1 *Tim.* 6. 12. Fight the good fight of faith, lay hold on eternall life, and 1 *Pet.* 2. 11. and *Jam.* 4. 1. there is speech of the fight of our lusts, and *Ephes.* 6. 11. he bids them put on armour, but it is to

resist the Devill, not flesh and bloud, not to fight against their brethren, towards whom he forbids all bitternesse and clamour, &c. *Eph.* 4. And when he speaks of spirituall weapons, 2 *Cor.* 10. he doth not draw them out against the persons of brethren, but against high thoughts and imaginations, &c. And if Mr. *Wheel.* had found out any such among us, and planted his battery against them by sound arguments, he had followed our Apostolike rule; Christ indeed threatneth to fight against the Nicholaitans with the sword of his mouth, and if Mr. *Wheel.* had knowne any such here, as certainly as Christ knew those, he might have beene justified by the example, otherwise not.

Therefore to conclude, seeing there be of those who dissent from Mr. *Wheel.* his doctrines, who have denied themselves for the love of Christ as farre as he hath done, and will be ready (by Gods grace) to doe and suffer for the sake of Christ, and the honour of Free-grace as much as himselfe, for such to be publikely defamed, and held forth as enemies to the Lord   [59] Jesus, and persecutors like *Herod* and *Pilate,* and the uncircumcised heathen, &c. cannot proceed from a charitable mind, nor doth it savour of an Apostolike, Gospel-like, brotherly spirit.

Mistris *Hutchison* being banished and confined, till the season of the yeere might be fit, and safe for her departure; she thought it now needlesse to conceale herselfe any longer, neither would Satan lose the opportunity of making choyce of so fit an instrument, so long as any hope remained to attaine his mischievous end in darkning the saving truth of the Lord Jesus, and disturbing the peace of his Churches. Therefore she began now to discover all her mind to such as came to her, so that her opinions came abroad and began to take place among her old disciples, and now some of them raised up questions about the immortality of the soule, about the resurrection, about the morality of the Sabbath, and divers others, which the Elders finding to begin to appeare in some of their Churches, they took much paines (both in publike and private) to suppresse; and following the sent from one to another, the root of all was found to be in Mistris *Hutchison;* whereupon they resorted to her many times, labouring to convince her, but in vaine; yet they resorted to her still, to the end they might either reclaime her from her errours, or that they might beare witnesse against them if occasion were: For in a meeting of the Magistrates and Elders, about suppressing these new sprung errours, the Elders of *Boston* had declared their readinesse to deale with Mistris *Hutchison* in a Church way, if they had sufficient testimony: for though she had maintained some of them sometimes before them, yet they thought it not so orderly to come in as witnesses; whereupon other of the Elders, and others collecting which they had heard from her owne mouth at severall times, drew them into severall heads, and sent them to the Church of *Boston,* whereupon the Church (with leave of the Magistrates, because she was a prisoner) sent for her to appeare upon a Lecture day, being the fifteenth of the first moneth, and though she were at her owne house in the Towne, yet she came not into the Assembly till the Sermon and Prayer were ended, (pretending bodily infirmity) when she was come, one of the ruling Elders called her forth before the Assembly, (which was very great from all the parts of the Countrey) and telling her the cause why the Church had called her, read the severall heads, which were as followeth.

1. That the soules of all men (in regard of generation) are mortall like the beasts, *Eccl.* 3. 8.

2. That in regard of Christs purchase they are immortall, so that Christ hath purchased the soules of the wicked to eternall paine, and the soules of the elect to eternall peace.

3. Those who are united to Christ have in this life new bodies, and 2 bodies, 1 *Cor.* 6. 19. she knowes not how Jesus Christ should be united to this our fleshly bodies.

4. Those who have union with Christ, shall not rise with the same fleshly bodies, 1 *Cor.* 15. 44.

5. And that the resurrection mentioned there, and   [60] in *John* 5. 28. is not meant of the resurrection of the body, but of our union here and after this life.

6. That there are no created graces in the Saints after their union with Christ, but before there are, for Christ takes them out of their hands into his owne.

7. There are no created graces in the humane nature of Christ, but he was onely acted by the power of the God-head.

8. The Image of God wherein *Adam* was made, she could see

no Scripture to warrant that it consisted in holinesse, but conceived it to be in that he was made like to Christs manhood.

9. She had no Scripture to warrant that Christs manhood is now in Heaven, but the body of Christ is his Church.

10. We are united to Christ with the same union, that his humanity on earth was with the Deity, *Jo.* 17. 21.

11. She conceived the Disciples before Christ his death were not converted, *Matth.* 18. 3.

12. There is no evidence to be had of our good estate, either from absolute or conditionall promises.

13. The Law is no rule of life to a Christian.

14. There is no Kingdome of Heaven in Scripture but onely Christ.

15. There is first engraffing into Christ before union, from which a man might fall away.

16. The first thing God reveales to assure us is our election.

17. That *Abraham* was not in a saving estate till the 22. *chap.* of *Gen.* when hee offered *Isaac,* and saving the firmenesse of Gods election, he might have perished notwithstanding any work of grace that was wrought in him till then.

18. That union to Christ is not by faith.

19. That all commands in the word are Law, and are not a way of life, and the command of faith is a Law, and therefore killeth; she supposed it to be a Law from *Rom.* 3. 27.

20. That there is no faith of Gods elect but assurance, there is no faith of dependance but such as an hypocrite may have and fall away from, proved *John* 15. for by that she said they are in Christ, but Christ is not in them.

21. That an hypocrite may have *Adams* righteousnesse and perish, and by that righteousnes he is bound to the Law, but in union with Christ, Christ comes into the man, and he retaines the seed, and dieth, and then all manner of grace in himselfe, but all in Christ.

22. There is no such thing as inherent righteousnesse.

23. We are not bound to the Law, no not as a rule of life.

24. We are dead to all acts in spirituall things, and are onely acted by Christ.

25. Not being bound to the Law, it is not transgression against the Law to sinne, or breake it, because our   [61] sinnes they are inward and spirituall, and so are exceeding sinfull, and onely are against Christ.

26. Sanctification can be no evidence at all of our good estate.

27. That her particular revelations about future events are as infallible as any part of Scripture, and that she is bound as much to beleeve them, as the Scripture, for the same holy Ghost is the author of them both.

28. That so farre as a man is in union with Christ, he can doe no duties perfectly, and without the communion of the unregenerate part with the regenerate.

29. That such exhortations as these, to worke out our salvation with feare, to make our calling and election sure, &c. are spoken onely to such, as are under a Covenant of workes.

All which she did acknowledge she had spoken, (for a coppy of them had been sent to her divers dayes before, and the witnesses hands subscribed, so as she saw it was in vaine to deny them) then she asked by what rule such an Elder could come to her pretending to desire light, and indeede to entrappe her, to which the same Elder answered that he had beene twice with her, and that he told her indeed at St. *Ives,* that he had beene troubled at some of her speeches in the Court, wherein he did desire to see light for the ground and meaning of them, but he professed in the presence of the Lord, that he came not to entrap her, but in compassion to her Soule, to helpe her out of those snares of the Devill, wherein he saw she was entangled, and that before his departure from her he did beare witnesse against her opinions, and against her spirit, and did leave it sadly upon her from the word of God; then presently she grew into passion against her Pastor for his speech against her at the Court after the sentence was passed, which he gave a full answer unto, shewing his zeale against her errors, whereupon she asked for what errors she had beene banished, professing withall that she held none of these things she was now charged with, before her imprisonment; (supposing that whatsoever should be found amisse, would be imputed to that, but it was answered as the truth was, that she was not put to durance, but onely a favourable confinement, so as all of her Family and divers others, resorted to her at their pleasure.) But this allegation was then proved false, (and at her next convention more fully) for there were divers present, who did know she spake untruth. Her answer being demanded to the first Articles, she maintained her assertion that the Soules were mortall, &c. alledging the place in the *Eccles.* cited in the Article, and some other Scriptures nothing to the purpose, she insisted much upon that in *Gen.* 1. In the day thou eatest, &c. thou shalt dye, she could not see how a Soule could be immortally miserable, though it might be eternally miserable, neither could shee distinguish betweene the Soule and the Life; and though she were pressed by many Scriptures and reasons al- leadged by the Elders of the same, and other Churches, so as she could not give any answer to them, yet she stood to her opinion, till at length a stranger[71] being desired to speake to the point, and hee opening to her the difference betweene   [62] the Soule and the Life, the first being a spirituall sub- stance, and the other the union of that with the body; she then confessed she saw more light then before, and so with some diffi- culty was brought to confesse her error in that point. Wherein was to be observed that though he spake to very good purpose, and so clearly convinced her as she could not gain-say, yet it was evident shee was convinced before, but she could not give the honour of it to her owne Pastor or teacher, nor to any of the other Elders, whom she had so much slighted.

Then they proceeded to the third, fourth, and fifth Articles, about the body and the resurrection of the old, which shee main- tained according to the Articles, and though shee were not able to give any reasonable answer to the many places of the Scripture, and other arguments which were brought to convince her, yet shee still persisted in her errour, giving froward speeches to some that spake to her, as when one of the Elders used this argument, that if the resurrection were only our union with Christ, then all that are united, are the children of the resurrection, and therefore

---

71. Probably John Davenport (1597–1670), who arrived in Massachusetts in June, 1637. The following year he became one of the founders of New Haven, Connecticut.

are neither to marry, nor to give in marriage, and so by consequence, there ought to bee community of women; shee told him that hee spake like the Pharisees, who said that Christ had a devill, because that *Abraham* were dead and the Prophets, and yet hee had said, that those which eate his flesh, should never dye, not taking the speech in the true meaning, so did hee (said shee) who brought that argument, for it is said there, they should bee like the Angels, &c. The Elders of *Boston* finding her thus obstinate, propounded to the Church for an admonition to bee given her, to which all the Church consented, except two of her sons, who because they persisted to defend her, were under admonition also. Mr. *Cotton* gave the admonition, and first to her sons, laying it sadly upon them, that they would give such way to their naturall affection, as for preserving her honour, they should make a breach upon the honour of Christ, and upon their Covenant with the Church, and withall teare the very bowels of their soule, by hardning her in her sin: In this admonition to her, first, hee remembred her of the good way shee was in at her first comming, in helping to discover to divers, the false bottom they stood upon, in trusting to legall works without Christ; then hee shewed her, how by falling into these grosse and fundamentall errors, shee had lost the honour of her former service, and done more wrong to Christ and his Church, then formerly shee had done good, and so laid her sin to her conscience with much zeale and solemnity, hee admonished her also of the height of spirit, then hee spake to the sisters of the Church, and advised them to take heed of her opinions, and to with-hold all countenance and respects from her, lest they should harden her in her sin: so shee was dismissed and appointed to appeare againe that day sevennight.

The Court had ordered that shee should return to *Roxbury* again, but upon intimation that her spirit began to fall, shee was permitted to remain at Mr. *Cottons* house (where *Davenport* was also kept) who before her next appearing, did both take much pains with her, and prevailed so far, that shee did   [63] acknowledge her errour in all the Articles (except the last) and accordingly shee wrote down her answers to them all, when the day came, and shee was called forth and the Articles read again to her, shee delivered in her answers in writing, which were also read, and being then willing to speak to the Congregation for their further satisfaction, shee did acknowledge that shee had greatly erred, and that God had left her to her self herein, because shee had so much under-natured his Ordinances, both in slighting the Magistrates at the Court, and also the Elders of the Church, and confessed that when shee was at the Court, shee looked only at such failings as shee apprehended in the Magistrates proceedings, without having regard to the place they were in, and that the speeches shee then used about her revelations were rash, and without ground, and shee desired the prayers of the Church for her.

Thus farre shee went on well, and the Assembly conceived hope of her repentance, but in her answers to the severall articles, shee gave no satisfaction, because in diverse of them shee answered by circumlocutions, and seemed to lay all the faults in her expressions, which occasioned some of the Elders to desire shee might expresse her self more cleerly, and for that ever shee was demanded about the Article, whether shee were not, or had not been of that judgement, that there is no inherent righteousnesse in the Saints, but those gifts and graces which are ascribed to them that are only in Christ as the subject? to which shee answered, that shee was never of that judgement, howsoever by her expressions shee might seem to bee so; and this shee affirmed with such confidence as bred great astonishment in many, who had known the contrary, and diverse alledged her own sayings and reasonings, both before her confinement and since, which did manifest to all that were present, that shee knew that shee spake untruth, for it was proved that shee had alledged that in *Esay* 53. By his knowledge shall my righteous servant justifie many; which shee had maintained to bee meant of a knowledge in Christ, and not in us; so likewise that in *Galatians,* I live by the faith of the Son of God, which shee said was the faith of Christ, and not any faith inherent in us; also, that shee had maintained, that Christ is our sanctification in the same sort that hee is our justification, and that shee had said, that shee would not pray for grace, but for Christ, and that (when she had been pressed with diverse Scriptures, which spake of washing and creating a new heart, and writing the Law in the heart, &c.) shee had denyed, that they did mean any sanctification in us: There were diverse women also with whom shee had dealt about the same point, who (if their modesty had not restrained them) would have born witnesse against her herein, (as themselves after confessed) wherefore the Elders pressed her very earnestly to remember her self, and not to stand so obstinately to maintain so manifest an untruth, but shee was deafe of that eare, and would not acknowledge that shee had been at any time of that judgement, howsoever her expressions were; Then Mr. *Cotton* told the Assembly, that whereas shee had been [64] formerly dealt with for matter of doctrine, he had (according to the duty of his place being the teacher of that Church) proceeded against unto admonition, but now the case being altered, and she being in question for maintaining of untruth, which is matter of manners, he must leave the businesse to the Pastor, Mr. *Wilson* to goe on with her, but withall declared his judgement in the case from that in *Revel*. 22. that such as make and maintaine a lye, ought to be cast out of the Church; and whereas two or three pleaded that she might first have a second admonition, according to that in *Titus* 3. 10. he answered that that was onely for such as erred in point of doctrine, but such as shall notoriously offend in matter of conversation, ought to be presently cast out, as he proved by *Ananias* and *Saphira,* and the incestuous Corinthian; (and as appeares by that of *Simon Magus*) and for her owne part though she heard this moved in her behalfe, that she might have a further respite, yet she her selfe never desired it: so the Pastor went on, and propounding it to the Church, to know whether they were all agreed, that she should be cast out, and a full consent appearing (after the usuall manner) by their silence, after a convenient pause he proceeded, and denounced the sentence of excommunication against her, and she was commanded to depart out of the Assembly. In her going forth, one standing at the dore, said, The Lord sanctifie this unto you, to whom she made answer, The Lord judgeth not as man judgeth, better to be cast out of the Church then to deny Christ.

Thus it hath pleased the Lord to have compassion of his poore Churches here, and to discover this great imposter, an instrument of Satan so fitted and trained to his service for interrupting the passage, [of his] Kingdome in this part of the world, and poysoning the Churches here planted, as no story records the like of a woman, since that mentioned in the *Revelation;* it would make a large volume to lay downe all passages, I will onely observe some few, which were obvious to all that knew her course.

1. In her entrance I observe,
$$\begin{cases} 1. \text{ Her entrance.} \\ 2. \text{ Her progresse.} \\ 3. \text{ Her downfall.} \end{cases}$$

1. The foundation she laid was (or rather seemed to be) Christ and Free-Grace.

2. Rule she pretended to walke by, was onely the Scripture.

3. The light to discerne this rule, was onely the holy Ghost.

4. The persons she conversed with were (for the most part) Christians in Church Covenant.

5. Her ordinary talke was about the things of the Kingdome of God.

6. Her usuall conversation was in the way of righteousnesse and kindnesse.

Thus she entred and made up the first act of her course.

In her progresse I observe,

First, her successe, she had in a short time insinuated her selfe into the hearts of much of the people (yea of many of the most wise and godly) who grew into so reverent an   [65] esteeme of her godlinesse, and spirituall gifts, as they looked at her as a Prophetesse, raised up of God for some great worke now at hand, as the calling of the Jewes, &c. so as she had more resort to her for counsell about matter of conscience, and clearing up mens spirituall estates, then any Minister (I might say all the Elders) in the Country.

Secondly, Pride and arraigning of her spirit.

1. In framing a new way of conversation and evidencing thereof, carried along in the distinction betweene the Covenant of workes, which she would have no otherwise differenced, but by an immediate Revelation of the Spirit.

2. In despising all (both Elders and Christians) who went not her way, and laying them under a Covenant of workes.

3. In taking upon her infallibly to know the election of others, so as she would say, that if she had but one halfe houres talke with a man, she would tell whether he were elect or not.

4. Her impatience of opposition, which appeares in divers passages before.

Thirdly, Her skill and cunning to devise.

1. In that she still pretended she was of Mr. *Cottons* judgement in all things.

2. In covering her errors by doubtfull expressions.

3. In shadowing the true end, and abuse of her weekely meetings under the name of repeating Mr. *Cottons* Sermons.

4. In her method of practise to bring the conscience under a false terror, by working that an argument of a Covenant of workes, which no Christian can have comfort without, viz. of sanctification, or qualifications, (as she termed it.)

5. In her confident profession of her owne good estate, and the clearnesse and comfort of it, obtained in the same way of waiting for immediate Revelation which she held out to others.

In her downefall there may be observed the Lords faithfulnesse in honouring and justifying his owne Ordinances.

1. In that hee made her to cleare the justice of the Court, by confessing the vanity of her revelations, &c. and her sinne in despising his Ministers.

2. In that the judgement and sentence of the Church hath concurred with that of the Court in her rejection, so that she is cast out of both as an unworthy member of either.

3. The Justice of God in giving her up to those delusions, and to that impudency in venting and maintaining them, as should bring her under that censure, which (not long before) she had endeavoured and expected to have brought upon some other, who opposed her proceedings.

4. That she who was in such esteeme in the Church for soundnesse of Judgement and sincerity of heart (but a few moneths before) should now come under admonition for many foule and fundamentall errors, and after be cast out for notorious lying.

5. That shee who was wont to bee so confident of her spirituall good estate, and ready (undesired) to hold   [66] it forth to others (being pressed now at her last appearance before the Church to give some proofe of it) should bee wholly silent in that matter.

6. Whereas upon the sentence of the Court against her, shee boasted highly of her sufferings for Christ, &c. it was noted by one

of the Elders (who bare witnesse against her errors) that the spirit of glory promised in *Pet.* to those who suffer for well-doing, did not come upon her, but a spirit of delusion, and damnable error, which as it had possessed her before, so it became more effectuall and evident by her sufferings.

7. Here is to bee seen the presence of God in his Ordinances, when they are faithfully attended according to his holy will, although not free from human infirmities: This *American Jesabel* kept her strength and reputation, even among the people of God, till the hand of Civill Justice laid hold on her, and then shee began evidently to decline, and the faithfull to bee freed from her forgeries; and now in this last act, when shee might have expected (as most likely shee did) by her seeming repentance of her errors, and confessing her undervaluing of the Ordinances of Magistracy and Ministracy, to have redeemed her reputation in point of sincerity, and yet have made good all her former work, and kept open a back doore to have returned to her vomit again, by her paraphrasticall retractions, and denying any change in her judgement, yet such was the presence and blessing of God in his own Ordinance, that this subtilty of Satan was discovered to her utter shame and confusion, and to the setting at liberty of many godly hearts, that had been captivated by her to that day; and that Church which by her means was brought under much infamy, and neere to dissolution, was hereby sweetly repaired, and a hopefull way of establishment, and her dissembled repentance cleerly detected, God giving her up since the sentence of excommunication, to that hardnesse of heart, as shee is not affected with any remorse, but glories in it, and feares not the vengeance of God, which she lyes under, as if God did work contrary to his own word, and loosed from heaven, while his Church had bound upon earth.

FINIS.

CHAPTER 9

The Examination of Mrs. Anne Hutchinson
at the Court at Newtown

THE following account of Mrs. Hutchinson's examination by the General Court in November, 1637, is an important supplement to the abbreviated report included in the *Short Story.* Not only does the longer account contain many details missing in the *Short Story,* it also reveals that Mrs. Hutchinson parried the accusations of her examiners with a wit and verve that reduced them to confusion. Since she had not participated in the Antinomians' political protests, the Court could only charge her with "countenancing" those who did. The Court's other accusations concerned her weekly meetings and her attacks upon the ministers for preaching "works." But her dramatic statement that she received divine revelations became the pretext for her banishment.[1]

This report of the examination first appeared as an appendix to the second volume of Thomas Hutchinson's *History of the Colony and Province of Massachusetts Bay* (Boston, 1767). Hutchinson, a notable historian and an important political figure in prerevolutionary Massachusetts, was also the great-great-grandson of Anne. For his history of the colony he assembled a large collection of documents, among them an "ancient manuscript," now lost, containing the account of the examination. The manuscript may have disappeared in the sacking of Hutchinson's house during the Stamp Act riots of 1765. As reprinted below, the text follows the first edition of Hutchinson's *History.* It was previously reprinted in Adams.

1. Cf. Edmund S. Morgan, "The Case against Anne Hutchinson," *New England Quarterly 10* (1937), 675–697.

November 1637.

The Examination of Mrs. Ann Hutchinson at the court at New-town.

Mr. Winthrop, governor.   Mrs. Hutchinson, you are called here as one of those that have troubled the peace of the commonwealth and the churches here; you are known to be a woman that hath had a great share in the promoting and divulging of those opinions that are causes of this trouble, and to be nearly joined not only in affinity and affection with some of those the court had taken notice of and passed censure upon, but you have spoken divers things as we have been informed very prejudicial to the honour of the churches and ministers thereof, and you have maintained a meeting and an assembly in your house that hath been condemned by the general assembly as a thing not tolerable nor comely in the sight of God nor fitting for your sex, and notwithstanding that was cried down you have continued the same, therefore we have thought good to send for you to understand how things are, that if you be in an erroneous way we may reduce you that so you may become a profitable member here among us, otherwise if you be obstinate in your course that then the court may take such course that you may trouble us no further, therefore I would intreat you to express whether you do not hold and assent in practice to those opinions and factions that have been handled in court already, that is to say, whether you do not justify Mr. Wheelwright's sermon and the petition.

Mrs. Hutchinson.   I am called here to answer before you but I hear no things laid to my charge.

Gov.   I have told you some already and more I can tell you. (*Mrs. H.*) Name one Sir.

Gov.   Have I not named some already?

Mrs. H.   What have I said or done?

Gov.   Why for your doings, this you did harbour and countenance those that are parties in this faction that you have heard of.   (*Mrs H.*) That's matter of conscience, Sir.

Gov.   Your conscience you must keep or it must be kept for you.

Mrs. H.   Must not I then entertain the saints because I must keep my conscience.

Gov.   Say that one brother should commit felony or treason and come to his other brother's house, if he knows him guilty and conceals him he is guilty of the same. It is his conscience to entertain him, but if his conscience comes into act in giving countenance and entertainment to him that hath broken the law he is guilty too. So if you do countenance those that are transgressors of the law you are in the same fact.

Mrs. H.   What law do they transgress?

Gov.   The law of God and of the state.

Mrs. H.   In what particular?

Gov.   Why in this among the rest, whereas the Lord doth say honour thy father and thy mother.

Mrs. H.   Ey Sir in the Lord.   (*Gov.*) This honour you have broke in giving countenance to them.

Mrs. H.   In entertaining those did I entertain them against any act (for there is the thing) or what God hath appointed?

Gov.   You knew that Mr. Wheelwright did preach this sermon and those that countenance him in this do break a law.

Mrs. H.   What law have I broken?

Gov.   Why the fifth commandment.

Mrs. H.   I deny that for he saith in the Lord.

Gov.   You have joined with them in the faction.

Mrs. H.   In what faction have I joined with them?

Gov.   In presenting the petition.[2]

Mrs. H.   Suppose I had set my hand to the petition what then?   (*Gov.*) You saw that case tried before.

Mrs. H.   But I had not my hand to the petition.

Gov.   You have councelled them.   (*Mrs. H.*) Wherein?

Gov.   Why in entertaining them.

Mrs. H.   What breach of law is that Sir?

Gov.   Why dishonouring of parents.

Mrs. H.   But put the case Sir that I do fear the Lord and my

---

2. The petition the Antinomian party presented to the General Court in March, 1637.

parents, may not I entertain them that fear the Lord because my parents will not give me leave?

Gov.   If they be the fathers of the commonwealth, and they of another religion, if you entertain them then you dishonour your parents and are justly punishable.

Mrs. H.   If I entertain them, as they have dishonoured their parents I do.

Gov.   No but you by countenancing them above others put honor upon them.

Mrs. H.   I may put honor upon them as the children of God and as they do honor the Lord.

Gov.   We do not mean to discourse with those of your sex but only this; you do adhere unto them and do endeavour to set forward this faction and so you do dishonour us.

Mrs. H.   I do acknowledge no such thing neither do I think that I ever put any dishonour upon you.

Gov.   Why do you keep such a meeting at your house as you do every week upon a set day?

Mrs. H.   It is lawful for me so to do, as it is all your practices and can you find a warrant for yourself and condemn me for the same thing? The ground of my taking it up was, when I first came to this land because I did not go to such meetings as those were, it was presently reported that I did not allow of such meetings but held them unlawful and therefore in that regard they said I was proud and did despise all ordinances, upon that a friend came unto me and told me of it and I to prevent such aspersions took it up, but it was in practice before I came therefore I was not the first.

Gov.   For this, that you appeal to our practice you need no confutation. If your meeting had answered to the former it had not been offensive, but I will say that there was no meeting of women alone, but your meeting is of another sort for there are sometimes men among you.

Mrs. H.   There was never any man with us.

Gov.   Well, admit there was no man at your meeting and that you was sorry for it, there is no warrant for your doings, and by what warrant do you continue such a course?

Mrs. H.   I conceive there lyes a clear rule in Titus, that the elder women should instruct the younger[3] and then I must have a time wherein I must do it.

Gov.   All this I grant you, I grant you a time for it, but what is this to the purpose that you Mrs. Hutchinson must call a company together from their callings to come to be taught of you?

Mrs. H.   Will it please you to answer me this and to give me a rule for then I will willingly submit to any truth. If any come to my house to be instructed in the ways of God what rule have I to put them away?

Gov.   But suppose that a hundred men come unto you to be instructed will you forbear to instruct them?

Mrs. H.   As far as I conceive I cross a rule in it.

Gov.   Very well and do you not so here?

Mrs. H.   No Sir for my ground is they are men.

Gov.   Men and women all is one for that, but suppose that a man should come and say Mrs. Hutchinson I hear that you are a woman that God hath given his grace unto and you have knowledge in the word of God I pray instruct me a little, ought you not to instruct this man?

Mrs. H.   I think I may. — Do you think it not lawful for me to teach women and why do you call me to teach the court?

Gov.   We do not call you to teach the court but to lay open yourself.

Mrs. H.   I desire you that you would then set me down a rule by which I may put them away that come unto me and so have peace in so doing.

Gov.   You must shew your rule to receive them.

Mrs. H.   I have done it.

Gov.   I deny it because I have brought more arguments than you have.

Mrs. H.   I say, to me it is a rule.

Mr. Endicot.   You say there are some rules unto you. I think there is a contradiction in your own words. What rule for your practice do you bring, only a custom in Boston.

---

3. Titus 2.3, 4, 5.

Mrs. H.   No Sir that was no rule to me but if you look upon the rule in Titus it is a rule to me. If you convince me that it is no rule I shall yield.

Gov.   You know that there is no rule that crosses another, but this rule crosses that in the Corinthians.[4] But you must take it in this sense that elder women must instruct the younger about their business, and to love their husbands and not to make them to clash.

Mrs. H.   I do not conceive but that it is meant for some publick times.

Gov.   Well, have you no more to say but this?

Mrs. H.   I have said sufficient for my practice.

Gov.   Your course is not to be suffered for, besides that we find such a course as this to be greatly prejudicial to the state, besides the occasion that it is to seduce many honest persons that are called to those meetings and your opinions being known to be different from the word of God may seduce many simple souls that resort unto you, besides that the occasion which hath come of late hath come from none but such as have frequented your meetings, so that now they are flown off from magistrates and ministers and this since they have come to you, and besides that it will not well stand with the commonwealth that families should be neglected for so many neighbours and dames and so much time spent, we see no rule of God for this, we see not that any should have authority to set up any other exercises besides what authority hath already set up and so what hurt comes of this you will be guilty of and we for suffering you.

Mrs. H.   Sir I do not believe that to be so.

Gov.   Well, we see how it is we must therefore put it away from you, or restrain you from maintaining this course.

Mrs. H.   If you have a rule for it from God's word you may.

Gov.   We are your judges, and not you ours and we must compel you to it.

Mrs. H.   If it please you by authority to put it down I will freely let you for I am subject to your authority.

---

4. 1 Corinthians 14.34, 35.

Mr. Bradstreet.[5]   I would ask this question of Mrs. Hutchinson, whether you do think this is lawful? for then this will follow that all other women that do not are in a sin.

Mrs. H.   I conceive this is a free will offering.

Bradst.   If it be a free will offering you ought to forbear it because it gives offence.

Mrs. H.   Sir, in regard of myself I could, but for others I do not yet see light but shall further consider of it.

Bradst.   I am not against all women's meetings but do think them to be lawful.

Mr. Dudley, dep. gov.[6]   Here hath been much spoken concerning Mrs. Hutchinson's meetings and among other answers she saith that men come not there, I would ask you this one question then, whether never any man was at your meeting?

Gov.   There are two meetings kept at their house.

Dep. Gov.   How; is there two meetings?

Mrs. H.   Ey Sir, I shall not equivocate, there is a meeting of men and women and there is a meeting only for women.

Dep. gov.   Are they both constant?

Mrs. H.   No, but upon occasions they are deferred.

Mr. Endicot.[7]   Who teaches in the men's meetings none but men, do not women sometimes?

Mrs. H.   Never as I heard, not one.

Dep. gov.   I would go a little higher with Mrs. Hutchinson. About three years ago we were all in peace. Mrs. Hutchinson from that time she came hath made a disturbance, and some that came over with her in the ship did inform me what she was as soon as she was landed. I being then in place dealt with the pastor and teacher of Boston and desired them to enquire of her, and then I was satisfied that she held nothing different from us, but within half a year after, she had vented divers of her strange opinions and had made parties in the country, and at length it comes that Mr. Cotton and Mr. Vane were of her judgment, but Mr. Cotton hath

---

5. Simon Bradstreet, an assistant in the General Court.
6. Thomas Dudley, then deputy governor of the colony.
7. John Endicott, an assistant in the General Court.

cleared himself that he was not of that mind, but now it appears by this woman's meeting that Mrs. Hutchinson hath so forestalled the minds of many by their resort to her meeting that now she hath a potent party in the country. Now if all these things have endangered us as from that foundation and if she in particular hath disparaged all our ministers in the land that they have preached a covenant of works, and only Mr. Cotton a covenant of grace, why this is not to be suffered, and therefore being driven to the foundation and it being found that Mrs. Hutchinson is she that hath depraved all the ministers and hath been the cause of what is fallen out, why we must take away the foundation and the building will fall.

Mrs. H.   I pray Sir prove it that I said they preached nothing but a covenant of works.

Dep. Gov.   Nothing but a covenant of works, why a Jesuit may preach truth sometimes.

Mrs. H.   Did I ever say they preached a covenant of works then?

Dep. Gov.   If they do not preach a covenant of grace clearly, then they preach a covenant of works.

Mrs. H.   No Sir, one may preach a covenant of grace more clearly than another, so I said.

D. Gov.   We are not upon that now but upon position.

Mrs. H.   Prove this then Sir that you say I said.

D. Gov.   When they do preach a covenant of works do they preach truth?

Mrs. H.   Yes Sir, but when they preach a covenant of works for salvation, that is not truth.

D. Gov.   I do but ask you this, when the ministers do preach a covenant of works do they preach a way of salvation?

Mrs. H.   I did not come hither to answer to questions of that sort.

D. Gov.   Because you will deny the thing.

Mrs. H.   Ey, but that is to be proved first.

D. Gov.   I will make it plain that you did say that the ministers did preach a covenant of works.

Mrs. H.   I deny that.

D. Gov.   And that you said they were not able ministers of the new testament, but Mr. Cotton only.

Mrs. H.   If ever I spake that I proved it by God's word.

Court.   Very well, very well.

Mrs. H.   If one shall come unto me in private, and desire me seriously to tell them what I thought of such an one. I must either speak false or true in my answer.

D. Gov.   Likewise I will prove this that you said the gospel in the letter and words holds forth nothing but a covenant of works and that all that do not hold as you do are in a covenant of works.

Mrs. H.   I deny this for if I should so say I should speak against my own judgment.

Mr. Endicot.   I desire to speak seeing Mrs. Hutchinson seems to lay something against them that are to witness against her.

Gover.   Only I would add this. It is well discerned to the court that Mrs. Hutchinson can tell when to speak and when to hold her tongue. Upon the answering of a question which we desire her to tell her thoughts of she desires to be pardoned.

Mrs. H.   It is one thing for me to come before a public magistracy and there to speak what they would have me to speak and another when a man comes to me in a way of friendship privately there is difference in that.

Gov.   What if the matter be all one.

Mr. Hugh Peters.[8]   That which concerns us to speak unto as yet we are sparing in unless the court command us to speak, then we shall answer to Mrs. Hutchinson notwithstanding our brethren are very unwilling to answer.

Govern.   This speech was not spoken in a corner but in a public assembly, and though things were spoken in private yet now coming to us, we are to deal with them as public.

Mr. Peters.   We shall give you a fair account of what was said and desire that we may not be thought to come as informers against the gentlewoman, but as it may be serviceable for the country and our posterity to give you a brief account. This gentle-

---

8. Hugh Peter (1599–1660), minister at Salem, 1636–1641. His role in the Antinomian Controversy is described by Raymond Stearns in *The Strenuous Puritan, Hugh Peter* (Urbana, Ill., 1954), 112–124.

woman went under suspicion not only from her landing, that she was a woman not only difficult in her opinions, but also of an intemperate spirit. What was done at her landing I do not well remember, but assoon as Mr. Vane and ourselves came[9] this controversy began yet it did reflect upon Mrs. Hutchinson and some of our brethren had dealt with her, and it so fell out that some of our ministry doth suffer as if it were not according to the gospel and as if we taught a covenant of works instead of a covenant of grace. Upon these and the like we did address ourselves to the teacher of that church, and the court then assembled being sensible of these things, and this gentlewoman being as we understood a chief agent, our desire to the teacher was to tell us wherein the difference lay between him and us, for the spring did then arise as we did conceive from this gentlewoman, and so we told him. He said that he thought it not according to God to commend this to the magistrates but to take some other course, and so going on in the discourse we thought it good to send for this gentlewoman, and she willingly came, and at the very first we gave her notice that such reports there were that she did conceive our ministry to be different from the ministry of the gospel, and that we taught a covenant of works, &c. and this was her table talk and therefore we desired her to clear herself and deal plainly. She was very tender at the first. Some of our brethren did desire to put this upon proof, and then her words upon that were The fear of man is a snare why should I be afraid.[10] These were her words. I did then take upon me to ask her this question. What difference do you conceive to be between your teacher and us? She did not request us that we should preserve her from danger or that we should be silent. Briefly, she told me there was a wide and a broad difference between our brother Mr. Cotton and our selves. I desired to know the difference. She answered that he preaches the covenant of grace and you the covenant of works, and that you are not able ministers of the new testament and know no more than the apostles did before the resurrection of Christ. I did then put it to her,

9. Hugh Peter and Sir Henry Vane both arrived in Massachusetts in early October, 1635. Winthrop, *History, 1,* 202–203.
10. Proverbs 29.25.

What do you conceive of such a brother? She answered he had not the seal of the spirit. And other things we asked her but generally the frame of her course was this, that she did conceive that we were not able ministers of the gospel. And that day being past our brother Cotton was sorry that she should lay us under a covenant of works, and could have wished she had not done so. The elders being there present we did charge them with her, and the teacher of the place said they would speak further with her, and after some time she answered that we were gone as far as the apostles were before Christ's ascension. And since that we have gone with tears some of us to her.

Mrs. H. If our pastor would shew his writings you should see what I said, and that many things are not so as is reported.

Mr. Wilson. Sister Hutchinson, for the writings you speak of I have them not, and this I must say I did not write down all that was said and did pass betwixt one and another, yet I say what is written I will avouch.

Dep. Gov. I desire that the other elders will say what Mr. Peters hath said.

Mr. Weld. Being desired by the honoured court, that which our brother Peters had spoken was the truth and things were spoken as he hath related and the occasion of calling this sister and the passages that were there among us. And myself asking why she did cast such aspersions upon the ministers of the country though we were poor sinful men and for ourselves we cared not but for the precious doctrine we held forth we could not but grieve to hear that so blasphemed. She at that time was sparing in her speech. I need not repeat the things they have been truly related. She said the fear of man is a snare and therefore I will speak freely and she spake her judgment and mind freely as was before related, that Mr. Cotton did preach a covenant of grace and we a covenant of works. And this I remember she said we could not preach a covenant of grace because we were not sealed, and we were not able ministers of the new testament no more than were the disciples before the resurrection of Christ.

Mr. Phillips.[11] For my own part I have had little to do in

---

11. George Phillips (1593–1644), minister of Watertown, 1630–1644.

these things only at that time I was there and yet not being privy
to the ground of that which our brother Peters hath mentioned
but they procuring me to go along with them telling me that they
were to deal with her; at first she was unwilling to answer but at
length she said there was a great deal of difference between Mr.
Cotton and we. Upon this Mr. Cotton did say that he could have
wished that she had not put that in. Being asked of particulars she
did instance in Mr. Shephard that he did not preach a covenant
of grace clearly, and she instanced our brother Weld. Then I
asked her of myself (being she spake rashly of them all) because
she never heard me at all. She likewise said that we were not able
ministers of the new testament and her reason was because we
were not sealed.

Mr. Simmes.[12]   For my own part being called to speak in this
case to discharge the relation wherein I stand to the common-
wealth and that which I stand in unto God, I shall speak briefly.
For my acquaintance with this person I had none in our native
country, only I had occasion to be in her company once or twice
before I came, where I did perceive that she did slight the ministers of the word of God. But I came along with her in the ship, and
it so fell out that we were in the great cabin together and therein
did agree with the labours of Mr. Lothrop[13] and myself, only there
was a secret opposition to things delivered. The main thing that
was then in hand was about the evidencing of a good estate, and
among the rest about that place in John concerning the love of
the brethren.[14] That which I took notice of was the corruptness
and narrowness of her opinions, which I doubt not but I may call
them so, but she said, when she came to Boston there would be
something more seen than I said, for such speeches were cast about
and abused as that of our saviour, I have many things to say but
you cannot bear them now. And being come and she desiring to
be admitted as a member, I was desired to be there, and then Mr.
Cotton did give me full satisfaction in the things then in question.
And for things which have been here spoken, as far as I can re-

---

12. Zechariah Symmes (1599–1671), minister of Charlestown, 1634–1671.
13. John Lothrop (1584–1653), who emigrated to New England in 1634
on the same ship as Symmes, was minister in Scituate and Barnstable.
14. 1 John 3.14, a text invoked frequently in the Controversy; see p. 105.

member they are the truth, and when I asked her what she thought of me, she said alas you know my mind long ago, yet I do not think myself disparaged by her testimony and I would not trouble the court, only this one thing I shall put in, that Mr. Dudley and Mr. Haines[15] were not wanting in the cause after I had given notice of her.

Mr. Wilson. I desire you would give me leave to speak this word because of what has been said concerning her entrance into the church. There was some difficulty made, but in her answers she gave full satisfaction to our teacher and myself, and for point of evidencing justification by sanctification she did not deny, but only justification must be first. Our teacher told her then that if she was of that mind she would take away the scruple: for we thought that matter, for point of order we did not greatly stand upon, because we hoped she would hold with us in that truth as well as the other.

Mr. Shephard. I am loth to speak in this assembly concerning this gentlewoman in question, but I can do no less than speak what my conscience speaks unto me. For personal reproaches I take it a man's wisdom to conceal. Concerning the reproaches of the ministry of our's there hath been many in the country, and this hath been my thoughts of that. Let men speak what they will not only against persons but against ministry, let that pass, but let us strive to speak to the consciences of men, knowing that if we had the truth with us we shall not need to approve our words by our practice and our ministry to the hearts of the people, and they should speak for us and therefore I have satisfied myself and the brethren with that. Now for that which concerns this gentlewoman at this time I do not well remember every particular, only this I do remember that the end of our meeting was to satisfy ourselves in some points. Among the rest Mrs. Hutchinson was desired to speak her thoughts concerning the ministers of the Bay. Now I remember that she said that we were not able ministers of the new testament. I followed her with particulars, she instanced myself as being at the lecture and hearing me preach when as I

---

15. John Haynes, governor of Massachusetts 1635–36, emigrated to Connecticut in May, 1637.

gave some means whereby a christian might come to the assurance of God's love.[16] She instanced that I was not sealed. I said why did she say so. She said because you put love for an evidence. Now I am sure she was in an error in this speech for if assurance be an holy estate then I am sure there are not graces wanting to evidence it.

Mr. Eliot.[17]   I am loth to spend time therefore I shall consent to what hath been said. Our brethren did intreat us to write and a few things I did write the substance of which hath been here spoken and I have it in writing therefore I do avouch it.

Mr. Shephard.   I desire to speak this word, it may be but a slip of her tongue, and I hope she will be sorry for it, and then we shall be glad of it.

Dep. Gov.   I called these witnesses and you deny them. You see they have proved this and you deny this, but it is clear. You said they preached a covenant of works and that they were not able ministers of the new testament; now there are two other things that you did affirm which were that the scriptures in the letter of them held forth nothing but a covenant of works and likewise that those that were under a covenant of works cannot be saved.

Mrs. H.   Prove that I said so.   *(Gov.)* Did you say so?

Mrs. H.   No Sir it is your conclusion.

D. Gov.   What do I do charging of you if you deny what is so fully proved.

Gov.   Here are six undeniable ministers who say it is true and yet you deny that you did say that they did preach a covenant of works and that they were not able ministers of the gospel, and it appears plainly that you have spoken it, and whereas you say that it was drawn from you in a way of friendship, you did profess then that it was out of conscience that you spake and said The fear of man is a snare wherefore should I be afraid, I will speak plainly and freely.

Mrs. H.   That I absolutely deny, for the first question was thus answered by me to them. They thought that I did conceive

---

16. The sermons Shepard was preaching during these years were later published as *The Parable of the Ten Virgins Opened & Applied* (London, 1660). For Shepard's doctrine of assurance, see p. 19.

17. John Eliot (1604–1690), minister of Roxbury, 1632–1690.

there was a difference between them and Mr. Cotton. At the first I was somewhat reserved, then said Mr. Peters I pray answer the question directly as fully and as plainly as you desire we should tell you our minds. Mrs. Hutchinson we come for plain dealing and telling you our hearts. Then I said I would deal as plainly as I could, and whereas they say I said they were under a covenant of works and in the state of the apostles why these two speeches cross one another. I might say they might preach a covenant of works as did the apostles, but to preach a covenant of works and to be under a covenant of works is another business.

Dep. Gov. There have been six witnesses to prove this and yet you deny it.

Mrs. H. I deny that these were the first words that were spoken.

Gov. You make the case worse, for you clearly shew that the ground of your opening your mind was not to satisfy them but to satisfy your own conscience.

Mr. Peters. We do not desire to be so narrow to the court and the gentlewoman about times and seasons, whether first or after, but said it was.

Dep. Gov. For that other thing I mentioned for the letter of the scripture that it held forth nothing but a covenant of works, and for the latter that we are in a state of damnation, being under a covenant of works, or to that effect, these two things you also deny. Now the case stands thus. About three quarters of a year ago I heard of it, and speaking of it there came one to me who is not here, but will affirm it if need be, as he did to me that he did hear you say in so many words. He set it down under his hand and I can bring it forth when the court pleases. His name is subscribed to both these things, and upon my peril be it if I bring you not in the paper and bring the minister (meaning Mr. Ward[18]) to be deposed.

Gov. What say you to this, though nothing be directly proved, yet you hear it may be.

Mrs. H. I acknowledge using the words of the apostle to the

---

18. Nathaniel Ward, in Massachusetts from 1634–1646, part of the time as minister of Ipswich.

Corinthians unto him, that they that were ministers of the letter
and not the spirit did preach a covenant of works. Upon his saying there was no such scripture, then I fetched the Bible and
shewed him this place 2 Cor. iii. 6. He said that was the letter of
the law. No said I it is the letter of the gospel.[19]

Gov.   You have spoken this more than once then.

Mrs. H.   Then upon further discourse about proving a good
estate and holding it out by the manifestation of the spirit he did
acknowledge that to be the nearest way, but yet said he, will you
not acknowledge that which we hold forth to be a way too wherein
we may have hope; no truly if that be a way it is a way to hell.

Gov.   Mrs. Hutchinson, the court you see hath laboured to
bring you to acknowledge the error of your way that so you might
be reduced, the time now grows late, we shall therefore give you
a little more time to consider of it and therefore desire that you
attend the court again in the morning.

The next morning.

Gov.   We proceeded the last night as far as we could in hearing of this cause of Mrs. Hutchinson. There were divers things
laid to her charge, her ordinary meetings about religious exercises, her speeches in derogation of the ministers among us, and
the weakning of the hands and hearts of the people towards them.
Here was sufficient proof made of that which she was accused of
in that point concerning the ministers and their ministry, as that
they did preach a covenant of works when others did preach a covenant of grace, and that they were not able ministers of the new
testament, and that they had not the seal of the spirit, and this was
spoken not as was pretended out of private conference, but out of
conscience and warrant from scripture alledged the fear of man
is a snare and seeing God had given her a calling to it she would
freely speak. Some other speeches she used, as that the letter of the
scripture held forth a covenant of works, and this is offered to be
proved by probable grounds. If there be anything else that the
court hath to say they may speak.

---

19. 2 Corinthians 3.6: Who also hath made us able ministers of the new
testament; not of the letter, but of the spirit: for the letter killeth, but the
spirit giveth life.

Mrs. H.   The ministers come in their own cause. Now the Lord hath said that an oath is the end of all controversy; though there be a sufficient number of witnesses yet they are not according to the word, therefore I desire they may speak upon oath.

Gov.   Well, it is in the liberty of the court whether they will have an oath or no and it is not in this case as in case of a jury. If they be satisfied they have sufficient matter to proceed.

Mrs. H.   I have since I went home perused some notes out of what Mr. Wilson did then write and I find things not to be as hath been alledged.

Gov.   Where are the writings?

Mrs. H.   I have them not, it may be Mr. Wilson hath.

Gov.   What are the instructions that you can give, Mr. Wilson?

Mr. Wilson.   I do say that Mr. Vane desired me to write the discourse out and whether it be in his own hands or in some body's else I know not. For my own copy it is somewhat imperfect, but I could make it perfect with a little pains.

Gov.   For that which you alledge as an exception against the elders it is vain and untrue, for they are no prosecutors in this cause but are called to witness in the cause.

Mrs. H.   But they are witnesses of their own cause.

Gov.   It is not their cause but the cause of the whole country and they were unwilling that it should come forth, but that it was the glory and honour of God.

Mrs. H.   But it being the Lord's ordinance that an oath should be the end of all strife, therefore they are to deliver what they do upon oath.

Mr. Bradstreet.   Mrs. Hutchinson, these are but circumstances and adjuncts to the cause, admit they should mistake you in your speeches you would make them to sin if you urge them to swear.

Mrs. H.   That is not the thing. If they accuse me I desire it may be upon oath.

Gov.   If the court be not satisfied they may have an oath.

Mr. Nowel.[20]   I should think it convenient that the country

---

20. Increase Nowell of Charlestown, an official of the colony.

also should be satisfied because that I do hear it affirmed, that things which were spoken in private are carried abroad to the publick and thereupon they do undervalue the ministers of congregations.

Mr. Brown.[21]   I desire to speak. If I mistake not an oath is of a high nature, and it is not to be taken but in a controversy, and for my part I am afraid of an oath and fear that we shall take God's name in vain, for we may take the witness of these men without an oath.

Mr. Endicot.   I think the ministers are so well known unto us, that we need not take an oath of them, but indeed an oath is the end of all strife.

Mrs. H.   There are some that will take their oaths to the contrary.

Mr. Endicot.   Then it shall go under the name of a controversy, therefore we desire to see the notes and those also that will swear.

Gov.   Let those that are not satisfied in the court speak.

Many say. — We are not satisfied.

Gov.   I would speak this to Mrs. Hutchinson. If the ministers shall take an oath will you sit down satisfied?

Mrs. H.   I can't be notwithstanding oaths satisfied against my own conscience.

Mr. Stoughton.   I am fully satisfied with this that the ministers do speak the truth but now in regard of censure I dare not hold up my hand to that, because it is a course of justice, and I cannot satisfy myself to proceed so far in a way of justice, and therefore I should desire an oath in this as in all other things. I do but speak to prevent offence if I should not hold up my hand at the censure unless there be an oath given.

Mr. Peters.   We are ready to swear if we see a way of God in it.[22]

---

21. Richard Brown, a deputy from Watertown to the General Court.

22. Puritans took the third commandment seriously. "Whosoever taketh an Oath," declared the Westminster Confession, "ought duly to consider the weightiness of so solemn an act, and therein to avouch nothing but what he is fully perswaded is the truth." The ministers were simply not *that* sure of what had been said eleven months ago; hence their reluctance to take the oath.

Here was a parley between the deputy governor and Mr. Stoughton about the oath.

Mr. Endicot.   If they will not be satisfied with a testimony an oath will be in vain.

Mr. Stoughton.   I am persuaded that Mrs. Hutchinson and many other godly-minded people will be satisfied without an oath.

Mrs. H.   An oath Sir is an end of all strife and it is God's ordinance.

Mr. Endicot.   A sign it is what respect she hath to their words, and further, pray see your argument, you will have the words that were written and yet Mr. Wilson saith he writ not all, and now you will not believe all these godly ministers without an oath.

Mrs. H.   Mr. Wilson did affirm that which he gave in to the governor that then was to be true.   *(Some reply)* But not all the truth.

Mr. Wilson.   I did say so far as I did take them they were true.

Mr. Harlakenden.[23]   I would have the spectators take notice that the court doth not suspect the evidence that is given in, though we see that whatever evidence is brought in will not satisfy, for they are resolved upon the thing and therefore I think you will not be unwilling to give your oaths.

Gov.   I see no necessity of an oath in this thing seeing it is true and the substance of the matter confirmed by divers, yet that all may be satisfied, if the elders will take an oath they shall have it given them.

Dep. Gov.   Let us join the things together that Mrs. Hutchinson may see what they have their oaths for.

Mrs. H.   I will prove by what Mr. Wilson hath written that they never heard me say such a thing.

Mr. Sims.   We desire to have the paper and have it read.

Mr. Harlakenden.   I am persuaded that is the truth that the elders do say and therefore I do not see it necessary now to call them to oath.

Gov.   We cannot charge any thing of untruth upon them.

---

23. Roger Harlakenden of Cambridge, an assistant in the General Court.

Mr. Harlakenden.   Besides, Mrs. Hutchinson doth say that they are not able ministers of the new testament.

Mrs. H.   They need not swear to that.

Dep. Gov.   Will you confess it then.

Mrs. H.   I will not deny it nor say it.

Dep. Gov.   You must do one.

Mrs. H.   After that they have taken an oath, I will make good what I say.

Gov.   Let us state the case and then we may know what to do. That which is laid to Mrs. Hutchinson's charge is this, that she hath traduced the magistrates and ministers of this jurisdiction, that she hath said the ministers preached a covenant of works and Mr. Cotton a covenant of grace, and that they were not able ministers of the gospel, and she excuses it that she made it a private conference and with a promise of secrecy, &c. now this is charged upon her, and they therefore sent for her seeing she made it her table talk, and then she said the fear of man was a snare and therefore she would not be affeared of them.

Mrs. H.   This that yourself hath spoken, I desire that they may take their oaths upon.

Gov.   That that we should put the reverend elders unto is this that they would deliver upon oath that which they can remember themselves.

Mr. Shepard.   I know no reason of the oath but the importunity of this gentlewoman.

Mr. Endicot.   You lifted up your eyes as if you took God to witness that you came to entrap none and yet you will have them swear.

Mr. Harlakenden.   Put any passage unto them and see what they say.

Mrs. H.   They say I said the fear of man is a snare, why should I be afraid. When I came unto them, they urging many things unto me and I being backward to answer at first, at length this scripture came into my mind 29th Prov. 15. The fear of man bringeth a snare, but whoso putteth his trust in the Lord shall be safe.

Mr. Harlakenden.   This is not an essential thing.

Gov.   I remember his testimony was this.

Mrs. H.   Ey, that was the thing that I do deny for they were my words and they were not spoken at the first as they do alledge.

Mr. Peters.   We cannot tell what was first or last, we suppose that an oath is an end of all strife and we are tender of it, yet this is the main thing against her that she charged us to be unable ministers of the gospel and to preach a covenant of works.

Gover.   You do understand the thing, that the court is clear for we are all satisfied that it is truth but because we would take away all scruples, we desire that you would satisfy the spectators by your oath.

Mr. Bishop.[24]   I desire to know before they be put to oath whether their testimony be of validity.

Dep. Gov.   What do you mean to trouble the court with such questions. Mark what a flourish Mrs. Hutchinson puts upon the business that she had witnesses to disprove what was said and here is no man to bear witness.

Mrs. H.   If you will not call them in that is nothing to me.

Mr. Eliot.   We desire to know of her and her witnesses what they deny and then we shall speak upon oath. I know nothing we have spoken of but we may swear to.

Mr. Sims.   Ey, and more than we have spoken to.

Mr. Stoughton.   I would gladly that an oath should be given that so the person to be condemned should be satisfied in her conscience, and I would say the same for my own conscience if I should join in the censure — *Two or three lines in the MS. are defaced and not legible.*

Mr. Coggeshall.[25]   I desire to speak a word — It is desired that the elders would confer with Mr. Cotton before they swear.

Govern.   Shall we not believe so many godly elders in a cause wherein we know the mind of the party without their testimony?

Mr. Endicot to Mr. Coggeshall.   I will tell you what I say. I think that this carriage of your's tends to further casting dirt upon the face of the judges.

Mr. Harlakenden.   Her carriage doth the same for she doth

---

24. Townsend Bishop, a deputy from Salem to the General Court.

25. John Cogshall, a deputy from Boston who had previously signed the remonstrance protesting the Court's action against Wheelwright.

not object any essential thing, but she goes upon circumstances and yet would have them sworn.

Mrs. H.　This I would say unto them. Forasmuch as it was affirmed by the deputy that he would bring proof of these things, and the elders they bring proof in their own cause, therefore I desire that particular witnesses be for these things that they do speak.

Gov.　The elders do know what an oath is and as it is an ordinance of God so it should be used.

Mrs. H.　That is the thing I desire and because the deputy spake of witnesses I have them here present.

Mr. Colborn.[26]　We desire that our teacher may be called to hear what is said. — Upon this Mr. Cotton came and sat down by Mrs. Hutchinson.

Mr. Endicot.　This would cast some blame upon the ministers. — Well, but whatsoever he will or can say we will believe the ministers.

Mr. Eliot. ⎱　We desire to see light why we should take
Mr. Shepard. ⎰ an oath.

Mr. Stoughton.　Why it is an end of all strife and I think you ought to swear and put an end to the matter.

Mr. Peters.　Our oath is not to satisfy Mrs. Hutchinson but the court.

Mr. Endicot.　The assembly will be satisfied by it.

Dep. Gov.　If the country will not be satisfied you must swear.

Mr. Shepard.　I conceive the country doth not require it.

Dep. Gov.　Let her witnesses be called.

Gov.　Who be they?

Mrs. H.　Mr. Leveret and our teacher and Mr. Coggeshall.

Gov.　Mr. Coggeshall was not present.

Mr. Coggeshall.　Yes but I was, only I desired to be silent till I should be called.

Gov.　Will you Mr. Coggeshall say that she did not say so?

Mr. Coggeshall.　Yes I dare say that she did not say all that which they lay against her.

---

26. William Colburn, a deputy from Boston to the General Court. He had also signed the remonstrance.

Mr. Peters.   How dare you look into the court to say such a word?

Mr. Coggeshall.   Mr. Peters takes upon him to forbid me. I shall be silent.

Mr. Stoughton.   Ey, but she intended this that they say.

Gov.   Well, Mr. Leveret, what were the words? I pray speak.

Mr. Leveret.[27]   To my best remembrance when the elders did send for her, Mr. Peters did with much vehemency and intreaty urge her to tell what difference there was between Mr. Cotton and them, and upon his urging of her she said. The fear of man is a snare, but they that trust upon the Lord shall be safe. And being asked wherein the difference was, she answered that they did not preach a covenant of grace so clearly as Mr. Cotton did, and she gave this reason of it because that as the apostles were for a time without the spirit so until they had received the witness of the spirit they could not preach a covenant of grace so clearly.

Gov.   Don't you remember that she said they were not able ministers of the new testament?

Mrs. H.   Mr. Weld and I had an hour's discourse at the window and then I spake that, if I spake it.

Mr. Weld.   Will you affirm that in the court? Did not I say unto you, Mrs. Hutchinson, before the elders. When I produced the thing, you then called for proof. Was not my answer to you, leave it there, and if I cannot prove it you shall be blameless?

Mrs. H.   This I remember I spake, but do not you remember that I came afterwards to the window when you was writing and there spake unto you?

Mr. Weld.   No truly. (*Mrs. H.*) But I do very well.

Gov.   Mr. Cotton, the court desires that you declare what you do remember of the conference which was at that time and is now in question.

Mr. Cotton.   I did not think I should be called to bear witness in this cause and therefore did not labour to call to remembrance what was done; but the greatest passage that took impression upon me was to this purpose. The elders spake that they had heard that she had spoken some condemning words of their min-

---

27. Thomas Leverett, ruling elder of the Boston Church.

istry, and among other things they did first pray her to answer
wherein she thought their ministry did differ from mine, how the
comparison sprang I am ignorant, but sorry I was that any comparison should be between me and my brethren and uncomfort-
able it was, she told them to this purpose that they did not hold
forth a covenant of grace as I did, but wherein did we differ? why
she said that they did not hold forth the seal of the spirit as he
doth. Where is the difference there? say they, why saith she speaking to one or other of them, I know not to whom. You preach of
the seal of the spirit upon a work and he upon free grace without
a work or without respect to a work, he preaches the seal of the
spirit upon free grace and you upon a work. I told her I was very
sorry that she put comparisons between my ministry and their's,
for she had said more than I could myself, and rather I had that
she had put us in fellowship with them and not have made that
discrepancy. She said, she found the difference. Upon that there
grew some speeches upon the thing and I do remember I instanced to them the story of Thomas Bilney in the book of martyrs[28] how freely the spirit witnessed unto him without any respect unto a work as himself professes. Now upon this other
speeches did grow. If you put me in mind of any thing I shall
speak it, but this was the sum of the difference, nor did it seem
to be so ill taken as it is and our brethren did say also that they
would not so easily believe reports as they had done and withal
mentioned that they would speak no more of it, some of them
did; and afterwards some of them did say they were less satisfied
than before. And I must say that I did not find her saying they
were under a covenant of works, nor that she said they did preach
a covenant of works.

    Gov.   You say you do not remember, but can you say she did
not speak so —— *Here two lines again defaced.*

    Mr. Cotton.   I do remember that she looked at them as the
apostles before the ascension.

    Mr. Peters.   I humbly desire to remember our reverend
teacher. May it please you to remember how this came in.
Whether do you not remember that she said we were not sealed
with the spirit of grace, therefore could not preach a covenant of

---

28. See p. 94.

grace, and she said further you may do it in your judgment but not in experience, but she spake plump that we were not sealed.

Mr. Cotton. You do put me in remembrance that it was asked her why cannot we preach a covenant of grace? Why, saith she, because you can preach no more than you know, or to that purpose, she spake. Now that she said you could not preach a covenant of grace I do not remember such a thing. I remember well that she said you were not sealed with the seal of the spirit.

Mr. Peters. There was a double seal found out that day which never was.

Mr. Cotton. I know very well that she took the seal of the spirit in that sense for the full assurance of God's favour by the holy ghost, and now that place in the Ephesians[29] doth hold out that seal.

Mr. Peters. So that was the ground of our discourse concerning the great seal and the little seal.

Mr. Cotton. To that purpose I remember somebody speaking of the difference of the witness of the spirit and the seal of the spirit, some to put a distinction called it the broad seal and the little seal. Our brother Wheelwright answered if you will have it so be it so.

Mrs. H. Mr. Ward said that.

Some three or four of the ministers. Mr. Wheelwright said it.

Mr. Cotton. No, it was not brother Wheelwright's speech but one of your own expressions, and as I remember it was Mr. Ward.

Mr. Peters. . . . . . .

Mr. Cotton. Under favour I do not remember that.

Mr. Peters. Therefore her answer clears it in your judgment but not in your experience.

Mrs. H. My name is precious and you do affirm a thing which I utterly deny.

D. Gov. You should have brought the book with you.

Mr. Nowell. The witnesses do not answer that which you require.

Gov. I do not see that we need their testimony any further.

---

29. Ephesians 1. 13, 14.

Mr. Cotton hath expressed what he remembred, and what took impression upon him, and so I think the other elders also did remember that which took impression upon them.

Mr. Weld. I then said to Mrs. Hutchinson when it was come to this issue, why did you let us go thus long and never tell us of it?

Gov. I should wonder why the elders should move the elders of our congregation to have dealt with her if they saw not some cause.

Mr. Cotton. Brother Weld and brother Shepard, I did[30] then clear myself unto you that I understood her speech in expressing herself to you that you did hold forth some matter in your preaching that was not pertinent to the seal of the spirit —— *Two lines defaced.*

Dep. Gov. They affirm that Mrs. Hutchinson did say they were not able ministers of the new testament.

Mr. Cotton. I do not remember it.

Mrs. H. If you please to give me leave I shall give you the ground of what I know to be true. Being much troubled to see the falseness of the constitution of the church of England, I had like to have turned separatist; whereupon I kept a day of solemn humiliation and pondering of the thing; this scripture was brought unto me — he that denies Jesus Christ to be come in the flesh is antichrist[31] — This I considered of and in considering found that the papists did not deny him to be come in the flesh, nor we did not deny him — who then was antichrist? Was the Turk antichrist only? The Lord knows that I could not open scripture; he must by his prophetical office open it unto me. So after that being unsatisfied in the thing, the Lord was pleased to bring this scripture out of the Hebrews.[32] He that denies the testament denies the testator, and in this did open unto me and give me to see that those which did not teach the new covenant had the spirit of antichrist, and upon this he did discover the ministry unto me and ever since. I bless the Lord, he hath let me see which was the clear ministry and which the wrong. Since that time I confess I have been more choice and he hath let me to dis-

30. Later editions of Hutchinson's *History* include a "not": "I did not."
31. 1 John 2.18.
32. Hebrews 9.16.

tinguish between the voice of my beloved and the voice of Moses, the voice of John Baptist and the voice of antichrist, for all those voices are spoken of in scripture. Now if you do condemn me for speaking what in my conscience I know to be truth I must commit myself unto the Lord.

Mr. Nowell. How do you know that that was the spirit?

Mrs. H. How did Abraham know that it was God that bid him offer his son, being a breach of the sixth commandment?

Dep. Gov. By an immediate voice.

Mrs. H. So to me by an immediate revelation.

Dep. Gov. How! an immediate revelation.

Mrs. H. By the voice of his own spirit to my soul. I will give you another scripture, Jer. 46. 27, 28 — out of which the Lord shewed me what he would do for me and the rest of his servants. — But after he was pleased to reveal himself to me I did presently like Abraham run to Hagar. And after that he did let me see the atheism of my own heart, for which I begged of the Lord that it might not remain in my heart, and being thus, he did shew me this (a twelvemonth after) which I told you of before. Ever since that time I have been confident of what he hath revealed unto me.

Obliter- ⎫ another place out of Daniel chap. 7. and he and for
ated ⎭ us all, wherein he shewed me the sitting of the judgment and the standing of all high and low before the Lord and how thrones and kingdoms were cast down before him. When our teacher came to New-England it was a great trouble unto me, my brother Wheelwright being put by also. I was then much troubled concerning the ministry under which I lived, and then that place in the 30th of Isaiah was brought to my mind. Though the Lord give thee bread of adversity and water of affliction yet shall not thy teachers be removed into corners any more, but thine eyes shall see thy teachers. The Lord giving me this promise and they being gone there was none then left that I was able to hear, and I could not be at rest but I must come hither. Yet that place of Isaiah did much follow me, though the Lord give thee the bread of adversity and water of affliction. This place lying I say upon me then this place in Daniel[33] was brought unto me and

---

33. Daniel 6.4,5.

did shew me that though I should meet with affliction yet I am the same God that delivered Daniel out of the lion's den, I will also deliver thee. —— Therefore I desire you to look to it, for you see this scripture fulfilled this day and therefore I desire you that as you tender the Lord and the church and commonwealth to consider and look what you do. You have power over my body but the Lord Jesus hath power over my body and soul, and assure yourselves thus much, you do as much as in you lies to put the Lord Jesus Christ from you, and if you go on in this course you begin you will bring a curse upon you and your posterity, and the mouth of the Lord hath spoken it.

Dep. Gov.   What is the scripture she brings?

Mr. Stoughton.   Behold I turn away from you.

Mrs. H.   But now having seen him which is invisible I fear not what man can do unto me.

Gov.   Daniel was delivered by miracle do you think to be deliver'd so too?

Mrs. H.   I do here speak it before the court. I look that the Lord should deliver me by his providence.

Mr. Harlakenden.   I may read scripture and the most glorious hypocrite may read them and yet go down to hell.

Mrs. H.   It may be so.

Mr. Bartholomew.[34]   I would remember one word to Mrs. Hutchinson among many others. She knowing that I did know her opinions, being she was at my house at London, she was afraid I conceive or loth to impart herself unto me, but when she came within sight of Boston and looking upon the meanness of the place, I conceive, she uttered these words, if she had not a sure word that England should be destroyed her heart would shake. Now it seemed to me at that time very strange that she should say so.

Mrs. H.   I do not remember that I looked upon the meanness of the place nor did it discourage me, because I knew the bounds of my habitation were determined, &c.

Mr. Bartholomew.   I speak as a member of the court. I fear that her revelations will deceive.

---

34. William Bartholomew, a deputy from Ipswich to the General Court.

Gov. Have you heard of any of her revelations?

Mr. Barthol. For my own part I am sorry to see her now here and I have nothing against her but what I said was to discover what manner of spirit Mrs. Hutchinson is of; only I remember as we were once going through Paul's church yard[35] she then was very inquisitive after revelations and said that she had never had any great thing done about her but it was revealed to her beforehand. (*Mrs. H.*) I say the same thing again.

Mr. Bartholomew. And also that she said that she was come to New-England but for Mr. Cotton's sake. As for Mr. Hooker (as I remember) she said she liked not his spirit, only she spake of a sermon of his in the low countries wherein he said thus — it was revealed to me yesterday that England should be destroyed. She took notice of that passage and it was very acceptable with her.

Mr. Cotton. One thing let me intreat you to remember, Mr. Bartholomew, that you never spake any thing to me.

Mr. Barth. No Sir, I never spake of it to you and therefore I desire to clear Mr. Cotton.

Gov. There needs no more of that.

Mr. Barth. Only I remember her eldest daughter said in the ship that she had a revelation that a young man in the ship should be saved, but he must walk in the ways of her mother.

Mr. Sims. I could say something to that purpose, for she said — then what would you say if we should be at New-England within these three weeks, and I reproved her vehemently for it.

Mr. Eliot. That speech of Mr. Hooker's which they alledge is against his mind and judgment.[36]

Mr. Sims. I would intreat Mrs. Hutchinson to remember, that the humble he will teach — I have spoken before of it and therefore I will leave the place with her and do desire her to consider of many expressions that she hath spoken to her husband, but I will not enlarge myself.

---

35. St. Paul's Church in London.

36. John Eliot had been closely associated with Hooker while the two were in England, and presumably spoke with authority. Nevertheless Hooker did prophesy that England was doomed to destruction unless the people renewed their covenant. Thomas Hooker, *The Danger of Desertion: or A Farwell Sermon of Mr. Thomas Hooker . . . Preached immediately before his departure out of old England* (London, 1641).

Mr. Endicot. I would have a word or two with leave of that which hath thus far been revealed to the court. I have heard of many revelations of Mr.[37] Hutchinson's, but they were reports, but Mrs. Hutchinson I see doth maintain some by this discourse, and I think it is a special providence of God to hear what she hath said. Now there is a revelation you see which she doth expect as a miracle. She saith she now suffers and let us do what we will she shall be delivered by a miracle. I hope the court takes notice of the vanity of it and heat of her spirit. Now because her reverend teacher is here I should desire that he would please to speak freely whether he doth condescend to such speeches or revelations as have been here spoken of, and he will give a great deal of content.

Mr. Cotton. May it please you Sir. There are two sorts of revelations, there are   [*defaced*]   or against the word besides scripture both which   [*defaced*] tastical and tending to danger more ways than one —— there is another sort which the apostle prays the believing Ephesians may be made partakers of, and those are such as are breathed by the spirit of God and are never dispensed but in a word of God and according to a word of God, and though the word revelation be rare in common speech and we make it uncouth in our ordinary expressions, yet notwithstanding, being understood in the scripture sense I think they are not only lawful but such as christians may receive and God bear witness to it in his word, and usually he doth express it in the ministry of the word and doth accompany it by his spirit, or else it is in the reading of the word in some chapter or verse and whenever it comes it comes flying upon the wings of the spirit.

Mr. Endicot. You give me satisfaction in the thing and therefore I desire you to give your judgment of Mrs. Hutchinson; what she hath said you hear and all the circumstances thereof.

Mr. Cotton. I would demand whether by a miracle she doth mean a work above nature or by some wonderful providence for that is called a miracle often in the psalms.

Mrs. H. I desire to speak to our teacher. You know Sir what he doth declare though he doth not know himself

---

37. Apparently a misprint for "Mrs."

[something wanting.]

now either of these ways or at this present time it shall be done, yet I would not have the court so to understand me that he will deliver me now even at this present time.

Dep. Gov.   I desire Mr. Cotton to tell us whether you do approve of Mrs. Hutchinson's revelations as she hath laid them down.

Mr. Cotton.   I know not whether I do understand her, but this I say, if she doth expect a deliverance in a way of providence — then I cannot deny it.

Dep. Gov.   No Sir we did not speak of that.

Mr. Cotton.   If it be by way of miracle then I would suspect it.

Dep. Gov.   Do you believe that her revelations are true?

Mr. Cotton.   That she may have some special providence of God to help her is a thing that I cannot bear witness against.

Dep. Gov.   Good Sir I do ask whether this revelation be of God or no?

Mr. Cotton.   I should desire to know whether the sentence of the court will bring her to any calamity, and then I would know of her whether she expects to be delivered from that calamity by a miracle or a providence of God.

Mrs. H.   By a providence of God I say I expect to be delivered from some calamity that shall come to me.

Gover.   The case is altered and will not stand with us now, but I see a marvellous providence of God to bring things to this pass that they are. We have been hearkening about the trial of this thing and now the mercy of God by a providence hath answered our desires and made her to lay open her self and the ground of all these disturbances to be by revelations, for we receive no such made out of the ministry of the word and so one scripture after another, but all this while there is no use of the ministry of the word nor of any clear call of God by his word, but the ground work of her revelations is the immediate revelation of the spirit and not by the ministry of the word, and that is the means by which she hath very much abused the country that they shall look for revelations and are not bound to the ministry of the word, but God will teach them by immediate revelations and this hath been the ground of all these tumults and troubles, and I would that those were all cut off from us that trouble us, for this is the thing that hath been the root of all the mischief.

Court. We all consent with you.

Gov. Ey it is the most desperate enthusiasm in the world, for nothing but a word comes to her mind and then an application is made which is nothing to the purpose, and this is her revelations when it is impossible but that the word and spirit should speak the same thing.

Mr. Endicot. I speak in reference to Mr. Cotton. I am tender of you Sir and there lies much upon you in this particular, for the answer of Mr. Cotton doth not free him from that way which his last answer did bring upon him, therefore I beseech you that you'd be pleased to speak a word to that which Mrs. Hutchinson hath spoken of her revelations as you have heard the manner of it. Whether do you witness for her or against her.

Mr. Cotton. This is that I said Sir, and my answer is plain that if she doth look for deliverance from the hand of God by his providence, and the revelation be in a word or according to a word, that I cannot deny.

Mr. Endicot. You give me satisfaction.

Dep. Gov. No, no, he gives me none at all.

Mr. Cotton. But if it be in a way of miracle or a revelation without the word that I do not assent to, but look at it as a delusion, and I think so doth she too as I understand her.

Dep. Gov. Sir, you weary me and do not satisfy me.

Mr. Cotton. I pray Sir give me leave to express my self. In that sense that she speaks I dare not bear witness against it.

Mr. Nowell. I think it is a devilish delusion.

Gover. Of all the revelations that ever I read of I never read the like ground laid as is for this. The Enthusiasts and Anabaptists had never the like.

Mr. Cotton. You know Sir, that their revelations broach new matters of faith and doctrine.

Gover. So do these and what may they breed more if they be let alone. I do acknowledge that there are such revelations as do concur with the word but there hath not been any of this nature.

Dep. Gov.   I never saw such revelations as these among the Anabaptists, therefore am sorry that Mr. Cotton should stand to justify her.

Mr. Peters.   I can say the same and this runs to enthusiasm, and I think that is very disputable which our brother Cotton hath spoken   [*wanting*]

an immediate promise that he will deliver them [*wanting*]   in a day of trouble.

Gover.   It overthrows all.

Dep. Gov.   These disturbances that have come among the Germans have been all grounded upon revelations, and so they that have vented them have stirred up their hearers to take up arms against their prince and to cut the throats one of another, and these have been the fruits of them, and whether the devil may inspire the same into their hearts here I know not, for I am fully persuaded that Mrs. Hutchinson is deluded by the devil, because the spirit of God speaks truth in all his servants.

Gov.   I am persuaded that the revelation she brings forth is delusion.

All the court but some two or three ministers cry out, we all believe it — we all believe it.

Mr. Endicot.   I suppose all the world may see where the foundation of all these troubles among us lies.

Mr. Eliot.   I say there is an expectation of things promised, but to have a particular revelation of things that shall fall out, there is no such thing in the scripture.

Gov.   We will not limit the word of God.

Mr. Collicut.[38]   It is a great burden to us that we differ from Mr. Cotton and that he should justify these revelations. I would intreat him to answer concerning that about the destruction of England.

Gov.   Mr. Cotton is not called to answer to any thing but we are to deal with the party here standing before us.

Mr. Bartholomew.   My wife hath said that Mr. Wheelwright was not acquainted with this way until that she imparted it unto him.

---

38. Richard Collicott, a deputy from Dorchester to the General Court.

Mr. Brown.   Inasmuch as I am called to speak, I would therefore speak the mind of our brethren. Though we had sufficient
ground for the censure before, yet now she having vented herself
and I find such flat contradiction to the scripture in what she
saith, as to that in the first to the Hebrews — God at sundry times
spake to our fathers — For my part I understand that scripture
and other scriptures of the Lord Jesus Christ, and the apostle
writing to Timothy saith that the scripture is able to make one
perfect — therefore I say the mind of the brethren — I think she
deserves no less a censure than hath been already past but rather
something more, for this is the foundation of all mischief and of
all those bastardly things which have been overthrowing by that
great meeting. They have all come out from this cursed fountain.

Gov.   Seeing the court hath thus declared itself and hearing
what hath been laid to the charge of Mrs. Hutchinson and especially what she by the providence of God hath declared freely
without being asked, if therefore it be the mind of the court,
looking at her as the principal cause of all our trouble, that they
would now consider what is to be done to her. ——

Mr. Coddington.   I do think that you are going to censure
therefore I desire to speak a word.

Gov.   I pray you speak.

Mr. Coddington.[39]   There is one thing objected against the
meetings. What if she designed to edify her own family in her own
meetings may none else be present?

Gov.   If you have nothing else to say but that, it is pity Mr.
Coddington that you should interrupt us in proceeding to censure.

Mr. Coddington.   I would say more Sir, another thing you
lay to her Charge is her speech to the elders. Now I do not see any
clear witness against her, and you know it is a rule of the court
that no man may be a judge and an accuser too. I do not speak to
disparage our elders and their callings, but I do not see any thing
that they accuse her of witnessed against her, and therefore I do
not see how she should be censured for that. And for the other

39. William Coddington, a deputy from Boston to the General Court,
and a supporter of Mrs. Hutchinson.

thing which hath fallen from her occasionally by the spirit of God, you know the spirit of God witnesses with our spirits, and there is no truth in scripture but God bears witness to it by his spirit, therefore I would entreat you to consider whether those things you have alledged against her deserve such censure as you are about to pass, be it to banishment or imprisonment. And again here is nothing proved about the elders, only that she said they did not teach a covenant of grace so clearly as Mr. Cotton did, and that they were in the state of the apostles before the ascension. Why I hope this may not be offensive nor any wrong to them.

Gov. Pass by all that hath been said formerly and her own speeches have been ground enough for us to proceed upon.

Mr. Coddington. I beseech you do not speak so to force things along, for I do not for my own part see any equity in the court in all your proceedings. Here is no law of God that she hath broken nor any law of the country that she hath broke, and therefore deserves no censure, and if she say that the elders preach as the apostles did, why they preached a covenant of grace and what wrong is that to them, for it is without question that the apostles did preach a covenant of grace, though not with that power, till they received the manifestation of the spirit, therefore I pray consider what you do, for here is no law of God or man broken.

Mr. Harlakenden. Things thus spoken will stick. I would therefore that the assembly take notice that here is none that condemns the meeting of christian women; but in such a way and for such an end that it is to be detested. And then tho' the matter of the elders be taken away yet there is enow besides to condemn her, but I shall speak no further.

Dep. Gov. We shall be all sick with fasting.

Mr. Colburn. I dissent from censure of banishment.

Mr. Stoughton. The censure which the court is about to pass in my conscience is as much as she deserves, but because she desires witness and there is none in way of witness therefore I shall desire that no offence be taken if I do not formally condemn her because she hath not been formally convicted as others are by witnesses upon oath.

Mr. Coddington. That is a scruple to me also, because Solomon saith, every man is partial in his own cause, and here is none that accuses her but the elders, and she spake nothing to them but in private, and I do not know what rule they had to make the thing publick, secret things ought to be spoken in secret and publick things in publick, therefore I think they have broken the rules of God's word.

Gov.   What was spoken in the presence of many is not to be made secret.

Mr. Coddington.   But that was spoken but to a few and in private.

Gov.   In regard Mr. Stoughton is not satisfied to the end all scruples may be removed we shall desire the elders to take their oaths.

Here now was a great whispering among the ministers, some drew back others were animated on.

Mr. Eliot.   If the court calls us out to swear we will swear.

Gov.   Any two of you will serve.

Mr. Stoughton.   There are two things that I would look to discharge my conscience of, 1st to hear what they testify upon oath and 2dly to ——

Gov.   It is required of you Mr. Weld and Mr. Eliot.

Mr. Weld. ⎫
Mr. Eliot. ⎬ We shall be willing.

Gov.   We'll give them their oaths. You shall swear to the *Mr. Peters held up* ⎫ truth and nothing but the truth as far as *his hand also.* ⎰ you know. So help you God. What you do remember of her speak, pray speak.

Mr. Eliot.   I do remember and I have it written, that which she spake first was, the fear of man is a snare, why should she be afraid but would speak freely. The question being asked whether there was a difference between Mr. Cotton and us, she said there was a broad difference. I would not stick upon words — the thing she said — and that Mr. Cotton did preach a covenant of grace and we of works and she gave this reason — to put a work in point of evidence is a revealing upon a work. We did labour then to convince her that our doctrine was the same with Mr. Cotton's: She said no, for we were not sealed. That is all I shall say.

Gov.   What say you Mr. Weld?

Mr. Weld.   I will speak to the things themselves — these two things I am fully clear in — she did make a difference in three things, the first I was not so clear in, but that she said this I am fully sure of, that we were not able ministers of the new testament and that we were not clear in our experience because we were not sealed.

Mr. Eliot. I do further remember this also, that she said we were not able ministers of the gospel because we were but like the apostles before the ascension.

Mr. Coddington. This was I hope no disparagement to you.

Gov. Well, we see in the court that she doth continually say and unsay things.

Mr. Peters. I was much grieved that she should say that our ministry was legal. Upon which we had a meeting as you know and this was the same she told us that there was a broad difference between Mr. Cotton and us. Now if Mr. Cotton do hold forth things more clearly than we, it was our grief we did not hold it so clearly as he did, and upon those grounds that you have heard.

Mr. Coddington. What wrong was that to say that you were not able ministers of the new testament or that you were like the apostles — methinks the comparison is very good.

Gov. Well, you remember that she said but now that she should be delivered from this calamity.

Mr. Cotton. I remember she said she should be delivered by God's providence, whether now or at another time she knew not.

Mr. Peters. I profess I thought Mr. Cotton would never have took her part.

Mr. Stoughton. I say now this testimony doth convince me in the thing, and I am fully satisfied the words were pernicious, and the frame of her spirit doth hold forth the same.

Gov. The court hath already declared themselves satisfied concerning the things you hear, and concerning the troublesomeness of her spirit and the danger of her course amongst us, which is not to be suffered. Therefore if it be the mind of the court that Mrs. Hutchinson for these things that appear before us is unfit for our society, and if it be the mind of the court that she shall be banished out of our liberties and imprisoned till she be sent away, let them hold up their hands.

All but three.

Those that are contrary minded hold up yours,
  Mr. Coddington and Mr. Colborn, only.

Mr. Jennison.[40]   I cannot hold up my hand one way or the other, and I shall give my reason if the court require it.

Gov.   Mrs. Hutchinson, the sentence of the court you hear is that you are banished from out of our jurisdiction as being a woman not fit for our society, and are to be imprisoned till the court shall send you away.

Mrs. H.   I desire to know wherefore I am banished?

Gov.   Say no more, the court knows wherefore and is satisfied.

---

40. William Jennison, a deputy from Watertown to the General Court.

CHAPTER 10

A Report of the Trial of Mrs. Anne Hutchinson
before the Church in Boston

AFTER the General Court sentenced Mrs. Hutchinson to banishment from the colony, she passed the winter of 1637–38
as a prisoner in the Roxbury home of Joseph Weld, Thomas
Weld's brother. In March, 1638, she was brought to trial again,
this time by the Boston Church. In that setting Anne Hutchinson confronted her antagonists for the last time.

Her trial illustrates the Congregationalists' handling of
church discipline. They believed that each church was founded
on a covenant that obliged the members (in the words of the Boston Church covenant) to "walke . . . according to the Rule of the
Gospell, & in all sincere Conformity to His holy Ordinaunces."
Anyone violating this covenant was subject to censure by the
church according to the procedures outlined in Matthew 18.15–
18. In ordinary cases the offender received an admonition, which
"doth therby with-hold or suspend him from the holy fellowship
of the Lords Supper, till his offence be removed by penitent confession."[1] In extreme cases, the punishment was excommunication: literally, being cast out of the church. No punishment could
be imposed without the consent of the church members. Whether
their consent must be unanimous became an issue at Mrs. Hutchinson's trial, as did the question of whether the ministers could
testify publicly if they had not first dealt with her "privately."[2]

---

1. Walker, *Creeds and Platforms of Congregationalism*, 131, 227.
2. Matthew 18.15: Moreover if thy brother shall trespass against thee, go
and tell him his fault between thee and him alone.

If the trial seems harsh to the modern reader, its role within the Puritan context was punitive only in a limited sense. Punishment by the church was meant to inspire repentance, and a genuine act of repentance could lead to the restoration of church membership. Those who prosecuted Mrs. Hutchinson hoped that she would confess her errors, as, for a moment, she did. But in the end she stood her ground and the church had no other choice than to cast her out.

The text of the proceedings at her trial comes from an eighteenth-century copy of the seventeenth-century original. The original has apparently disappeared, but the copy, made by Ezra Stiles, a minister in Newport who later was president of Yale, survives in the Stiles Papers, Yale University Library. The manuscript has been printed before in the *Proceedings of the Massachusetts Historical Society, 24*, 161–191, and in Adams. Both of these texts purport to be literal reproductions of Stiles' manuscript, although in fact the punctuation, capitalization, and spelling have frequently, and inconsistently, been changed. Punctuation in the original is so erratic as to make the manuscript almost unintelligible. In the text below, punctuation has been kept to a minimum, and only introduced where warranted by the sense. The ellipses occur in the manuscript itself.

A Report of the Trial of Mrs. Ann Hutchinson before the Church in Boston, March, 1638.

"By My Brother Willson. (Before Mrs. Hutchinsons Examination and her Answer in the Meetinghouse at Boston in New England one the Lecture Day March 15. 1638 whan she was accused of divers Errors and unsound Opinions which she held; as was taken from her owne Mouth by Mr. Shephard and Mr. Wells[3] Ministers and proved by fuer Witnesses."

"We have herd this day very sweetly that we are to cast downe all our Crownes at the feete of Christ Jesus. Soe let every one be content to deny all Relations of Father, Mother, Sister, Brother, Friend, Enemy and to cast downe all our Crownes and whatsoever

---

3. Thomas Weld.
* See new note p. xx.

Judgment or Opinion that is taken up may be cast downe at the Feete of Christ, and let all be carried by the Rules of Gods Word and tried by that Rule and if thear be any Error let no one Rejoyce. None but the Divells in Hell will rejoyce, but in all our proceedings this day, let us lift up the name of Christ Jesus and so proceed in Love in this day's proceedinge.

Mr. Olliver.[4] I am to acquaynt all this Congregation, that whereas our Sister Hutchinson was not hear at the Beginninge of this Exercise, it was not out of any Contempt or Neglect to the Ordinance, but because she hath bine longe [under] Durance. She is so weake that she conceaves herselfe not fitt nor able to have bine hear soe longe togeather. This she sent to our Elders.

Mr. Leverit our other Elder. I am to request those that are Members of the Congregation, that thay would draw as neare togeather as they can, and into such places as thay may be distinguished from the rest of the Congregation, that whan thear Consent or Dissent is required to the Things which shall be read: we may know how thay doe express themselves ayther in the allowinge or condemninge of them.

Mr. Leverit. Sister Hutchinson: hear is divers Opinions layd to your charge by Mr. Shephard and Mr. Frost,[5] and I must request you in the name of the Church to declare whether you hould them or renounce them as thay be read to you.

1. That the Soules Ecclesiastes 3.18–21 of all men by Nature are mortal.

2. That those that 1 Corinthians 6.19 that are united to Christ have 2 Bodies, Christs and a new Body and you knew not how Christ should be united to our fleshly Bodys.

3. That our Bodies shall not rise 1 Corinthians 15.4. with Christ Jesus, not the same Bodies at the last day.

4. That the Resurrection mentioned 1 Corinthians 15 is not of our Resurrection at the last day, but of our Union to Christ Jesus.

---

4. Thomas Oliver and Thomas Leverett were the two "ruling elders" of the Boston Church; the primary function of their office was to handle cases of discipline.

5. Probably Edmund Frost, ruling elder of the church at Cambridge. (Adams.)

5. That thear be no created graces in the humane Nature of Christ nor in Beleevers after Union.

6. That you had no scripture to Warrant Christ beinge now in Heaven in his humane Nature.

7. That the Disciples wear not converted at Christs Death.

8. That thear is no Kingdom of Heaven but Christ Jesus.

9. That the first Thinge we receave for our Assurance is our Election.

These are alledged by Mr. Shephard. Next from Roxberie

1. That Sanctification can be no Evidence of a good Estate in no wise.

2. That her Revelations about futire Events are to be beleeved as well as Scripture because the same holy Ghost did indite both.

3. That Abraham was not in savinge Estate till he offered Isack and so savinge the firmnes of Gods Election he might have perished eternally for any Worke of Grace that was in him.

4. That an Hipocrite may have the Righteousness of Adam and perish.[6]

5. That we are not bound to the Law, not as a Rule of Life.

6. That not beinge bound to the Law, no Transgression of the Law is sinfull.

7. That you see no Warrant in Scripture to prove that the Image of God in Adam was Righteousness and trew Holiness.

These are aledged agaynst you by Mr. Wells and Mr. Eliott.

Mr. Leverit. It is desired by the Church Sister Hutchinson that you expresse whether this be your opinion or not.

Mrs. Hutchinson. If this be Error than it is myne and I ought to lay it downe. If it be truth it is not myne but Christ Jesus and than I am not to lay it downe. But I desire of the Church to demand one Question. By what Rule of the Word whan these Elders shall come to me in private to desire Satisfaction in some poynts, and doe professe in the sight of God that thay did not come to Intrap nor insnare me, and now without speakinge to me and expressinge any Unsatisfaction would come to bringe it publickly

---

6. This was one of the questions Thomas Shepard raised in his letter to John Cotton.

unto the Church before thay had privately delt with me? For them to come and inquire for Light, and afterwards to bare Witness against it, I thinke it is a Breach of Church Rule, to bringe a Thinge in publicke before thay have delt with me in private.

Mr. Cotten. To answer this, indeed if thear be any playne Breach of Rule then you may. But if thear be not a manifest Breach than the church hath not power to make Inquisition in a doubtful Case.

Mr. Shephard. I desire to aske this Question of Mrs. Hutchinson, Whether she accuse any of us or no of such a Breach of Rule?

Mrs. Hutchinson. I aske a Question. There was none with me but myselfe and I may not accuse an Elder under 2 or 3 Witnesses.

Mr. Cotten. Brother Shephard if you cane expres any thinge that concerns this Matter, you shall doe well to give God Glory and speake.

Mr. Shephard. For my first cominge to Mrs. Hutchinson, I lyinge in the Towne all night was . . . importuned by some theare to goe and see Mrs. Hutchinson. And soe I did goe to desire further Satisfaction from her, for some speeches that she had used in the Court which I did not well understand. At my second cominge to her be[ing] sent by special providences of God, and I did tell her, that I came not to Intrap her nor had not than any Thought nayther doe I know wherein I could deale more lovingly with this your Sister than to bringe her thus before you. And whearas she sayeth that we delt not with her, I must needs say that I never came to her but I bare Witness and left some Testimony behind me agaynst her Opinions. Yet I did not publish any Thinge of the Conference but kept it in my own Brest. But seeinge the Flewentness of her Tonge and her Willingness to open herselfe and to divulge her Opinions and to sowe her seed in us that are but highway side and Strayngers to her and therefore would doe much more to her owne Jaolosie and to them that are mor nearly like to her, for I account her a verye dayngerous Woman to sowe her corrupt opinions to the infection of many and therefore the more neede you have to looke to her. And therefore at my third Cominge to her I tould her that I came to deale with her and labour to reduce her from her Errors and to bare witness against them therefor I do marvell that she will say that we bringe it into publicke before I delt with her in private. Hebrews 4. 12.

Mrs. Hutchinson. I did not hould divers of these Thinges I am accused of, but did only ask a Question Ecclesiastes 3.18–21.

Mr. Shephard. I would have this Congregation know that the vilest Errors that ever was brought into the Church was brought by way of Questions 42.7.[7]

Mr. Cotton. Brother we consent with you. Therefor Sister Hutchinson it will be most satisfactorie to the Congregation for you to answer to the Things as thay are objected against you in order.

Mrs. Hutchinson. I desire thay may be read.

Mr. Cotten. Your first opinion layd to your Charge is *That the Soules of all Men by nature are mortall and die like Beastes,* and for that you alledge Ecclesiastes 3.18–21.

Mrs. Hutchinson. I desire that place might be answered; the spirit that God gives returns.

Mr. Cotton. That place speaketh that the spirit ascends upwards, soe Ecclesiastes 12.7. Mans spirit doth not returne to Dust as mans body doth but to God. The soul of man is immortall.

Mrs. Hutchinson. Every Man consists of Soul and Body. Now *Adam dies not except his soule and Body dye.* And in Hebrews 4 the word is lively in Operation, and devides between *soule and Spirit: Soe than the Spirit that God gives man, returned to God indeed, but the Soule dyes* and That is the spirit Ecclesiastes speakes of, and not of the Soule. Luke 19.10.

Mr. Cotton. If you hould that Adams Soule and body dyes and was not redeemed or restored by Christ Jesus it will overthrough our Redemption. Both Soule and Body is bought with a price Luke 19.10 I come to seek and save what was lost. 1 Corinthians 6.E. [to the end of the chapter].

Mrs. Hutchinson. I acknowledged I am redeemed from my vayne conversation and other Redemptions but it is no whare sayd that he came to redeem the seed of Adam but the seed of Abraham.

---

7. Apparently a misreading of the manuscript, as no Biblical text seems to fit.

Brother Willson. I desire befor you lay downe your Scruples that you would seriously consider of the places alledged and of that in 1 Corinthians 6 end: the spirit of God needs no Redemption, but he speaks thear neyther of Gods Spirit but of our Spirits.

Mrs. Hutchison. I speake not of Gods Spirit now: but I will propound my mayne scruple and that is *how a Thinge that is Immortally miserable can be immortally happie.*

Mr. Cotten. He that makes miserable can make us happy.

Mrs. Hutchison. I desire to hear God speak this and not man. Shew me whear thear is any Scripture to prove it that speakes soe.

Mr. Cotten. *You doe not say that the soule is not immortal but that this Imortalety is purchased from Christ.*

Mrs. Hutchison. Yes Sir.

Mr. Cotten. That in Ecclesiastes proveth that the soule is the Gift of God and that it hath no Relation to such fadinge and destroyinge matter as his Body was made of. Matthew 10.28, 1 Thessalonians 5.23.

Mrs. Hutchison. Doe you thinke his naturall Life is gone into Heaven, and that we shall goe into Heaven with our naturall Life?

Mr. Cotten. Thear is a soule that is immortal Matthew 10.28. and our nature shall goe into heaven but not our corrupt Nature.

Mrs. Hutchison. Than you have both a Soule and Spirit that shall be saved. I desire you to answer that in 1 Thessalonians 5.23. Your hole *Spirit Soule and body,* and that in Psalms he hath redeemed his soule from hell.

Mr. Cotten. Sister doe not shut your Eyes agaynst the Truth. All these places prove that the soule is Immortall.

Mrs. Hutchison. *The Spirit is immortall indeed but prove that the Soule is.* For that place in Matthew which you bringe of Castinge the soul into hell is ment of the Spirit.

Mr. Cotten. Thease are principles of our christian Fayth, and not denyed. The Spirit is sometimes put for the Contience and for the Giftes of the Spirit that fitts the soule for Gods Service.

Mrs. Hutchison. The holy Ghost makes this Distinction between the soule and Body and not I.

Mr. Cotten. *If wicked men have the Immortalitie of thear*

Soules purchased to them by Christ Jesus than the Divells have Immortalitie purchased to them by Christ.

Governor.   She thinkes that the Soule is annihilated by the Judgment that was sentenced upon Adam. Her Error springs from her Mistaking of the Curse of God upon Adam, for that Curse doth not implye Annihilation of the soule and body, but only a dissolution of the Soule and Body.

Mrs. Hutchison.   I will take that into Consideration for it is of more wayte to me than any thinge which yet hath bine spoken.

Governor.   As the Body remaynes an Earthly substance after Dissolution, soe the Soule remaynes a spirituall Substance after the Curse, though we see not what substance it is turned into after Dissolution.

Mr. Eliot.   She thinkes the Soule to be Nothinge but a Breath, and so vanisheth. I pray put that to her.

Mrs. Hutchison.   I thinke the soule to be nothing but Light.

Brother Willson.   If the Soule be but a Breath, than how doth Christ say that a mans Soule is better than the whole World.

Mr. Cotten.   The Sume of her Opinion is that the soules of men by Creation is no other or better than the soules of beastes which dye and *are mortall, but are made immortall* by the Redemption of Christ Jesus, to which hath bine Answered that Soule is Imortall by Creation and some places brought to prove that thay are, namely, the soules of the wicked [are] cast into Hell forever, and the soules of the godly are kept in a blameless frame unto Immortall Glory.

Mr. Leverit.   The Church is desired to expres whither what you have heard give you Satisfaction and sufficient Light in the poynt in Question.

Sargeon Savidge.[8]   My Scruple is seeing the Church is not accused of this Opinion, but one partie, whether we should presently express our Consent or Dissent whan the partie that houlds it is not satisfied nor convinced, but rather that the church may have Time first to consider of it.

Brother Willson.   It was usiall in the former Times whan

---

8. Thomas Savage married a daughter of Mrs. Hutchinson and went into exile with her in 1638.

any Blasphemie or Idolatrie was held forth thay did use to rent thear Garments and tare thear hare of thear heads in signe of Lothinge. And if we deny the Resurrection of the Body than let us turne Epicures. Let us eate and drinke and doe any Thinge, to morrow we shall dye: and whan all the Priests of Baall pleaded for Baall and Eliah proved the Lord to be God, if any one had a scruple . . . and was not satisfied but Baall was still God, should one mans scruple or doubte hinder all the rest of the Congregation which are satisfied to crye out, that the Lord is God, the Lord is God and the Lord only is the Lord?

Governor.   The whole Congregation but one Brother is sufficiently satisfied with what hath bine allready spoken to this poynt to be sufficient: therefor let us proceed to the next.

Brother Willson.   I desire to hear our Sister speake, what becomes of that Spirit whan the body dyes. For I thinke she contradicts herselfe.

Mrs. Hutchison.   *I spake of the Spirit that God gave* that returnes to God that gave it.

Mr. Cotten.   We are not to hear what naturall affection will say, for we are to forsake Father and Mother, Wife and children for Christ Jesus 1 Corinthians 5.12.

Brother Willson.   This that will not confesse me before men: him will not I confesse befor my father which is in Heaven: this is the Rule of God by which the church should proceed.

Mr. Cotten.   You see how far naturall affection doth prevayle with Children to speake for thear Mother, and thearfor it concerns others of the Congregation to take heed how thay linke themselves with any that hould . . . damnable Errors. And I am sorry to hear any of our Brethren to be soe brought up that thay should not hear of the Immortalletie of the soule.

Governor.   I wonder thear should be any scruple in this Thinge which is practised in all the Churches, to give some signe whether what hath bine spoken doe give satisfaction to the Church or no, that soe we may proceed.

Mr. Cotten.   I would ask our sister this Question, *whether the Soule body and spirit be not Immortal* 1 Peter 3.19.

Mrs. Huchison.   It is more than I know. How doe we *prove that both soule and body are saved?*

Brother Willson.   I pray God kepe your hole body soule and body may be kept blamless to Salvation.

Mrs. Hutchison.   It is sayd thay are kept blameles to *the coming of Christ Jesus not to Salvation.*

Brother Willson.   What doe we mene by the Cominge of Christ Jesus?

Mrs. Hutchison.   By Cominge of Christ thear he meanes his *cominge to us in Union.* 1 46 4[9]

Brother Willson.   I looke at this Opinion to be dayngerous and damnable and to be no lesse than Sadducisme and Athiisme and therefore to be detested.

Mrs. Hutchinson.   If Error be the Thinge you intend, than I desire to know what is the Error for which I was banished for I am suer this is not, for then thear was no such Expression from me on this. The most part of the Church did express themselves satisfied with what hath bine spokin and *by Lifting up of thear hands did show thear Dislike of it and did condemn it as an Error.*

Mr. Dampford.[10]   Whan it comes to a case of Testimony and a baringe Witness to a Truth of God and than whan the Truth is like to [be] cried downe, than it is time to speak. This Question of the Immortalitie of the soule is not new, but an Ayntient Heresie and most censurable and gives way to Libertanisme. And *this poynt was disputed a whole day togeather befor Adrian the Pope:* who like a Beast concluded this, that *he that speakes for the Immortallitie of the soule speakes most like to the Scriptures, but he that speakes of the Mortalletie of the soul speakes most to my minde and desire.* And soe it is in this very Thinge. Thay that speake for the Mortalitie of the soule speake most for Licentiousnesse and sinfull Liberty. Therefore ... Questions that have bine started about this hath bine, as hath bine sayd, from naturall Affection. And for any scruple of Contience that some made whether thay may expres thear Judgments by Vote or no: I thinke it is according to the Rule and doe not see how we cane bare Witnesse to the Truth or agaynst any Error but by expressinge their Assents or Dissents, ayther by silence or Liftinge up thear Hands. That in Matthew 18 in case of offendors brought to the Church

---

9. Adams suggests that the reference is to Romans 6.4.
10. John Davenport.

the Rule is if they will not hear the Church let him be as an Heathen or Publican. Now what is ment by Church only the Officers or the whole Church? Now it is playne it is the whole Church. Now how can the Church expresse themselves, but ayther by thear *Votes* or *Silence,* and soe in castinge out the Incestious person in 1 Corinthians 5. How shall the Churches consent be knowen except thay expresse it one way or other: therefor I thinke that should be no Scruple.

Mr. Cotten. We come to the second poynt. By the purchase and Redemption of Christ the Soules are made immortall though by Creation they are mortall.

Mrs. Hutchison. The Soule is immortall by Redemption.

Mr. Cotten. You have no scripture to prove this. Therefor you ought not to prostitute your Fayth to any one no not to your owne Inventions. And you have herd playne places against it as that the *Spirits of wicked men are in Hell:* and you have herd that the soules of the faythfull are in Heaven.

Mr. Damphord. A soule may be Immortall and not miserable. Now the Curse is this, that Missery is annexed to Immortalitie. Immortalitie was a Gift to the Spirit in thear very Beinge. The *soule cannot have Imortaletie in itselfe but from God from whom it hath its beinge.*

Mrs. Hutchison. I thanke the Lord I have Light. And I see more Light a greate deale by Mr. Damphords opening of it.

Mr. Cotten. Than you revoke what you have delivered or held in this Poynt.

Mrs. Hutchison. Soe far as I understand Mr. Damphord. I pray let some body open this. How the soul is Imortall by Creation.

Mr. Damphord. It is immortall as the Ayngells are by Creation.

Mrs. Hutchison. If the soule be Immortall by Christ how can the Soule dye but the Curse sayeth that in the day thou eatest thereof thou shalt dye.

Mr. Damphord. The soule doth not dye, but the Person of Adam, and not the soule. *But the person of Adam is redeemed by Christ Jesus. Now the Ayngells and Divells are Imortall not by the Redemption of Christ, but by Nature and Creation.*

Mr. Cotten. Sister the Comparison is familliar and usiall.

Mr. Damphord. You must distinguish betwene the *life of the Soule and the Life of the Body.* The Life of the Body is mortall but the Life of the Soule is immortall Ecclesiastes 12. thear the Spirit signifies the soule, in Isaiah 53. 10. 11. he shall make his soule an offering for sine.

Mrs. Hutchison. *I am clear in this now.*

Mr. Damphord. Than you renounce what you held in both those poynts.

Mrs. Hutchison. *Yes I doe, takinge Soule as Mr. Damphord doth. Soe thear was my Mistake. I tooke Soule for Life.*

Mr. Damphord. The Spirit is not a Third Substance but the Bent and Inclination of the soule and all the facultis thearof. Now this is not a substance differinge from the soule, and that Spirit in *Ecclesiastes is ment of the Soule,* the Spirit returns to God that gave it, that is, the soule or substance thereof.

Mrs. Hutchison. I doe not differ from Mr. Damphord, as he expresseth himselfe.

Mr. Damphord. The *Spirit* thear in Thessalonians is as the Bias to the Soule.

Brother Willson. But the Question is *whether that Spirit in Thessalonians be Imortall or not.*

Mr. Damphord. *That Word Spirit* in Ecclesiastes *is ment the Soule, and that Spirit in Thessalonians is not the substance of the soule but a Qualitie of it.* That soule which Christ speakes of in Matthew He casts both soule and Body into Hell *thear soule is not ment spirit but soule.*

Mrs. Hutchison. I may speake playnelye whether you thinke that the *soules of men are Imortall by Generation or . . . mortall,* and soe fadeth away like the soule of a Beast.

Mrs. Hutchison. Now Mr. Damphord hath opened it, it is cleare to me or God by him hath given me Light.

Mr. Cotten. Sister, speake to this: Whether you conceave that the devine and gracious Qualeties of the soules of Beleevers be Immortall or no and shall goe with the soule into Heaven and whether you thinke the Evell Qualleties of the soules of wicked men and thear Evell Dispositions shall goe with thear Soules to Hell or no.

Mrs. Hutchison. I know not presantly what to say to this.

Mr. Damphord. You doe than consent to the two first Questions that *the Coming of Christ in Thessalonians to the soule is not ment of Christs Cominge in Union but of his Cominge at the day of Judgment.*

Mrs. Hutchison. I doe not acknowledge it to be an Error but a Mistake. *I doe acknowledge my Expression to be Ironious but my Judgment was not Ironious,* for I held befor as you did but could not express it soe. John 12 [1] Corinthians 4.16. 3 Things. That men whan thay beleeve have a New Body and thay have 2 bodies. 1 Corinthians 15.44.37.

Mr. Cotten. If you meane thay have 2 bodies one of sine and another of death, and one outward body and an Inward Body of Graces.

Mrs. Hutchison. I meane as that Scripture meanes 1 Corinthians 4.16.

Mr. Cotten. You say you doe not know whether Jesus Christ be united to this body of ours or . . . our fleshly bodies. Thear lies the scruple and the absurdetie of it. Therefor, remember, both soule and body are united to Christ. In our spirituall Estate the Body is a sanctified Instrument to hear and to be holy and Christ is united to that body which we made the body of an Harlot. *Your bodies are the Temples of the* Holy Ghost: that very body that befor we had taken and made the Members of Harlots.

Mrs. Hutchison. I desire you to speake to that place in 1 Corinthians 15.37.44 for I doe question whether the same Bodies that dies, shall rise agayne.

Mr. Damphord. The same Body that is sowen the same Body shall rise agayne. It is sowen a naturall Body but it shall rise a spirituall Body.

Mrs. Hutchison. We all rise in Christ Jesus. In Romans 6 he showes that he dyes.

Mr. Damphord. That is another kind of Death. But speak first of the other Death and [it is] clear that he rayseth us the same Body and not another Body for substance.

Mrs. Hutchison. I question whether your body be sowen or no.

Mr. Damphord. Whan I dye than my body is sowen: and turned into Corruption and dust. And that dust which is sowen shall rise agayne in a body.

Mrs. Hutchison. Than come to Romans 6. 1. 2–7: thear is no death of a Child of God: but a puttinge of our Tabernacle. Revelation 20.

Mr. Damphord. This Death and Resurrection hear spoken of is not a naturall Death nor a naturall Resurrection but a spirituall one. But that Death in 1 Corinthians 15 is spoken of a naturall and bodely Death and Resurrection. Matthew 22.

Mrs. Hutchison. There is another place in Revelation 20 whear he speakes of the first Resurrection.

Mr. Damphord. Thear is no first and second Resurrection of one and the same Body, for that implyes a second Resurrection. Now some understand that of the Resurrection of the Martirs, others of a spiritual Resurrection, as is ment in Romans 6 a spiritual Resurrection both which we enjoy in this Life, but that in 1 Corinthians is ment of a Bodely Resurrection after this Life. Therefor are you clear in that place?

Mrs. Hutchison. No not yet.

Mr. Buckle.[11] I desire to know of Mrs. Hutchison whether you hould any other Resurection than that of . . . Union to Christ Jesus. And whether you hould that foule, groce, filthye and abbominable opinion held by Familists,[12] *of the Communitie of Weomen.* Job 19.25. Philippians 3.

Mrs. Hutchison. *I hould it not.* But Christ Answers now, I know thou hast a Divell. That was the Conclusion thay made agaynst Christ *when he sayd thay that beleeve in me shall not dye:* I doe not beleeve that Christ Jesus is united to our Bodies.

Brother Willson. God forbid.

Mr. Damphord. Avoyd . . . Mr. Buckles question for it is a right principle for if the Resurrection be past than Marriage is past: for it is a waytie Reason; *after the Resurrection is past, marriage is past. Than if thear be any Union betwene man and woman it is not by Marriage but in a Way of Communitie.*

Mrs. Hutchison. If any such practice or Conclusion be drawen from it than I must leave it, *for I abhor that Practise.*

Governor. The Familists doe not desire to evade that question for thay practise the Thinge. And thay bringe this very place

---

11. Peter Bulkeley.

12. The Familists, a heretical sect of the sixteenth century, were popularly (and incorrectly) supposed to believe in "free love" between the sexes.

to prove thear Communitie of Weomen and to justify thear ab-
hominable Wickedness. It is a dayngerous Error.

Mr. Leverit. But our sister doth not deny the Resurrection
of the Body.

Mrs. Hutchison. No.

Mr. Simes.[13] She denies the Resurrection of the same Body
that dyes. Therefore to prove that the same body that dyes shall
rise agayne, I prove it Job 19.35 and . . . .

Mrs. Hutchison. That it is all the question for *I doe not
thinke the Body that dyes shall rise agayne.*

Mr. Damphord. *You tell us of a new Body and of 2 bodies;
that is three. Now which of these Bodies do you hould shall rise
agayne.*

Mr. Eliot. We are altogether unsatisfied with her answer
and we thinke it is very dayngerous to dispute this Question soe
longe in this Congregation. She that hath come of in her other
Answer, to say it was not an Error but a mistake of so groce and so
dayngerous an opinion as this is, we much fear her spirit.

Mr. Buckle. In Hebrews 6.1. the Holy Ghost thear makes
the denyinge of the Resurrection to be the denyinge of a fundamentall Truth of Religion. Thearfor for any to hould thear is no
Resurrection I thinke it is as dayngerous an Heresie, and we are
to hould them as dayngerous Heriticks as any are.

Mr. Simes. I desire to propound one place more 1 Corinthians 15.13. *if thear be no Resurrection then our fayth is in vayne*
and preachinge is in vayne: and all is in vayne.

Mrs. Hutchison. I confess if thear be no Resurection than
all is in vayne, both preaching and all. *I scruple not the Resurrection but what Body shall rise,* it shall rise, that is in Christ we
shall rise.

Governor. I desire to propound this to Mrs. Hutchison. It
is sayd whan Christ arose many of those dead bodies of the Saints
did arise out of thear Graves, and did accompany Christ into the
holy Cittie. Now I would know what Bodies those wear that rose,
whether it be not the same Bodies that wear dead and layd in
thear Graves.

---

13. Zechariah Symmes.

Mrs. Hutchison. I know not but thay may be the same Bodies.

Mr. Governor. Than the poynt is at an End.

Mrs. Hutchison. I am not clear in the poynt. I cannot yet see that Christ is united to these fleshly Bodies. And if he be not united to our fleshly Bodies, than those Bodies cannot rise.

Mr. Damphord. The fleshly *Bodies of the wicked are not united to Christ yet thay shall rise agayne.*

Mrs. Hutchison. Thay shall rise to Condemnation.

Mr. Damphord. That is nothinge. And soe the Bodies of the Saints shall rise to Salvation.

Mr. Peters. I would aske Mrs. Hutchison this Question whether you thinke that the *very Bodys of Moses Eliah and Enoch were taken up into the Heavens,* or no.

Mrs. Hutchison. *I know not* that I scruple the former than much more this.

Mr. Damphord. Thease are Opinions that cannot be borne. They shake the very foundation of our fayth and tends to the Overthrough of all Religion. Thay are not slight matters [but] of greate Wayte and Consequence.

Brother Willson. If the Church be satisfied with the Arguments that have been propounded that thay are convinced in thear Judgments that thease are Errors, *Let them expres it by thear usiall sign of houldinge up thear Hands,* and that thay looke at them as groce and damnable Heresies. And because it is very late and many Thinges yet to goe over the Church thinkes it meete to refer farder Dealinge with our sister till the next Lecture day.

Mr. Hutchison. I desire to know by what Rule I am to expres myselfe in my Assent or Dissent whan yet *my Mother* is not convinced. For I hope she will not shut her Eyes agaynst any Light.

Brother Willson. Brother you may as well make Question whether God will confesse you before his Father which is in Heaven, whan you deny to confesse his Truth befor Men though agaynst your owne Mother.

Mr. Damphord. You are not to be led by naturall Affection but to declare your opinion for the Truth and agaynst Error, though held by your owne Mother. The Question was not whether the Arguments were waytie enough to convince your Mother, but whether you have Light enough to satisfie your Contience that thay are Errors.

Mr. Hutchison. Than I consent to them as far as I know that thear is a Resurection etc.

Mr. Sheppard. If thear be any of this Congregation that doe hould the same opinions I advise them to take heed of it, for the hand of the Lord will finde you out. And for Mrs. Hutchison I would wish her to consider by what spirit and Light she is lead. For she hath often bosted of the Guidance of Gods Spirit and that her Revelations are as trew as the scriptures. But she hath allready confessed her Mistake in the 2 first poynts by the Light she hath receaved from Mr. Damphord. Now than her spirit hath led her into some Errors therfor I hope she will see the rest to be Errors and to suspect herselfe and to know it is not Gods Spirit but her owne Spirit that hath guided her hitherto, a spirit of Delusion and Error. And for my owne part I must needes say that I know not what Course better to take: nor wherein I might show more love to her Soule than in bringinge her to her owne Congregation of which she is a Member to answer to thease dayngerous and fearfull Errors which she hath drunke in, that thay under God which have the Care of her soule may deale with her for them, and wach mor narrowly over her for time to come, and seeke to reclayme her. For she is of a most dayngerous Spirit and likely with her fluent Tounge and forwardnes in Expressions to seduce and draw away many, Espetially simple Weomen of her owne sex.

Brother Willson. *If the church* be satisfied with what hath bine spoken: and that thay *conceave we ought to proceed to Admonition, we will take thear Silence for Consent: if any be otherwise minded, thay may expres themselves.*

Sargeon Savidge. For my part I am not yet satisfied. Nayther doe I see any Rule why the church should proceed to Admonition: seeinge that in the most Churches thear hath bine some Errors or Mistakes held. Yea and in this very Church of Corinth there was many unsound opinions and in particular some amongst them that held this very opinion: about the Resurection as appears by Paulls arguments in 15 Chapter yet we doe not read that the Church did admonish them for it. Indeed in poynt of fact as in the Case of Incest the church proceeded to Excommunication because it was groce and abominable but not for opinion: now *my Mother* not beinge accused for any haynous fact but *only for opinion and that wherin she desires Information and Light,* [rather] than peremptorelye to hould, *I cannot consent that the church should proceed yet to admonish her for this.*

Mr. Cotten.   *Your Mother though she be not accused of any thinge in poynt of fact or practise nayther for my owne part doe I know thear is any cause.* Yet she may hould Errors as dayngerous and of worse Consequence than matters of practise cane be, and therfor I see not but the church may proceed to Admonition. And whereas you say *she seekes Light and Information rather than houlds them peremptorily,* you hear that thear hath bine much paynes taken and many Arguments brought not only from ourselves but from divers of the Elders of other Churches which gives satisfaction to the rest of this Assembly and which she is no wayes able to answer. And yet she persists in her Opinion; besides *the Apostle did admonish for poynt of Opinion.* For *Himeneus* and *Philetus* thay held thinges of this Nature. The Apostle doth give thear an Admonition for it therfor you doe a very evell office out of your naturall not religious Affection to hinder the Church in her proceeding and to be a meanes to harden your Mothers Heart in thease dayngerous Opinions and so keepe her from Repentance. I pray consider of it.

Liuetenant Gibbens.[14]   I desier Leave of the church for one word; not that I would open my mouth in the least kinde to hinder the Churches proceedinge in any way of God. *For I looke at our sister as a lost Woman* and I blesse God to see the paynes that is taken to reduce her: but I would humbly propose this to the churches Consideration seeing *Admonition is one of the greatest Censures* that the Church can pronounce agaynst any offender and one of the last next to Excommunication and to be used agaynst Impenitent Offendors, but seinge God hath turned her hart about allready to see her Error *or Mistake as she calls it* in some of the poynts. Whether the Church had not better wayte a

---

14. Edward Gibbons, a Boston merchant.

little longer to see if God will not help her to see the rest and to acknowledge them, than the Church may have no occasion to come to this Censure.

Mr. Simes. I am much greved to hear that soe many in this Congregation should stand up and declare themselves unwillinge that Mrs. Hutchison should be proceded agaynst for such dayngerous Errors. I fear that if by any meanes this should be carried over into England, that in New England and in such a Congregation thear was soe much spoken and soe many Questions made about *soe playne an Article of our fayth as the Resurrection is,* it will be one of the greatest Dishonors to Jesus Christ and of Reproch to thease Churches that hath bine done since we came heather.

Mr. Damphord. I thinke it is meete that if any of the Brethren hav any Scruples upon thear Spirits about this or any other Poynt that shall be discussed, that thay should have free Leave to propound it that it may be taken off and thear Doubts removed. And if thease Brethren that withstand the Church in proseedinge to Admonition did but consider *that Admonition is an Ordinance of God* and sanctified of him for this very End as a spetiall and powerfull meanes to convince the partie offendinge as well as Arguments and reasons given; than thay would not oppose it. The want of that Consideration is the Cause of thear present scruple herin.

Elder Oliver. I desier to be satisfied in one Thinge and I am glad that I have soe good an Opertunitie to propound my Doubt at such a Time whan God hath furnished us with such store of Elders and Men of able parts from other Churches, that may resolve the same: And that is How the church cane or *whether it may proceede to any Censure whan all the Members doe not consent thearto: or whether the Church hath not power to lay a Censure upon them that doe hinder the Churches proseedinges.*

Mr. Cotten. I thinke Bretheren are to be satisfied: the church ought as much as in them lies to remoove all Scruples that if it may be the whole Church may proseede with one Consent in the Act to be done; but if the Church doe take paynes and doe bringe Arguments such as satisfies the whole Congregation to be sufficient to remoove such Scruples, if yet some Bretheren will

persist in thear Dissent upon no Ground but for by Respects of
thear owne or out of naturall affection than the Church is not to
stay her proseedinge for that.

Mr. Damphord.   I doe not see but that the Church is satisfied. I perceive none doth oppose the Church: some only 2 or 3
which are tied to her by Naturall Relation; for these others that
have spoken thay did propound it but as Scruples and thay have
receaved satisfaction. And therfor I see nothinge that may hinder.

Sargion Oliver.   I desire to propound this one Thinge to the
Church befor you proseed to admonition. I doe blesse God to see
soe much Care and faythfullnes shewed to the soule of this our
Sister: and it doth rejoyce my Soule to see soe much paynes taken
and so many effectuall Arguments brought to reduce her from
her Errors and goinge astray. And it is of no lesse greife to my
Spirit to see thease two Bretheren to speake soe much and to
scruple the proseedinges of the Church in that way of God that is
in hand. Therefore I would propound this seeing that all the proseedinges of the Churches of Jesus Christ now should be accordinge to the *Patterne of the primative Churches: And the primative pattern was that all Thinges in the Church should be done
with one hart and one soule and one Consent; that any act and
every Act done by the Church may be as the Act of one Man.*
Therefor whether it be not meete to *lay thease two Bretheren
under an Admonition with thear Mother;* that soe the church
may proseed on without any further Opposition.

Brother Willson.   I thinke you speake very well: it is very
meete.

The whole Church by thear Silence Consented to the Motion:
and soe thay proceded to Admonition. The rest of our Elders requested Mr. Cotten to give the Admonition as one whose Wordes
by the Blessinge of God may be of more Respect and sinke deeper
and soe was likely to doe more good upon the partie offendinge
than any of theas. And it was alsoe left to him to doe as God
should incline his hart whether to lay any admonition upon her
2. Sonnes or no with her selfe.

Mr. Cotten.   I doe in the first place blesse the Lord: and
thanke in my owne Name and in the Name of our Church theas
our Bretheren the Elders of other Churches for thear Care and

faythfullnes in waching over our Churches and for bringinge to Light what our selves have not bine soe ready to see in any of our Members and to take soe much paynes to seeke to reduce any of ours from goinge astray; and I shall desier that this faythfull and wachfull Care of thears towards [us] may still be continued: and I doubt not but the Lord Jesus Christ who is the head of the whole Church will reward it into thear Bosoms. I confes I have not bine ready to beleeve Reports and have bine slowe of proseedinge agaynst any of our Members for want of sufficient Testimony to prove that which hath bine layd to thear Charge. But now thay have proceded in a way of God and doe bringe such Testimonie as doth Evince the Truth of what is affirmed, it would be our sine if we should not joyne in the same which we are willinge to doe. And therfor in the first place I shall direct my speech and admonition to you that are her sonnes, and sonne in Law; and let me tell you from the Lord; though naturall affection may leade you to speake in the Defence of your Mother and to take her part and to seeke to keepe up her Credit and respect, which may be lawfull and comendable in some Cases and at some times, yet in the Cause of God you are nayther to know Father nor mother sister nor Brother, but to say of them all as Levie did what have we to doe with them. And though the Credit of your mother be dear to you, and your Regard to her Name, yet the Regard you should have of Christs Name and your Care of his Honour and Credit should outway all the other. Yea and as you have herd you must cast downe her Name and Credit, though it be the chiefest Crowne that ayther yourselves or your mother hath, at the Feete of Jesus Christ and let that be trampled upon soe his Crowne may be exalted. And I doe *admonish you both* in the name of Christ Jesus and of his Church to consider how ill an office you have performed to your Mother this day to be Instruments of hardninge her Hart and Nourishinge her in her unsound Opinions by your pleadinge for her and hindringe the proceedings of the Church agaynst her which God hath directed us to take to heale her soule, and which God might have blessed and made mor effectuall to her had not you intercepted the Course. And how insteed of lovinge and naturall Children *you have proved Vipers to Eate through the very Bowells of your Mother,* to her Ruine if God doe not gratiously prevent. Therefor I advise you both and admonish you in the Lord that you desist from such practise and take heed how you by your flattery or mourninge over her: aplaudinge of her in her Opinion or takinge part with her whan you come home, do hinder the Work of Repentance in her and keepe her from seeinge thease Evells in her selfe: but looke up to Christ Jesus and address yourselves to her with all faythfull and gratious Counsells to her, that you may doe what you cane to bring her to a sight of her wronge way and to reduce her from it. Than shall you performe the parts of faythfull Children indeed. The Lord will blesse you. If you doe otherwise Looke that the Lord will bringe you to an Account for it.

Next let me say somewhat to the Sisters of our owne Congregation, many of whom I fear have bine too much seduced and led aside by her; therfore *I admonish you* in the Lord to looke to your selves and to take heed that you reaceve nothinge for Truth which hath not the stamp of the Word of God from it. I doubt not but some of you have allsoe received much good from the Conference of this our Sister and by your Converse with her: and from her it may be you have reaceved helpes in your spirituall Estates, and have bine brought from Restinge upon any Duties or Workes of Righteousnes of your owne. But *let me say this to you all, and to all the Sisters of other Congregations. Let not the good you have receved from her, make you to reaceve all for good that comes from her;* for you see she is but a Woman and *many unsound and dayngerous principles are held by her,* therfor whatsoever good you have reaceved owne it and keepe it carefully, but if you have drunke in with this good any Evell or Poyson, make speed to vomit it up agayne and to repent of it and take [care] that you doe not harden her in her Way by pittyinge of her or confirminge her in her opinions, but pray to God for her and deale faythfully with her soule in baringe Witnesse agaynst any unsound Thinge that at any Time she hath held forth to you.

And now, Sister, let me adresse myselfe to you. The Lord put fitt Words into my Mouth, and carry them home to your Soule for good. It is trew whan you came first over into this Cuntrye we herd some thinge of some opinions that you held: and vented upon the Seas, in the Ship whan you came, which whan you came to be propounded for a Member, we had some Conference with you about them hear in which you ded give us such satisfaction that after some little stay to your Admition you wear reaceved in amongst us.[15] And since that admission I would speake it to Gods Glory you have bine an Instrument of doing some good amongst us. You have bine helpfull to many to bringe them of from thear unsound Grounds and Principles and from buildinge thear good Estate upon thear owene duties and performances or upon any Righteousness of the Law. And the Lord hath indued yew with good parts and gifts fitt to instruct your Children and Servants and to be helpfull to your husband in the Government of the famely. He hath given you a sharpe apprehension, a ready utterance and abilitie to exprese yourselfe in the Cause of God. I would deal with you as Christ Jesus deales with his Churches whan he goes to admonish them to take a Vew and to call to your mind the good Thinges that he hath bestowed upon you. Yet Notwishstandinge: we have a few Thinges agaynst you and in some sence not a few but such as are of great Wayte and of a heavy Nature and dayngerous Consequences. Therefore let me warne you and admonish you in the Name of Jesus Christ to consider of it seriously, how the Dishonour you have brought unto God by thease unsound Tenets of yours, is far greater than all the honor you have brought to him. And the Evell of your Opinions doth outway all the good of your Doinges. Consider how many poore soules you have mislead, and how you have convayed the poyson of your unsound principles into the harts of many which it may be will never be reduced agayne. Consider in the fear of God that by this one Error of yours in denyinge the Resurection of thease very Bodies you doe the uttermost to rase the very foundation of Religion to the Ground and to destroy our fayth yea all our preachinge and your hearinge and all our sufferinges for the fayth to be in vayne if thear be no Resurection than all is in vayne and we of all people are most miserable. Yea consider *if the Resurection be past than you cannot Evade the Argument* that was prest

---

15. Mrs. Hutchinson was admitted to the Boston Church on "The 2d of the 9th," 1634, a week after her husband, and nearly two months after her arrival in the colony. *Publications of the Colonial Society of Massachusetts, 39,* 19.

upon you by *our Brother Buckle* and others, that filthie Sinne of the Comunitie of Woemen and all promiscuus and filthie cominge togeather of men and Woemen without Distinction or Relation of Marriage, will necessarily follow. And though I have not herd, nayther do I thinke, you have bine unfaythfull to your Husband in his Marriage Covenant, *yet that will follow upon it,* for it is the very argument that the Saduces bringe to our Saviour Christ agaynst the Resurrection: and that which the Annabaptists and Familists bringe to prove the Lawfullnes of the common use of all Weomen and soe more dayngerous Evells and filthie Unclenes and other sines will followe than you doe now Imagine or conceave.

Mrs. Hutchison. I desire to speake one word befor you proceed: I would forbar but by Reason of my Weakness. I fear I shall not remember it whan you have done.

Mr. Cotten. You have Leave to speake.

Mrs. Hutchison. All that I would say is this that *I did not hould any of thease Things before my Imprisonment.*

Mr. Cotten. I confesse I did not know that you held any of thease Things nor heare till hear of late. But it may be it was my sleepines and want of wachfull care over you, but you see the daynger of it and how God hath left you to your selfe to fall into thease dayngerous Evells, for I must needs say that *I have often feared the highth of your Spirit and being puft up with your owne parts,* and therfore it is just with God thus to abase you and to leave you to thease desperat falls for the Lord looketh upon all the children of pride and delights to abase them and bringe them lowe. And soe the other Thinges that you hould of the *Mortalletie of the Soule by Nature,* and that *Christ is not united to our Bodies:* and that *the Resurrection* spoken of at his appearinge is ment of his *appearinge to us in Union,* thease are of dayngerous Consequence and set an open Doore to all Epicurisme and Libertinisme; if this be soe than come let us eate and drinke for to morrow we shall dye, than let us nayther fear Hell nor the losse of Heaven; than let us beleve thare is nayther Ayngelles nor Spirits. What need we care what we speake, or doe, hear if our Soules perish and dye like beasts. *Nay though you should not hould thease Things possitively,* yet if you doe but make a Question of them and propound them as a doubt for satisfaction, yet others that hear of it will conclude them possitively and thay will thinke: suer thear is some thinge in it if Mrs. Hutchison makes a Question of it, if those that have greate parts of Wisdome and Understandinge and if such eminent Christians make a Question of them, Thear is something that needs further Serch and Inquirie about them. And soe your opinions frett like a Gangrene and spread like a Leprosie, and infect farr and near, and will eate out the very Bowells of Religion, and hath soe infected the Churches that God knowes whan thay will be cured. Therfor that I may draw to an End; I doe Admonish you and alsoe charge you in the Name of Christ Jesus in whose place I stand and in the Name of the Church who hath put me upon this service, that you would sadly consider the just hand of God agaynst you, *the greate hurt you have done to the Churches, the great Dishonour you have brought to Jesus Christ* and the Evell that you have done to many a poore soule, and *seeke unto him to give you Repentance for it,* and a hart to give satisfaction to the Churches you have offended hereby; and bewayle your Weaknes in the Sight of the Lord, that you may be pardoned, and consider the great Dishonor and Reproch that hereby you have brought upon this Church of ours wherof you are a Member, how you have layd us all under a Suspition, yea, and a Censure of houldinge and mayntayne Errors. Therefor thinke of it and be jelious of your owne Spirit in the rest and take heed how you Leaven the hartes of younge Weomen with such unsound and dayngerous principles, but Labor rather to recover them out of the Snaers as opertunetie shall serve; which you have drawn them to, and soe the Lord carry home to your Soule what I have spoken to you in his Name.

Mr. Shephard. Lest the Crowne should be set on her Hed in the day of her Humiliation I desier Leave to speake one Word befor the Assemblie break up. It is no little Affliction nor Grefe to my Spirit to hear what Mrs. Hutchison did last speake, it was a Trouble to me to see her interrupt you, by speaking in the midest of her Censure; unto which she ought to have attended, with fear and Tremblinge; but it was an Astonishment to me to hear that she should thus Impudently affirme soe horrible an Untruth and falshood in the midest of such a sollomne Ordinance of Jesus Christ and befor such an Assembly as this is; yea in the face of the Church *to say she held none of thease Opinions befor her*

Imprisonment, whan she knowes that she used this Speech to me, whan I was with her and delt with her about thease opinions, and she had fluently and forwardly expressed herself to me, yet she aded If I had but come to her befor her Restraynt, she would have opened herselfe mor fully to me and have declared many other Thingcs about them, yea of thease very Opinions. Therfor I am sorry that Mrs. Hutchison should soe far forget herselfe; it showes but little frute of all the paynes taken with her. This makes me mor to fear the unsoundnes of her hart than all the rest.

Mr. Eliot. It was the same Trouble and Greife allsoe to my selfe.

Brother Willson. Sister Huchison, I requier you in the Name of the Church to present yourselfe hear agayne, the next Lecture day, Viz this day Sevennight to give your *Answer to such other Thinges as this Church or the Elders of other Churches have to charge you withall,* Concerninge your Opinions, whether you hould them or no, or will revoke them.

Mrs. Hutchisons *second Examination* in Boston Church. one Thirsday Lectuer day after Sermon: March: 22th. 1638, *before all the Elders of other Churches,* and the Face of the Cuntry.

Elder Leveret. Sister Huchison, you are farther to make Answer to other Thinges layd to your Charge: But first I would have the Members of our owne Church draw near to expresse thear Consent or Dissent to the Things in hand which doth most concerne them. Mrs. Huchison, the Things further layd to your Charge are these

1. Those that have Union with Christ shall not rise in these Bodyes.
2. The Resurrection in 1 Corinthians 15 is not spoken of our Resurrection at the last day but of our Union to Christ Jesus.
3. That thear is no created Graces in Belevers after Union. Befor Union ther is, but after Union Christ takes them out of us into himselfe.
4. That in Christ thear is no created Graces.
5. That thear is an Ingraftinge into Christ befor our Union with him, from which we may fall away.
   Hear is further agaynst you
1. That your particular Revelations about futire Events

wear as infaliable as the scriptures them selves. That you wear bound to beleeve them as well as the Scriptures: because the Holy Ghost was the Author of both.

2. That Sanctification could be no Evidence of a good Estate at all.

3. That Union to Christ Jesus is not by Fayth.

4. That an Hipocrite may have Adams Righteousnes and perish.

5. That we have no Grace in our Selves but all is in Christ and thear is no inherent Righteousnes in us.

To the 3 first from N. Towne you gave no satisfaction. Therefor an Admonition past agaynst you. Therfor you are now to give further satisfaction about them.

Mrs. Huchison.   For the first, I doe acknowledge I was deeply deaceved, the opinion was very dayngerous. 1 Corinthians 6. 19.18.

2. *Though I never doubted that the Soule was Imortall yet . . . Things I renounce, as that the Soule was purchased to eternall payne.*

3. I acknowledge my Mistake of Belevers haveing two Bodies. Soe now I see that the Apostle in 1 Corinthians 6.14.15. speakes of persons in one place and of bodies in another.

4. I acknowledge and I doe thanke God that I better see that Christ is united to our Fleshlye Bodies as 1 Corinthians 6.18.19. *I doe acknowledge that the same Body that lies in the Grave shall rise agayne and renounce the former as eronious* Isaiah 11.2.

5. For no Graces beinge in Beleevers I desier that to be understood that thay are *not in us but as thay flow from Christ.* And I doe not acknowledge any Graces in us, accompanying Salvation before Union.

6. I acknowledge that thar is Graces created in Christ Jesus as Isaiah 11.2, 2 Peter 4.24, Colossians 3.10.

8. I doe see good Warrant that Christs Mantion is in heaven as well as his Body.

9. I have considered some Scriptures that satisfie me that the Image of Adam is Righteousnes and Holiness.

10. I hould that to be a dayngerous Error which than I held.

11. *I confes now the Law is a Rule of Life* and I acknowledge
the other to be a hateful Error and that which openeth a
Gap to all Lisentiousnes. And I beleve the Law is a Rule
of our Life and if we doe any Thing contrary to it it is a
grevous Sine.

Thus she answered to the first sixteen Objections.

Have you any Answer to the rest?

Answer to Mr. Wells Articles

1. That Sanctification cant be an Evidence but as it flowes
from Christ and is witnessed to us by the Spirit.

2. For these Scriptures that I used at the Court in Censur-
inge the Cuntrie I confes I did it rashly and out of heate
of Spirit and unadvisedly, and have cause to be sorry for
my unreverent Cariage to them and I am hartely sorry
that any Thinge I have sayde have drawn any from hearinge any of the Elders of the Bay.

3. I acknowledge the command of fayth is a part of the Doctrine of the Gospell.

4. That thear *is no fayth of Gods Elect but Assurance,* and
that thear is no Fayth of Dependance but such as Hipocrits may have.

Mrs. Huchison.   I never held any such Thing.

Elder Leverett.   It semes you did hould it, though after
you revoked it.

5. I doe not beleeve that a Hipocrite cane attayne to Adam's
Righteousnes.

6. We are dull to act in spirituall Thinges savingly, but as
we are acted by Christ.

For the 9th *I deny it, that not beinge bound to the Law
it is no Transgression to breake it. I never held it for I acknowledge any Breach of the Law is a sine,* and the former
is a hatefull Error.

Brother Willson.   Thear is one Thinge that will be necessary
for you Sister to answer to which was objected to you the last
meetinge, but it beinge soe late we could not take your Answer.
And that was that you denied you held none of those Thinges but
since your Durance wheras he aledged to you that you expressed
befor the contrary.

Mrs. Huchison.   As my sine hath bine open, soe I thinke it needfull to acknowledge how I came first to fall into thease Errors. Instead of Lookinge upon myselfe I looked at Men, I know my Dissemblinge will doe no good. I spake rashly and unadvisedly. *I doe not allow the slightinge of Ministers nor of the Scriptures* nor any Thinge that is set up by God. If Mr. Shephard doth conceave that I had any of these Things in my Minde, than he is deceaved. It was never in my hart to slight any man but only that man should be kept in his owne place and not set in the Roome of God.

Elder Leverit.   That the Assemblie may know what you have delivered, as our Honored Governor hath mooved, it is meet some body should expres what you say to the Congregation which heard not.

Mr. Cotten.   The Sume of what she sayd is this, that she did not fall into thease groce and fundamentall Errors till she came to Roxbery. And the Ground was this her Miscariage and disrespect that she showed to the Magistrats whan she was befor them who are set up by . . . . . and those that doe soe lead themselves into Errors, and she doth utterly disalow herselfe and condemne herselfe for that Cariage: and she confesseth the Roote of all was the hight and Pride of her Spirit. Soe for her slighting the Ministers she is hartely sorry for it. For her particular Relation in her Spech to the Disgrace of him She is sorry for it and desiers all that she hath offended to pray to God for her to give her a hart to be more truly humbled.

Mr. Shephard.   If this day whan Mrs. Hutchison should take Shame and Confusion to herselfe for her groce and damnable Errors, she shall cast Shame upon others and say thay are mistaken, and to turne of many of those groce Errors with soe slight an Answer as *your Mistake,* I fear it doth not stand with true Repentance. I confes I am wholy unsatisfied in her Expressions to some of the Errors. Any Hereticke may bringe a slye Interpritation, upon any of thease Errors and yet hould them to thear Death: therfor I am unsatisfied, I should be glad to see any Repentance in her: that might give me Satisfaction.

Mr. Elliot.   Mrs. Hutchison did affirme to me, as she did to Mr. Shephard, that if we had come to her before her restraynt or Imprisonment she could and would have tould me many Things of Union etc. but now we had shut and debarred ourselves from that Helpe by impresinge and procedinge agaynst her, and she did produce some Scriptures to me.

Mr. Shephard.   She puts of many Thinges with her Mistake, as in union with Christ, Christ takes all these Graces he finds in us into ourselves, and transacts us him selfe.

Mr. Cotten.   Sister was thear not a Time whan once you did hould that thear was *no distinct graces inherent in us but all was in Christ Jesus?*

Mrs. Hutchison.   *I did mistake the word Inherent,* as Mr. Damphord can tell who did cause me first to see my Mistake in the word inherent.

Mr. Elliot.   We are not satisfied with what she sayth that she should say now *that she did never deny Inherence of Grace in us, as in a subject,* for she beinge by us pressed soe with it she denyed that thear was *no Graces inherent in Christ himselfe.*

Mr. Shephard.   She did not only deny the word inherent, but denyed the very Thinge itself. Than I asked her if she did beleave that the spirit of God was in Beleevers.

Mrs. Hutchison.   *I confes my Expressions was that way but it was never my Judgment.*

Mr. Damphord.   It requiers you to answer playnly in thease Thinges.

Mr. Elliot.   She did playnly expres herselfe to me that thear was *no difference betweene the Graces that are in Hipocrits and those that are in the Saints.*

Mr. Cotten.   Thear is 2 thinges to be clerd, 1. what you doe now hould. 2ly what you did hould.

Mrs. Hutchison.   My Judgment is not altered though my Expression alters.

Brother Willson.   This you say is most dayngerous, for if your Judgment all this while be not altered but only your Expressions, whan your Expressions are soe contrary to the Truth.

Mr. Simes.   I should be glad to see any Humiliation in Mrs. Hutchison. I am afrayd that she lookes but to Spriges,[16] for I fear thease are no new Thinges but she hath ayntientlye held them

16. Not improbably the original was here copied wrong; but possibly "spriges" is used for the old English "sprigges" — small sprouts or outshoots; or, yet more possibly, for "springes" in the sense in which the word is used by Shakespeare: — "Springes to catch woodcocks." — Adams.

* See new note p. xx.

and had need to be humbled for her former Doctrines and for her abuse of divers Scriptures. And if she held no new Thinge yet she ought to be humbled for what she hath held formerly as *A christians beinge dead to all spirituall Actinge after thay are united to Christ* and soe that of Graces. She hath brought that place in Isaiah that all flesh is grasse and poor witheringe Thinges and soe other Things to the like purpose.

Mr. Peters.   We did thinke she would have humbled herselfe for denyinge Graces this day, for her opinions are dayngerous and fundamentall and such as takes downe the Articles of Religion, *as denying the Resurrection* and fayth and all Sanctification, so that some Elders have made whole Sermons for fayth as if fayth should never hould up her Hed agayne in this Cuntrye; as it hath done in our Native Cuntry.

Deputie.[17]   Mrs. Hutchisons Repentance is only for Opinions held since her Imprisonment, but befor her Imprisonment she was in a good Condition, and held no Error, but did a great deale of Good to many. Now I know no Harme that Mrs. Hutchison hath done since her Confinement, therfor I think her Repentance will be worse than her Errors, for if by this meanes she shall get a partie to herselfe, and what cane any Heretick in the World desier more. And for her forme of Recantation, her *Repentance is in a paper,* whether it was drawn up by herself, or whether she had any helpe in it I know not, and will not now Inquier to, but suer *her Repentance is not in her Countenance,* none cane see it thear I thinke. Therfor I speak this only to put the Elders in minde to speake to this whether she did not hould errors before her Imprissonment.

Mr. Wells.   I must needs say that before this she hath sayd to me whan I spake of Graces that she would not pray for fayth nor for patience and the like. Which whan I asked her if she would stand to that and tooke out my pen and Inke to have writ it downe, than she turns it this way, *I will not pray for Patience but for the God of Patience.*

Governor.   I must put Mrs. Hutchison in minde of a paper that she sent to me, wherin she did very much slight fayth.

Mrs. Hutchison.   Those papers wear not myne.

---

17. Deputy-governor Thomas Dudley.

Mr. Peters.   I would say this, whan I was once speakinge with her about the *Woman of Elis:* she did exceedingly magnifie her to be a Womane of 1000 hardly any like to her. And yet we know that the *Woman of Elis:* is a dayngerous Woman and houlds forth greevous Things and ferfull Errors. And whan I tould her that hear was divers worthy and godly Weomen Even amongst us and than she sayd she ment she was better than soe many Jewes. Soe that I beleeve that she hath vilde Thoughts of us and thinkes us to be nothinge but a company of Jewes and that now God is con-virtinge of Jewes.

Mrs. Hutchison.   I sayd of the Woman of Elis but what I herd, for I knew her not nor never sawe her.[18]

Brother Willson.   I must needs say this and if I did not say soe much I could not satisfie my owne Contience herin, for wheras you say that the Cause or Root of thease your Errors, was your slightinge and Disrespect of the Magistrates and your unreverent Carriage to them; which though I thinke that was a greate Sine, and it may be one Cause why God should thus leave you, but that is not all, for I fear and beleve thar was another and a greater Cause, and that is the *slightinge of Gods faythfull Ministers and contemninge and cryinge downe them as Nobodies.* And wheras you say that one Cause was the settinge up of men in the Roome of God and a to high and honorable Esteme of them, I doe not deny but it may be you might have an honorable Esteme of some one or 2. Men as our Teacher and the like. Yet I thinke it was to set up *your selfe in the Roome of God above others that you might be extolled and admired and followed after, that you might*

---

18. A possible explanation of this reference is suggested by Emery Battis: "This rather puzzling exchange is considerably illuminated by the following passage in Thomas Edwards, *Gangraena* [London, 1646], Part II, 29: 'There are also some women preachers in our times, who keep constant lectures, preaching weekly to many men and women. In Lincolnshire, in Holland and those parts there is a woman preacher who preaches (it's certain), and 'tis re-ported also she baptizeth, but that's not so certain. *In the Isle of Ely (that land of errors and sectaries) is a woman preacher also.*' In indexes of English towns Ely is the only town which even approximates in sound or appearance the word, 'Elis,' and the identification seems reinforced by the fact that Ely had long been notorious as a gathering place for radical sectaries." *Saints and Sectaries,* 43n.

be a greate Prophites . . . and Undertake to expound Scriptures, and to interpret other Mens Sayings and sermons after your minde. And therefor I beleve your Iniquite hath found you out, and wheras befor if any delt with you about any Thinge you called for Witnesses and for your Accusers, and who can lay it to your Charge, now God hath left you to your selfe, and you have hear confessed that which befor you have called for Witnesses to prove. Therfor it greves me that you should soe mince *your dayngerous soule and damnable Herisies* whereby you have soe wickedly departed from God and done soe much hurt.

Mr. Shephard.   I thinke it is needles for any other now to speake and useless for the Case is playne, and hear is Witnesses enough.

Mr. Elliot.   Some will acknowledge the Word Gifts and Frutes but thay deny the word Graces: thay acknowledge actings of the Spirit: and by such Distinctions, I could wipe of all her Repentance in that paper, therfore she shall doe well to express her selfe playnly what her Judgment now is in thease Thinges.

Mrs. Huchison.   Our Teacher knowes my Judgment, for I never kept my Judgment from him.

Deputie.   I doe remember, that whan she was examined, about the six Questions or Articles, about Revelations etc., that she held nothinge but what Mr. Cotten held.

Mr. Wells.   I cane affirme the same to, for whan I spake with her she tould me that Mr. Cotten and she was both of one minde and she held no more than Mr. Cotten did in thease Thinges. And whan I told her that then she was lately chaynged in her Opinion, and I urged her with some Thinges that Mr. Cotten had left, some Thinges in Writinge expressly agaynst some of the opinions she held; *she affirmed still that thear was no difference betwene Mr. Cotten and She.*

Sargeon Oliver.   I know the Time whan Mrs. Hutchison did plead for Creature Graces and did acknowledge them and stood for them; but since she hath used these Expressions in way of Dislike I have pleaded as much for Graces as others. Now if you doe not deny *created Graces in us* than cleer that Expression.

Mrs. Hutchison.   I confesse I have denyed the Word Graces but not the Thinge itselfe, and whan I sayd I had pleaded for them as much as others, *I ment only in seekinge Comfort from them.*

Mr. Simes. In the Ship[19] she may remember that she was often *offended at the Expression of growinge in Grace* and laying up a *Stock of Grace* and that *all Grace is in Christ Jesus.*

Brother Willson. I know she hath sayd it and affirmed it dogmatically, *that the Graces of God is not in us* and we have no Graces in us but only the Righteousnes of Christ Imputed to us, and if thear be any Actinge in us it is Christ only that acts. 53 Isaiah. Galatians 2.

Mr. Mather.[20] Mrs. Hutchison may remember that in her Speakinge with me that she denyed all Graces to be in us. That thear was nayther faith, nor knowledge nor Gifts and Graces no nor Life itselfe but all is in Christ Jesus. And she brought some Scriptures to prove her Opinions, *as that befor Union, thear was Graces and Fayth in us but not after Union,* and she Coted Romans 11 *Thou standest by Fayth be not high minded but fear, lest thou also be cut of,* whar sayth she, befor Union thear is Fayth thou standest by fayth, but if you be high minded you shall be cut of. And for knowledge it is not in us but in Christ and soe than you brought Isaiah 53 by his Knowledge shall my Righteous Servant Justifie many, thear, sayth she, *we are Justified by his Knowledge that is in him* and not by our Knowledge, and for [so] sayth that in Galatians 2 You brought I live but not I but Jesus Christ lives in me. Therfor I wonder that Mrs. Hutchison doth so far forget herselfe as to deny that she did not formerly hould this Opinion of denying Gifts and Graces to be in us.

Mr. Peters. I would desier Mrs. Huchison in the name of the Lord that she would serch into her hart farther to helpe on her Repentance. For though she hath confessed some Thinges yet it is far short of what it should be, and therfore

1. I fear you are not well principled and grounded in your Catechisme.
2. I would commend this to your Consideration that you have

---

19. The ship *Griffin* on which Mrs. Hutchinson and Symmes travelled together to New England in 1634.

20. Richard Mather (1596–1669), minister of Dorchester.

stept out of your place, *you have rather bine a Husband than a Wife and a preacher than a Hearer; and a Magistrate than a Subject.* And soe you have thought to carry all Thinges in Church and Commonwealth, as you would and have not bine humbled for this.

Governor. Seinge divers Sisters of the Congregation have builded upon her Experience, therfor I thinke it would be very Expedient and much to Gods Glory if she would declar har what here Estate is or wherin her good Estate is if not by Ingraftinge into Christ Jesus, for the Estate she held out before the Elders was not by Ingrafting into Christ for a *Man may be ingrafted into Christ Jesus and yet fall away.*

Mr. Wells. I desire that Motion may go on.

Mr. Shephard. You have not only to deale with a Woman this day that houlds diverse erronius Opinions but with one that never had any trew Grace in her hart and that by her owne Tenect. Yea this day she hath shewed herselfe to be a Notorius Imposter, it is a Tricke of as notorious Subtiltie as ever was held in the Church, to say thear is no Grace in the Saints and now to say she hath, and that she all this while hath not altered her Judgment, but only her Expressions.

2. I would have you question whether she was ever in a state of Grace or no, [seeing] her horrible Untruths that she hath affirmed in the Congregation and proved by many Witnesses and yet she hath not confessed it before the Lord.

3. *I would have the Congregation judge whether ever thear was any Grace in her hart or no;* or whither the Spirit of Glory rests upon her in the Cause she suffers. Soe her Cause were good, for which she suffers and doth not suffer as an evell doer, than the spirit of Glory and Christ shall rest upon tham that suffer as Peter speaks. Now if in her Restraynt God hath soe left her soe far to her selfe as she hath now confessed, that she never held any of thease Opinions till her Imprissonment, which is the Time of her Humiliation: and persecution she thinkes, therfor by Peter her sufferings is not for good because such an evell spirit hath rested upon her in this Time of her Humilliation.

4. Upon this Ground I thinke you are to deale with her not only for her Opinions as with one who is to be questioned whether ever she was in a good Estate, because the Ground of her Opinions hath bine built upon fayned and fantasticall Revelations as she held forth 2. in the Court, one for the certayne Destruction of Ould England and another for the Ruine of this Cuntrie and the people thereof for thear proceedinge agaynst her. Therefor I pray consider of it, and the rather I note this that all those Weomen and others that have bine led by her and doted soe much upon her and her Opinions.

Mr. Peters.   We are not satisfied in her Repentance, in that she hath expressed, wherin she layes her Censuer or Imprissonment to be the Cause of all her Errors as if she wear Inocent befor.

Brother Willson.   I cannot but reverence and adore the wise hand of God in this thinge, and canot but acknowledge that the Lord is just in leavinge our Sister to pride and Lyinge, and out of hith Spirit to fal into Errors and divers unsound Judgments. And I looke at *her as a dayngerus Instrument of the Divell* raysed up by Sathan amongst us to rayse up Divissions and Contentions and to take away harts and affections one from another. Wheras befor thear was much Love and Union and sweet agreement amongst us before she came, yet since all Union and Love hath bine broken and thear hath bine Censurings and Judgings and Condemnings one of another. And I doe conceve all these wofull Opinions doe come from this Botome, for if the Botome hath bine unsound and corrupt, than must the Building be such, and the Misgovernment of this Woman's Tounge hath bine a greate Cause of this Disorder, which hath not bine to set up the Ministry of the Word ayther hear or elce whear, but to set up her selfe and to draw deciples after her, and therfor she sayth one Thinge to day and another thinge to morrow: and to speake falsely and doubtfully and dullye wheras we should speake the Truth playnly one to another. I doe therfor this conceave in the poynt of Religion and in the poynt of Doctrine, thay take away the bottome, woe be to that soule that shall build upon such botoms. Our soules should abhor and loth to come soe far short in Repentance, therfor I thinke as she was lyable to an Admonition befor soe thear should be a . . .

of our Church and a proceedinge therin, to Ease our selves of such a member, Espetially for her untruth or Lyes, as that she was allways of the same Judgment, only she hath altered her Expressions. Therfor I leave it to the Church to consider how safe it is to suffer soe eronius and soe schismaticall and soe unsound a member amongst us, and one that stands guiltie of soe foule a falshood. Therfor consider whether we shall be faythfull to Jesus Christ or whether it cane stand with his honor to suffer such an one any longer amongst us, if the blind lead the blind whether shall we goe. Consider how we cane or whether we may longer suffer her to goe on still in seducinge to seduce and in deacevinge to deceave and in lyinge to lye and in condemninge Authoritie and Magistracie still to contemne. Therfor we should sine agaynst God if we should not put away from us soe Evell a Woman, guiltie of such foule Evells. Therfor if the church be of an other minde Let them express themselves, if she may not be seperated from the Congregation of the Lord.

Elder Oliver.   I did not thinke the Church would have come thus far soe soone, espetially seinge whan I taulked with her in the morninge I saw her to come of soe freely in her Confession of her sine in contemninge Magistrats and Ministers.

Mr. Elliot.   It is a wonderfull Wisdom of God to let them fall by that whearby they have upheld thear Opinions, and carried them as to let her fall into such Lies as she hath done this day, for she hath caried on all her Erors by Lies, as that she held nothinge but what Mr. Cotten did, and that he and she was all one in Judgment. And soe it fared with divers others that we have cast out of our Church of these opinions. [Revelation] 22.15.

Mr. Cotten.   The matter is now translated, the last day she was delt with in poynt of Doctrine, now she is delt with in poynt of practice. And soe it belongs to the Pastors Office to instruct and also to correct in Righteousnes whan a Lye is open and persisted in, in the face of the Congregation after proved by Witnes. I know not how to satisfye myselfe in it but accordinge to that in Revelation 22.15. If it come to this to the makinge of a Lye; than without shall be doges and such as love and makes lyes. Therfor though she have confessed that she sees many of the Thinges which she held to be Errors and that it proceded from the Roote Pride of

Spirit, yet I see this pride of Harte is not healed but is working still, and therfor to keep secret some unsound Opinions. God hath lett her fall into a manifest Lye, yea to make a Lye and therfor as we receaved her in amongst us I thinke we are bound upon this Ground to remove her from us and not to retayne her any longer, seeinge she doth prevaricate in her Words, as that her Judgment is one Thinge and her Expression is another.

Mr. Damphord. God will not bare with Mixtures in this kinde. Therfor you must freely Confess the Truth, take Shame to your selfe that God may have the Glory, and I fear that God will not let you see your sine and confes it, till the Ordinance of God hath taken place agaynst you. Soe that it semes to me God hath a purpose to goe on in the Course of his Judgment agaynst you.

Question. I desire to be satisfied in this how the Church may proseed to *Excommunication* whan the Scripture saythe he that confesseth and forsaken sine shall have Mercy, and whether we should not bare with Patience the contrary minded.

Mr. Cotten. Confession of Sine thear is ment withall the Agrivations of it . . which yet hath not appeared to us. And by baring with the contrary minded is ment of those that are without.

Mr. Scot.[21] I desire to propound this one Scruple which keepes me that I canot soe freely in my spirit give way to Excommunication. Whether it wear not better to give her a little time to consider of the Thinges that is . . . vised agaynst her, because *she is not yet convinced of her Lye* and soe things is with her in Distraction, and she canot recollect her Thoughts.

Mr. Cotten. This now is not for poynt of Doctrine, wherin we must suffer her with Patience, but we now deal with her in poynt of fact or practise, as the makinge and houldinge of a Lye. Now in poynt of groce fact thear may be a present proceedinge.

Mr. Shephard. I perceve it is the Desire of many of the Brethren to stay her Excommunication, and to let a second Admonition lye upon her; but now for one not to drop a Lye, but to make a Lye, and to mayntayne a Lye: and to doe it in a day of

---

21. Richard Scott, a shoemaker in Boston, was Anne Hutchinson's brother-in-law.

Humilliation, and in the sight of God, and such a Congregation as this is, I would have this Church consider whether it will be for the Honor of God and the honor of this Church to bare with patience soe groce an offendor.

Mr. Mather. The Apostle sayth an Hereticke after once or twise Admonition reject and cut of like a Gangrene as the word signifies: now she hath bine once admonished allready, why than should not the Church proceed.

Mr. Leverit. The Word is after once or twice by a Copulative.[22]

Deputie. I would answer this to Mr. Leverit, to his Objection after twise Admonition; Now Mrs. Huchison hath bine delt [with] and admonished not once, twise nor thrice but many Times by privat Bretheren and by Elders of other Congregations and by her owne Church. Therfor that should be no scruple. Besides, I thinke that text doth not speake of the Admonition of the Church but of privat Admonition.

Straynger. I would desier to knowe, if the Church prosedes agaynst her whether it be for Doctrine or for her Lye. If for her Lye than I consent. If it be for her Doctrine, she hath renounced that as Eroneus and than I want Light to goe with the Church in it.

Brother Willson. For my part, if the Church proceds I thinke it is and it should be for her Errors in Opinion as well as for poynt of Practise, for though she hath made some showe of Repentance yet it doth not seme to be cordial and sincere, and that of *Achan though he did confes and acknowledge his sine, yet Joshua, and that by the apoyntment of God did proced agaynst him,* and in Corinth as soon as ever the Apostle herd of that sine committed agaynst them, he writes his Letter *to cast them out forthwith without delay.*

Mr. Cotten. For you to propound Termes of Delay: what Rule have you for it, whan in poynt of practise thear hath bine a presant proseedinge as in Acts 5. *as soon as ever Annanias had tould a Lye the Church cast them out.*

---

22. Titus 3.10: A man that is an heretic, after the first and second admonition reject.

Brother Willson. The Church consentinge to it we will proced to

Excommunication.

Forasmuch as you, Mrs. Huchison, have highly transgressed
and offended and forasmuch as you have soe many ways *troubled
the Church with your Erors* and have drawen away many a poor
soule and have *upheld your Revelations:* and forasmuch as *you
have made a Lye,* etc. Therefor in the name of our Lord Jesus
Christ and in the name of the Church I doe not only pronounce
you worthy to be cast out, but *I doe cast you out* and in the name
of Christ *I doe deliver you up to Sathan* that you may learne no
more to blaspheme to seduce and to lye. And I doe account you
from this time forth to be a Hethen and a Publican and soe to be
held of all the Bretheren and Sisters of this Congregation, and of
others. Therfor *I command you* in the name of Christ Jesus and
of this Church *as a Leper to withdraw your selfe out of the Congregation;* that as formerly you have dispised and contemned the
Holy Ordinances of God and turned your Backe one them, soe
you may now have no part in them nor benefit by them.

CHAPTER II

Proceedings of the Boston Church
against the Exiles

DISCIPLINARY action by the Boston Church did not come to an end with Mrs. Hutchinson's excommunication. A year later the Church was still concerned about the members who accompanied her to Rhode Island. According to the Congregational conception of church membership, these "wandringe sheepe" were still within the church covenant until they were dismissed from Boston to another congregation. To remind these members of their obligations, as well as to check on the spiritual state of Mrs. Hutchinson and others who were under a sentence of discipline, the Church dispatched three messengers, Edward Gibbons, William Hibbins, and John Oliver, to Rhode Island early in 1639. Leaving Boston on February 24, these men completed their mission and reported back to the Church on March 16. Their report survives in the notebook of Robert Keayne, a Boston merchant who kept a personal record of the Church's affairs.[1] His account was published in George E. Ellis, *Life of Anne Hutchinson* (The Library of American Biography, second series, 6, Boston, 1845), 329–337; it was reprinted in Adams's collection and so is included here. The original manuscript is at the Massachusetts Historical Society.

---

1. Robert Keayne's interesting career in New England is described in Bernard Bailyn, "The Apologia of Robert Keayne," *William and Mary Quarterly* 3d series 7 (1950), 568–587.

Robert Keayne's Report of Boston Church Action

PASTOR. These 3 Brethren that was sent by the church to those wandringe sheepe at the Iland[2] beinge now returned, accordinge to the custome of the churches and servants of god in the scripture when thay did returne thay gave an account to the church of gods dealinge with them and the passages of his providences and how god carried them a Longe, it is expected of the church that some one of you or all of you one after another should declare the same that the church may have matter to prayse god with you.

Brother Hibbens. We thinke it our dutie to give an account to the church of gods dealinge with us in our jorny out and in and of the successe of our bussines when we came to our jornies end at the Iland. The second day of the weeke we reached the first night to mount wollistone, whear we were refreshed at our Brother Savidges House[3] wherby we were comfortablly fitted for our jorny the next day in which by the good mercy of god and the helpe of yor prayers god did accompany us with seasonable weather, and in our jorny the first observable providence of god that presented it selfe to our vew and espetially to my owne observation, which was in providinge for me a comfortable Lodginge, that second Night, which was the thinge I most feared becas I never was used to lye with out a Bead, and there was one that mett us in the way that came from Cohannet, who had a House to him selfe and he of his owne accord did give us Leave to Lodg and abide in his House that night, where myselfe especially, and all of us had comfortable Lodginge for that night which was a greate refreshinge to us and a deliverance from my fear.

The next providence of god that fell out in our jorny was some manifestations of gods hand agaynst us, for being the 4th day to passe over a River in a Canew in which was 8 of us our Canowe did hange upon a Tree, to [our] very great daynger, the water runninge swiftly away now my Ignorance was Such that I feared no daynger though those which had more skill sawe we were in Iminent daynger, here our god delivered us.

But now we Cominge safe over the water it pleased god to ex-

---

2. Newport Island.
3. The home of Thomas Savage, Anne Hutchinson's son-in-law.

ercise us much in the Losse of our Brother Oliver, whose Company we mist and did not perceave it, he fallinge into mr. Luttalls Company that was a goinge that way to the Iland then thay Lost thear way. And as our hartes was full of fear and care for our Brother soe was his of us and the fear was incresed one both sides becaus thear fell a greate snowe and very hard weather upon it, and it was to our greate rejoysinge when we met one another agayne in helth and safetoe accordinge to the good hand of our god that was upon us in our jorny and thay had bine exposed to much daynger in that could season for want of a fiar and all meanes to make it, had not the Lord beyond expectation provided for them, to bring forth a litle powder through the shott of the peece, now the 5th day we were to goe over another River where we were in greate daynger our Canow fallinge upon a Rocke, which had not some of our Brethren mor skilfull steped out of the Rocke and put of the Canow our daynger had bine very greate, but god brought us safe at Last one the 6th day viz 28 day of the 12th month to our greate rejoysinge.[4]

Brother Oliver. Now for the success of our jorny to our Brethren at the Iland we acquaynted them with our purpose in Cominge, and desired that they would procure us a meetinge that daye, but for reasons in their owne brest and because of the snowe thay did not thinke meete then to give us a meetinge but the next day thay promised and did give us a meetinge, mr Ashpinwall our Brother Baulston, Brother Sanphard and others and we delivered our message and the churches Letter, which thay Read and gave us satisfactory Answers. The next day we went to portsmouth where being entertayned at our Brother Cogshalls[5] House we desired them to procure us a meetinge, to deliver our message and the churches Letter, But when we expected a meetinge mr Cogshall sent us word that by reson of a Civell meetinge that was befor apoynted; But for a meetinge thay did not know what power one church hath over an other church and thay denyed our Comis-

---

4. The route the messengers took is identified in Adams's notes to the text.

5. Aspinwall, William Balston and Cogshall had signed the remonstrance concerning Wheelwright; further information on them and on John Sanford is in Battis, *Saints and Sectaries*.

sion and refused to Let our Letter be read. And they Conseave one church hath not power over the members of another church, and doe not thinke thay are tide to us by our covenant and soe were we fayne to take all thear Answers by goinge to thear severall Houses, mr Hutchison tould us he was more nearly tied to his wife than to the church, he thought her to be a dear saint and servant of god.

We came then to mrs Hutchison and told her that we had a message to doe to her from the Lord and from our church.

She answered, There are Lords many and gods many but I acknowledge but one Lord, which Lord doe you meane.

We Answered we Came in the Name but of one Lord and that is god. Than sayth she soe far we agree and where we doe agree, Let it be set downe. Then we tould her we had a message to her from the church of christ in Boston.

She replyed she knew no church but one we told her in scripture the Holy Ghost calls them churches. She sayd Christ had but one Spouse we tould her he had in some sort as many spouses as saints, but for our church she would not acknowledg it any church of Christs.

Mr. Cotton. Time beinge farr spent it will not be seasonable to speake much, we blesse god with our Brethren for thear protection in thear jorny assunder and together and we finde thay have faythfully and wisely discharged the trust and care put upon them.

For the Answers of our Brethren at the Iland they are divers, as for those at Portsmouth that thay would not reaseve thear message and Comission except thay would present it to thear church which had bine to have acknowledged them a Lawfull church which thay had no Comission to doe, now these doe wholy refuse to hear the church or to hold any submission or subjection to the church: I would not expect any Anser now but that the church Consider of it till the next day now, Consider

1 Whether this be not a transgression of that Rule in Matthew 18 if thay will not hear you tell the church and soe fall under the sensure of the church.

2 Thay were in Covenant with us as a wife to the Husband (1

Corinthians 7.15) but like a Harlot she welbe gone for all her Covenant now if thay will goe whether we be not discharged of our Covenant with them and soe cut them of as no members, we shall Consider with Elders of other churches what is best to be done in such Cases.

Others doe not refuse to hear the church but Anser as farr as thay cane goe only some scruple the Covenant, and others other things but doe not reject the church: but doe honor and esteme of us as churches of Christ. Now Consider whether, it is not meete that we should first wright to them and Labor to satisfi them and to take of thear groundes and see if thay may be redused befor we goe to farther prosedinges with them. And I would knowe how farr the wives doe Consent or dissent from thear Husbands or whether thay be as resolut and obstinate peremptory as thay.

Thear is another sort and that was of such as are excommunicate, now we have gone as far with them as I thinke we cane go except thay did showe some pertenacy and obstenacy agaynst Christ Jesus and then the greate Censure of Anathama Marinatha[6] that is for mrs Hutchison. But such as start aside from church Censure and Rules out of Ignorance, another corse is to be taken with them to reduse them agayne if we cane, as mrs Harding and mrs dyar,[7] who acknowledgeth the churches and desiar Communion with us still. And for mr Ashpinwall, he now beinge satisfied of the Righteous and just proseedings of the church in castinge out some of our members and soe refuseth to have any Communion with them in the thinges of god.

I pray Consider of these thinges agaynst the next Lords day accordinge to the distributions of the qualetie and nature of thear offenses, as those that are necessarily tied thear for a home as children to thear Parents and wives to Husbands, and others that stand out of obstenacy.

I see the divel goes about to harden the harts of Brethren agaynst church Censure and soe to dispise all church proseedings and therupon question church Covenant to shake all churches

---

6. Consigned to damnation; cf. 1 Corinthians 16.22.
7. See p. 280.

and to question it alltogeather, or some parts of it, and how fare it
bindes and whether it be a part of the covenant of grace or no,
which I hope wilbe more and more cleared up and manafested.

[Two weeks intervened before the matter was again submitted to the church. On the 30th of March, after the Teacher,
Cotton, had concluded his discourse, Mr. Wilson made the following statement to the congregation:][8]

Pastor. Brethren you know the Bussines of the Iland hath
bine a Longe time propounded, and taken by the church into
Consideration: and now we should drawe to some Issue and de-
termination you know the Cases of them thear doe much differ
some are under admonition and some under excommunication:
and some have given satisfaction in part to the church and doe
hould them selves still as members of the church and doe yet
harken to us and seeke to give satisfaction and others thear be that
doe renounce the power of the church and doe refuse to hear the
church as mr Coddington mr Dyar and mr Cogshall, the 2 first
have [been] questioned in the church and delt with and are under
Admonition and have bine soe Longe yet this act of the church
hath Bine so farr from doinge them any good that thay are rather
growen worse under the same, for mr Coddington beinge delt
withall about hearinge of excommunicat persons Prophecy he
was sensable of an Evell in it, and sayd he had not before soe well
Considerd of it, yet since he hath not only hearde such by accident as befor But hath him selfe and our Brother diar and mr
Cogshall have gathered them selves into church fellowship not
regardinge the Covenant that thay have made with this church
neyther have taken our advise and consent herin neyther have
they regarded it, but thay have joyned them selves in fellowship
with some that are excomunicated wherby thay come to have a
constant fellowship with them and that in a church way and
when we sent the messengers of the church to them to admonish
them and treate with them about such offences, thay wear soe
farr from expressing any sorrow or givinge any Satisfaction, that
thay did alltogether refuse to hear the church and in this Case the
Rule of Christ is playne we know not how otherwise to proseed

_____

8. Adams's note.

with such than by Cuttinge them of from us: thay that will not hear the church, Let them be to you as a Heathen and a Publicane,[9] yet because we know not how far god may worke relentinge in any of thear hartes since the churches messengers came from them, it is thought meete to forbare our proseedinge yet a litle Longer, agaynst them and patiently to wayte a while to see if yet thay will indeavor to give satisfaction, if not we shall take a seasonable time to proceed with them.[10]

---

9. Matthew 18.17: And if he shall neglect to hear them, tell it unto the church: but if he neglect to hear the church, let him be unto thee as a heathen man and a publican.

10. For the sequel, see Ellis, *Life of Anne Hutchinson*, 338–346. Larzer Ziff provides an interesting commentary on the church proceedings in "The Social Bond of the Church Covenant," *American Quarterly 10* (1958), 454–462.

CHAPTER 12

John Cotton, *The Way of Congregational*
Churches Cleared

THE Antinomian Controversy had an international significance. Puritans in England followed the conflict closely
(they bought up three editions of the *Short Story*), hoping to find
in it the answers to several questions. One of these was how to
combat the English Antinomians who appeared after the Puritan
Revolution began in 1640. Another was how the Congregational
form of church government had fared in the new world. This
question was especially important because English Puritans
could not agree among themselves on the model of church government that should replace Episcopacy. Since the colonists
claimed that the "New England Way" was the exemplary model
for England to follow, the success or failure of their experiment
became a matter of controversy among English Congregationalists and Presbyterians. Congregationalists cited (or wanted to cite)
the success of the emigrants as proof that Congregationalism was
best, but Presbyterians insisted that it was a failure: witness the
Antinomian Controversy!

Of the many Presbyterians who charged the colonists with
failure, the most important was Robert Baillie, a minister in the
Church of Scotland. A delegate to the Westminster Assembly,
Baillie was dismayed when the Assembly fell to quarreling over
the merits of the Scottish system, and even more alarmed when
radical sects began springing up in England. He tried to discredit
these sects, as well as Congregationalism, in *A Dissuasive against*
the Errours of the Time (London, 1645). In writing about New
England, Baillie made John Cotton his principal target, since

396

Cotton was the best-known figure among the emigrants, had written several books defending Congregationalism, and was involved in the Antinomian Controversy. Baillie's strategy was simple: emphasizing Cotton's role in the Controversy, he argued that a man who erred in theology could not be trusted when he wrote about the church.

To the *Dissuasive* (and other attacks) Cotton replied in *The Way of Congregational Churches Cleared* (London, 1648). *The Way Cleared,* besides presenting Cotton's version of the Controversy, also contains another set of his answers to theological questions. Though Cotton is vague about dates and careless with chronology, he seems to indicate that this set of questions and answers is contemporaneous with the synod of 1637. There is little that is new in these answers except Cotton's willingness to recognize the legitimacy of his colleagues' position. Whether that willingness makes these answers "strangely different from his previous statements," as Perry Miller argued, is doubtful.[1]

Only those sections of *The Way Cleared* directly concerned with the Antinomian Controversy are included below. The same sections appeared in Adams's edition.

The Way Cleared

Sect. 13. Of Cottons pretended Antinomianisme and Familisme.

The Disswader proceedeth to point at (as hee calleth it) "another more dangerous fall of mine, which in his Margent, he nameth Mr. *Cottons* Antinomianisme, and Familisme: and within a few lines, his wandring into the horrible Errors of the Antinomians, and Familists, with his dear friend   [39] Ms. *Hutchinson,* so far that he came to a resolution to side with her, and to Separate from all the Churches in *New-England,* as legall Synagogues."

If all this charge were true (as indeed, in all parts of it, it is false:) yet the errors of Antinomianisme, and Familisme, then

---

1. Miller, " 'Preparation for Salvation' in Seventeenth-Century New England," *Nature's Nation,* 65.

stirring in the Countrey, and condemned in the Synod at *New-Towne,* were not more dangerous, then the old Montanisme.[2] I confesse, the Familisme afterwards broached by Mr. *Garton,*[3] and his followers, the same which *Calvin* in his *Opuscula* refuteth (in his *Instructio adversus Libertinos*)[4] as *Calvin* judgeth it more dangerous then Popery, so I conceive it to be as dangerous as Montanisme, though I cannot say more dangerous: for both of them overthrow al principles & foundations of Christian Religion. But for the making good of this charge upon me, let Mr. *Baylie* be pleased to instance in those horrible errors either of Antinomianisme or Familisme, whereunto I either wandred or fell: Or let him make it appeare "that I came to such a Resolution, to side with my dear friend Ms. *Hutchinson,* and to separate from all the Churches in *New England,* as legall Synagogues."

Let us examine his proofes and Testimonies.

"1. The first is from the parties themselves, the followers of Ms. *Hutchinson,* who (saith he) boast of Mr. *Cotton* for their Master and Patron."

And it is true, they professed so: just as *Wightman* who was burnt at *Lichfield* for Montanisme, (avouching himself to be the Holy Ghost) professed he had received all his grounds from Mr. *Hildersam.*[5] And I confesse my self, being naturally (I thank God) not suspicious, hearing no more of their Tenents from them, then what seemed to mee Orthodoxall, I beleeved, they had been far off from such grosse errors, as were bruited of them. But when some of my fellow-Brethren (the Elders of Neighbour Churches) advertised me of the evill report that went abroad of

---

2. Montanism was a heretical movement of the second century. Its principal characteristic was an insistence upon the direct inspiration of the Holy Spirit.

3. Samuel Gorton (1592–1677) emigrated to Boston in 1637 and was banished from Massachusetts in 1644 for maintaining heresies similar to those of the Antinomians.

4. John Calvin, *Contre La Secte Phantastique et Furieuse des Libertins* (Geneva, 1545).

5. Edward Wightman was burned at the stake in England in 1612; Arthur Hildersam (1563–1632) was a well-known Puritan preacher. Cotton wrote a preface to Hildersam's *Lectures upon the fovrth of Iohn* (London, 1629).

* See new note p. xx.

their corrupt Tenents, I desired to know what the Tenents were, which were corrupt, and which they had vented here and there, in my name. They mentioned some to mee, some of those which are published in the short story of that Subject: and named also to me the persons, who had uttered the same. I therefore dealt with Mris. *Hutchinson* and others of them, declaring to them the erroneousnesse of those Tenents, and the injury done to my self in fathering them upon mee. Both shee, and   [40] they utterly denyed, that they held such Tenents, or that they had fathered them upon mee. I returned their Answer to the Elders, who had spoken to mee of them: and I inquired, if any two of them, or of their Neighbours could bear witnesse in this case. They answered me, they had but one witnesse of any corrupt Tenent: and that one, loth to be known to bee an accuser of them. I replyed, what course would you then advise mee to take? They answered, that I could not indeed bring the matter to the Church for want of witnesses:[6] But the best way would bee, publikely and privately to bear witnesse against such errors. I tooke their counsell, and bare witnesse against the errors complained of, as well publikely as privately. Which when some Elders and Brethren heard, meeting soon after with some of these Opinionists: "Loe, say they, now wee have heard your Teacher bearing witnesse openly against those very points, which you falsely father on him. No matter (say the other) what you heare him say in publick: we know what hee saith to us in private." This answer bred in some of my Brethren and friends, a jealousie, that my selfe was a secret fomenter of this spirit of Familisme, if not leavened my self that way. Whereupon sundry Elders and Brethren perceiving these Errors to spread, secretly and closely, they consulted among themselves, and with me what I thought of a Synod, whether it might bee of use in such a case for the clearing of these Points, and the allaying of the jealousies and differences in the Countrey? I answered, yea. Thereupon, with consent of the Magistrates, a time, and place was appointed for a Synodicall

---

6. Cotton refers to the procedure of church discipline outlined in Matthew 18.15–16, according to which two witnesses were required if an offender were brought before the church.

meeting, and sundry Elders were sent for, from other jurisdictions, and messengers from all the Churches in the Country to assist in this worke.

Against which time three things principally were attended for preparation.

1. A Solemne Fast kept in all the Churches: in which it fell out, that Mr. *Whelewrights* Sermon was apprehended to give too much encouragement to the Opinionists. And himself hath since confessed, that being but new come into the Countrey, having but little acquaintance but with his kindred, and their friends, (who were many of them levened this way) he spake some things, which if he had before discerned their Familisme, he would not have expressed himself as he did.[7]

The 2. thing attended to, for preparation to the   [41] Synod, was, the gathering up of all the corrupt and offensive Opinions that were scattered up and down the Countrey, and to commend them to Publique Disquisition in the Synod: that howsoever, the Authours of them were loth to owne them publikely, yet at least, they might see them publickely tryed, confuted, and condemned. The which was accordingly done in the Synod: and the Opinions with their Confutations are since printed in the short story, whence Mr. *Baylie* fetcheth many Testimonies.

The 3. thing thought needfull for preparation to the Synod, was, to gather out of my Sermons to the people, and my conferences (in word and writing) with the Elders, all such opinions of mine as were conceived by some, to bee erroneous: and having gathered them together, to inquire in a brotherly conference with mee, how far I would own them, or how I did understand them, that so the true state of the questions in difference might appeare; and withall, if there were any aguish distemper, or disaffection growen in any of our spirits amongst our selves, it might be healed in a private brotherly way, and mutuall satisfaction given and taken on all hands. Accordingly we had such a meeting

---

7. In 1643 Wheelwright apologized to the Massachusetts General Court for adhering "to persons of corrupt judgment." *John Wheelwright,* ed. Bell, 48.

in private; wherein five questions were propounded unto mee, with desire of my plaine and explicite answer to the same: which also upon their demand, I gave suddenly.

Quest. 1.

"Whether our Union with Christ be compleat before and without Faith?"

Where I gave this answer, which was taken in writing: "Not without, nor before the habit (or gift) of Faith, but before the act of Faith; that is, not before Christ hath wrought Faith in us (for in uniting himself to us, he worketh Faith in us:) yet in order of nature, before our faith doth put forth it self to lay hold on him."[8]

For indeed I looked at Union with Christ, as equipollent to Regeneration. And looke as in Generation we are in a passive way united to *Adam:* so in Regeneration wee are united to Christ. And as the soule *habet se mere passive*[9] (in the judgement of our best Divines) in Regeneration, so also in union, and by the judgment of Christ himself, who saith, without Christ abiding in us (and so united to us) we can doe nothing, not   [42] bring forth any spiritual fruit at all: much lesse can we before union with Christ, unite our selves to Christ, which is the greatest and most spirituall fruit of all. I was not ignorant, that some of the Schoolmen (even some Dominicans) & out of them *Ferius,*[10] and some others, (even of judicious Protestants) are of opinion, that Christ doth give the Soule by the Almighty power of the *auxilium efficax*[11] of his Spirit, to put forth an act of Faith, to lay hold on Christ, before hee give them a habit or gift of Faith. But I could not understand how this could stand with Christs Word, *That without Christ abiding in us, wee can doe nothing.* Which argueth, no spirituall act can bee done by us without Christ habitually permanent in us. And as acute and judicious *Baynes* saith, (in Ephes. 1.)[12] This were to give a man to see, without an eye to see withall: which though God can doe by his Al-

---

8. See p. 194.

9. Leaves itself wholly passive.

10. Probably Paul Ferry (1591–1669), a Huguenot minister.

11. Powerful aid.

12. Paul Baynes, *A Commentarie upon the First Chapter of the . . . Ephesians* ([London], 1643). Baynes (d. 1617) was a Puritan minister.

mighty power, yet as the Philosopher said of *Entia:* so it may be much more said of *Miracula* (which are extraordinary *Entia*) *Miracula sine necessitate non sunt multiplicanda.*[13]

Quest. II.

Whether Faith be an instrumentall cause in applying Christs righteousnesse to our Justification.

Whereto I answered,

"Faith is an instrument to receive the righteousnesse of Christ applyed to us of God, for our Justification: but not properly an instrumentall cause."

Where I understood Instrument, as the Hebrews doe, יְלִי which they indifferently put for Instrument, or Vessell: For Faith emptying the soule of all confidence in its own righteousnesse, is a fit vessell or instrument to receive the righteousnesse of Christ offered and imputed; and so I tooke Faith rather as a fit disposition of the subject to be justified, then as a proper instrumentall cause of our justification: like the empty vessels of the Prophets widow, which whilst they were empty, the oyle ran forth into them (the empty vessels being fit to receive it:) But yet the empty vessels were not properly instrumentall causes of the running forth of the Oyle, but onely fit instruments to receive it.[14]

Quest. 3.   [43]

Whether the Spirit of God in evidencing our Justification doth beare witnesse in an absolute promise of free Grace, without Qualification, or condition.

My answer was,

"The Spirit in evidencing our Justification doth bear witnesse either in an absolute promise, or in a conditionall: in case, the condition bee understood, or applyed absolutely, not attending the condition as the ground or cause of the assurance, but as the effect and consequence of it: or (as I might have added, as before) as a fit disposition of the subject to receive it."

For I conceived, though the Spirit may evidence to us our

---

13. Miracles must not be multiplied without need.
14. The same language is used in Cotton's exchange with Bulkeley; see p. 35.

Justification in a Qualification or condition: yet sometime the condition is not there before the promise, but freely given with the promise, as *Acts* 10. 43, 44. where though *Cornelius* and his houshold were beleevers, yet many of his kindred and friends were not: who yet upon hearing the promise of Remission (or Justification) unto Faith, they received both Faith and Justification, and the evidence of both, all together: as did also the Jailor in the like sort, *Act.* 16. 31. Sometime, though the Qualification or condition bee there before, and the Spirit doe bear witnesse to our Justification in that condition: yet the condition is not the cause either of justification, or of the evidence of it, as in *Luke* 7. 47. Christ beareth evident witnesse of the Remission or Justification of *Mary Magdalen,* in her love to him. Neverthelesse her love was not the cause, neither of her Justification, nor of the assurance of it, but an effect of both. For shee expressed those evidences of her love to Christ, because her sins were forgiven her, and because her self was assured of the forgivenesse of them.

Sometimes the Qualification or condition mentioned in the promise, though it bee in the soule before, yet it is not evident there before. And then the evidence of Justification springeth not from the condition, but from the Grace of the promise, clearing and evidencing both the condition and the Justification. Thus Christ applyeth himselfe by his Spirit, to bruised Reeds, or broken hearts. *Isa.* 57. 15.

Lastly, if Faith it self bee meant to be the saving qualification or condition, and be also found, and that [44] evidently in the soul to whom the Promise of Justification is made; yet the Spirit may bear witnesse in the Promise of Grace to the Justification of such a soul, without either the word expressing the Condition in that place, or the soul attending the Condition at that time: As when Christ said to the Woman, *Luk.* 7. 48. *Thy sinnes are forgiven thee,* He neither mentioneth her Faith in that word, nor doth it appear, that she did reflect upon her Faith in receiving that Promise at that time. Many an Israelite stung by the fiery Serpents in the wildernesse, might look up to the brazen Serpent for healing, and yet at that time not look to their eye, nor think upon their eye by which they looked. And though afterwards Christ doe make expresse mention of the womans Faith, to which he attributeth her salvation, (*Woman,* saith he, *thy Faith hath saved thee,* ver. 50.) Nevertheless, that Faith, though it be an Evidence of Assurance in the subject Person of his Justification: yet it is also an Effect or Consequence of the Evidence and Assurance of the Object, that is, of the grace and mercy of God clearly revealed and applyed to the soul in the Promise, even to the begetting of Faith it self, and the Assurance of it. As when Christ did promise (by the Ministery of *Paul*) salvation to the Jaylor in Beleeving; the Grace of Christ clearly revealed and applyed in the Promise did beget Faith in the Jaylor, and the Assurance of Faith. And so his Faith, and the Assurance of it was an Effect and Consequence of the Grace and Assurance of it offered to him in the Promise. Faith though it be an Evidence of things not seen (with bodily eye;) yet it is an effect of a former Evidence, even of the light of Gods Countenance shining forth through Christ in the Promise of Grace upon the soul, to the begetting of Faith, and the assurance of it.

But howsoever, Faith being always of a self humbling efficacy, it is a fit disposition of the subject to receive comfort and assurance, *Isa.* 57. 15.

Calvin defineth Faith to be *Divinæ ergo nos benevolentiæ firmam certamque cognitionem, quæ gratuitæ in Christo Promissionis veritate fundata, per Spiritum Sanctum & revelatur mentibus nostris & cordibus obsignatur. Institut. l. 3. c. 2. Sect.* 7.[15] Now when hee cometh to expound what he meaneth by the free promise of grace in Christ, upon which this knowledg (or assurance) of Faith is founded, he maketh it to be, not   [45] conditionall. And he giveth this reason, "*Quoniam* (saith he) *Conditionalis Promissio quâ ad opera nostra remittimur, non aliter vitam promittit, quàm si perspiciamus esse in nobis sitam. Ergo, nisi Fidem tremere, ac vacillare volumus, illam*

---

15. "Now we shall possess a right definition of faith if we call it a firm and certain knowledge of God's benevolence toward us, founded upon the truth of the freely given promise in Christ, both revealed to our minds and sealed upon our hearts through the Holy Spirit." Calvin, *Institutes,* trans. Battles, III.ii.8.

*Salutis Promissione fulciamus oportet, quæ à Domino ultrò ac
liberaliter, potiusque miseriæ nostræ quàm dignitatis respectu of-
feratur; ibidem Sect. 29.*"[16]

But what was the occasion of this Question [whether] from any
speech or writing of mine, I cannot call to minde, unlesse it were
concerning the First evidence of justification, which is the purport of the next Question. For otherwise, if Faith and Assurance
be first founded and bottomed upon a Promise of Free-grace, I
never doubted, but that Sanctification or Faith, (any saving qualification) may be, (and is by the help of the Spirit) a clear and certain Evidence of Justification. So that put the Question *in terminis,*

"Whether the Spirit of God in Evidencing our Justification
doth bear witness in an absolute Promise of Free-Grace, without
qualification or condition?"

I should answer plainly and roundly, The Spirit doth Evidence our Justification both wayes, sometime in an absolute
Promise, sometime in a conditionall.

Quest. 4.

*Whether some Saving Qualification may be a first Evidence of
Justification?*

Hereto I answered,

"A man may have an argument from thence, (yea, I doubt not
a firm and strong argument) but not a first Evidence."

For I conceived, Faith it self, which is an evidence of things
not seen, and the first saving Qualification that doth Evidence
Justification, is it self founded upon a former evidence, even the
Free-grace of God in Christ, revealed in the promise of Grace, and
applyed to the soul effectually by the Spirit of grace both in our
effectuall Calling (even to the begetting of Faith) and in our Justification. Accordingly, the Apostle reckoning the Evidences that
bear witness of our life in Christ, giveth the first place to the

---

16. "For a conditional promise that sends us back to our own works does
not promise life unless we discern its presence in ourselves. Therefore, if we
would not have our faith tremble and waver, we must buttress it with the
promise of salvation, which is willingly and freely offered to us by the Lord
in consideration of our misery rather than our deserts." Ibid., III.ii.29.

Spirit, before any fruit of the Spirit; There are three (saith he)
that bear witnesse on earth, the Spirit, the Water, and
the Blood, 1 *Joh.* 5. 8. First, the Spirit, to wit, of illu-   [46]
mination and drawing, whereby he revealeth Christ to
us, and worketh Faith in us, 2 *Cor.* 4. 6. *Ephes.* 1. 17, 18. *Joh.* 6.
44. 45. Secondly, the water of Sanctification. And thirdly, the
Blood of atonement (or pacification) pacifying the conscience.

    Calvin also is of the same judgment in this Question, in 2 *Pet.*
1. 10. & in 1 *Joh.* 3. 14. & 19.[17]

    And *Zanchy* likewise doth at large dispute this Question, and
conclude it against Dr. *Marbachius* in his *Miscellanies,* in that
part of it entituled, *Disceptatio inter duos Theologos,* from *pag.*
598. to *pag.* 605. *Editionis in quarto.*[18]

Quest. 5.

*Whether Christ and his benefits be dispensed in a Covenant
of Works?*

    Whereunto my answer was,

    "Christ is dispensed to the Elect in a Covenant of Grace: to
others he may be dispensed in some sort, (to wit, in a taste of him)
either in a Covenant of works, or in a Covenant of grace legally
applyed."

    To give an hint of the reason of mine answer. The Covenant
on Mount *Sinai,* (wherein Christ was dispensed in sacrifices and
ceremonies) though to the faithfull seed of *Abraham* it was a Covenant of Grace, (wherein they saw Christ and his benefits graciously dispensed to them, *Psal.* 51, 7.) yet to the carnall seed, it
seemed to me to be a Covenant of Works, to prepare them for the
saving benefits of that Covenant of Grace which was formerly
given to *Abraham* and his seed, (but neglected by them in *Egypt*)
and afterwards renewed in the plains of *Moab, Deut.* chap. 29 &
Chap. 30. And so *Paul* maketh that Covenant on Mount *Sinai,* to
be expresly a different Covenant from that of grace, to wit, a
Covenant gendring unto bondage, *Gal.* 4. 24, 25. and the other
Covenant (*Deut.* 30.) to be of Grace, *Rom.* 10. 6, 7, 8. *Moses* also

---

    17. For earlier citations of Calvin on these same texts, see p. 185.

    18. Girolamo Zanchy, *Disceptatio Inter Duos Theologos,* in *Omnium
Operum Theologicorum* (Geneva, 1619), *3,* second pagination, 208–453. Jo-
hann Marbach (1521–1581) was a German theologian.

himself, having recited the Covenant on Mount *Sinai* (*Deut.* 5.)
he maketh the observation of all the Commandements to be the
righteousnesse of the people, *Deut.* 6. 25. and their life, *Levit.*
18. 4. And so *Paul* understandeth him, *Rom.* 10. 5. *Gal.* 3. 12.
Now that Covenant which gendreth unto bondage, and
holdeth forth righteousnesse and life upon obedience to   [47]
all the Commandements, it is a Covenant of Works.

And so have the chiefest Germane Divines, as well as *Piscator,*
and *Polanus,* taken the Covenant on Mount *Sinai* to bee a covenant of Workes. See *Piscator, Ezek.* 16. *Observat, ultima in vers.*
60. 62. & *Polanus ibidem.*[19]

How far there arose any consent or dissent about these questions, between my Fellow-Brethren (the Elders of these churches)
& my self, it is not materiall now to particularize; it is enough, that
upon our clear understanding of one anothers mindes & judgments, and upon the due proceeding of our Church against convinced notorious errors and scandalls, wee have ever since (by the
Grace of Christ) much amiable and comfortable Communion
together in al brotherly kindness. But this short relation may
suffice.

To let Mr. *Baylie* know, and all them that shall read his Book,
to consider, what slender "ground hee had to speak of my wandring into the horrible Errors of the Antinomians, and Familists,
and siding therein with Mistris *Hutchinson,* and therein to tell
the world of a more dangerous fall of mine, then that of Montanisme: And withall to clear up to him, what little ground Mistris
Hutchinson had, to pretend, that shee was of Mr. *Cottons* judgement in all things:" that so Mr. *Baylie* may likewise observe what
ground himself had to take up such a report against me, upon her
testimony. Which yet will the more fully appeare, if I proceed to
relate a principall passage or two in the Synod, after it was assembled. It was the first act of the Synod (after Prayer and choice of
Moderators) to propound the severall offensive opinions, which
had been dispersed up and downe in the Countrey, and briefely

19. Johannes Piscator, *In Prophetam Ezechielem Commentarius* (Herborn, 1614). Amandus Polanus, a Reformed theologian of the sixteenth century, wrote *The Substance of Christian Religion* [London, 1608].

to argue them, and bear witnesse against them. The opinions were about fourescore (more or lesse) which being orderly propounded and argued against, I perceived that some of the Members & Messengers of our Church, were ready to rise up, and plead in defence of sundry corrupt Opinions, which I verily thought had been far from them; especially such as concerned union with Christ before Faith, Iustification without Faith, inherent righteousnes, and evidencing a good estate by it at all, first or last. Whereupon assoon as I could get liberty of speech with them, "Brethren (said I) if you be of that judgment, which you plead for, all these Bastardly Opinions, which are justly offensive to the Churches, will be fathered upon *Boston."* They answered me again, "Though they were not clear for those   [48] Opinions, which they spake for, yet neither were they clear for condemning of them, considering the tendernesse of some Consciences: I replyed, if they were doubtfull of the Erroneousnesse and danger of such Opinions, they should have dealt openly with the Church at home, when they were chosen Messengers, and should have declared their judgments before the Church: as knowing such points amongst others were likely to come into agitation in the Synod: whereas now looke what they speak, it is conceived by the whole Countrey to bee the judgment of our Church."

Hereupon some of the Messengers of our Church withdrew themselves, and appeared no more in the Synod, such as did appear, did much what forbear any prosecution of argument in such causes. But that (to my remembrance) was the first time of my discerning a real and broad difference, between the judgments of our Brethren (who leaned to Mistris *Hutchinson*) and my self. And therefore to clear my self, and the sounder Members of our Church from partaking in those manifold errors there presented, I declared my judgment openly before all the assembly, "That I esteemed some of the Opinions, to bee blasphemous: some of them, hereticall: many of them, Erroneous: and almost all of them, incommodiously expressed: as intending to except those chiefly, wherein I had declared mine own opinion, as before."

But because I would deale openly and ingenuously with Mr. *Baylie,* and hide nothing from him, that might fortify his accusation against me, there was some colour of my leaning to one Antinomian Tenent in one day of the Synod. For though in answer to the questions of the Elders before the Synod, I had affirmed Faith to be an instrument for the receiving the righteousnesse of Christ to our justification: yet for as much as some great Divines had let fall some expressions, that seemed to favour the Antinomian party in a contrary Tenent, I was desirous to hear that Point a little further ventilated, and to see the difficulties a little more fully cleared. Dr. *Twisse* (not suspected for an Antinomian, much lesse for a Familist) in his *vindiciæ gratiæ, de electione, Parte 2. Section. 25. Numero 5.* bringeth in *Arminius,* arguing against Mr. *Perkins,* thus:[20] "The righteousnesse of Christ wrought or performed, is not ours, as wrought or performed, but as by Faith imputed to us. Whereto the Dr. answereth,

Before Faith, this Righteousnesse of Christ was ours,   [49] and in the intention of God the Father, and of Christ our Mediator, was wrought for us. And because it is wrought for us, therefore God in his own time will give it us, and Grace of every kind, even Faith it self amongst the rest. But Faith coming, (which the Holy Ghost kindleth in our hearts) then at length this love of God to us in *Christ,* is acknowledged & perceived. Whence it is, that the Righteousnesse of Christ is said to bee imputed to us, by Faith, because it is not descerned to be imputed to us, but by Faith: and then we are said to be justified with that kind of Justification, & absolution from sin, which breedeth peace in our Consciences."

"And this (saith he) I confirm by two arguments. 1. Because by the Righteousnesse of Christ, wee obtain not onely Remission

---

20. William Twisse (1578?–1646) was a famous Puritan theologian who served as moderator of the Westminster Assembly. He criticized Cotton's stand on the doctrine of reprobation in *A Treatise of Mr. Cottons Clearing Certain Doubts Concerning Predestination, Together with an Examination Thereof* (London, 1646) from a strict Calvinist point of view; hence the irony of Cotton's remark, "not suspected for an Antinomian." Against the Dutch theologian James Arminius (1560–1609), whose name became synonymous with a modification of Calvinism in the direction of free will, Twisse wrote *Vindiciae gratiae, potestatis . . . ad examen libelli Perkinsiani, De Praedestinationis modo & ordine, Institutum à Iacobo Arminio, responsio scholastica* (Amsterdam, 1632).

of sinnes, but Faith it self, and Repentance, as it is writen, God hath blessed us with all spirituall blessings in Christ, *Ephes.* 1. 3. Therefore even before Faith and Repentance, the Righteousnesse of Christ is applyed to us, as for which wee obtain Grace effectuall to believe in Christ, and to repent. 2. Because Justification and absolution, as they signify an immanent act in God, are *ab æterno,* &c."[21]

"Whereto he subjoyneth the Poets ingenuous verse to the reader.

> '*Si quid novisti rectius istis,*
> *Candidus imperti; si non, his utere mecum.*' "[22]

Before Dr. *Twisse, Chamier* (a Divine, as free as the other from suspition of Antinomianisme) denyeth Faith to bee a cause of Justification; "For if it were (saith hee) Justification should not be of Grace, but of us. But Faith is said to justifie, not because it effecteth Justification, but because it is effected in the justified person, and requisite to be found in him." *De Fide libr.* 13. *cap.* 6. And to the same purpose, *De Justificatione, libr.* 22. *cap.* 12. hee contendeth, "that Faith as it doth not merit, nor bring Justification, so neither doth it (*impetrare*) obtain it. For if it were so, then *tum ratione, tum tempore Fides præcederet Justificationem,* Faith should goe before Justification, both in nature and time: Which (saith hee) in no sort may be granted. For Faith is it self a part of Sanctification; but there is no Sanctification, but after Justification, *quæ & re, & naturâ prior est,* which both in the thing it self, and in nature is before it."[23]

To the like purpose doth Mr. *Pemble* deliver his judgment in his Book of the Nature and Properties of Grace and Faith, *Page* 24. 26. of his Edition in Folio.[24]   [50]

The Discrepance of all these Divines from the received expressions of the most, gave just occasion, why in such an Assembly, the judgment of sundry acute and judicious Elders, might be enquired. Accordingly, in one day of their dispute in

---

21. Twisse, *Vindiciae Gratiae,* Bk. 1, 276–277.

22. "If you know anything better than those, then frankly share your knowledge; if not, adopt these principles with me."

23. Chamier, *Panstratiae Catholicae, 3,* 960.

24. William Pemble (1592?–1623), a Puritan minister; Cotton refers to *Vindiciae Gratiae. A Plea for Grace* (London, 1629).

* See new note p. xxi.

the Synod (with Mr. *Whelewright,* if I forget not) I interposed such a word as this, God may bee said to justifie me before the habit, or act of Faith, and the habit is the effect of my Justification, intending the same sense, as hath been expressed out of those Divines: upon which, the next day was taken up in disputing and arguing that Point with mee. And when I saw their apprehensions, that they were suitable to Scripture phrase, and the contrary difficulties might bee removed *sano sensu,*[25] I the next morning did of my self freely declare to them publikely, my consent with them in the point, which (as they professed) they gladly accepted.

Now upon all this relation (which is the substance of the whole Truth in this cause) I desire Mr. *Baylie* might consider what ground hee had, "either to report mee to the World as sometimes dangerously fallen into the horrible Errors of Antinomianisme, and Familisme: or to take Ms. *Hutchinsons* report in this cause, That she was of Mr. *Cottons* judgment in all things." Let him please to read the short story of the Errors and heresies, for which shee was admonished publickly in *Boston* Church, and compare them with the Tenents of mine now mentioned, and let him judge of himself, whether she was of Mr. *Cottons* judgment in all things.

I would not have enlarged my self so much, either to clear her testimony, or to elevate it, were it not to take off some scruples and surmises in Mr. *Baylie* of some dangerous guilt in me of Antinomian, and Familisticall errors, which he thinkes cannot be avoided by what he collecteth from other testimonies, as well as hers which may fully be prevented and avoided by this relation of the true state of things.

But before I leave speech of her, let me speak a word to Mr. *Baylie* of the Epithet hee is pleased to give her, "when hee styleth her, my dear friend, with whom I resolved to side and separate from all the Churches in *New-England,* as Legall Churches."

At her first comming she was well respected and esteemed of me, not onely because herself and her family   [51] were well beloved in *England* at *Allford* in *Lincolnshire* (not far beyond *Boston:*) nor onely because she with her

---

25. Through sound thinking.

family came over hither (as was said) for conscience sake: but chiefly for that I heard, shee did much good in our Town, in womans meeting at Childbirth-Travells, wherein shee was not onely skilfull and helpfull, but readily fell into good discourse with the women about their spiritual estates: And therein cleared it unto them, That the soul lying under a Spirit of Bondage, might see and sensibly feel the hainous guilt, and deep desert of sin, and thereby not onely undergoe affliction of Spirit but also receive both restraining, and constraining Grace likewise, (in some measure:) restraining from all known evill (both courses, and companies) (at least for a season) and constraining to all knowen duties, as secret Prayer, Family Exercises, Conscience of Sabbaths, Reverence of Ministers, Frequenting of Sermons, Diligence in calling, honesty in dealing and the like: yea and that the Soul might find some tastes and flashes of spirituall comfort in this estate, and yet never see or feel the need of Christ, much lesse attain any saving Union, or Communion with him, being no more but Legall work, even what the Law, and the Spirit of bondage (breathing in it) might reach unto. By which means many of the women (and by them their husbands) were convinced, that they had gone on in a Covenant of Works, and were much shaken and humbled thereby, and brought to enquire more seriously after the Lord Jesus Christ, without whom all their Gifts and Graces would prove but common, and their duties but legall, and in the end wizzen and vanish. All this was well (as is reported truely, *page* 31. of her Story) and suited with the publike Ministery, which had gone along in the same way, so as these private conferences did well tend to water the seeds publikely sowen. Whereupon all the faithfull embraced her conference, and blessed God for her fruitfull discourses. And many whose spirituall estates were not so safely layed, yet were hereby helped and awakened to discover their sandy foundations, and to seek for better establishment in Christ: which caused them also to blesse the Lord for the good successe, which appeared to them by this discovery.[26]

---

26. In this paragraph, as at the church trial (see p. 371), Cotton suggests the congruence of his message and that of Mrs. Hutchinson; both attacked assurance based on the performance of duties.

Hitherto therefore shee wrought with God, and with the Ministers, the work of the Lord. No marvell therefore if at that time, shee found loving and dear respect both from our Church-Elders and Brethren, and so from my self also   [52] amongst the rest.

Afterwards, it is true, she turned aside not only to corrupt opinions, but to dis-esteem generally the Elders of the churches, (though of them shee esteemed best of Mr. *Shepheard:*) and for my selfe, (in the repetitions of Sermons in her house) what shee repeated and confirmed, was accounted sound, what shee omitted, was accounted Apocrypha. This change of hers was long hid from me: and much longer the evidence of it, by any two clear witnesses. I sent some Sisters of the Church on purpose to her Repetitions, that I might know the truth: but when shee discerned any such present, no speech fell from her, that could be much excepted against. But further discourse about her course is not pertinent to the present businesse. But by this Mr. *Baylie* may discerne, how farre Ms. *Hutchinson* was dear unto mee, and if hee speak of her as my deare friend, till shee turned aside, I refuse it not.

But yet thus much I must professe to him, That in the times of her best acceptance, shee was not so dear unto mee, but that (by the help of Christ) I dealt faithfully with her about her spirituall estate. Three things I told her, made her spirituall estate unclear to mee. 1. "That her Faith was not begotten nor (by her relation) scarce at any time strengthened, by publick Ministery, but by private Meditations, or Revelations onely.

"2. That shee clearly discerned her Justification (as shee professed:) but little or nothing at all, her Sanctification: though (she said) shee beleeved, such a thing there was by plain Scripture.

"3. That she was more sharply censorious of other mens spirituall estates and hearts, then the servants of God are wont to be, who are more taken up with judging of themselves before the Lord, then of others."

Now a word of that other passage, in Mr. *Baylies* speech, "touching my resolution to side with Ms. *Hutchinson,* and to separate from all the Churches of *New-England,* as legall Synagogues." The truth is, I did intend to remove, but not to Separate; much lesse with Ms. *Hutchinson,* and least of all from all the

---

* See new note p. xxi.

Churches of *New-England:* and yet lesse then the least of all, to separate from them, as legall Synagogues.

The occasion of my intent of removall was this. After the banishment of Ms. *Hutchinson* and sundry   [53] others by occasion of her,[27] the generall court made an order, that none should be received to abide as Inhabitants in this Jurisdiction, unlesse they were allowed under the hand of the Governour, or two Assistants. The Assistants are our Magistrates. When this Law came to be put in use, I was informed that some godly passengers who hither arrived out of *England,* were refused to sit down amongst us, because (upon tryall) they held forth such an union with Christ by the Spirit giving Faith, as did precede the acting of Faith upon Christ: and such an evidence of that union, by the favour of God shed abroad in their hearts by the Holy Ghost, as did precede the seeing (though not the being) of Sanctification.

This took the deeper inpression upon me, because I saw by this meanes, wee should receive no more Members into our Church, but such as must professe themselves of a contrary judgment to what I beleeved to bee a Truth. Besides I was informed, that it was the judgment of some of place, in the Countrey, that such a Doctrin of Union, and evidencing of Union, as was held forth by mee, was the *Trojan* Horse, out of which all the erroneous Opinions and differences of the Countrey did issue forth.

Hereupon, fearing this might in time breed a renewall of Paroxysmes, I called to mind the intent of my comming hither, which was, not to disturb, but to edify the Churches here: and therefore began to entertain thoughts rather of peaceable removall then of offensive continuance. At the same time there was brought to mee a writing, subscribed with about threescore hands to encourage me to removall, and offering their readinesse to remove with mee into some other part of this Countrey.

I considered, If wee removed, it would be matter of much

---

27. Writing carelessly and from memory, Cotton here falls into an error as to the sequence of events. The Alien Law of 1637 was passed at the May session of the General Court of that year; Mrs. Hutchinson was tried and banished in the following November by another General Court chosen in October. — Adams

various construction amongst such as knew us, both in *Old-Eng-land*, and *New;* and I was loth to doe any thing, (especially of importance) but what I might give account of before God, and his people; I took advice therefore of some friends here, especially Mr. *Davenport*, and resolved, first to clear the certainty of the grounds of the information given mee of the rejections of those godly persons (of whom I had heard) for their judgments sake in those points. 2. To see if my continuance here would certainly, or probably breed any further offensive agi-   [54] tation: And 3. If both those things were found clearly, then to take opportunity with common consent to remove to *Quinipyatk*[28] whereto at that time a door was opened.

But when I came to enquire the certainty of these informations, in conference with some of our chief Magistrates and others, I found, though there had speach been about such points between themselves, and some passengers: yet their refusall of such passengers was not upon those points, but (as I remember) upon denyall of inherent righteousnesse in beleevers, and of any evidence of a good estate from thence, first or last. Withall, they declared to mee their minds touching such points of Union, or evidencing of Union, which I had taught, that they did not looke at them to bee of such Fundamentall concernment either to civill or Church-Peace, as needed to occasion any distance in heart, (much lesse in place) amongst godly brethren. Which when I heard from them, and found upon search, the mis-informations given mee, were but misprisions, I then layed down all thoughts of removall, and sat down satisfied in my aboad amongst them, and have so continued (by the help of God) to this day. By all this may appear the truth of what I said, that though I had thoughts of removall, yet not with Ms. *Hutchinson,* shee being gone to *Road Island,* but I intending *Quinipyack*. Much lesse had I any thoughts of Separation from all the Churches of *New-England:* for the Churches in *Quinipiack* are in *New-England*. And those Churches at the *Bay* (amongst whom I lived) It was far from my

---

28. Quinipyatk was the Indian name for the area later designated as New Haven; John Davenport, who arrived in Massachusetts in the summer of 1637, founded New Haven in the spring of 1638.

thoughts to separate from them, whom I ever truely honored as the holy Spouses of Jesus Christ. Nor did I ever look at such Points, as any just ground of Separation from any Church, (so much as in place, much lesse in Communion:) no nor any just ground of removall from them, unlesse a man were compelled to professe contrary to his judgment. And least of all durst I turn my back upon such Churches as Legall Synagogues, who do all of us hold Union with Christ, and evidencing of Union by the same Spirit, and the same Faith and the same holinesse: though some may conceive the Union wrought in giving the habit, and others rather refer it to the act: and some may give the second place to that, whereto others give the first.

It was therefore too much credulity in Mr. *Baylie*, either to take up the former testimony from Ms. *Hutch-* [55] *inson,* or this latter from Mr. *Williams:*[29] though if both of them had joyned in one and the same Testimony, (which they doe not) yet the Testimony of two excommunicate Persons doth not make up *idoneum Testimonium* in Ecclesiasticall causes.

"No? Saith Mr. *Baylie,* if I mistake not the humor of the man, (Mr. *Williams* he meaneth) he is very unwilling to report a lie of his greatest enemy."

I look not at my self, as his greatest, or least, or any enemy at all. I doe not know, that I did ever walke towards him either in the affection, or action of an enemy, notwithstanding the provoking injuries, and indignities hee hath put upon mee.

Nor would I call it any mans humor (as Mr. *Baylie* calleth it, Mr. *Williams* his humor) "to be very unwilling to report a lye of his greatest enemy."

But this I say, Mr. *Williams* is too too credulous of surmises and reports brought to him, and too too confident in divulging

---

29. Roger Williams, in his controversy with Cotton over the issue of religious toleration, charged that Cotton "was upon the Point" of separating from the churches in Massachusetts "as Legall." *Mr. Cottons Letter lately printed, Examined and Answered* (London, 1644), reprinted in *Publications of the Narragansett Club* (Providence, 1866), *1,* 337. Cotton denied the charge in *A Reply to Mr. Williams his Examination* (London, 1647), reprinted in *Publications of the Narragansett Club* (Providence, 1867), 2, 80–84.

of them. Which if Mr. *Baylie* know not, hee may (at his leisure, if hee think it worth the while) peruse the Reply, I have made to his answer of my Letter, as also my answer to his bloody Tenent.[30]

But Mr. *Baylie* giveth the more credit to Mr. *Williams* his Testimony, because Mr. *Williams* saith in his examination of my Letter, "How could I possibly (saith hee) bee ignorant of their estate, when being from first to last in fellowship with them, an Officer amongst them, had private and publick agitation concerning their Estate, with all, or most of their Ministers?"

The answer is very easie both to Mr. *Williams,* and Mr. *Baylie* too, that Mr. *Williams* speaketh of the times before his banishment: then indeed he had some fellowship with us, and might have had more, but that hee suspected all the *Statos conventus*[31] of the Elders to bee unwarrantable, and such as might in time make way to a Presbyteriall government. But this Testimony, which hee giveth about my neerenesse to Separation from these Churches, was many yeares after his banishment from us, when hee was in no fellowship with us, sacred nor civill, nor came any whit neer any private or publick agitation amongst us, nor could have any intelligence of our affaires, but by report and fame, which is *tam ficti pravique tenax, quam nuncia veri,*[32] and is indeed in this point, most false.

"But yet (saith Mr. *Baylie*) the truth of this horrible   [56]
fall (of Mr. *Cotton*) if you will not take it, neither from
the followers of Ms. *Hutchinson,* nor from the Testimony of Mr. *Williams:* yet wee may not reject the witnesse of Mr. *Winthrop,* and of Mr. *Wells* in their printed relations of the Schismes there.

"Both these, albeit, with all care and study, they endeavour to save Mr. *Cottons* credit: yet they let the truth of Mr. *Cottons* Seduction fall from their Pens in so clear termes, as cannot bee avoided: yea so clear, as no Art will get Mr. *Cotton* cleared."

---

30. Cotton refers to *The Bloudy Tenent, washed, And made white in the bloud of the Lambe* (London, 1647), his reply to Williams's *The Bloudy Tenent, of Persecution, for cause of Conscience, discussed, in A Conference betweene Truth and Peace* (London, 1644).

31. Regular meetings.

32. Which holds fast to the fictitious and wicked rather than announces the truth.

Notwithstanding al this confident charge of Mr. *Baylie,* there will be no need at al of any Art to clear Mr. *Cotton,* from seduction into any such horrible fall, the naked truth (by the helpe of Christ) will clear both it self, and him. The Testimonies of Mr. *Winthrop,* and Mr. *Wells,* are all delivered (as it seemeth) in the short Story. There

In the Preface, *page* 7. "It is said, by this time, they had to patronise them, some of the Magistrates, and some men eminent for Religion, Parts and Wit."

Answ. 1. This were something, if there were no more men eminent for Religion, Parts and Wit, in the Country but my self, who professe no eminency in any of these in respect of many of my Brethren. But if I were eminent, the testimony concludeth not. Let not Art judge, whether the conclusion will follow from both the premises particular: but let common sense judge of such men, as then lived in the Countrey, whether there were not many eminent persons for Religion, Parts, and Wit, who did patronise them, though I had been out of the Countrey.

2. I willingly confesse, that I my self, though I did not patronise them, yet I did countenance them (in my measure) whilst they held forth (to my knowledge) no more then I have formerly delivered of my own Tenents: which yet I hope he will not again tax, as an horrible fall into Antinomianisme and Familism. When their Errors were brought to me, I bare publike witnesse against them, even before I was fully perswaded that those persons were guilty of them.

His next Testimony (which hee quoteth from *page* 25. of the short Story) the former part of it concerneth Mr. *Whelewright,* and not mee: though I must confesse I doe not know how it can be collected from Mr. *Whelewrights* doctrin,   [57] unlesse it were by a forestalled mis-apprehension and mis-application of those hearers, who were leavened with corrupt Opinions. The latter part of the testimony, "That the former Governor never stirred out, but attended by the Serjants with Halberts or Carrabines, but the present Governor was neglected": I do not remember, that ceremony was any more then once neglected: and when I heard it, I bore witnesse against it. And they excused their former observance, by the eminency of the person.

But sure I am, the present Governor (as he well deserveth all honor from this People, so) he is seldome or never seen in publick, but in like sort attended with Halberts or Carrabines.

Next, he alledgeth a testimony from the Court, which (it is likely) was delivered by Mr. *Winthrop,* being then Governor, *page* 35. of the short Story: "They soon profited so well, as in a few moneths, they outwent their Teacher."

Answ. This testimony is so far from taxing mee of any horrible fall, that it clearly acquiteth mee from the fellowship thereof. For if they outwent their Teacher, as the Court said (and said truely:) then I went not along with them in their Tenents. And Teacher I was called, and their Teacher, as being called to that Office in that Church, whereof many of them were Members.

The next testimony (from *page* 33. of the story) expresseth, "That upon the countenance it took from some eminent Persons, her Opinions began to hold up their heads in Courts of Justice."

Answ. This might indeed argue, that some Magistrates leaned more or lesse to that way: but it reacheth not me, who am seldome present at any Courts, but when with other Elders I am sent for. And let it not be forgotten, what I related above, that many held with those Opinionists (as they were called) when they knew of no other opinions held forth by them, but what was publickly taught in our Church: but after they were discovered to overgoe not so much their Teachers, as the truth, and that so evidently, as could clearly be convinced by the testimony of two or three witnesses, they were soon forsaken by those, who esteemed better of them before.

His next testimony is from the story *page* 32. "It was a wonder, upon what a suddain, the whole Church of *Boston* (some few excepted) were become her new Converts,   [58] and infected with her Opinions."

"And Preface *page* 7. most of the Seducers lived in the Church of *Boston.*"

Answ. That most of the Church of *Boston* consented with Ms. *Hutchinson,* (whilst shee openly held forth no more, then what was publickly taught) is true; but nothing to prove Mr. *Cottons* horrible fall, for after shee fell into any horrible, or evident erors, it may clearly appear, the whole Church were not become her con-

verts, by this undenyable evidence, that the whole body of the
Church (except her own son) consented with one accord, to the
publick censure of her, by admonition first, and excommunication after.

"But (saith Mr. *Baylie*) None of these erroneous persons were
ever called to account by the Presbytery of that Church, till after
the Assembly, though the Pastor of the Church, Mr. *Wilson* was
alwayes exceeding zealous against them."

Answ. 1. Mr. *Baylie* is mistaken, when he saith, Mr. *Wilson*
was always exceeding zealous against them. For the whole
Church will bear him witnesse, hee was a long time full of much
forbearance towards them, and thought well of them, and bare
witnesse to the wayes of free Grace in such manner, as testified his
good will to them and the Truth. Afterwards in some private conference, which one or more of them had with him, and (our beloved Sister) his Wife, he discerned some more rottennesse in
them, and their way, then he suspected before: And after that
time indeed, he grew more zealous against them, but the occasion
of the offence was private, and (for a good space) unknown both
to mee and the Church.

2. But why they were not called to account by the Presbytery
of the Church, the reason was evident: because their grosse errors
were not confirmed unto us, by two or three witnesses. And this I
can truely professe, That when the Elders of other Churches acquainted mee with some of their Errors, (even when the noise of
them was spred far and neer:) yet they acknowledged, the Erroneous persons were so cautious, that they would never vent any
grosse Errors before two witnesses. And this I can further truely
avouch, that my self dealt sadly and seriously with some chief
leaders of them, both by word, and writing to recover them from
the Error of their way: which though they would argue for, yet they would ever excuse themselves from   [59]
setling upon any such things. I dealt also with others
(whom I began to suspect might be leavened by their Leaders)
and earnestly charged them to beware what Tenents they received from them, lest by that means they might be corrupted
themselves, and their Leaders hardned. But they would not bee
known to me, that they drunke in any such dregs, as afterwards
appeared.

His next testimony is taken from Ms. *Hutchinsons* speach in the open Court, "Preferring my Ministery in holding forth free Grace, above some, or most of the other Elders." But of the invalidity of her testimony in these things I have spoken, (I suppose) enough above. An evill Spirit (which sometimes breatheth both in good and bad persons,) may give a glorious testimony to some servants of God, not so much to honour them, or their doctrine, as either to cover themselves under their shadow, or else (but that was not her aime) to bring them and their Doctrin into suspition, and trouble, as the Spirit of the *Pythonesse* did to *Paul* and *Silas, Act.* 16, 17, to 20. That speach of hers, I bore witnesse against it, as prejudiciall and injurious both to them and mee.

Another testimony hee alledgeth out of the Story, *Page* 50. "That all the Ministers consented in bearing some witnesse against Mr. *Whelewright,* except their Brother the Teacher of *Boston.*"

Answ. The Story relateth those words, as the speach of the Elders; that they speak of me, as their Brother, to wit, the brother of the Elders, lest any should misconceive of their speach, as ranking me in a Brotherhood with erroneous persons.

That I did not consent with the rest of my Brethren (the Elders) in drawing the inference out of Mr. *Whelewrights* Sermon, which they (being required) presented to the Court, I had a twofold reason for it. 1. Because I was not present with them, when they searched Mr. *Whelewrights* Sermon, and gathered that inference from it.

2. Because I could not speake it of mine own knowledge, "That the Elders of the Country did walk in or teach such a way of Salvation, and evidencing thereof, as Mr. *Whelewright* describedeth, and accounteth to bee a Covenant of Works."

They knew what themselves taught in that point, better then I. The Elders might testifie what they knew: [60] I could not testifie, what I knew not. But it seemeth any testimonies will serve turn, when such as these are thought unavoidable, to lay me under the guilt of an horrible fall.

Yet one more remaineth, from *page* 21. "That albeit the Assembly of the Churches had confuted and condemned most of these new opinions, and Mr. *Cotton* had in publick view consented with the rest: yet the leaders in those Erroneous wayes stood still to maintain their New Light. Mr. *Whelewright* also continued his Preaching, and Ms. *Hutchinson* her wonted meetings: and much offence was stil given by her, and others in going out from the Pastors Exercise."

Answ. 1. As the Assembly of the Churches confuted and condemned those Errors, so I will not say, That the motion of confuting them (as I remember) arose from my self. And my self also had an hand in confuting such of them, as the Elders committed to my hand, as themselves took severall likewise taskes, none of us confuted all. My consent to the confutation, I have expressed above, and in what sense. What I did in publick view (as the Story expresseth it) I spake before the Lord, and from the truth of my heart.

That notwithstanding this Act of the Assembly against the Errors, the leaders still stood to maintain their way, it was because the Assembly did not fasten these Errors upon any Persons either in our own, or other Churches. And what corrupt opinions were maintained by our Members, it was done in private, and not before such witnesses, as might reach to publick conviction.

Mr. *Whelewrights* continuance in his preaching, was 8. or 9. miles distance from us. And having been put into that place before by the Church, whilst the Farmers there belonged to our Church, (which by reason of the distance, wee soon after dismissed into a Church-estate amongst themselves)[33] wee that were Elders could not (if wee would) discharge him from that worke, without the consent of the Church. But though hee gave some offence in some passages at the Assembly, (which hee since upon further conference and consideration retracted:) yet neither the Church, nor my self (notwithstanding those unsafe expressions) did ever look at him either as an Antinomian or Familist. Many of us knew that hee had taken good paines against both, and in that very place, where hee was wont to preach; insomuch that one of his hearers (who since joyned to Mr.   [61] *Gortons* society) openly contested against his doctrine as false and Antichristian. And when Mr. *Whelewright* was put out

---

33. The "Farmers" were inhabitants of Boston who moved out to present-day Braintree in order to be closer to their land. See Darrett B. Rutman, *Winthrop's Boston* (Chapel Hill, 1965), 95.

of this Countrey (though hee be since restored)[34] yet if hee had cleaved to the Errors which Ms. *Hutchinsons* company fell into, he would never have refused their earnest invitation and call of him, to Minister unto them. They sent to him, and urged him much to come to them, to a far richer soyle, and richer company then where hee lived: yet hee constantly refused, and upon that very ground, because of the corruption of their judgments: "Professing often, whilst they pleaded for the Covenant of Grace, they took away the Grace of the Covenant."

Ms. *Hutchinsons* continuance of her weekly meetings we could not proceed to the suppression thereof, with consent of the Church, before wee received the conviction of her personall Errors, which shee still closely carryed, till after her civill censure. And then shee declared her self more plainly, and witnesses arose more fully, and the Church proceeded against her accordingly.

The going of her self and others out of the Congregation when our Pastor began to Exercise, though many feared it was a turning their backs upon his Ministery: yet the most of them were women, and they pretended many excuses for their going out, which it was not easie to convince of falshood in them, or of their contempt of him.

But in fine, when her Antinomian and Familisticall Errors were held forth by her before sufficient witnesses, our Church (as I said before) proceeded without delay, first, to admonish her according to the rule, *Tit.* 3. 10, 11. Afterwards when upon serious paines taken with her, Mr. *Davenport,* and my self (as wee thought) had convinced her of her erroneous wayes in judgment and practice, so as that under her hand, shee presented a Recantation before the whole Church, (indeed before many Churches then assembled at *Boston*) yet withall, (after some passages of speach) "Professing that shee never was of any other judgment, then what she now held forth, so many witnesses forthwith rose up to convince the contrary, that with common consent both of the

---

34. In May, 1644, the Massachusetts General Court passed the following vote: "Mr. Wheelwright (upon particular, solemne and serious acknowledgment and confession by letter, of his evill carriages and of the Courts justice upon him for them) hath his banishment taken of, and is received in as a member of this commonwealth." *Massachusetts Records, 2,* 67.

Elders and Brethren of our Church, shee was cast out of our Communion."

And now that (by the help of Christ) I have perused all the testimonies, which Mr. *Baylie* hath alledged to [62] convince me of an horrible fall into Antinomianism, and Familism, I desire him in the fear of God to consider, whether any or all these testimonies severally or jointly, will amount to make good such grievous scandalls, as hee hath charged upon mee. Which if they neither will, nor can reach unto, let him remember his promise in his Epistle Dedicatory, "That in all which he hath said over and above (just testimony) he will undertake to give ample satisfaction, wherein so ever he hath given the least offence to any. Meane while the Lord lay not this sin to his charge."

SECT. 14. *Of* Cottons *humiliation upon his former fall, as is reported by Mr.* Baylie.

But yet let me adde a word more, to a word of Mr. *Baylies* in his entrance of this discourse of my Antinomianism, and Familism, which may else leave an impression upon the minds of some Reader, as if I had acknowledged this my dangerous fal, and had been much humbled for it.

"This other more dangerous fall (saith hee) as it hath already much humbled his Spirit, and opened his eare to instruction, and I trust will not leave working, till it have brought him yet nearer to his Brethren: so to the worlds end, it cannot but be a matter of fear and trembling to all, who shall know it, and of abundant caution, to bee very wary of receiving any singularity from his hand, without due tryall."

Answ. 1. Suppose all this were true *in terminis,* as Mr. *Baylie* hath expressed it, yet this were no impeachment at all to the doctrin and practice of that (which hee calleth) our Independent Church way; nor is it any just ground of caution to bee wary of receiving my testimony to it. *Peters* dangerous and dreadfull fall into the denyall of Christ, (though hee seemed to be a pillar) was no impeachment, but advancement to Christianity. And if my fall were so dangerous, walking in this Church-way, and stumbling so foully in it, the greater Grace and witnesse from heaven was upon his Churches in this way, who by the blessing of God were instruments of recovering me out of this fall, even by a con-

sultatory conference in a Synod, which did not assume to themselves any power of Church-censures. Let mee be accounted to
have fallen, and to have fallen (as Mr. *Baylie* represent-
eth it) horribly, so that the truth and wayes of Christ   [63]
may stand and find free passage.

Neither is this fall of mine such a just ground of caution (as he
would make it) unto any, to bee very wary of receiving my testimony to this Church way. For the way is no way of singularity
from my hand, but that which the body of the rest of my Brethren,
and of the Churches in this Country doe walk in with mee.

Answ. 2. But yet, let not Mr. *Baily* make further speech or use
of my humiliation, then was performed, or intended by me. For
God hath not given mee to this day (upon my best search) to discerne any such dangerous fall into Antinomianisme, or Familisme, as either hath, or might much humble my spirit.

It is true, my spirit had much cause to be humbled, (and so
through mercy it was) upon many just occasions at that time. As
first, that so many Erroneous and Hereticall opinions should be
broached in the Country, and carried on with such Arrogancy,
and Censoriousnesse, and guile of spirit.

Secondly, That the principall offenders in this kind were
members of our own Church, and some of them such as had neer
relation to my self.

Thirdly, that my self should be so sleepy and invigilant, as that
these (not Tares onely, but Bryers) should be sowen in our Field,
and my self not discerne them, till sundry persons up and down
the Countrey were leavened by them.

Fourthly, that such as endeavored the healing of these distempers, did seeme to me to be transported with more jealousies,
and heates, and paroxysmes of spirit, then would well stand with
brotherly love, or the rule of the Gospel.

The bitter fruits whereof doe remaine to this day, in the Letters sent over that year from hence to *England*. Whence also it
came to passe finally, that in the course taken for the clensing of
Gods Field, it seemed to me, that some good Wheat was pluckt up
with the Tares, some simple hearted honest men, and some truths
of God, fared the worse for the resemblance which the tares bare
to them.

Upon all which grounds, my self with our whole Church thought it needfull to set a day apart for publick humiliation before the Lord, wherein these and the like, both in Prayer and Preaching, were opened more at large before the Lord and his people.

But all this will not amount to make good Mr. *Bay-*   [64]
lies word, "That my dangerous fall into Antinomianisme and Familisme hath much humbled my Spirit."

Nor can I say (as he doth) that it hath opened mine eares to instruction. For I doe not know, that they have been shut to it, when I discerned the Spirit, and Word of truth breathing in it.

Nor can I say after him, "That the humbling of my spirit for those dangerous errours, will not leave working till it have brought me yet nearer to my brethren."

For though I blesse the Lord, who hath brought me nearer to my brethren, and them also nearer to me, which I trust will still grow whilst our selves grow (in all the duties of brotherly love, wherein we have much sweet and frequent intercourse:) yet I doe not interpret this as the fruit of my spirits humiliation for my Antinomy, and Familisme: but as the fruit of our clearer apprehension, both of the cause and of the state of our differences, and of our joynt consent and concurrence in bearing witnesse against the common heresies, and errors of Antinomianisme, and Familisme, which disturbed us all.

But Mr. *Baily* as he began his discourse of my dangerous fall with relation of my humiliation for it: so hee shutteth it up, *pag.* 58. with a like close of my griefe of mind, and confusion for it.

"I have been informed (saith he) by a gratious Preacher who was present at the Synod in *New-England,* that all the Brethren there, being exceedingly scandalized with Mr. *Cottons* carriage, in Mistris *Hutchinsons* processe, did so farre discountenance, and so severely admonish him, that hee was thereby brought to the greatest shame, confusion and griefe of mind, that ever in all his life he had endured."

Answ. 1. I conceive it is not allowable in Presbyteriall discipline, (sure I am, not in Congregationall) that an accusation shall be received against an Elder under one witnesse, though he gratious and a Preacher: especially when this gratious Preacher is namelesse, and his testimony hovereth in generalities, without instance in particular offences: as "That all the Brethren were exceedingly scandalized with Mr. *Cottons* carriage in Mistris *Hutchinsons* processe," but not expressing what carriage, nor what processe, nor wherein they were scandalized.

"And that all the Brethren did so far discountenance   [65] him, and severely admonish him, as that he was thereby brought to the greatest shame, and confusion, and grief of minde, that ever in all his life he endured." But no mention for what offence they did so severely admonish him, nor wherein they did so farre discountenance him.

Such words of infamy, and reproach may passe for Table talke, (which yet morall Philosophy would not approve:) but surely in orderly Church-Discipline, such dealing could not passe without just reproof, unlesse there were too much prejudice or partiality, the rule is plain and obvious, and not now the first time violated in the Disswasive, 2 *Tim.* 5. 19.

Answ. 2. I must (as justly I may) protest against that testimony, not onely as violating the rule of Love, but of Truth also. For,

1. It is untrue, that all the Brethren were scandalized with my carriage, much lesse exceedingly scandalized at the Synod, or in any processe about Ms. *Hutchinson.* There were sundry godly brethren otherwise minded, and otherwise affected.

2. It is untrue also, that such as were scandalized, did so severely admonish me, or discountenance me; for I can neither call to mind any such deep discountenance, nor any such severe admonition of Brethren, and yet I had reason to know it, and to remember it well, as well as any Brother at the Synod: the matter so neerly concerning my self, and more neerly and deeply, then any man else.

3. It is most untrue, that I was so far discountenanced, "and so severely admonished, as that I was brought to the greatest shame, confusion and grief of mind, that ever in all my life I had endured."

I should have little comfort in my own spirit, to look either God or man in the face, "if the discountenance or admonition of men (especially for such carriage) were the greatest shame, and confusion, and grief of mind, that ever in all my life I had en-

dured." The rebukes of God upon the soule for sin will put a man
to far greater shame, and confusion and grief of mind, then any
discountenance, or admonition from Brethren, (especially for
such offences) *Psal.* 76. 7.[35] But whatsoever discountenance, or
dis-respect I met withal, from one hand or other, till the true state
of my judgment, and carriage was clearly manifested, I
have long agoe left with the Lord: But I conceive I have   [66]
met with more hard measure in Letters to *England,* and
in ungrounded reports there, then ever I found from the admonition, or discountenance of any brethren here.

.   .   .   .

SECT. 18. *Of the third shamefull absurdity said to bee*   [82]
found in our way of Independency.

Come wee now to consider of the third shamefull Absurdity,
"which Mr. *Baylie* maketh the fruit of our Independency, breaking forth in the practises and profession of the most, who have
been admitted as very fit, if not the fittest Members of our
Churches."

And these evill fruits hee brancheth out into five sorts:

"1. (Saith he) in the vilenesse of their Errors.

2. In the multitude of the erring persons.

3. In the hypocrisie joyned with their Errors.

4. In malice against their Neighbors, and contempt
of their superiors, Magistrates and Ministers for opposi-   [83]
tion to their evill way.

5. In their singular obstinacy, stiffly sticking unto their errors,
&c."

Answ. 1. Suppose all this to bee true: yet this is so far from
discrediting the way of Independency, or arguing the Tree to be
bad by these bad fruits, that it doth rather justifie the way to be of

---

35. On March 27, 1638, Cotton expressed similar feelings in a letter to
Samuel Stone, the minister at Hartford: "I willingly heare your Counsell of
becoming so wise, and fearfull of my self, as not to vent new things without
sufficient Arguments. I may truly confesse . . . surely I am more foolish, than
any man . . . . But for Fearfulnesse of my selfe, though I have just and sad
Cause to abhor sin and unmortifyed selfishnesse still remayning: yet I may
truely tell you, God hath so often exercised me with renewed Fears and
Agonyes about mine owne spirituall Estate . . . that I could not Rest mine
owne Spirit." Cotton Papers, Boston Public Library.

God, which so easily hath either healed, or removed, so many, so vile, so generall, so subtle, so headstrong corruptions, and them that maintained them. *Non seclus, non scelerum varietas aut atrocitas,* is *dedecus Politiæ, sed scelerum impunitas.*[36] The Church of *Ephesus* was not blamed by Christ, because false Apostles and Nicolaitans were found amongst them: but commended, because she could not beare them, *Rev. 2. 2. 6.* Nor is *Thyatira* blamed, that *Jezabell* was found amongst them, but that they suffered her, *Rev. 2. 20.* What if so many, so hideous vile Errors were found in our Churches? What if the number of erring persons were (as he speaketh) incredible? "Multitudes of men and women every where infected? almost no Society, nor Family in the Land free from the pest? *Boston* (which he is pleased to style, the best and most famous of our Churches) so far corrupted, that few were untainted? What if they accounted the late Governour their true friend, and thought no lesse of Mr. *Cotton,* and Mr. *Whelewright* whom they adored? What if they had drawn to their sides not onely multitudes of the people, but the ablest men for parts, in all Trades, especially the Souldiers? What if all these evills were carried forth with presumptuous contumacy against godly Magistrates, and the Orthodox Ministers? yea, what if to all the rest, they added obstinacy against al wholsome meanes of redresse and remedy?"

Is it not therefore the more evident Demonstration of the gratious presence, and mighty power of God, in the Discipline of our Churches, that did so effectually, so speedily, so safely, so easily, purge out all this Leaven, either out of the hearts of the people, out of their Families, and Churches, or else out of the Country?

Whence the argument seemeth to mee to arise unavoidably.

Those evills, which Independency doth either heal, or remove, they are not the fruits of Independency.

But all these grievous and dangerous evils, Independency did either heal or remove.

Therefore these grievous and dangerous evills were   [84] not the fruits of Independency.

Again, That government, which by the blessing of Christ,

---

36. It is not wickedness, not the variety or the severity of wickedness that is a disgrace to the Polity, but the failure to punish wickedness.

doth safely, speedily, and effectually purge out such grievous and dangerous evills, as threaten the ruine of Church and State, that government is safely allowed, and justly and wisely established in any civill State.

But Independency by the blessing of Christ doth speedily, safely, and effectually purge out such grievous and dangerous evills, as threaten the ruine of Church and State: therefore Independency is safely allowed, and justly, and wisely established in any civill State.

Ob. 1. But this purging and healing of these grievous and dangerous evills was not the fruit of their Independent-Church-Government, but of their civill Government. "We have oft marvelled, that the Eldership of *Boston* did never so much, as call Ms. *Hutchinson* before them, to be rebuked for any of her errors, though their generall Assembly had confuted them, and condemned them: yet still shee was permitted to goe on, till the zeal of the new Governour, and the generall Court did condemne her to perpetuall banishment. Then, and not till then, so far as wee can perceive by the story, did the Church of *Boston* bring a processe against her. And when the processe was brought to an end, Mr. *Cotton* would by no meanes put it in execution; that burden was layed upon the back of Mr. *Wilson* his Colleague, how ever not the fittest Instrument, being the person to whom Ms. *Hutchinson* had professed greatest opposition. And when the sentence was pronounced against her, they tell us, that the great cause of it was none of her Errors or Heresies, but her other practises, specially her grosse lying."

Answ. 1. Whatever assistance the civill Government gave to the purging and healing of these evils, it was the fruit of Independent Church Government. For whether the Neighbour Churches suspected our Church of *Boston* might bee partiall, and indulgent to these erroneous persons: or whether they saw, we wanted sufficient witnesses upon which wee might proceed against them in a Church way, they took a right course (according to the principles of the Independent Government) to gather into a Synod with the consent of the civill Magistrates: [85] and in the Synod to agitate, convince and condemne the Errors, and the offensive carriages then stirring. Whereat the Magistrates being present, they saw just cause to proceed against the chief of those whom they conceived to have bred any civill disturbance: and the Churches saw cause to proceede against their Members, whom they found to bee broachers or maintainers of such heresies.

Answ. 2. It hath been declared above, why "the Eldership of *Boston* did not call Ms. *Hutchinson* before them to rebuke her for her Errors, or to restraine her from going on, though the generall Assembly had confuted and condemned her Errors and course."

For though the Errors were condemned, (and by the Elders of *Boston,* as well as others:) yet the errors were not fastened personally upon her: nor had we any two witnesses, that would affirm it to us, that shee did broach or maintain such errors or heresies, till after her sentence unto banishment by the generall Court; And then indeed, as she was more bold and open in declaring her judgment before many witnesses: so the Elders of the Church of *Boston* called her to account before the Church, and convinced her of her Errors, and with the consent of the Church, layed her, and one or two more of her abettors under the censure of an admonition even for those corrupt opinions, which were charged upon her, and proved against her.

"*Ob.* 1. Yea but Mr. *Cotton* would by no means put the censure in execution upon her, that burden must be layed upon the back of Mr. *Wilson, &c.*"

Answ. The censure of admonition, because it was for matter of Erroneous doctrine, it was thought meet to bee dispensed and administred by Mr. *Cotton,* who was their Teacher: which also (by the help of Christ) hee did performe, setting before her both the corrupt causes of her errors, and the bitter fruits of them: and charging her solemnly before the Lord, and his Angells, and Churches then assembled, to return from the Error of her way.

Afterwards, when upon further serious debate and conference with her by Mr. *Davenport,* and my selfe, she was convinced of all her errors in particular, shee being called againe before the Church, did openly recant every errour and heresie, and professed her repentance for every miscarriage against Magistrates and Elders: which farre exceeded the expecta-   [86] tion of the whole Congregation, which then consisted of many Churches, and strangers. But when shee had done, she added withall, "That she had never been of other judgement, howsoever her expressions might seem to vary." This sounded so harshly, and falsly in the eares of many witnesses, that many rose up to convince her of her falshood and lying, in so saying. Which when shee did not hearken to, shee was esteemed, by the judgement of the Elders, and our whole Church, to be justly subject to excommunication. Which though I did not think meet to bee dispensed by my self (because the offence was not in matter of Doctrin, but of practise, which more properly belonged to the Pastours Office, or ruling Elders:) yet I declared to the whole Congregation the righteousnesse of the censure, and satisfyed the Scruples of some Brethren, who doubted of it. But yet if the Church, or other Elders had put that taske upon me, I should no more have refused the dispensing of the censure of excommunication upon her, then I did before of admonition. Neither was her opposition against Mr. *Wilson* any just reason of exempting him from that duty. For shee saw, wee all with one accord, concurred in that sentence: it was no partiall act of his, but the common vote both of the Presbytery, and Fraternity. And what if she had professed her opposition against us all? had that been a just excuse to exempt any of us from performing a service due to God, and the Church, yea and to herself also?

Object. 2. "But when the sentence was propounded against her, they tell us, the great cause of it was none of her Errours, and Heresies, but for other practises, especially her grosse lying."

Answ. Wee could not justly pronounce the cause of her sentence to be her errors and heresies, which she had openly recanted, and given her recantation under her handwriting. Neither did any of us say, That such Heresies did not deserve the censure of excommunication, if she had continued obstinate in them: but wee thought it needfull to follow the rule of the Apostle, not to reject an Heretick till after once or twice admonition, *Tit.* 3. 10. under which if the Heretick relent, the Church proceeding stayeth, unlesse some other offence set it forward, as it did in her case.

SECT. 19. *Tending to rectifie some mistakes of Mr.*   [87] Baylie *in relating the former absurdities.*

But before I leave this close of Mr. *Baylies* third Chapter, touching the evill fruits of Independency, let mee advertise him of some few further mistakes in his Narration of the same.

First, when he reckoneth in the front of vile errours, the inhabitation of the person of the Spirit in all the godly, let him weigh what hath been said above, touching that point. And if hee cleare it to be an errour, I willingly shall acknowledge, hee shall teach me that, which I yet know not. I professe my self willing to learn of a meaner man, then Mr. *Baylie.*

"Secondly, when he maketh the number of the erring persons incredible, almost no society, no family free from that pest, *Boston* it self so farre infected, that few there were untainted": let him be pleased to consider, whether his testimony will make it good. His testimonies (recited in his Markes *FF. GG.*) speak to the utmost of truth, but not so much as he avoucheth. The short Story in Preface, *pag.* 7. saith indeed, "They had some of all sorts and qualities in all places to patronize and defend them: and almost in every family some were ready to defend them as the Apple of their own eye."

But this will not make it good, that almost in every family some were infected with the pest of their errours. It is one thing to speak in the defence of erroneous persons, another to speak in defence of errours. Multitudes there were, that thought well of the persons, who knew nothing of their errours, but heard onely of their unbottoming sandy foundations of a spirituall estate, which hath been mentioned above, Chap. 3.

Which may also truely be said even of *Boston* likewise. The body of the Church, the greatest part of them were like those members of the Church in *Thyatira,* of whom it is said (*Rev.* 2. 24.) They knew not the depths of Satan. The truth whereof may evidently appeare by this, That when those errors of Mistris *Hutchinson* were publickly charged upon her before the Church, and proved by sufficient witnesses, the whole body of the Church, and all the Brethren with one accord (save   [88] onely her sonne) consented readily to her censure: which they would not have done, "if the whole Church of *Boston* (some excepted) had become her converts, and were infected with her opinions."

"Thirdly, when hee saith, they adored some of their Ministers, and instanceth in Mr. *Cotton,* and Mr. *Whelewright.*"

Adoration is too vast an Hyperbole to be made good by just

testimonies. All hyperbolicall praises, though they may farre exceed the bounds of truth in comparisons of men with men; yet they will not reach adoration, which is divine worship. Neither will it bee made good, That they magnified either Mr. *Whelewright,* or me, for the defence of their errors. Yea they soon forsooke Mr. *Whelewright* (as well as he them) when they saw his judgement (as well as mine) against Antinomianisme, and Familisme.

Fourthly, when he saith, "Mistris *Hutchinson,* and the late Governour, kept almost every day, so private and long discourse with Mr. *Cotton,* that made them conclude all was their own."

I must needs professe, that cannot be made good by any witnesse of truth, Mistris *Hutchinson* seldome resorted to mee: and when she did, she did seldome or never enter into any private speech between the former Governour and my self. And when she did come to me, it was seldome or never (that I can tell of) that she tarried long. I rather think, she was loath to resort much to me, or, to conferre long with me, lest she might seeme to learne somewhat from me. And withall I know (by good proof) she was very carefull to prevent any jealousie in mee, that shee should harbour any private opinions, differing from the course of my publick Ministery. "Which she could not well have avoyded, if she had kept almost every day so private and long discourse with me."

But what Testimony, or proof doth Mr. *Baylie* alledge for this our private and long conference, almost every day? His marke (*YY*) referreth us to the short story, where it is said, "They made full account the day had been theirs."

But did they make this account upon occasion of these our private, and long, and frequent conferences every day? not a syllable of proofe for this point. It is not righteous dealing, large charges, and narrow proofs.

Fourthly, that which Mr. *Baylie* further relateth from the testimony of Mr. *Williams,* is as farre from [89] truth, as the former.

"Mr. *Williams* (saith Mr. *Baylie*) told me, that he was employed to buy from the Savages, for their late Governour, and Mr. *Cotton,* with their Followers, a portion of Land without the *English* Plantation whither they might retire and live according to their mind, exempt from the jurisdiction of all others, whether Civill or Ecclesiastick, Mr. *Williams* was in so great friendship with the late Governour, when he told me so much, that I beleeve he would have been loth to have spoken an untruth of him."

Answ. But this I dare be bold to say, if Mr. *Williams* told Mr. *Baylie* so much, that he was imployed by me to buy any Land from the Savages, for mee and my followers (as he calls them) he spake an untruth of me, whatsoever he did of the Governour. Yet because I would not speake nor thinke worse of Mr. *Williams* then necessitie constrayneth, I cannot say but that he might speak as he thought, and as he was told; for it may well bee, that such as abused the Governours name to him for such an end, might also more boldly abuse mine. But I must professe, I neither wrote, nor spake, nor sent to Mr. *Williams* for any such errand. If ever I had removed, I intended *Quinipyack,* and not *Aquethnick.* And I can hardly beleeve the Governour would send to him for any such end, who I suppose never thought it likely, that himself should tarry longer in the Countrey, then he tarried in the *Bay.*

Fiftly, when Mr. *Baylie* objecteth the prophanenesse of these erroneous persons, and justifieth it by the testimonies of Mr. *Weld* and my self, "And aggravateth the same by their profession of Piety (so farre, that they avow their standing loose from all reformed Churches as uncleane, because of their mixture with the prophane Multitude.)"

Let him be pleased to consider; First, what was said above, *Non scelus, sed sceleris impunitas,*[37] is the guilt of a society, whether civill or sacred.

Secondly, what Mr. *Weld* meant by fouler sinnes then pride, or lying, found in those persons, I cannot guesse: nor have I heard of them: unlesse hee meant the adultery of one, who upon his own confession was cast out of the Church for that crime.

As for the testimony of mine, which hee quoteth from some words in the vialls,[38] wherein the sinnes of   [90] the people were reproved, let him not improve them

---

37. Not wickedness, but the failure to punish wickedness.
38. Cotton refers to his sermons on the book of Revelation, *The Powrring out of the Seven Vials* (London, 1642).

further then they will bear. Such reproofs doe not alwayes argue sinnes of our Church members: or if they did, yet not, that those sinnes are openly known: or if openly known, yet not, that they were tolerated. And yet all these must concurre, or else the vices found amongst professors, will not argue the viciousnesse either of their doctrine or worship, or Church Government.

Luther complaineth, *in Postill. super Evangel. Dom. adventus, Sunt nunc homines magis vindictæ cupidi, magis avari, magis ab omni misericordiâ remoti, magis immodesti, & indisciplinati, multoque deteriores, quam fuerunt sub papatu.*[39] And *Chrysostome, (in opere imperfect. in Matth. Hom. 49.)*[40] speaketh of Christians as becomming like the Hereticks, or Pagans, or worse.

Yet I suppose he that should improve the words either of *Chrysostome,* to argue the discipline of Christians, worse then that of the Pagans: or of *Luther,* to argue the discipline of Protestants to be worse then that of Papists, he shall doubtlesse stretch their words upon the Rack, farre beyond the scope of their meaning. The words I spake, were in comparison between the godly Professors in *England,* and ours here, and at such a time, when Episcopall persecution made them draw the nearer to God, and to walke the more circumspectly before men. But Sheepe set at libertie from the feare of Wolves, will straggle further from their Shepheard, then when they resent danger.

Thirdly, it is too grosse and heavy an aggravation, which Mr. *Baylie* putteth upon us, if he meane it of us, "That our profession of pietie is so faire that wee stand aloofe from all reformed Churches as uncleane, because of their mixture with the prophane multitude."

For it is more then he can prove, or we doe professe. Though in the Bishops time, we did not forthwith receive all the members of the Church of *England* into the fellowship of our Churches: yet (for ought I know) wee are not likely to stand aloofe from Pres-

---

39. Men nowadays are more vengeful, more avaricious, more removed from any compassion, more impure and undisciplined, and much worse than under the papacy: Luther, *A Very Comfortable Sermon Concerning the Comming of Christ* (London, 1578).

40. John Chrysostome (c. 345–407) reputedly wrote an *Incomplete Work on Matthew;* an edition was published at Strasbourg, 1466(?).

byteriall Churches faithfully administred, nor from the testimony which they shall give of their members, that may have occasion to Traffick hither. And the like doe I conceive of other reformed Churches in other Nations of Christendome. Presbyterian Churches faithfully administred, are not wont to admit a mixt prophane multitude to the Lords Table.

Sixtly, let me take off one instance more, which Mr.   [91]
Baylie giveth of one abomination, which to him seemeth strange. "That the Midwives to our most zealous women, should not onely have familiarity with the Devill, but also in that service commit devillish Malefices: which so farre as they tell us, were not onely past over without punishment, but never so much as enquired after."

Answ. This accusation is indeed of some weight, because it is of a grievous, and devillish crime, and it tolerated. But how doth it appeare to him, that it was tolerated? "not onely past over without punishment, but never so much as enquired after?"

Why, saith he, so farre as they tell us. So farre as they tell us? Is the silence of a short story of this or that fact, a good argument, *a non dici, ad non esse?*[41] yea it is a good argument on the contrary, that there was inquiry made after that Midwife, and diligent search into her, or else it would have been recorded, as some close conveyance of the erroneous party. The truth is, the woman, though she offered her self to the Elders of our Church, yet was not received, upon discovery of some unsound principles in her judgement. Being then no member, the Church had no power to deale with her. But when suspition grew of her familiarity with the Devill, especially upon that occasion, which the short story relateth, shee was convented before the Magistrates, and diligently examined about that, and other evills. But though no familiarity with the Devill could be proved against her; yet because of some other offences in dealing with young women, she was forbidden to stay in the Countrey.[42]

---

41. Arguing from the fact that it is not mentioned to the fact that it does not exist.

42. See p. 281, and *Massachusetts Records, I,* 224.

A Note on the Transcription of Manuscripts

ALL of the documents of the Antinomian controversy existed initially as manuscripts. Some of these manuscripts (or, more likely, copies of them) were sent to England and first put in print as *Antinomians and Familists Condemned* (1644; reprinted, with Thomas Weld's additions, as *A Short Story*). Other documents remained in manuscript. In 1676 the Quaker Samuel Groom owned a copy of John Wheelwright's fast-day sermon and a transcript of Wheelwright's "trial" before the General Court. Several other copies of the Wheelwright sermon were in circulation, and two have survived; but the contents of the transcript are known only from the portions Groom printed in *A Glass for the People of New England* ([London], 1676) . In 1743 Charles Chauncy, the minister of Boston First Church, had access to "an ancient Manuscript Copy of the Proceedings of the Synod, in 1637." His two quotations from this copy (in *Seasonable Thoughts on the State of Religion in New-England*), which are reproduced on pages xix–xx, indicate that it included material omitted from *A Short Story*. The correspondence between Thomas Hutchinson and Ezra Stiles (printed in *New England Historical and Genealogical Register* 26 [1882], 161–64) reveals that Stiles received his copy of the church trial of Mrs. Hutchinson from her great-grandson. The provenance of the manuscript that I published in 1968 from the collections of the Massachusetts Historical Society is unknown. It is always possible that other manuscripts relating to the controversy may turn up in English and American archives. Sargent Bush is preparing for publication the letters of John Cotton, several of which are important supplements to the letters included in this book. He will also argue in a forthcoming essay that John Wheelwright was not the author of *Mercurius Americanus*.

439

Bibliographical Note

THE following note is intended as a guide to the literature of the Antinomian Controversy that falls outside this collection. The literature breaks down into two groups: *primary,* the materials that could be considered documents (in the broadest sense) of the Controversy, and *secondary,* the historiography of New England Puritanism.

Primary

OF the documents that have been omitted from this collection, the most significant is John Winthrop, *History of New England.* The *History* is available in various editions, the best being the one edited by James Savage (Boston, 1853). The *Winthrop Papers,* volumes 3 and 4 (Boston, 1943–44), contain many items of importance, ranging from personal letters to formal arguments about theology. Especially interesting in view of the problem of assurance is John Winthrop's "Relation of his Religious Experience," written in January, 1637. Winthrop and Henry Vane argued the validity of the General Court order controlling further emigration to the colony in a series of essays that were first printed in Thomas Hutchinson, ed., *A Collection of Original Papers Relative to the History of the Colony of Massachusetts-Bay* (Boston, 1769). The *Records of the Governor and Company of the Massachusetts Bay in New England,* ed. N. B. Shurtleff, volume 1 (Boston, 1853) provide further information on the role of the General Court in the Controversy. Finally, John Wheelwright wrote a rebuttal to the *Short Story* entitled *Mercurius Americanus, or, Mr. Welds his Antitype* (London, 1645). It has been reprinted in *John Wheelwright, His Writings,* ed. Charles Bell (Boston, 1876).

Equally relevant to an understanding of Antinomianism in Massachusetts are the sermons of John Cotton and his fellow ministers that were published in the seventeenth century. A few of these sermons bear dates and can be related directly to the Controversy. Thomas Shepard began to preach the sermons later published as *The Parable of the Ten Virgins Opened & Applied* (London, 1660) in June, 1636. The treatise is reprinted in *The Works of Thomas Shepard,* ed. John A. Albro (Boston, 1853), volume 2. In 1638 or 1639, Peter Bulkeley commenced on the sermons collected in *The Gospel-Covenant; or The Covenant of Grace Opened* (London, 1646; second edition, 1653). Thomas Hooker was preaching in 1640 the sermons contained in *The Application of Redemption* (London, 1657). Two of John Cotton's published books can be dated: *A Treatise: I. Of Faith . . .* (n.p., [1713]) was probably written in 1634 or 1635, while *A Sermon Preached . . . At Salem* (Boston, 1713) was delivered in June, 1636. Both provide revealing parallels between Cotton's preaching and the rhetoric of the Antinomians. *The New Covenant, or, A Treatise, unfolding the order and manner of the giving and receiving of the Covenant of Grace to the Elect* (London, 1654), subsequently reprinted under different titles, contains sermons Cotton preached in Massachusetts, perhaps at the time of the Controversy. A list of treatises in which the Antinomian Controversy figures as an echo would, in effect, be a complete bibliography of the writings of the first generation of ministers.

Other responses to Antinomianism are reported in the polemical literature dealing with Congregationalism, and in contemporary histories of Massachusetts. Edward Johnson, *The Wonder-working Providence of Sion's Saviour in New England* (London, 1654, under a different title; New York, 1959), is an important history. Another is William Hubbard, *A General History of New England* (Boston, 1848). And though not by a contemporary, Cotton Mather's *Magnalia Christi Americana* (London, 1702; reprinted Hartford, 1854–55) is a significant source of information.

Unprinted sources include other items in the Cotton Papers (Boston Public Library) and the Hutchinson Papers (Massachusetts State Archives).

Secondary

THERE is scarcely a book about seventeenth-century New England that fails to touch on the Antinomian Controversy. Useful guides to the historiography of Puritan New England are the bibliographies in the paperback edition of Perry Miller and Thomas H. Johnson, eds., *The Puritans, A Sourcebook of Their Writings* (New York, 1963). On the Antinomian Controversy itself, the most recent bibliography is in Emery Battis, *Saints and Sectaries* (Chapel Hill, 1963). Battis has written the fullest account of the Controversy, though it is somewhat marred by an unsubstantiated interpretation of Anne Hutchinson. Another good general narrative is in Charles F. Adams, *Three Episodes of Massachusetts History* (Boston, 1892).

The recovery of the theological dimension of the Controversy began with the essay by Perry Miller, " 'Preparation for Salvation' in Seventeenth Century New England" (1943, now reprinted in *Nature's Nation*, Cambridge, 1967). Miller argued that the Puritans developed the doctrine of preparation for grace as a way of getting around the determinism in Calvin's theology. John Cotton was a more consistent Calvinist than his fellow ministers, and the Antinomian Controversy grew out of his objections to their use of the doctrine. The role of the doctrine of preparation in the Antinomian Controversy is the subject of a more recent study by Norman Pettit, *The Heart Prepared* (New Haven, 1966). Pettit provides a much fuller reading of the ministers' theology and corrects Miller's interpretation on a number of points. In " 'The Heart of New England Rent': The Mystical Element in Early Puritan History," *Mississippi Valley Historical Review* 42 (1956), 621–652, James F. Maclear relates Anne Hutchinson and the New England "Antinomians" to the mystical strain in Puritanism. Though the Controversy does not figure in Geoffrey Nuttall, *The Holy Spirit in Puritan Faith and Experience* (Oxford, 1946), his discussion of the doctrine of the Holy Spirit helps to explain the spiritualism of Mrs. Hutchinson and John Cotton. Two recent biographies of Cotton carry on the analysis of his theology: Larzer Ziff, *The Career of John Cotton* (Princeton, 1962), and

Everett H. Emerson, *John Cotton* (New York, 1965). On Puritanism in general, the outstanding study is Perry Miller, *The New England Mind: The Seventeenth Century* (New York, 1939). It is complemented by William Haller, *The Rise of Puritanism* (New York, 1938).

The social, political, and institutional setting of the Antinomian Controversy has also been reinvestigated since Charles F. Adams rendered his *obiter dictu*. The most important study is Battis, *Saints and Sectaries,* which contains elaborate tables defining the Antinomian party in terms of occupation and economic status. Some of the identifications of persons as "Antinomians" may be questionable. The town of Boston is analyzed in an important book by Darrett B. Rutman, *Winthrop's Boston* (Chapel Hill, 1965). In *The New England Merchants of the Seventeenth Century* (Cambridge, 1956), Bernard Bailyn describes the development of the professional group from which came the most prominent of the Antinomians. Around the figure of John Winthrop, Edmund S. Morgan has woven a general interpretation of Puritanism in *The Puritan Dilemma, The Story of John Winthrop* (Boston, 1958). Morgan's is the best brief account of the political evolution of Massachusetts during the 1630s. The ecclesiastical setting of the Antinomian Controversy is described in another book by Morgan, *Visible Saints, The History of a Puritan Idea* (New York, 1963), which treats the colonists' conception of church membership. Also useful are Williston Walker, *The Creeds and Platforms of Congregationalism* (New York, 1893), and Perry Miller, *Orthodoxy in Massachusetts* (Cambridge, 1933). Samuel Eliot Morison has related the Antinomian Controversy to the establishment of Harvard in *The Founding of Harvard College* (Cambridge, 1935).

A Selective Bibliography of Recent Work

Adams, Charles F., *The Antinomian Controversy*, edited and with an introduction by Emery Battis (New York, 1976).

Barker-Benfield, Ben, "Anne Hutchinson and the Puritan Attitude Toward Woman," *Feminist Studies* 1 (1973): 65–96.

Bush, Sargent, Jr., " 'Revising What We Have Done Amiss': John Cotton and John Wheelwright, 1640," *William and Mary Quarterly*, 3d ser. 45 (1988): 733–50.

———, *The Writings of Thomas Hooker: Spiritual Adventure in Two Worlds* (Madison, Wis., 1980).

Caldwell, Patricia, *The Puritan Conversion Narrative: The Beginnings of American Expression* (New York, 1983).

Cohen, Charles Lloyd, *God's Caress: The Psychology of Puritan Religious Experience* (New York, 1986).

Cohen, Ronald D., "Church and State in Seventeenth-Century Massachusetts: Another Look at the Antinomian Controversy," *Journal of Church and State* 12 (1970): 475–94.

Colacurcio, Michael J., "Footsteps of Anne Hutchinson: The Context of *The Scarlet Letter*," *English Literary History* 39 (1972): 459–94.

Dailey, Barbara, "Root and Branch: New England's Religious Radicals and Their Transatlantic Community, 1600–1660" (Ph.D. thesis, Boston University, 1984).

Delamotte, Eugenia, "John Cotton and the Rhetoric of Grace," *Early American Literature* 21 (1986): 49–74.

Delbanco, Andrew, *The Puritan Ordeal* (Cambridge, Mass., 1989).

Endy, Melvin, *William Penn and Early Quakerism* (Princeton, N.J., 1973).

Etulain, Richard, "John Cotton and the Anne Hutchinson Controversy," *Rendezvous* 2 (1967): 9–18.

Fiering, Norman, "Benjamin Franklin and the Way to Virtue," *American Quarterly* 30 (1978): 199–223.

Foster, Stephen, *English Puritanism and the Shaping of New England Culture, 1570–1700* (Chapel Hill, N.C., 1991).

———, "New England and the Challenge of Heresy, 1630–1660: The Puritan Crisis in Transatlantic Perspective," *William and Mary Quarterly*, 3d ser. 38 (1981): 624–60.

Gura, Philip, *A Glimpse of Sions Glory: Puritan Radicalism in New England, 1620–1660* (Middletown, Conn., 1983).

Hall, David D., "On Common Ground: The Coherence of American

Puritan Studies," *William and Mary Quarterly*, 3d ser. 44 (1987): 193–229.

———, "Understanding the Puritans," in *The State of American History*, ed. Herbert Bass (Chicago, 1970): 330–49.

———, *Worlds of Wonder, Days of Judgment: Popular Religious Belief in Early New England* (New York, 1989).

Habegger, Alfred, "Preparing the Soul for Christ: The Contrasting Sermon Forms of John Cotton and Thomas Hooker," *American Literature* 41 (1969): 342–54.

Hill, Christopher, *The World Turned Upside Down: Radical Ideas During the English Revolution* (New York, 1972).

Holifield, E. Brooks, *The Covenant Sealed: The Development of Puritan Sacramental Theology in Old and New England, 1570–1720* (New Haven, 1974).

Huber, Elaine C., *Women and the Authority of Inspiration: A Reexamination of Two Prophetic Movements from a Contemporary Feminist Perspective* (Lanham, Md., 1985).

Karlsen, Carol F., *The Devil in the Shape of a Woman* (New York, 1987).

Kendall, R. T., *Calvin and English Calvinism to 1649* (Oxford, 1979).

Kevan, Ernest F., *The Grace of Law: A Study of Puritan Theology* (London, 1976).

Kibbey, Ann, *Rhetoric, Prejudice, and Violence: The Interpretation of Material Shapes in Puritanism* (New York, 1985).

Knight, Janice L., "The Garden Enclosed: The Rhetoric of the Heart in Puritan New England" (Ph.D. thesis, Harvard University, 1988).

Koehler, Lyle, *A Search for Power: The "Weaker Sex" in Seventeenth-Century New England* (Urbana, Ill., 1980).

Lang, Amy, "Antinomianism and the 'Americanization' of Doctrine," *New England Quarterly* 54 (1981): 225–42.

Lewis, Mary Jane, "Anne Hutchinson," in *Portraits of American Women*, ed. G. J. Barker-Benfield and Catherine Clinton (New York, 1990).

———, "A Sweet Sacrifice: Civil War in New England" (Ph.D. thesis, State University of New York, Binghamton, 1986).

Lovejoy, David S., *Religious Enthusiasm in the New World* (Cambridge, Mass., 1985).

McGiffert, Michael, "From Moses to Adam: The Making of the Covenant of Works," *Sixteenth Century Journal* 19 (1988), 131–55.

———, "Grace and Works: The Rise and Division of Covenant Theology in Elizabethan Puritanism," *Harvard Theological Review* 75 (1982): 463–502.

Mack, Phyllis, "Women as Prophets During the English Civil War," *Feminist Studies* 8 (1982): 19–45.

Maclear, James F., "Anne Hutchinson and the Mortalist Heresy," *New England Quarterly* 54 (1981): 74–103.

Moss, Jean Dietz, " 'Godded with God': Henrik Niclaes and His Family of Love," *American Philosophical Society Transactions* 71, pt. 8 (Philadelphia, 1981).

Pettit, Norman, "Cotton's Dilemma: Another Look at the Antinomian Controversy," *Colonial Society of Massachusetts, Publications* 59 (Boston, 1982): 393–413.

Pudaloff, Ross J., "Sign and Subject: Antinomianism in Massachusetts Bay," *Semiotica* 54 (1985): 147–63.

Rosenmeier, Jesper, "New England's Perfection: The Image of Adam and the Image of Christ in the Antinomian Crisis, 1634 to 1638," *William and Mary Quarterly*, 3d. ser. 27 (1970): 435–59.

Selement, George, "John Cotton's Hidden Antinomianism: His Sermon on Revelation 4:1–2," *New England Historical and Genealogical Register* 129 (1975): 278–94.

Shuffelton, Frank, *Thomas Hooker 1586–1647* (Princeton, N.J., 1977).

Stoever, William K. B., *'A Faire and Easie Way to Heaven': Covenant Theology and Antinomianism in Early Massachusetts* (Middletown, Conn., 1978).

Toulouse, Teresa, *The Art of Prophesying: New England Sermons and the Shaping of Belief* (Athens, Ga., 1987).

von Rohr, John, *The Covenant of Grace in Puritan Thought* (Athens, Ga., 1986).

Williams, Selma, *Divine Rebel: The Life of Anne Marbury Hutchinson* (New York, 1981).

Withington, Ann Fairfax, and Jack Schwartz, "The Political Trial of Anne Hutchinson," *New England Quarterly* 51 (1978): 226–40.

Index

449

David D. Hall is Professor of American Religious History and Bartlett Lecturer in New England Church History, Harvard University Divinity School. He is the author of *The Faithful Shepherd: A History of the New England Ministry in the Seventeenth Century* (1972) and *Worlds of Wonder, Days of Judgment: Popular Religious Belief in Early New England* (1989).

Library of Congress Cataloging-in-Publication Data

The Antinomian controversy, 1636–1638 : a documentary history / edited
with introduction and notes by David D. Hall.—2nd ed.

p.   cm.

Includes bibliographical references.

ISBN 0–8223–1083–X.—ISBN 0–8223–1091–0 (pbk.)

1. Hutchinson, Anne Marbury, 1591–1643.   2. Massachusetts—
History—Colonial period, ca. 1600–1775.   3. Antinomianism—History
of doctrines—17th century.   4. Massachusetts—Church history—17th
century.   5. Puritans—Massachusetts—History—17th century.

I. Hall, David D.

F67.H92A58   1990

273′.6′09744—dc20

90–3237

CIP